Sandy Denny

A People's History

The Adam & Eve
SPA ROAD S'OTON.
TOMORROW, SATURDAY
Personal appearance of Radio 1 DJ
MIKE RAVEN
7.30—1 a.m. Licensed Bars.
Members: 7/6.
Wednesday, February 26
FAIRPORT CONVENTION
Advance ticket now on sale—10/-.
ROYAL FESTIVAL HALL
GENERAL MANAGER JOHN DENISON, C.B.E.
THE FAIRPORT CONVENTION
WED., 24 SEPTEMBER, 1969
8. p.m.
Management: Peter Bowyer
TERRACE
GANGWAY 10
ROW
SEAT
GREEN SIDE
Please enter the auditorium by
DOOR
5
LEVEL
MATTHEWS SOUTHERN COMFORT
FOTHERINGAY
10 PM
ERS: BRING A CUSH
E THEATRE
vid Ginges presents
NDY DENNY and
ORT CONVENTION
MAY
SUN., 20 MAY
p.m.
LS
8.30 p.m.
STALLS
10 AA 10
the Edward Herbert Building on SATURDAY
th June Doors Open 7.30 pm.
AIRPORT CONVENTION
ATURING SANDY DENNY
ckets £1·00 in advance
ith S.U.card.
therwise £1·20 (Inc VAT)
NO persons under 16 admitted
R.O.A.R.
LOUGHBOROUGH UNIVERSITY ENTS
FOTHERINGAY
MATTHEW'S SOUTHERN COMFORT
Friday, November 20th
10/- Members
Others
No. 1573
"NOTHING MORE"
THE COLLECTED
FOTHERINGAY
BBC Music Day
ALEXANDRA ELENE
MACLEAN
'SANDY' DENNY
1947-1978
Influential folk rock singer-songwriter
with Fairport Convention
Played her final gig at Byfield Village Hall
1st April 1978
Awarded by
BBC Radio Northampton
British Plaque Trust

Sandy Denny

A People's History

Georgia Rose Lucas

SPENWOOD BOOKS

First published in Great Britain 2026 by Spenwood Books Ltd

1 Totnes Road, Manchester, M21 8XF, United Kingdom

A CIP record for this book is available from the British Library.

ISBN 978-1-915858-52-8

Design by Bruce Graham, The Night Owl
Editors: Dawn Kemp & Nigel Schofield

Manufactured in Czech Republic

spenwoodbooks.com

MIX
Paper | Supporting responsible forestry
FSC® C014138

In the end I want to be remembered for my singing and my songwriting: I don't want to become an answer in a pop trivia quiz: you know, 'Name the only female singer to appear on a Led Zeppelin album'
Sandy Denny

Sandy hated rehearsals
Richard Thompson

We only slept together once
Simon Nicol

One of England's greatest singer/songwriters
Dave Pegg

She was one of the most talented and wonderful people I've had the good fortune to work with
Dave Mattacks

I have never got over her dying
Dave Swarbrick

Thank you, Sandy, you beautiful soul, for allowing me to be part of your magical space in the time we called Fairport
Iain Matthews

Sometimes it's better not to know. There's a lot to be said for leaving things mysterious
Sandy Denny

ABOUT THE AUTHOR

Georgia Rose Lucas is the daughter of Sandy Denny and Trevor Lucas. She lives in Sydney, Australia.

Georgia Rose Lucas at the Sandy Denny Exhibition, Brasenose Arms, Cropredy, 2025

DEDICATION

For Shannon, Ariel, Jahmira, Liam and the rest of my family. I love you with all my heart.

And for my mum, with love always, I miss what I'll never know.

FOREWORD

Sandy hated rehearsals. When I was in her band in 1971, with Timi Donald and Pat Donaldson, we would use the upstairs room at the Railway Tavern in West Hampstead, and nominally start at noon – although we had to have tea first. We might run through one song before lunch break, then another song before tea break about half an hour later. Sometimes there was the question of the freshness of the strings on Sandy's guitar. She never changed them, but would give me a pleading look, as if this was a masonic ritual beyond her powers of understanding, and I would sigh and go off into a corner and put fresh ones on – and that would be another half an hour. Another tea break or two, and we would have run through about three songs, and could then feel justified in stopping for the day.

When it was desperate, usually at the sound check before the first show of a tour, Sandy would finally get focused, and the real rehearsal would happen. The shows, of course, went off without a hitch.

RICHARD THOMPSON

Sandy aged 6, 1953 (Sandy Denny Archive)

PREFACE

I want to say thank you. Thank you to every single person who has contributed their story to this book. Reading through these pages has brought me a huge amount of joy and given me a new insight into my mum's life and music. Through your words, your memories, the way you describe hearing her voice for the first time, be it on a late-night radio station, a friend playing you a favourite album or standing at the front of a stage with your whole life ahead of you, I am reminded of how much my mum has touched the lives of so many people. She was funny, boisterous, sensitive, spiritual, sometimes difficult, sometimes sad but enormously brave and with an exceptional gift for communicating emotion. She had a life that was full and complicated and real.

People have had the most intimate personal relationships with my mum and her music, relationships that belong entirely to them, private and precious. Thank you for sharing those memories here. I know for some of you they were not easy to revisit but they matter to me, more than you could know.

One story especially has stayed with me. It is from a woman who was 16 when she first heard my mum on an underground radio station in Philadelphia in 1970. She tracked down import copies of her albums, spent hours every day listening to them, stood at the front of stages and carried Sandy in her heart for the rest of her life. She is now 70. She wrote that it is truly possible to grieve forever for someone you never met. I read that and I had to put the book down for a moment because I understand that. I was nine months old when my mum died, I still grieve for her and the life we might have had together.

For such a long time I couldn't listen to my mum's music, partly because I couldn't understand why people would choose to listen to music that would make them cry.

It wasn't until I got sick with cancer in 2016 that I finally stopped running from everything and started really listening to my mum's music. And when I did, something shifted in me that I can't quite put into words. Some of these stories made me laugh. Some made me reach for the tissues. All of them reminded me that my mum touched people in ways that go far beyond music — she touched their lives and shaped the way they've experienced the world.

Special thanks to Richard Houghton for inviting me to be part of this beautiful project. I am humbled and grateful. I hope in some small way this book brings the 'Sandy Community' a little closer together. That feels like exactly what she would have loved.

With so much love and gratitude.

GEORGIA ROSE LUCAS

INTRODUCTION

Sandy Denny's name was already familiar when the music press announced she had joined Fairport Convention. Aside from working with The Strawbs (with whom she had made an LP – unreleased at the time – that included the first recorded version of 'Who Knows Where The Time Goes?'), she also recorded with Johnny Silvo and as a solo artist, appearing on the 1967 album *Alex Campbell And Friends.*

It's often said that Sandy replaced Judy Dyble in Fairport Convention. But as the band moved to a harder rocky sound, Judy's vocals simply weren't strong enough (though ironically the next band she worked with was a nascent King Crimson) and Ashley Hutchings, as de facto band leader, was given the unenviable task of asking her to leave.

Fairport's Simon Nicol said, 'It was actually a few weeks before it dawned on us that Judy had made more of an impression on the audiences than we thought. When we went back to played gigs that we'd done with Judy, people were asking, 'Where's the girl gone?', 'What's happened to the chick singer?' We realised we'd established ourselves as a band with a female lead vocalist and we bowed to the inevitable. We had to find another one.

'We advertised for a new singer, inviting people to auditions. We also asked around to see whether anyone could suggest someone suitable. We auditioned about a dozen girls who were hopefuls. Some played guitar; some just sang. If there's anything worse than going to an audition, it's holding one. By the end we thought we were never going to find the right person. It was both embarrassing and difficult. You have to remember that we were still young, but we were a band with an album to our credit, a contract with Island and already quite a reputation. Then Sandy appeared.'

Fairport may have thought they were auditioning a potential lead vocalist. Sandy had other ideas.

'I'd worked for a while with The Strawbs and enjoyed the experience of being part of a band. My mental approach was that I was auditioning Fairport as a backing group, which is not how they were thinking of it.'

She played her first gig with Fairport at Middle Earth in London on 20

May 1968. A week later, she recorded a radio session with Fairport for *Top Gear*.

Even after joining Fairport Convention, Sandy maintained folk connections: she fulfilled her bookings, kept in contact with the likes of Anne Briggs and Bert Lloyd, and had a series of famous-folk-name boyfriends after Jackson C Frank's return to America ended their relationship. She even played on a session for The Young Tradition.

However, her lifestyle also embraced the rock ethos: her contemporaries attest to the prodigious amounts she could (and did) drink, make reference to her drugtaking and, as Al Stewart put it, her lifestyle that 'made Janis Joplin look like Mother Teresa'.

Fairport gigged extensively, building their reputation as a live act. They were regular guests on the newly established Radio 1, a frequency that producer John Walters put down to: 'The three Ps – prepared, professional and polite. They were not like other bands – they were musically interesting, not concerned about plugging a new release, always offering something different and surprising.'

The events surrounding Fairport's less than reliable Transit van on the return journey from a gig at Mothers in Birmingham on 11 May 1969 are part of music legend. Their roadie lost control of the vehicle, which left the road, scattering equipment and band members across the adjacent field. Only Simon Nicol remained inside, escaping serious injury.

Sandy had chosen to travel with her boyfriend Trevor Lucas and guitarist Gary Boyle from the band Eclection, who were also playing in Birmingham that night.

After *Liege & Lief*, Sandy left Fairport and formed a new band named after her song that opened her first album with Fairport, Fotheringay. It meant she could work with Trevor and follow her vision of folk rock, writing songs inspired by the tradition. They toured the university circuit and those sixties clubs that were still surviving, as well as concert venues opening up to rock music.

They made one album, including the epic 'Banks Of The Nile' (described by *Rolling Stone* as 'the best ever rock arrangement' before Fotheringay fell apart during the recording of their second album, some of which contributed to Sandy's next career move.

When one refers to Sandy's solo career, one is really talking about several different things. There was her initial folk-singer career. There were her noteworthy guest appearances (aside from recording with Led Zep, she also made a brief but memorable appearance in the all-star version of The Who's *Tommy*.) There were solo albums today regarded as classics – the sublime *Sandy* with its David Bailey cover, its outstanding songs and a gathering of musicians even more impressive than the first (add to the previous list Linda Thompson, Dave Swarbrick, John Kirkpatrick, Sneaky Pete Keinow, John Bundrick, Timi Donald plus brass arrangement by Allan Toussaint); the luscious *Like An Old Fashioned Waltz* featuring not only the classic 'Solo' but also a couple of jazz standards with Diz Disley, Danny Thompson et al.

After a couple of years struggling to get a workable Fairport line-up together, Daves Pegg and Swarbrick recruited Trevor Lucas and Jerry Donahue from the wreckage of Fotheringay and persuaded Dave Mattacks (for the first but by no means last time) to rejoin Fairport Convention, usually known as the '*Nine* line-up'. Sandy would often accompany husband Trevor to gigs and sometimes she'd join them on stage and blast out a couple of rock 'n' roll numbers. A world tour was planned. Sandy, meanwhile, had planned a tour to promote *Like An Old Fashioned Waltz* but Island decided to postpone the release of the album and the tour became pointless.

Sandy: 'Back then, you didn't tour to make money – as Fairport were about to prove in spectacular fashion – you toured to promote and sell your latest record. That's where the money was. Although *Like An Old Fashioned Waltz* was finished, there were no scheduled plans to put it out and touring would have been a waste of time and money, which we had very little of at that point.'

Sandy decided to head off around the world with Fairport. 'To make it clear, I wasn't going with Fairport. Very specifically I was going with Trevor.'

Dave Pegg: 'Fairport Convention are on stage. Sandy Denny, one of the greatest singers in the world and at the time the band's most high-profile member, is sitting in the wings, knitting or whatever. It simply didn't make sense.' She agreed to come on as a surprise guest on the tour.

By the time Fairport's world tour reached Los Angeles, Sandy was firmly ensconced as part of the band and a grand piano was part of the required stage set up. She played some of her solo oldies and some covers but no old Fairport material apart from 'Matty Groves'. It was officially confirmed (via the *NME* on 14 February 1975) that Sandy had rejoined the band. But Fairport Convention included none of the band members who first auditioned her – and her them – back in May 1968.

Fairport ('now with added Sandy Denny', to quote one gauche poster) ended their first US tour of 1974 in May in Washington DC. On 19 June they began a UK tour in Harlow, Essex. One reviewer said, 'The gig felt like a Sandy Denny concert punctuated with high-speed instrumentals.' As was her wont, Sandy was subtly taking over. Some within the band and the Fairport fanbase objected. Journalist Karl Dallas didn't help matters by coining the name 'Fotheringport' in an article that misleadingly said that the sextet consisted of 'three members of Fairport and three from Fotheringay'. More generous, and more accurate, was an end-of-year piece in *Sounds* describing Fairport as 'probably the hardest working British band of 1974'.

Island finally released *Like An Old Fashioned Waltz*, reckoned by many to be Sandy's masterpiece, almost a year later than originally planned. Fairport's live album was due out two weeks later, meaning there was no chance for Sandy to promote her release. She dismissed it with, 'I made that record so long ago I really can't remember.'

It remained a gem for future fans gratefully to unearth. 'Solo', a counterpart to the material she would write for the Fairport album, struck chords very quickly, and half a dozen cover versions appeared on albums over the next few months. Sadly, for 18 months after its release, the solo Sandy album that many fans name as their favourite was overshadowed by the fact she was now most definitely back in Fairport.

A couple of years later, on 8 October 1975, in my first in-depth interview with Sandy, I asked her about the revised plans of the previous 22 months. 'I'm not really a planner,' she told me, 'Things tend to happen, or not. Or people tell me what's been arranged and I go along with it… usually. Planning ahead always seemed to me a pretty certain way to end up being disappointed.'

At the start of 1975, Sandy was back on the road and in the studio, working with Fairport. Her solo album had gone down well with fans ('people wrote to me to say how much the songs meant to them') and the planned new Fairport album, featuring mainly her songs, was headed in a more commercial direction. But Dave Pegg remembered it differently. 'We'd worked hard and earned almost nothing. It seemed like the end. We'd not finished songs and no one was talking to each other and we'd no drummer.'

Reports in the music press alluded to tensions within the band; musical differences, leadership struggles, heavy drinking, the strain on Sandy's marriage. The gossip and rumours seemed validated when first Dave Mattacks and, ten months later, Jerry Donahue decided to quit the fold. (Dave's departure, the result of a dispute with producer-for-hire Glyn Johns, led to album cover art with the drummer pictured with his back to the camera.)

Sandy: 'I hate all that band politics stuff. When Dave Mattacks left, finding a new drummer, which was urgent because we were booked for a lot of gigs, was awful and stressful.' Work on *Rising For The Moon* was squeezed into February and March 1975, with a pressing deadline created by another Australian tour.

The two Daves, Swarbrick and Peggy were old guard post-1970 Fairport. Sandy was from the Fairport before that and very much still considered the Fairport vocalist. Jerry Donahue and Sandy's husband, Trevor, were from Fotheringay and therefore deemed to be in Sandy's camp. Add to that the marital tensions between Sandy and Trevor. A couple of years on, Sandy summed it up perfectly: 'You can only live in each other's pockets for so long before you start to wear holes in them.'

Jerry Donahue: 'I had become unhappy with the way the band was working out. It wasn't anything to do with musicianship, as Fairport included some of the finest musicians I have ever worked with. I called Sandy to explain how I felt… She said she and Trevor were thinking of leaving too.' The three quit the band on the same day. Sandy had been a Fairport member for 24 months; in the late sixties, the period usually described as 'the Sandy Denny era' of Fairport, she had lasted 20 months. As ever with Sandy, perceptions skew the documented reality.

That year I asked her whether she had any regrets about putting her career on hold and joining Fairport: 'It wasn't me that put my solo career on hold, it was the record company. I had no control over that. Joining

– or rejoining – Fairport meant I could be with Trevor, and the rest of the band were mates, even the ones I hadn't been in a band with before. That was a good thing. We had some great times, played some great gigs, met some great people, made a great album. Did it help my career? Probably not.'

There was a definite sense of needing to make a new solo album before someone pulled the plug.

In December 1975, Sandy withdrew to the rural retreat of The Twistle in Byfield in Northamptonshire to take a well-deserved rest, consider her future and begin writing new songs. By April 1976, she had more than enough to begin work on a new album. Seeking the elusive sound that would provide a long-desired breakthrough into the mainstream, Trevor recorded her at Island Studios, Basing Street Studios and CBS (London) Studios.

Rendezvous did not hit the shops until May 1977. There were other changes in Sandy's life too. She was six months pregnant: her daughter Georgia Rose was born on 12 July. With no new album to promote, Sandy's working life had been spent either writing at home or recording in the studio.

When I interviewed her after the release of the album, she spoke about the 'frustrating delay' in getting the album released, adding that, 'In this business, it's something you have to get used to.'

The album had been completed, with tracks to spare, with a final session at Island Studios in June 1976. On 24 February 1977, she returned to the Basing Street Studio to record a cover of Elton John's 'Candle In The Wind'. On the album it replaced her own 'Still Waters Run Deep' which was relegated to the B-side of the single. Sandy was coy and evasive when I asked about the motivation for recording such a strange song choice. As it turned out, this was the final release of her lifetime. It was almost an obituary, except Sandy had written at least half a dozen better songs (including the B-side) with more authority and fewer clichés.

*

One of the questions I am regularly asked is, 'What year did Sandy Denny perform at Cropredy?'

The Festival, which is what people generally mean by the term, did not come into existence until 1979, the year after Sandy's death and also the year Fairport decided to call it a day – the local appearance was to be their farewell UK gig! So the answer is that Sandy never performed on the Cropredy stage – though Vikki Clayton is just one of those who will tell you that when you are up there performing a Sandy song, you certainly feel a presence on stage beside you.

In the early years of Cropredy, Fairport were happy to backtrack through their 'boy band' years but songs closely associated with Sandy were a different matter. The spell was first broken in 1983, when The Albion Band were on the bill, meaning that Ashley Hutchings could briefly rejoin the band, bringing with him Cathy le Surf to sing Sandy's songs.

Prior to that Ralph McTell had played 'White Dress' annually when he joined Fairport on stage at Cropredy. The song highlights issues raised by the term 'Sandy songs': written by Dave Swarbrick, it was the one song of his sung by Sandy on *Rising For The Moon*.

Cathy le Surf's first stint as 'Sandy stand in' saw her reviving songs from *Liege & Lief* as well as 'Learning The Game', 'Rising For The Moon', 'Genesis Hall', 'Percy's Song', 'Si Tu Dois Partir' and 'Who Knows Where The Time Goes?'. The last song reappeared over the next four years as Cathy returned to sing Sandy. She was the first in a long line of guest female singers to undertake that rôle as Cropredy guests: others include Sally Barker, Beth Nielsen Chapman, Vikki Clayton, the Parker sisters, Julianne Reagan, June Tabor, and Chris While.

Chris While has taken on the task more than anyone else. When Fairport received the Radio 2 award for most influential folk album, she sang with the reformed original *Liege & Lief* line-up at special complete performances of the album in London and Cropredy. In 2008, marking the thirtieth anniversary of Sandy's death, she featured in a tribute set that included Vikki Clayton, Julie Fowlis, Kellie While and Kristina Donahue who sang 'The Battle Of Evermore' with Robert Plant as the finale of the set-within-the-set. At the end of the song, Robert paid tribute to Sandy and then turned to face her portrait on the big screen, becoming the front man in the audience as we all listened to Sandy's voice. For many, this remains one of Cropredy's most memorable moments.

Another is when the Cropredy stage was left empty and Sandy's version of 'Quiet Joys Of Brotherhood' was played over the PA. As Sandy's solo and then self-harmonised voice rang out across the field, it seemed time stood still: people stopped what they were doing to look at the stage, conversations hushed, purchases at the concessions were put on hold. It felt reverential and, as someone nearby remarked as Fairport returned, 'The field just filled with love.'

Not counting over twenty versions by Sandy, almost 100 cover versions of 'Who Knows Where The Times Goes?' have been released. In 2007, almost thirty years after Sandy's death and forty since her first draft of the song, it was voted 'Favourite Folk Track Of All Time' by listeners to BBC Radio 2. It has featured on at least three film soundtracks and in several TV dramas.

Each member of Fairport has a story of the first time they heard it – an enquiry after hearing Judy Collins had recorded a song Sandy had written; a visit one sunny afternoon, when she was playing it to herself near an open window; warming up in her dressing room before a gig; a soundcheck; even, unlikely as this is, 'when we went to see her at a folk club'.

They eventually recorded it on 9 April 1969 for their third album. It was the last track recorded for *Unhalfbricking*, an unreleased elegy at the time of their motorway crash a month later. After the accident the song, along with all pre-May '69 songs, was dropped from Fairport's setlist, which means Fairport Convention played it for less than three months, When Sandy rejoined in 1974, the band began to play the song again. In the meantime, seven versions had been released including those by Nina Simone, Lonnie Donegan, Marianne Faithfull and Nana Mouskouri.

After Sandy left Fairport (for the second time), Fairport once more put the song back on the shelf. It was dusted down whenever a guest singer wanted to perform it at Cropredy. While Fairport delved more and more into their back catalogue, first for Cropredy flashbacks, then for songs in their touring set and ultimately for new recordings, 'Time Goes' remained untouched.

Simon Nicol explained, 'Recording that song was a big step. It was one of the things in our back catalogue which we had consciously avoided. It was also the first time we released something which reworked a song Fairport had released before, in a way that was so different to the original version. We'd played it at Cropredy a number of times, of course, but always with a guest vocalist. This was the first time it had become part of the band's repertoire proper, and even then, it was one of the two bonus live tracks on the CD.'

It has become a fixture and there are over thirty Fairport versions available on vinyl, cassette, VHS, CD and DVD; it has also been performed (and recorded) by ex-members Maartin Allcock, Dan ar Bras, Iain Matthews, Dave Swarbrick and Richard Thompson.

If Sandy's reputation rested on that one song alone, it would be sufficient, but as this collection of recollections shows, that is very far from the case.

Everyone who knew her or knows her music has their own Sandy. Clues to the real Sandy lie in the correct connection of the puzzle pieces herein. There you will find Sandy the person. Ultimately:

We've all gone solo
We all play solo
Ain't life a solo?

NIGEL SCHOFIELD

Sandy (on the left) with her aunt, her brother David & her cousins c1955

Pat Chaplin - her sister was Sandy's school friend

SANDY'S AUNT & UNCLE'S HOUSE
1955, LIVERPOOL, UK

HILARY ENGLISH (NÉE JONES), SANDY'S COUSIN

I've never met anyone like her since. I have stories that sound so chocolate-boxy that they couldn't be true. But that's the whole point. Sandy could be drama queen-ish sometimes, but underlying it all was this kindness.

She really did love her mother particularly. When we were about eight – this is going to sound ridiculous, but it really happened – she was with us at Easter again. They came back to pick her up. Just before they were due to get back, she asked my mother if she could go outside by herself for a while. She went out and, when her parents arrived, which wasn't much longer, she came back into the house and she had the most enormous bunch of daffodils you have ever seen in your life. Her arms were full. Imagine somebody with their arms out at right angles. Her arms were full, absolutely full, of daffodils. Her mother said, 'Sandy? What have you got there?' Sandy said, 'Oh, they're for you.' Her mother said, 'Did you buy those?' Which was a ridiculous question. She said, 'No, no, no, I picked them for you.' You could see her mother's face, thinking, 'Oh, good gracious, every house within five square miles being raided by this child.' And she said, 'I'm very sorry, Sandy, but you're going to have to take them back to every person you got them from and apologise.' Sandy said, 'No, I can't put them back, they'll die!' 'Well, you can't go picking them out of people's gardens.' Sandy said, 'No, I picked them from the field.'

What Edna (her mother) hadn't noticed was that in front of the house there was a little green, and then a huge hedge, and then a lake, and then another huge hedge, and on the other side of that was this huge, huge field of daffodils. Fields and fields of them, actually. What they'd do is they planted all of these and as soon as they came into flower the fields were full of women whose job it was to snap the heads off – because they were just growing them for the bulbs. So this had been her plot.

My mother explained that they were not being grown for the flowers anyway, they were being grown for the bulbs. Sandy said, 'Mummy, I got them for you, I knew that you had to have them, because this is your 'host of golden daffodils'.' It was this huge thing. My mother, who was always launching into poetry, had been saying all sorts of poems a few days before, including the one about the host of golden daffodils. So Sandy had spied these daffodils through the really thick hedge, found an opening, and then when her mother was due to come back, her mother was going to get a host of golden daffodils.

So we had to find huge amounts of newspaper and wet it all. The car was piled high with this 'host of golden daffodils'.

Other people would have admired the daffodils, other people might have taken one or two, but Sandy linked it with this poem and had to have a host of golden daffodils for her mother.

After Sandy died, the following fall, her parents planted a lot [a couple of hundred] of daffodils near the house they had down in Cornwall, that were left to be naturalised. I wondered if she remembered what Sandy had done as a child. She was very close to her mother. And her mother did think that Sandy was wonderful.

COOMBE COUNTY SECONDARY GIRLS' SCHOOL
1963-64, NEW MALDEN, SURREY, UK

PAT CHAPLIN

Sandy was my sister Barbara's friend at Coombe County School in New Malden in the 1960s. They were both interested in music and sang in the school's senior choir, which always sounded heavenly. Barbara remembers her playing the violin in the school orchestra, and I remember her sometimes playing the piano in the school's morning assembly.

Sandy and Barbara were four years older than me, but I do remember Sandy quite well as we often travelled to school together. When we travelled by train, Sandy joined us on the train at the station after ours. I remember looking out of the window as the train pulled into Sandy's station (Raynes Park) so that she could see which carriage we were in. I remember her being very funny and self-confident (unlike me) and I was always slightly afraid to say too much in case I said something silly, although I don't think she'd have been unkind if I had. She never seemed to be bothered about what people thought of her.

One very strong memory I have of her is when she joined us on the train and complained that some workmen had made fun of her socks. Unlike most teenagers, she and my sister didn't really keep up with the latest fashions. Most of us wanted to wear either white knee-length socks or tan-coloured stockings to school (in the days before tights!). On this particular day, Sandy was wearing what I would call 'fisherman's socks' which were slightly tweedy. Instead of being embarrassed like most teenage girls would have been, she was indignant and said something like, 'How dare they criticise my socks! What's it got to do with them?' Sometimes our dad would drive us to school and we would stop and pick Sandy up from her house.

Sandy came to some of my sister's birthday parties at our house. My dad always used to take photos of the group of girls at the parties, but sadly my mum destroyed a lot of photos when she developed dementia, including the party photos. Many photos were lost that way before we realised what she was doing.

I asked my sister what her memories of Sandy were. She said she remembers once in a Latin class Sandy translated a sentence as 'elephants on scooters!' She said Sandy did the first year of A-level music in the sixth form at Coombe but left after that, when I think they must have lost contact. My sister got on with the music teacher, but apparently Sandy didn't. (I wasn't keen on her either!) Barbara and Sandy both went on an educational school cruise to Madeira, Lisbon and Corunna and one day Sandy and some others were messing about in the dormitory and managed to flood the bathroom. They tried to mop it up, but I don't know how successful they were.

JEANNIE MACMEEKIN

We were in the same year at school. She was never in my form lower down, but by the time I got to the sixth form, there were eleven of us in the lower sixth and maybe four in the upper sixth. And Sandy was one of them. I think she took English, History and Music. I took at least one class the same as her, and I know she took music with the deputy head, whose name was Mr Fisher.

Jeannie MacMeekin was head girl at Sandy's school

The school was very *Prime of Miss Jean Brodie*-

ish. There were a lot of single women on the staff who felt very strongly about women's education. Ann Packer (who won a gold medal at the Rome Olympics) was our PE teacher, and our art teacher designed some of the tiles for the London Underground when they revamped it. He claimed to be a Polish count or something, and our French teacher, Mr Gander, had been heavily involved in refugee work. They were quite powerful teachers who were very keen on us not all ending up working in a factory. It was an era when we were being pushed to be outspoken. So there was a lot going on in school and it was a radical place to be in lots of ways.

The upper sixth didn't have a common room, but when there was going to be eleven of us in the lower sixth and it was too many to have us wandering about with nowhere to sit, we were given an old stationery cupboard as a common room. And lots of us, including Sandy, spent time painting this incredibly small room with a tiny window.

She was very musical right from day one as far as I remember, playing in the school orchestra and the choir and all that kind of stuff. Not that I was in the choir because I'm rubbish at that kind of thing.

The school made me head girl because I was terribly shy and they thought it would be really good for me. And several of the girls they promoted as prefects, including Sandy and a girl called Diana Wignall, were very much anti prefects.

We were supposed to do things like enforce school uniforms and stuff, and they were adamantly against all that and said, 'No, we're never going to do that.' And I was constantly being asked to try and persuade them to toe the line, which didn't work. And she was never turning up for prefects' meetings: 'No, I'm not going to do that.'

I always remember having what you might call unruly hair, which didn't go down very well. You were supposed to keep it respectable. And we had these ridiculous little Juliet caps with a tassel that we had to wear, which she adamantly refused to wear.

And we had to wear straw boaters in the summer. She always looked a bit messy, I suppose you'd say. But if you saw her outside of school, I think you could say she was specially dressed.

I went with a couple of friends to see her in a folk club in Kingston or somewhere like that, to give her a bit of moral support. It was very early on and she wasn't even sure whether they were going to let her sing. She rocked up with a guitar and just hoped that they would let her on. She sang a couple of songs. And then we all hurried away because we weren't really supposed to be there. I hadn't told my mum I was going!

I didn't see much of her after school finished. We all went our separate ways. I keep in touch with hardly anybody from school.

I followed her career from afar, and it was fascinating to think, 'Gosh, I know this person.' I wasn't altogether surprised that she made it because she was very good and very confident. She was always a bit of a 'taking no prisoners' kind of person. To be a singer was what she wanted to do with her life, so it didn't surprise me at all that that's what she ended up doing.

She was always sloping off PE because she hated it. She'd disappear into the loo and we had to flush her out and say, 'Come on, you've got to go to PE otherwise we'll all be in trouble.'

I wasn't entirely in her group. She had a life outside school that I didn't really have, because she was already involved in music at school. So that when she did start playing the folk clubs, it was just the obvious next step in cultivating us. Her life outside school was quite daring and grown up to us. She was going to the pub when she was in the fifth year.

My memory of being head girl is having constantly to say, 'Don't forget, you've got to come to this,' and, 'Don't forget to do so-and-so.' And she'd say, 'I can't be arsed.' It was very irritating when you wanted her to do something and she'd never be there. But she was in the school production of *The Mikado* as Nanki-Poo – the love interest, as it were.

Overall, they're fun memories. She was a laugh. And in a way, I quite admired her.

FOLK CLUB
1964-65, RICHMOND-UPON-THAMES, UK

BOB CARTWRIGHT

Back when the folk music revival was in full swing in London and other UK cities, I ran a small club in Richmond. The main aim was to promote local performers and raise money for Richmond Labour Party Young Socialists and other left-wing causes.

The club met on Saturday nights in the basement of the Labour Party offices. The room could accommodate about 80 people in comfort, but throughout its relatively short existence we attracted an audience of well over a hundred.

Even today, it seems remarkable how easy it was to run a small but popular folk club. At least, it was in Richmond. During the 1960s, Richmond boasted a plethora of establishments for jazz and rhythm and blues fans. But there was nothing for folk music fans, so a few of us decided to give it a go.

We thought we had a ready-made audience, the first requirement for success. In addition, there was an almost limitless number of local performers who jammed in local pubs and would play and sing in the club for the cost of a drink. The local talent was led by a former schoolmate of mine, Tony 'Duster' Bennett, who singly fronted the Jericho Jugband. More than that, we had a valuable friend in the formidable form of Theo Johnson, Richmond resident and manager of Bungies, one of London's best-known clubs. Bungies kicked off around midnight so Theo was more than happy to use our club as a warm up for the likes of Jackson C Frank, Lou Killen and Nigel Denver, and on one very memorable night he allowed us the first UK concert by Tom Paxton.

Sandy starting out (Sandy Denny Archive)

But there was one person, the best friend of one of my ex-girlfriends, who came to the club frequently, never pestered us to perform and gave no idea whatsoever of the enormous talent she was hiding. She only sprang to life at the end of an evening when we were clearing up. On Sunday mornings the room was rented to the Christadelphians for their church service, and hidden in the dark corner of the room was the

American harmonium they used for their hymns. The only person who showed the harmonium the slightest attention was this one girl, who would plead passionately for ten minutes on the instrument. The sound was amazing and she certainly knew how to get the best out of it.

The girl on the harmonium was Sandy Denny and, sadly, that was the only contribution she ever made to the folk club.

KINGSTON COLLEGE OF ART
1965, KINGSTON-UPON-THAMES, UK

PETE COLE

I was with Sandy at art college (now Kingston Uni). She was my partner for about six months. She had a bad experience when a part fell off her small clay sculpture. The others, including the tutor, laughed. She was crying but managed to hide it. I was very sad. She walked out of the room, telling me she'd be in the local pub, The Swan.

In the pub she told me she was leaving the course to concentrate on her music. The Swan hosted live rock'n'roll and Sandy, without telling many people, loved rock'n'roll. A band was rehearsing in the pub and I asked the boss to let Sandy get on stage and join the practice. With their backing, she sang an excellent Gene Vincent number and everyone applauded.

We split up because I couldn't do all the travel with her, although I had a good motor bike, which she loved being on with me for rides into the country.

I bumped into her a few years later, in a pub in Barnes. She was with her husband, and I was with my first wife and my children. I told her about Gene's death not long after, back in USA. We all agreed to meet again, but sadly she died not long after.

UNIVERSITY OF ESSEX FOLK CLUB
1966, COLCHESTER, UK

ANDREW PRING

In very early days while at Essex University, Sandy was a regular solo performer for our folk club before she moved to groups. She (as well as Davy Graham, Bert Jansch, John Renbourn and Roy Harper) was booked by Paul Adler.

THE TROUBADOUR
1966, LONDON, UK

RICHARD DIGANCE

My first recollections of Sandy go way, way back to 1966 and music sessions at the world-famous Troubadour coffee house in London's Old Brompton Road. Bob Dylan played there back in the day and Ed Sheeran in more modern times. The place probably held no more than 60 folkie fans, two of which were myself and Sandy. It was a handy venue for her as she worked just down the road for a short time at Brompton Hospital.

I would suggest The Troubadour to be a highly important factor of Sandy's career and social life. A tiny coffee house that would have looked more at home on a Paris street than round the corner from Earls Court, it was the meeting place for so many of us. In through the door, through tables, where mostly old men smoked like chimneys and played chess, to a set of stupidly steep wooden stairs on the far-right corner by the side of the counter that led down to the cellar, the music room. Saturday nights were hosted by Martin Windsor and Redd Sullivan and it was one such Saturday night I saw Sandy perform for the first time. There was no dressing room as such, just a curtain behind which was a small space around three feet by six feet.

PA system? You must be joking. She sat cross-legged on the floor, chatting with Linda Peters, later Richard Thompson's wife, another magnificent singer of course, and she got up and sang a few songs, just three if I remember correctly. Her vocals were angelic and revolutionary as most female singers at the time pretended to be American and sang like Hedy West, Joan Baez or Judy Collins. Sandy sounded English and it was so refreshing. She giggled and larked around in-between those songs, equally refreshing at a time when most of us folkies took ourselves far too seriously. At that time, she played a huge jumbo guitar, long before her well-known instrument. I can't remember the make. None of us could afford nice guitars at such an early stage of our careers.

Many will argue that Sandy's rise on the folk scene was attributed to the legendary Les Cousins club in Greek Street, a rare club, another cellar, that boasted three main acts each evening, but that isn't so. Sandy's appearances at Les Cousins were sparse, although I do recall her getting up one time with John Martyn. Her boyfriend Jackson C Frank played there often but Sandy not so much. (By the way I met him on, I think, three occasions and I never heard him speak.)

Impressed by her few songs, I saw Sandy's first full gig at the Hammersmith Folk Centre, run by Rod Hamilton in a pub not far from The Troubadour, The Prince of Wales. Sandy was no shrinking violet and she spoke to many of the couple of dozen that made up the audience, including me, and from that evening our friendship grew.

Sandy made a couple of albums on a cheap label, duetting with Alex Campbell and Johnny Silvo. I bought both and hated both. It wasn't the Sandy Denny I wanted to hear. One evening I met up with Sandy at The Holy Ground Folk Club in Bayswater, run by my good friend Ronnie Cairnduff. She had turned up to watch The Strawbs gig. I hasten to add the original Strawbs were two guitars and an upright string bass, long before the likes of Rick Wakeman and electricity pumped into instruments. She joined the embryonic Strawbs shortly afterwards and again, I felt a little disappointed, her vocals crashing with the violent raging vocals of Dave Cousins. But luckily for all Sandy's solo gigs were wondrous. Sometimes they fell apart and sometimes they didn't. Sandy was human and her frailties showed every time she got up on stage. That's what we all loved about Sandy Denny, the delicate, non-conformist in every way.

We all smoked and drank when we could afford it, but the sixties folk scene wasn't laced with drugs like the rock circuit. We were a skint tribe, possibly pioneers of the real ale movement, so we made do with fags and booze. It was years later that Sandy tangled with such demons.

In 1967 Sandy appeared at my local folk club, The Central, in Barking Road, East Ham for the second time. Being in the East End of London it was the opposite side of town to where she lived. The Central, above an old East End pub, now closed and a kid's play centre, boasted the time Sandy fell off her stool and broke her leg, yet carried on playing. The next time she came she missed her last Tube train back across London and so she stayed the night at my parents' council flat in Blaney Crescent. She became a big hit with my dad, an incredible statement as my dad didn't like too many of my hippie friends, and every time we met up, she asked after him. Sandy was very much the cheeky girl with a laugh as raucous as a drunken sailor and he loved that, as did I.

Having slept in my bed, the following morning my mum made Sandy a bacon sandwich before we set off on the long walk to East Ham station, chatting all the way. She told me how she didn't really know what she wanted at that time. I personally feel she never had the confidence to truly go it alone, thus her connection with Fairport Convention. Of course we kept in touch, but had she not joined Fairport there would be no electric folk rock scene today. Mark my words, that is true. It became the next chapter in the life of a muddled Sandy Denny. I watched her grow from a giggly teenager on stage in a far-too-revealing mini-skirt at times to the creative animal that started the electric folk boom that exists today.

So how do I rate Sandy Denny the singer, I who have toured Britain with Elkie Brooks, Joan Armatrading and even performed with Cher in America? She was the best British female vocalist of all time, so put that in your pipe and smoke it. Sandy would have. An honour to have been a friend.

UNKNOWN VENUE
1966, LEICESTER, UK

PJ WRIGHT, SANDY DENNY PROJECT

The only time I was in the same room as Sandy Denny was in 1966. I was a shy schoolboy in the audience at a tiny folk club in Leicester, where she played (I think) a Guild guitar and sang what I recall as a mainly folk song set. I was struck by her lovely pure voice! It was the first folk club I'd been to and in the three consecutive weeks I went the acts were Sandy, Martin Carthy and Hedy West. Alas, that is my only recollection of her. I didn't even say hello!

VIKING FOLK CLUB, DEANE ARMS HOTEL
SEPTEMBER – NOVEMBER 1966, RUISLIP, UK

FRANK WELCOMME, MUSICIAN

I left school and turned 18 in the summer of 1966. I was living in Bushey Heath, North London. I was a keen but totally incompetent musician. I found I could do some folk songs with some finger-picking guitar tips picked up from an Alan Lomax book. I looked around for a folk club to try these out at and found the Viking Folk Club at the Deane Arms Hotel in Ruislip. (It later became the Middlesex Arms.) I cycled the 45 minutes each way for several weeks – usually in the pouring rain – with my (first ever) guitar strapped to the luggage rack. I remember the backroom being uninviting - with the tiled floor being cold and usually wet (because of the rain). I stopped going because I moved away with work.

I recall a big thing being made of Sandy being a resident there on alternate weeks. There were other people also coming along who subsequently became famous. I think Bert Jansch was one.

I recall Sandy singing '3.10 To Yuma' and 'Milk And Honey' as well as 'Last Thing On My Mind' and 'I Loved A Lass'. She also kept going on about Jackson C Frank songs – but I was never really impressed by those.

She smoked incessantly (as did many in those days) and often stuck her cigarette on the string stubs on the head of her guitar while she sang, which was very distracting. One little comment she made was that she'd been slung out of the choir at school – because she couldn't sing!

I subsequently realised that she must be quite good because that December she was asked to sing at a Christmas concert at the Royal Albert Hall – at least, that was what was promoted in the club. I recall that because I was peeved that no one had asked me to sing there! (I had moved away by then so couldn't have gone anyway.)

I remember her being quite pretty and, it being the era of the mini skirt, her having short dresses. She sang sitting on a tall stool (but I was 18 and she was about 18 months older than me, and I wasn't interested in her like that).

LES COUSINS
1966, SOHO, LONDON, UK

ANNA HAGLEY

I remember Sandy very well from Les Cousins club in Greek Street, I used to see her there all the time. She was very complimentary about a particular red velvet dress I wore sometimes. She and I used to share cabs going home from Soho. I used to drop her at Wimbledon and I carried on to Wallington.

I remember one New Year's Eve I was with her and her parents at Les Cousins and Paul Simon walked in and came straight up to Sandy as he knew her. She was such a lovely person and I was really shocked to read about her death in *Time* magazine. She was such a loss to so many people.

RAY STEVENSON, PHOTOGRAPHER

One night at Les Cousins at the end of her set nobody clapped, just silence. In the corridor she was on the verge of tears to have got no applause at all. Linda Peters (aka Linda Thompson) set her straight. 'No, no, Sandy, it was so perfect that no-one wanted to break the mood.' That's how good she could be.

I was a sort of an evangelist for Sandy, telling anyone who would listen how good she was. Some already knew, others didn't like 'folk'. One rock guitarist told me 'girls can't sing'. Twenty years after her death, a friend with a state-of-the-art hi-fi put on a Fairport album. It was like she was in the room. I had to make him take it off, before I burst into tears.

REDCAR JAZZ CLUB
21 MAY 1967, REDCAR, UK

IAN TYZACK, MUSICIAN

Ian Tyzack first saw Sandy at Redcar Jazz Club

I first saw Sandy at Redcar Jazz Club and Fairport at Redcar Jazz Club (and later with Fotheringay) and then in either Edinburgh or Dundee. She was absolutely spectacular! Over time, I've performed 'Who Knows Where The Time Goes', 'Farewell, Farewell', 'The Deserter', 'The Sea', 'Matty Groves' and 'No End', amongst many others, at various folk and acoustic clubs. They're all evocative songs that will last forever.

HANGING LAMP FOLK CLUB
1967, RICHMOND-UPON-THAMES, UK

BOB WHITLEY

Sandy starting out (Ray Stevenson) (Sandy Denny Archive)

In the sixth form at Isleworth Grammar, I started attending the Hanging Lamp Folk Club where I saw Sandy for the first time. I was totally transfixed and from then on sought every opportunity I could to see her perform. I saw her perform several more times at the Hanging Lamp in 1967, '68 and '69, and also at Les Cousins in Soho. She was a significant influence in me wanting to turn from writing poetry to writing songs. Just before going to university in autumn 1969, I bought a cheap mandolin and gradually moved to mandola and much later guitar.

I saw Sandy with Fairport at the Royal Festival Hall on 24 September 1969 (I still have the ticket stub) with support from Nick Drake and John and Beverley Martin. (John was also a regular at the Hanging Lamp and Les Cousins).

I then saw the Fairport concert at Exeter University in about November 1969. I bought *What We Did On Our Holidays*, *Unhalfbricking* and *Liege & Lief* when they came out. At university I became a singer songwriter and ran a folk and poetry club and recall going to a Fairport concert at the Royal Albert Hall during this period.

When Sandy left Fairport, I followed Fotheringay and saw them at the Royal Festival Hall on 30 March 1970. When I left university, I married and had children. Sandy was played to our children throughout their early lives.

I have run folk clubs and performed regularly in later years. I now perform historical folk musicals in my retirement. My daughter has an amazing voice, developed by singing along to all Sandy's Fairport songs as a child. My youngest son has become a professional folk singer. His duo, Ninebarrow, are BBC folk award nominees. Being inspired by Sandy has transformed my life and that of my children.

VANLØSE BIO RECORDING STUDIO
JULY 1967, COPENHAGEN, DENMARK

DAVE COUSINS, THE STRAWBS

Karl Knudsen took us to the studio at the Vanløse Bio, an old cinema in the centre of Copenhagen. We were introduced to producer Gustav Winckler, the Danish Frank Sinatra, engineer Ivar Rosenberg and the top Danish drummer, Ken Gudmand. The studio was on the stage of the cinema, and we could only record during the day as the cinema was still in use. The 'multi-track tape machine' was a three-track, sprocket-driven, film soundtrack recorder. We didn't know any different at the time as we had only ever recorded straight to stereo. Apparently, many classical recordings in the 1950s were made on these machines, but to get the best 'audio fidelity' the placing of the microphones was crucial. Ivar Rosenberg was a master of microphone placement, and used only the very best Neumanns. The harmony vocals were double-tracked on to the third track, a totally new experience for us, and the three track recordings were mixed down to two-track stereo… Although audiophiles can hear an element of wow and flutter, the sound is remarkably fresh…

Sandy, Dave Cousins & Tony Hopper were cover stars on the album *All Our Own Work* (Ray Stevenson)

Sandy on the rear cover of the Strawbs album, 1967

Sandy and I had become good friends over the months we'd been rehearsing and recording together. I was married and there was no hint of a relationship. I became Sandy's confidant. Late one night in Copenhagen, she was desperately sad that her doctor had told her she could never have children. In retrospect it accounts for many of Sandy's personality traits that people have identified with – her irascibility, her frustrations, and her melancholy.

LIVINGSTON RECORDING STUDIO
1967, BARNET, LONDON, UK

GORDON GILTRAP MBE

I think the year was 1967. The location was the first site of the Livingston Recording Studio in Barnet. It was the first day of recording for my first ever album, for Transatlantic Records, and the producer was the legendary Bill Leader, who produced Bert Jansch, John Renbourn and many more besides.

Gordon Giltrap with Georgia Rose Lucas

I arrived early and was raring to go but time was being spent looking for a lost recording. It was Dave Swarbrick with his very pretty girlfriend who was, of course, Sandy Denny. All I remember is being taken by her quiet and almost shy presence.

The second time I encountered Sandy was at the legendary Les Cousins whilst attending a John Martyn gig. John was giving various name checks to friends in the audience but hadn't mention Sandy. I was standing next to her when she announced in a loud voice 'and Sandy Denny'. I can remember thinking that here was a strong lady making her presence felt.

Many years later, I had met up with her then husband, the lovely

Trevor Lucas. I had supported his band Eclection at a university gig. It was a great band and I was told that one of its members, Michael Rosen, was leaving and there might be a vacancy for a guitarist. I was so taken with the band and had a strong desire to be a part of it. We exchanged numbers and I was invited to attend a rehearsal in the back room of a pub in Ealing. I turned up with my trusty John Bailey acoustic along with a tiny Gibson amp.

I plugged in and thought to jam along with the piece they were rehearsing. Their keyboard player was a guy called John 'Poli' Palmer. There I was, merrily jamming along, when Mr Palmer asked me in no uncertain terms to stop playing because they were trying to rehearse! Needless to say, I felt devastated. I quietly packed my stuff and departed. I was almost out the door when Trevor came up full of sincere apologies and asked me to call him in a few days.

On 27 May, the day of my son's birthday. I rang Trevor's home and Sandy answered the phone. She was an absolute delight to talk to. She told me that Trev was out. She then went on to ask me what I was doing for the day. I told her it was my little boy's birthday and we were preparing a little tea party for his friends. Sandy then asked if there were going to be cakes and jelly. I said, 'Of course,' and she said, 'I wish I could be there with you because I just love birthday parties and cakes and jellies.'

She was so lovely and innocent and even child-like in her enthusiasm. The chat was utterly delightful and I shall never forget that this amazing songstress could be so joyful about a child's birthday party.

The last time I saw Sandy was at a fundraising concert in London for two amazing guys who ran the famous Troubadour club, Redd Sullivan and Martin Windsor. They were great characters and always found time to give me gigs there whenever I needed one. I was part of the bill that included Noel Murphy and Davy Johnson, an astonishing musician who became Elton John's guitarist and remains so right up until the present day. I can't remember who else was on but it was quite a line up. But I digress…

Word had got round that Fairport Convention might appear and a ripple of excitement ran through the proceedings at the prospect of this amazing band turning up. Sure enough, midway through the evening the stage door burst open and like a whirlwind the band came in ready to rock.

There was Sandy, cigarette in hand and wearing a fringed jacket, looking very rock and roll. I don't remember chatting with her as there was so much going on. Trevor was now a full-time member and I think the line-up was the classic one of Conway, Swarbrick, Peggy, Nicol, Thompson, Sandy and Trevor. Trevor wore a very smart three-piece suit and was playing a beautiful Gibson J-50.

All the above memories are quite fleeting, but very special to me.

THÉÂTRE 140
1 OCTOBER 1967, BRUSSELS, BELGIUM

OLIVIER LE DOUR

Jo Dekmine was the founder of Théâtre 140, a very well-known, if small, theatre in Brussels. He was well known for supporting promising talented artists, from the sixties until the 2010s. I once met a used record dealer who had a shop close to the Grand'Place and who told me that he had seen Sandy Denny (pre-Fairport) there on the same bill as Manfred Mann and Denny Laine (post-Moody Blues, pre-Wings).

A press report from that time says that Sandy accompanied herself on acoustic guitar, performing 'Who Knows Where

Promotional photo for Brussels British Week October 1967 (Sandy Denny Archive)

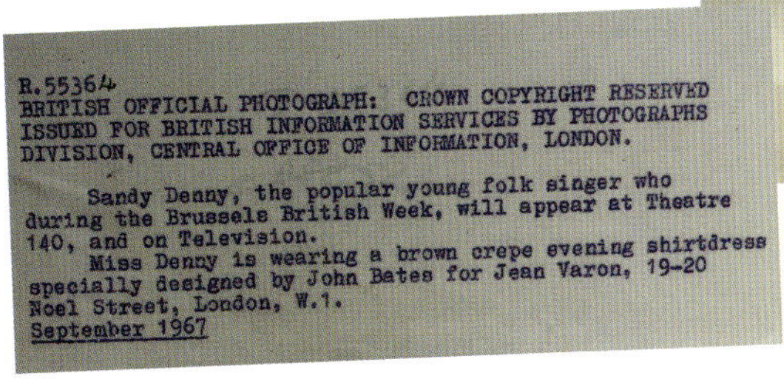

R.55364
BRITISH OFFICIAL PHOTOGRAPH: CROWN COPYRIGHT RESERVED
ISSUED FOR BRITISH INFORMATION SERVICES BY PHOTOGRAPHS DIVISION, CENTRAL OFFICE OF INFORMATION, LONDON.

Sandy Denny, the popular young folk singer who during the Brussels British Week, will appear at Theatre 140, and on Television.

Miss Denny is wearing a brown crepe evening shirtdress specially designed by John Bates for Jean Varon, 19-20 Noel Street, London, W.1.

September 1967

The Time Goes?' The record dealer remembered Sandy and Denny Laine talking loudly, a few seats from him, during Manfred Mann's set.

Given her fear of flying that led her to difficulties with Fairport, it is interesting that Sandy had crossed the Channel to perform solo. Her connection to Manfred Mann, which led to her singing on the *Swedish Fly Girl* soundtrack in 1972, might date back to these 1967 days?

LES COUSINS
1968, SOHO, LONDON, UK

RICHARD PEARL

I first saw Sandy perform at Les Cousins folk club in Greek Street, Soho. She did a guest spot singing 'She Moved Through The Fair' a cappella. It was so stunning that I was moved by the experience. A little later, I found out that she had joined my friend Richard Thompson's band Fairport Convention, as a replacement for Judy Dyble.

My friends and I went to a lot of Fairport's gigs in those days, and the combination of the vocals of Sandy and Iain Matthews was very remarkable for a burgeoning folk rock band. They did wonderful versions of songs like Richard Fariña's 'Reno, Nevada' and Leonard Cohen's 'Suzanne,' backed by RT, Simon Nicol, Ashley Hutchings (whom we knew as Tyger) and Martin Lamble.

I used to visit Richard's flat in Brent Cross, which he shared with school friends Paul Ghosh and Andy Horvitch. Iain Matthews also lived there for a while. Often, Sandy would be there and we would listen to the latest albums by The Band, Neil Young, Love and other American artists, and there were sometimes some practice sessions there too, on acoustic guitars. After I went to uni, I didn't see them much but I did hear how devastating the van crash on the M1 had been.

Les Cousins membership card

I remember listening to *Liege & Lief* for the first time and thinking, 'This is as good as it gets,' and I haven't changed my opinion. However, in my opinion Sandy's song 'Who Knows Where The Time Goes?' (from *Unhalfbricking*, which RT sometimes performs live), remains one of the finest contemporary songs ever written.

I continued to follow her career with Fotheringay (where she had a great rapport with Trevor Lucas) though I never saw them perform live. I was very sad to hear of her tragic death.

ROYSTON WOOD, THE YOUNG TRADITION

Bridget St John, John Altman, Diana Matheou, Georgia Rose Lucas & Steve Tilston, Les Cousins' 60th anniversary, 2025

Sandy sang with a bunch of guys who called themselves the Strawberry Hill Boys – later The Strawbs. In the alleged good old 1960s, when Les Cousins club in London's Soho used to hold all-night folk bashes, and the Young Tradition might stay on after a gig to sing, be raucous and get stoned with all the other up-and-comings, Sandy, under the influence of her American mentor and sometime lover Jackson Frank (he of the heart-stopping lyricism; oh, Jackson, a lovely man and fucked-up true poet as he was) made young Alexandra Denny sing the soul-ridden stuff she was made to sing.

When she later joined the growing Fairport Convention, she was becoming the person who wrote powerful, mysterious poems-to-music as even one Robert Zimmerman from Hibbing, Minnesota, couldn't do, she being from Scotland and all. And she sang her songs, and Dylan's songs, and traditional songs from Scotland and England, the songs whose canny subtleties she had learned from hearing people like The Young Tradition, singing into the multi-flavoured smoke at Les Cousins. But she sang them in her own smoky fashion and made something new out of them.

GUILDHALL
27 MAY 1968, PORTSMOUTH, UK

TIM M

On Fairport's third gig at Portsmouth someone was playing three-foot-tall bongos. I asked if I could have a go, and did so for one song, successfully, even though I didn't know the song or instrument. That probably got me the invite to the studio. Sandy asked me to sing – something that had always been strongly discouraged in my life. She coached me to the extent that she asked me to join in the chorus of a song. When I tried no sound came out! She gave me a swig of vodka, something I'd never drunk before, and I was able to join in with 'Eastern Rain'. It was a magical experience being so close to her beautiful voice. But I'd had enough vodka to make singing 'ooh, ooh' repeatedly seem hysterically funny. We managed to complete the take, but then I laughed so much I puked. The stench hung around for weeks, there being no air conditioning. In the end I paid Joe Boyd compensation for an extensive cleaning, which almost cleared the smell. Most of the band were

Sandy joins Fairport, signing the recording contract May 1968

annoyed Sandy had promoted someone who literally came out of the audience to influence their album, but Sandy was boss.

After some weeks the band asked me to join them, but I was just off to tour the world with the Moody Blues as their sound engineer. I bluffed my way in despite having no idea what the job entailed. I paid an engineer to teach me before we left.

UNIVERSITY OF EAST ANGLIA
22 JUNE 1968, NORWICH, UK

OLIVER GRAY

UEA's social secretary – a burly, determined Welshman called John Morgan – had an agenda of 'progressive rock'. He pulled off quite a coup by arranging for Pink Floyd to visit UEA, in a surprising but clever double bill with Fairport Convention (because both were represented by the Bryan Morrison Agency). Being now UEA's official Rock Bod, I was keen, if not confident, to try and do some interviews. But, apart from the friendly-looking Sandy Denny, the Fairports looked scary. Tyger Hutchings, in particular, seemed aloof and unsmiling, so I decided to go for the brilliant guitar player with the Bolan-style corkscrew hair.

With Fairport (Eric Hayes)

'Excuse me, have you got a few minutes to spare?'

'Only if you ask extremely intelligent questions.' (Despite the total change of appearance since those days, Richard Thompson was as affable then as he is now.)

This version of Fairport still contained Iain Matthews as well as Sandy Denny, who was cheerful and relaxed. On drums was Martin Lamble and later that night I met a girl who knew him from home in Golders Green. She went on to become his girlfriend and they were still going out together a few months later when Martin was tragically killed in a crash in the band's van.

My interview with Richard revealed exciting things such as the fact that they would describe their music as 'electric folk' (goodness), that they never had trouble winning over audiences and that, if they had to compare themselves to any other bands, they would say Big Brother and the Holding Company. At the time, I was astonished: there didn't seem to be any similarity between Sandy Denny and Janis Joplin. History was to prove, however, that there were, indeed, a number of similarities, not least in their volatility and their embracing of the darker side of the rock lifestyle.

The Fairports gave a revelatory performance. Sandy broke the audience's hearts with her versions of 'Who Knows Where The Time Goes?' and Leonard Cohen's 'Suzanne', and we sat cross-legged on the floor, enraptured. The atmosphere intensified with the arrival of the Floyd, who were headlining. The light show, so innovative for its time, wafted and flickered over the band as they played endless, mesmerising versions of 'Astronomy Domine' and 'Careful With That Axe, Eugene'. They looked so frightening on stage but they, too, were happy to be interviewed. Roger Waters was particularly magnanimous towards Fairport, calling them 'the best electric folk this side of anywhere'.

Fairport's return visit to UEA later that year, this time headlining, was not a success, because Sandy had a bad throat and was also in a black mood. At first, she refused to go on, but the Social Secretary waved the contract in her face and insisted. She coughed her way through the first song, but during the second, her voice gave out completely. The band left the stage and I had to rush back to my post to put on a record. Sitting backstage on a flight of steps was Sandy Denny, just in the process of lighting up a King Size Benson and Hedges.

'Do you think that's a good idea?' I enquired, remembering what a warm, friendly person she had been on the band's last visit.

'What do you mean?'

'Maybe smoking a cigarette isn't a very good idea if you've got a bad throat.'

'Well,' replied Sandy, 'you are just a pathetic little creep and you can fuck right off.'

PAUL FRINDLE

I was 17 years old. We had a band and we were gigging around East Anglia. There was a Pink Floyd gig at the new University of East Anglia in Norwich for which we had tickets – and went to with much excitement. However, the warm up act on a side stage playing this new folk rock was so great and exciting that we were completely enthralled by it. They were called the Fairport Convention and none of us had ever heard of them before – and their style of music was completely new to us. They had a girl singer.

Their set was so great and exciting that, when it finished, we went outside to smoke, drink beer and chat. And we chatted so much about what we'd heard that we lost interest in Pink Floyd entirely! When we went back into the hall, the Floyd seemed so dreary and dull that we didn't even stay for their whole set.

I subsequently bought Fairport's debut album, plus *What We Did On Our Holidays* and, later, *Liege & Lief*. We acquired a girl singer in our band and changed our whole repertoire from rock/blues to 'electric folk'. We got rave reviews at local gigs and in the press and many more local bookings.

Our band split up when two of our members went to live in Australia. Ultimately, myself and our lead singer went to live in Canterbury to involve ourselves in the music scene there, and I was offered a place with Barbara Gaskin in the band Spirogyra when they were going on tour round Europe. But by then I was employed as an electronic design engineer for a small local manufacturing company. I ended up working in Paris as a studio recording engineer, then in London at Trident, and after that at Virgin Records, etc.

COUNTRY CLUB
17 JULY 1968, BELSIZE PARK, LONDON, UK

NOTMEHIM

I was 16. A poor council boy like many others. Just as the sixties really exploded in London I was on the scene. There was a special club, anonymously called the Country Club, just behind Belsize Park Station and not far from the infamous Roundhouse. For some years most bands that played here became very famous, some later filling stadiums. Here I saw Chuck Berry (duckwalk), I saw BB King, Graham Bond, John Mayall, Deep Purple, Black Sabbath, and so many others that were later well known on the London circuit: Van der Graaf Generator, Soft Machine, Free, T.Rex, Roy Harper, the Pretty Things and many more.

So, the drill was, on a summer's eve, turn right out the station, walk to the end of the row of shops, turn hard right into an alleyway. Past a few shabby tennis courts, to a gravel driveway. Wait in line. Over your heads were light bulbs on a cord and the occasional speaker. People from the queue blew bubbles and the air smelt of Afghan Black. Before you was the club, which was a strange fortress-like building attached to the railway station. One iron door.

Fairport Convention in London, 1968

Waiting in the queue was part of the experience. You were part of a special community of musically enlightened people: 'heads'. Time to roll one, as you listened to Soft Machine's 'We Did it Again' on repeat.

Through the door the first thing one meets is a huge friendly giant, worthy of any Tolkien novel. An Irishman of the farm, about six foot six with a lovely warm smile. Beneath his elbow was a guy at a table, charging you two pounds for entry. This guy looked like Brian Jones, with dark beatnik glasses and a blond mop-top.

Into the building and it was a typical social club, a place of modest size. The tired carpet was brown paisley and brown. The stage was tiny, almost enough room for a four-piece. Such a room could be found in any working man's village.

The 'folk scene' was part of the 'underground'. The underground was a rebellion against the bland and safe BBC music scene with its bom-diddy-bom-bom beats and wiggling to the 'scene' by bimbos on boxes. It was *our* music, not *theirs*. Here I got stoned and listened to Fairport Convention deliver their album *What We Did On Our Holidays*.

I had no idea that, 50 years later, I would still remember this as an immense privilege. To this day her voice is matchless. This material was them in their prime.

The room was full of magic when she sung. All hearts were opened and the full inheritance of being a human was felt. I have never experienced it since. Sometimes, I used to lie on the carpet and simply fall asleep to her. Richard Thompson was also utterly divine. He gave the backing band their identity. Everything was so perfectly matched.

Shortly, 'Meet On The Ledge' hit the charts and they became famous. Their venues became larger. *Unhalfbricking* was released, but somehow this never grabbed me, then *Liege & Lief*, and the magic of the *What We Did* days was over.

There was a car crash. The line up changed for Fairport. Swarbrick changed the sound. Denny left and formed Fotheringay. Things were never to repeat.

Over half a century later, and I still feel these sessions. I foolishly thought that others would match her. I have never heard such a contender. I loved her then. I love her now. When I reflect on the time which has passed, I wonder again. Who knows where the time has gone.

8TH NATIONAL JAZZ & BLUES FESTIVAL
9-11 AUGUST 1968, SUDBURY-ON-THAMES, UK

CHRIS DRINKWATER

My cousin Martin Lamble was Fairport's first proper drummer and a founder member of the band until the tragic M1 motorway crash that tragically claimed his life and that of Richard Thompson's then girlfriend, Jeannie Franklyn.

I went to see Fairport perform quite a few times while Martin occupied the drum stool. I really enjoyed their music. I also got to know all the band members a little, including the newer members such as Iain Matthews and Sandy, after Sandy was brought in to replace Judy Dyble as lead vocalist. I didn't get to know Sandy very well, mainly exchanging a few 'hellos' when we saw each other. I loved her singing and songwriting, which brought something new and fresh to the band.

The Fairport Convention were included in the bill for the 8th National Jazz & Blues Festival, which also featured Jerry Lee Lewis, The Herd, The Crazy World of Arthur Brown, Jethro Tull, Chicken Shack, The Spencer Davis Group and The Incredible String Band among many other bands. I travelled there with Martin and was backstage while Fairport were preparing to go on stage to do their set.

A young lady approached me and asked me where Sandy was. I replied that I didn't know as I hadn't seen her yet. She said, 'Well if you do, can you tell her Little Mo is here and wants to see her?' to which I replied, 'Okay, if I see her, of course I will tell her.' I didn't get to see Sandy until sometime after Fairport had performed their set, by which time Little Mo and Sandy had managed to meet up. A happy ending!

THE COCKPIT, HYDE PARK
24 AUGUST 1968, LONDON, UK

DAVE CLEMO

The summer of 1968 was memorable for a series of free concerts held in Hyde Park. I missed the first but went to the second. It was a lovely summer's day with a great vibe. This was by far the best festival I ever attended, and while the ice cream van had a long queue all afternoon, there was a Coca-Cola lorry parked nearby under the trees where you

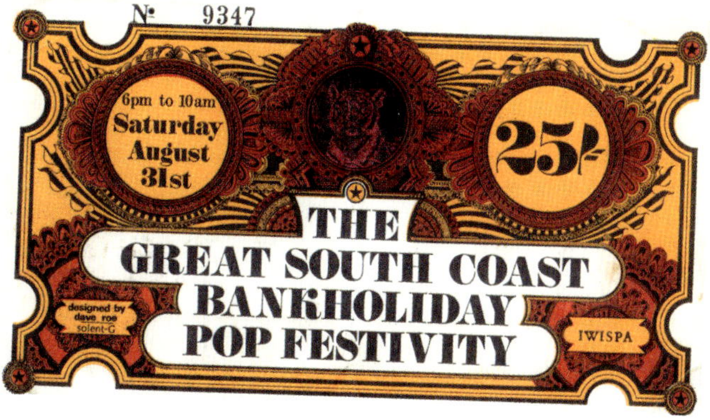

(Rob Whitmarsh)

could buy a warm can of fizziness for an eye watering two shillings (about two pounds in today's money.) That was the sum total of the catering facilities.

I arrived in good time before the music started. The stage was on the path with the Serpentine behind. The Cockpit was a sloping area of grass with shade provided by overhanging trees. About ten thousand of us sat in the sun and were royally entertained all afternoon, with performances by Ten Years After, Fleetwood Mac, Family and Peter Sarstedt.

The Fairports were amazing. Sandy had only been with the band for a matter of weeks, but it was a match made in heaven. They played just a few songs including The Farinas' 'Reno, Nevada', Tim Buckley's 'Morning Glory' and Leonard Cohen's 'Suzanne'.

PARLIAMENT HILL FIELDS
4 SEPTEMBER 1968, HAMPSTEAD, LONDON, UK

NIGEL SCHOFIELD

Much to Judy Dyble's disgust, Fairport used to be referred to as 'the English Jefferson Airplane'. But when they both played a free afternoon concert at Parliament Hill Fields, Fairport opened. Sandy was delayed and they began the set as an all-male act until Sandy joined them. It rained and only a few hundred people turned up. When the Airplane came on, they asked, 'What's wrong with you people? It's raining. Go home.' Then, with consummate grace Miss Slick introduced them. 'Hi. We're Jefferson Airplane. We are the American Fairport Convention.'

RICHARD LEWIS

The first time I saw Sandy was when she arrived late on the bandstand to join Fairport at a wind and rainswept free concert on London's

Sandy in the crowd at a festival
(Mike McCarthy, Island Records)

Parliament Fields. Appropriately one of the songs was 'It's Alright Ma, It's Only Witchcraft' with the lyrics, 'This is the season, stormy weather's on the way!' Even in the rain and the wind you could see Sandy smiling as Richard Thompson took one of his amazing guitar solos.

At their concert at The Royal Festival Hall three weeks later, as part of the Festival of Contemporary Song, I was able to hear what a difference Sandy's voice made to Leonard Cohen's 'Suzanne' and Dylan's 'I'll Keep It With Mine'.

I was lucky enough to be backstage at Middle Earth at the Royalty Theatre in Ladbroke Grove in March 1969 when they changed Dylan's 'If You Gotta Go, Go Now' into 'Si Tu Dois Partir'. It was obvious from the to and fro between all the Fairports how much Sandy was able to hold her own. No shrinking violet here.

After their horrible car crash in May 1969, I didn't know when or if I would see Fairport again. From reading the *International Times* I went to free concerts in Hyde Park, seeing Blind Faith in June and the Rolling Stones in July. Then in August I saw a tiny ad for a solo appearance by Sandy Denny at Les Cousins in London.

I went along to see a slightly nervous Sandy sing and play some of her favourite traditional folk songs including 'Nottamun Town', 'Come All You Fair And Tender Ladies' and 'Green Grow The Laurels'. She also sang in public, possibly for the first time, her own composition, 'The Pond And The Stream', which made my day!

Then in September I headed down to Devon with my friend Andy Brown to see Fairport's rebirth at the Van Dike Club in Plymouth. This was four days before their official public debut at the Royal Festival Hall. The club was quite small, hot, crowded and smoky and the stage seemed a bit cramped but the Fairports were having a ball. I got to hear for the first time 'Matty Groves', 'Reynardine', 'Tam Lin' and many others. During Richard or Swarb's solos, Sandy would stand to the side watching with a huge grin and obviously having a great time. I remember being surprised during the encore of 'Have You Had A Talk With Jesus?' as Swarb came forward to sing and Sandy picked up his fiddle to accompany him!

ROYAL FESTIVAL HALL
28 SEPTEMBER 1968, LONDON, UK

MICK HOUGHTON, SANDY'S BIOGRAPHER

When I was seventeen, it was a very good year. This was in 1968. At the very mid-point of that year, I turned 18 and in October I left home to go to University in Leicester to study politics. The week before, on 28 September, I attended The Festival of Contemporary Song at the Royal Festival Hall. As a gig goer, I was definitely making up for lost time. At the beginning of the month, I'd made the pilgrimage to see The Doors and Jefferson Airplane at the Roundhouse and, earlier that year, I'd seen the Incredible String Band with Tim Buckley opening, and Pentangle, both at the South Bank. Among others, I saw Pink Floyd in Hyde Park and the Byrds groundbreaking short-lived line up with Gram Parsons and Doug Dillard at Middle Earth in Covent Garden.

Mick Houghton's biography of Sandy

The Festival of Contemporary Song featured The Johnstons (with Paul Brady), Sandy's former boyfriend Jackson C Frank, Al Stewart, Joni Mitchell (promoting her debut LP) and Fairport Convention. I'd seen the original Fairport line up at Middle Earth back in February (with Blossom Toes and Marc Bolan's Tyrannosaurus Rex). It was my first bleary-eyed experience of an all-nighter where, shamefully, all I really took in about Fairport was Richard Thompson's remarkable soloing. It didn't escape my notice that they had a girl singer. I already knew that, having heard Fairport and, it almost goes without saying, all the above artists for the first time through listening to John Peel's *Perfumed Garden* on Radio London and his current *Nightride* and *Top Gear* shows on Radio One.

There was so much happening in 1968 that it was impossible to keep up. I'd read that Fairport's debut LP had been released in June, but I had no idea that original singer Judy Dyble had been replaced by Sandy Denny just weeks before the LP was released. Such antics and poor timing soon became something of a group trope. Much as I liked to think I was keeping up with the trends, it wasn't until I opened the programme for the Festival of Contemporary Song that I read that 'the most immediately outstanding member of the six-piece group is Sandy Denny'.

With hindsight, and thanks to Neil Garner's *The Peel Sessions* book, I'm now aware that she'd done two John Peel sessions with the group since joining, one transmitted the day before the concert. I should own up now that what I've written elsewhere about Sandy's first few months in Fairport Convention was slightly misinformed. What matters here, though, is that Fairport Convention were absolutely stunning at the Royal Festival Hall. They were clearly shedding their reputation as Britain's Jefferson Airplane and it wasn't just Richard who impressed. I remember thinking Martin Lamble's drumming was amazingly sensitive. What did I know about drumming? Iain Matthews was also superb, whether taking the lead – he was able to carry off Tim Buckley's 'Morning Glory' impeccably – as well as singing wonderfully in tandem with Sandy.

Even with the advantage of today's online research I've not been able to find a definitive set list. I always thought Sandy performed the traditional 'Nottamun Town', but I definitely remember hearing Joni Mitchell's 'Eastern Rain' and Dylan's then unreleased (by him) 'I'll Keep It With Mine'.

The tour de force, though, was the group's reimagining of Leonard Cohen's 'Suzanne'. Iain and Sandy were positioned on either side of the stage, both in their own reverie, swapping verses back and forth, their voices underpinned by Richard's dramatic staccato guitar. The two voices were perfectly synchronised, soaring above the group's unique arrangement of

Cohen's sedate love song. There's a moment when Sandy's voice comes in with the line, 'And Jesus was a sailor', and I swear it pierced my soul. 'Yeah right,' I hear you say, but it was a moment I've never forgotten.

On the Sunday, Peel repeated the group's recent session which, this time, added 'Suzanne'. If there was even a hint of disappointment with the group's second album, *What We Did On Our Holidays*, recorded later that year, but not released until January 1969, it was in not including 'Suzanne'. I didn't hear their version again until Ashley Hutching's *Heyday* collection of vintage Peel sessions appeared on cassette.

Of all the extraordinary and historic shows that I saw that year, seeing and hearing Sandy Denny with Fairport Convention that night stands out above Jim Morrison's theatrics, Tim Buckley's magical, breathtaking voice, even seeing Gram Parsons take control over the songs from *Sweetheart Of The Rodeo*. I can still picture Fairport on stage that night, looking like they'd just stepped out of a college lecture hall, and I can still remember how expertly they could evoke the changing moods of such varied material and how they were able to make other people's songs their own - even Leonard Cohen.

Time would tell how impactful that particular line up would become. These were still early days. What Sandy Denny had already brought to Fairport Convention was matched by what the group brought out in her. I left knowing I'd witnessed something very special.

NOTTINGHAM UNIVERSITY
LATE 1968, NOTTINGHAM, UK

MALCOLM SIMPSON

I had the huge privilege of seeing and hearing Sandy Denny perform (as a member of Fairport Convention) at Nottingham University in 1968 where I was an electrical engineering student. We had many excellent bands playing during this period but the concert was an absolute standout for me and it was Sandy's singing and stage presence that made it so. I was a member of the Nottingham University Technical Committee at the time and would either have been involved in the rigging of the lighting for the event or the recipient of one of the small number of free tickets that were allocated to the Technical Committee for providing free help during concerts. Most of the songs they did were from the then current Fairport album, *What We Did On Our Holidays*. I remember being absolutely stunned by her voice and singing. Regrettably I never managed to hear her again in a live performance.

UNIVERSITY OF ESSEX
1968, COLCHESTER, UK

ORLANDO GOODDEN

I saw Sandy perform with Fairport at Essex University in 1968. Years later I read in the sleeve notes of the CD version of *What We Did On Our Holidays* that the band, or at least Martin and Sandy, had drawn the cover picture of the album on a blackboard in a classroom at the university whilst waiting to go on stage. I was in my first year at art college in Colchester and went to many gigs at the university, including Pink Floyd with Syd Barrett and The Who. Fairport was one of my favourites. I bought their first album secondhand from a friend. In those far-off days we could see great bands at pocket money prices.

'MEET ON THE LEDGE'
RELEASED 29 NOVEMBER 1968

JOHN CLARE

John Peel always played stuff out of left field on his BBC Radio 1 *Top Gear* show and Fairport's 'If I Had a Ribbon Bow' was one such, I'm guessing in February 1968 when the single was released. After that, I forgot all about them until that lightbulb moment towards the end of the year, John Peel again – 'Meet On The Ledge'. What a single! I had to rush out and buy it with my Christmas money. I still have it and it is still one of my most treasured singles. I made a mental note that it had been written by group member, Richard Thompson. But it was that voice that beguiled me singing the second verse, 'The way is up, along the road, the air is getting thin' – the voice of an angel, Sandy Denny. Richard and Sandy were destined to become a lifelong hero and heroine of mine.

LONDON SCHOOL OF ECONOMICS
30 NOVEMBER 1968, ALDWYCH, LONDON, UK

GERALD HULL

My parents moved up to Fortis Green from Holloway in 1964 and the mock-Tudor 'Fairport' was my doctor's house – I remember going there for inoculations in 1968. My school friends knew of Fairport (Tyger Hutchings from Ally Pally had convinced himself to form the band at the John Baird pub across the road in 1966). The Kinks lived close by, opposite my father's pub, *The Clissold* (it has a shrine to them today). We knew of Fairport, but did not consider seeing them – we only had pocket money after all. To get a bit more pocket money (for Byrds and Lovin' Spoonful LPs) I got a Saturday job at Wood Green Library. There I met Judy Dyble.

'Judy Dribble' we called her, of course. She spoke of her group, but I did not pay much attention. A library assistant too, she wore two watches and heavy glasses. She was short and attractive, easy to talk to. I remembered I had heard her and the group do Lightfoot's 'Early Morning Rain' when hanging around outside The Country Club at Belsize Park.

I left school in 1968 and had more time to myself, taking a year out. I got another library job at the LSE off Fleet Street – the place had a great social life and a serious entertainments budget. A girl I knew there was a fan of The Incredible String Band and recommended Fairport. One Friday night in late November, as Roger and I were preparing to go to *the* club in Covent Garden, Middle Earth, to see Dylan's *Don't Look Back* we turned on the box. The programme was *How It Is* with Tony Palmer and there was Fairport doing 'Meet On The Ledge'. The structure, the vocals, the intensity blew me away – they were terrific. We would have to look out for them – they were good, we had missed out on something.

That night, in the club we were waiting downstairs to be allowed up for the film when I found myself standing next to Richard Thompson and Tyger, who had a large roll of notes. Thompson was smiling at someone stoned playing 'Crimson And Clover' (over and over). We went up for the film and I distinctly remember sitting, on the floor, behind Thompson in his cowboy coat, with his messy red-brown hair. When Joan Baez did 'Percy's Song' (in the film) is, I swear, when the possibility of chorus and slower melody line formed in Richard's mind. I would see Fairport do it in the new year.

I knew the exact seat below Muswell Hill Broadway where Tyger sat with Judy Dyble to fire her. The reasoning was correct. I'm not sure they had Sandy as their built-in choice for replacement then, but she was perfect. She, along with Thompson's guitar and their choice of songs, were the three reasons why people went to see Fairport.

I believe the photo of them performing on *Holidays* was taken at Barking Tech (where we saw them with the terrible Social Deviants, led by the lovely Mick Farren in the January). Fairport were our group after an amazing performance mid-December at LSE Refectory with Jethro Tull. This cost me nothing as I got in via the staff lift. Thompson was late ('They wouldn't let me in without a ticket – thought I was a student'). Sandy stood between him and Simon Nicol. She barely moved and let her strong voice do the work. When Richard took a solo in 'Reno Nevada' (or was it 'Jack O'Diamonds?') there was polite applause, as if this was intimate theatre.

They were about our age, north London (apart from Sandy and Iain) and played the folk-rock I had always loved from the previous five years – beginning with Dylan, The Byrds and Carolyn Hester et al.

This interest for me, and possibly for anyone else taking GCE English Literature in the mid-sixties, was fostered by *The Border Ballads* being on the London syllabus. Here, 'Mary Hamilton', 'Lord Grendall', 'Tam Lin' and others, often from Percy's *Reliques*, were to be found. This locked on perfectly to Dylan's early songs, which used such melodies and narratives (eg 'A Hard Rain's A-Gonna Fall' with the blue-eyed son), and Joan Baez's work.

At the time Fairport played songs with echo on the vocals – effective on 'She Moves Through The Fair', certainly. Sandy never played piano and I don't remember her with a guitar on stage before *Fotheringay.* They were concentrating on vocal balance, sound levels. They could do Muddy Waters, obscure Dylan stuff, Leonard Cohen ('Suzanne' was a favourite; they also did 'Bird On A Wire') and 'Gate Of Horn' as if they were Jefferson Airplane – with whom they were compared.

Their mix was eclectic – indeed Sandy's boyfriend Trevor Lucas played with Eclection on what was often a double bill for the two bands. Sandy would duet with Iain on this and others. At other times she would take full control, such as once I saw her doing a Janis Joplin mess-around. She was a little self-conscious with the band (they were never acoustic) and this meant she needed full power, with two guitars behind her. She always wore long, full, usually flowery dresses whenever I saw her. Her well-known clumsy mateyness on stage was clearly because she was nervous – and knew, anyway, that the band was great. I thought it was also an example of an inverted 'preciousness', and inevitable a teenage element. Yet, they were never ever sloppy.

DAVE CLEMO

I was walking past the London School of Economics in Aldwych with a couple of friends, when I heard the familiar sound of Fairport Convention coming from within. We blagged our way in and sat at the back listening to Sandy Denny and Fairport singing Dylan's song 'I'll Keep It With Mine'. It was as awesome as it was unexpected. Island released Fairport Convention's 'Meet on the Ledge' as a single at around the same time too. It was a buzz to hear it played on the radio, although it never troubled the compilers of the hit parade.

GRANADA TV
13 DECEMBER 1968, MANCHESTER, UK

STEPHEN DIGGLE

As a 15-year-old schoolboy in 1968 obsessed with music, I saw an unknown band play one song on local TV. This was on Granada TV, in the north west of England. The band were Fairport Convention, the track 'Meet On The Ledge'. Granada were years ahead of their time when it came to pop and rock music on TV.

Sometimes a song totally compels you to rush out and buy it, so the next day I raided my money box, got the bus into town and ordered the single from the Co-op record shop (the price of the album being further than my pocket money would stretch). The guy in the Co-op had never heard of Fairport Convention or 'Meet On The Ledge'. I wasn't sure if I'd got the name right, but he found the details in the Island Records releases booklet. A week later, I caught the bus into town again and came home clutching my precious, heavy vinyl, pink single with a big black logo in the middle. Needless to say, I played it to death.

When I'd saved up, I bought Unhalfbricking and played it relentlessly.

I'd never heard rock and folk mixed together like this. Sandy had a cold when they recorded 'A Sailor's Life'. But it remains a favourite to this day and is the very first electric folk song.

'Who Knows Where The Time Goes?' never fails to bring a lump to my throat. And, as we age, those lyrics just get more and more relevant and meaningful. BBC Radio 2 has *The Folk Show* with Mark Radcliffe. Every year 'Who Knows Where The Time Goes?' tops their poll of favourite songs.

An older school friend told me Sandy had left Fairport and formed a new band with Trevor Lucas called Fotheringay. They were playing Manchester Free Trade Hall. Sadly I was under 18 and skint so missed it. To my eternal regret I never saw them or their support that night, the legendary Nick Drake. However, my first ever gig did finally turn out to be Fairport in 1970 at the Free Trade Hall.

I have all the early Fairport albums and play them often, as I do Sandy Denny with The Strawbs, her solo albums and the *A Boxful Of Treasures* CDs containing her home-recorded stuff and demos, etc. I never caught Sandy live, but her songs, performances and albums showed a path to a music that remains important to this day to myself and to so many others.

WHAT WE DID ON OUR HOLIDAYS RELEASED DECEMBER 1968

JOE BOYD, PRODUCER

Sandy was a well-known name around the folk clubs. I had heard *of* her before hearing her at, I think, Les Cousins. I wasn't immediately interested – she sounded really loud, reminding me of Judy Henske or some of the belting girls of the American commercial folk scene. Once I met her, I realised she was remarkably intelligent, a completely original musical personality. When I heard

What We Did on Our Holidays, released December 1968 (chalk drawing by Sandy & Ashley Hutchings)

her record with The Strawbs, I was stunned by how good she sounded in a studio, when she wasn't trying to reach the back of a folk club without a microphone. Particular highlights from the material I produced with Fairport or Fotheringay that I would point a novice listener to are 'The Sea', 'She Moves Through The Fair', 'Crazy Man Michael' and 'Tam Lin'.

What We Did On Our Holidays (Richard Bennett Zeff)

'FOTHERINGAY'

ROSS PALMER

For Fairport Convention, convincing Sandy Denny to join the band was akin to a decent mid-table football team somehow landing the most prolific goalscorer in the league. Fairport's self-titled first album, on which vocals were handled by Iain Matthews and Judy Dyble, is really quite wet. The players, particularly Richard Thompson, show flashes of their later brilliance, but it was a record made of undistinguished original material and white-bread covers, sung by two of the folk revival's middling vocal talents. There's little that gives a clue as to the leap they were about to make.

In a field not short of remarkable singers, Denny remains the unchallengeable queen of English folk rock. That's how good she was. And it was all there – the singing and the songwriting – in 'Fotheringay', the first song on Fairport's second album, *What We Did On Our Holidays*. Hearing it must have stunned those who'd suffered through 'If (Stomp)' or their reading of 'Jack O' Diamonds' on *Fairport Convention*.

The song – a meditation on the final hours of Mary, Queen of Scots, imprisoned in Fotheringhay Castle in Northamptonshire and awaiting her execution – is lavishly beautiful and melancholy, with a gorgeous, unwinding melody. The chord sequence is rather more grandly baroque in places than is strictly period correct, but, accompanied as it is by wordless backing vocals from the band, it has a mournful dignity that feels entirely appropriate to the song's lyric.

SCOTT FISHKIND, SINGER SONGWRITER

It seems I had always known Sandy's name but the documentary *Sandy Denny: Folk Music's Unsung Pioneer* really moved me because it really got into so much of her history and progression over the years. It contained interviews with several of the Fairport members as well as legends like Martin Carthy. I sought out everything else I could find about her.

It was when I connected the dots of the song 'Fotheringay' that I realised the song was as much an autobiography of Sandy as it was about Mary Queen of Scots. That is, her own captivity of living with such a sensitive nature in such a harsh world. In a sense, she was a prisoner of her emotional world, yet trying to function as an artist and human being in the external world. The world never really gave her the type of worldwide recognition and success that so vast a talent deserved. Certainly, she was recognised in the musical community, but she should have been a household name, an equal to someone like Joni Mitchell.

Sandy seemed to have a real connection with the sea, which seems to represent freedom with its vastness, peacefulness and yet power, and a sense of the spiritual due to all those qualities.

Writing my song 'Sandy Shores' has been one of the most profound experiences as a songwriter that I've ever had. Sandy's story, and the way her music is so visceral, personal and timeless, meant that I had to dig into my deepest inner resources as a songwriter and try to find a way to express my gratitude for the gifts that Sandy gave to us all!

WENDY STEWART, SINGER SONGWRITER

I've loved Sandy Denny's voice and interpretation of English folk song ever since hearing her in the mid-seventies on my husband's collection of Fairport LPs. Effortless, yet so expressive and powerful, she felt like a combination of my other favourite female singers, Annie Briggs and Joni Mitchell.

I was brought up in a middle class Edinburgh family, listening to all kinds of music and with a father who played accordion and moothie. He loved listening to Scottish dance bands, Russian Army choirs and Gaelic psalm singing on Radio Scotland. Having taken up the clàrsach or Scottish lever harp when I was ten, I became immersed in the tradition and have performed, recorded and taught all over the world ever since.

Knowing my interest in early and Renaissance music as a teenager, my harp teacher Jean Campbell arranged and taught me a pavane from Thomas Wode's *Partbooks* of 1562. I knew well the story of Mary Stuart's life in Scotland, imprisonment in England and execution at Fotheringhay Castle in 1587. Though there is an old wire-strung harp in the National Museum in Edinburgh called the Queen Mary harp, she in fact played the stringed instrument, the mandour. Putting both ideas together, and realising the keys, feel and setting would work, I worked the song around the old tune that Mary herself might have played during her short life. I recorded the final arrangement in 1997 at Pier House Studios in Granton, Edinburgh and it appeared on my CD *About Time 2* released through Greentrax Recordings.

Sandy's songwriting on 'Fotheringay' and so many other songs was sublime and captured a perfect mix of authentic story telling with folk rock edge which attracted so many more listeners to the hinterland of the tales told. Her words convey Mary Stuart's tragic end so well that it is, to me, a classic timeless song, in the best tradition of the carrying stream and one I continue to love performing.

CHRIS BLACKWELL, ISLAND RECORDS

Sandy? Ohhh… what a voice. You know, I think we were very lucky, we had some of the greatest singers of that era who made records for us…

Fairport Convention 1968
(Richard Bennett Zeff)

Sandy didn't record very much at Basing Street. Only a couple of times I think, but she came in quite a bit because she and… yes, Trevor (Lucas) were together. So I did see her quite often. I liked her a great deal. Someone told me quite recently that 'Who Knows Where The Time Goes?' was one of the first songs she ever wrote. It's a magical song. Timeless. But not just on that, on some of her other songs too, she had this ability to… it's hard to explain. I'd say it was to fly above the music. There was a purity there, and a great range of emotion. Sandy Denny was a very special singer. I'm very proud she was signed to Island.

TOWN HALL
JANUARY 1969, WIMBLEDON, LONDON, UK

STEPHEN CLARKE

I grew up in Wimbledon, just down the hill from the Common, and spent my secondary school years on a scholarship at King's College School, right beside the Common. I was there from 1960 to 1967, in the junior and senior schools. When I joined the senior school in 1962 one of the school prefects, to whom, of course, we all looked up was a certain 'Denny, D' (in the language of the school lists). David was a very good sportsman (cricket, rugby and hockey) and impressed us all. He left school in 1963.

As tended to happen in the mid- to late-sixties, loud music became a central part of our lives and several schoolboy bands were formed, including one I drifted into, which went by a variety of names – Noos, Delta, Pictdiggers and, eventually, White Unicorn. I began trying to sing but ended up simply carting the equipment and being a general gofer, but there were several very good musicians in the band, not least the lead guitarist, Jon Cole. After a stellar career in academia (double first, Classics, Cambridge sort of thing), Jon developed his musical career with a band called The Movies in the seventies. But, for the purposes of this document, it was he who found Sandy fallen in Miranda's flat in April 1978.

But this isn't the memory, because in January 1969, Fairport played a wonderful gig in Wimbledon Town Hall to raise funds for a local church youth club, of all things. White Unicorn were the supporting act, played a blinder and Fairport recommended them to Island Records. It was also my last time of humping Marshall amps…

Fairport were on top form and I remember a storming rendition of Leonard Cohen's 'Bird On A Wire', with Sandy to the fore. White Unicorn had played alongside Fairport previously at one of those over-indulgent May Balls at King's College Cambridge, the previous June (1968). We shared the inevitable chicken salad with them and other bands in the college library. Good times.

But I said this was more about memory by association, which is where my brother, Geoff, comes in. He was five years older than me and a year ahead of David Denny in school. More significantly, before he went to King's, Geoff attended Old Central School, a primary school on Camp Road, across the Common. It was there that he first met a young Alexandra Denny, three years younger than him.

In the way of things in the late fifties and early sixties, later teenager friendships developed into loose-knit groups of people hanging out together, often based on particularly friendly houses (and parents), or music, or politics, or a combination. Geoff went 'left' – CND, Young Socialists, that sort of thing – which inevitably led him to protest music and, in turn, the early blooming of the folk revival. And, because she was part of the aforementioned groups, Sandy was around. Geoff mentioned several times her move towards the folk scene and a very early vinyl album appeared – possibly Sandy and Johnny?

Another feature of the teenage scene was, of course, the party, sometimes preceded by the pub and later by the inevitable Pipkin or Party Seven. Geoff and his then girlfriend were at one of these, apparently, when Sandy arrived late, enthusing about her visit that day to Fotheringhay Castle. The rest, as the saying goes, became a song. Geoff told this story every so often, with a smile.

And so life developed and the groups drifted apart and we all moved on. Through the rest of his life, although his politics changed, as did his outlook on life, Geoff retained a warm affection for those days and Sandy's music.

And me? Suffice to say that our second daughter, born 12 April 1978, bears the name Alexandra.

SOUTHAMPTON UNIVERSITY
18 JANUARY 1969, SOUTHAMPTON, UK

JOHN CLARE

In their infinite wisdom, Southampton University Student Union decided that both fifth and sixth year students from our school, Richard Taunton (and a couple of others), would be granted access to any of their concerts in both the Old Refectory and the Lecture Theatre. I'd already been to quite a few since my fifteenth birthday in June 1968, but Fairport Convention were not to be missed. I seem to remember that Ian Matthews was still in the band (just) and hadn't been ousted yet, but I don't really remember him doing much. The most mind-blowing experience was that they opened with a song called 'A Sailor's Life', with Sandy's voice soaring and a riveting Richard Thompson guitar solo.

More gems followed, particularly from the silver-throated Sandy, and included her mesmerising version of 'She Moved Through The Fair', as well as 'Autopsy' and 'Fotheringay'. Plus there was 'Meet On The Ledge'. The only downfall of the night was that we had to suffer the horrendous cacophony of support band Van der Graaf Generator first!

(This was the first performance of 'A Sailor's Life'.)

THE COUNTRY CLUB
2 FEBRUARY 1969, BELSIZE PARK, LONDON, UK

MICK DONOVAN

I saw Sandy perform with Fairport in the intimate surroundings of The Country Club in Belsize Park, near Hampstead in north London. I was tempted along after hearing her sing 'She Moves Through The Fair' and her own 'Fotheringay', the opener on her first album with Fairport, *What We Did On Our Holidays*, released a week or two earlier. Seeing and hearing her at that stageless venue standing a handful of yards in front of me sent me headlong into a lifelong love affair with my favourite singer. I was a Sandy Denny addict hoping a cure couldn't be found to ween me off that voice.

BRADFORD UNIVERSITY
6 FEBRUARY 1969, BRADFORD, UK

NIGEL SCHOFIELD

The first time I saw Sandy (though far from the first time I heard her) was when Fairport Convention made the long trip north to play at Bradford University. The gig was hosted by John Peel and also on the bill were Bridget St John and Principal Edwards Magic Theatre. Tickets cost six shillings (30p), slightly less than the price of a single. Sandy had been with the band for nine months; her first album with them, *What We Did On Our Holidays*, was new in the shops. However, the songs that stood out for me were 'A Sailor's Life', an entirely original approach to a traditional ballad and the starting point of British folk rock, and stately versions of Leonard Cohen's 'Suzanne' and Sandy's 'Who Knows Where The Time Goes?'. Ashley Hutchings informed us the last of these was 'not on the new album, but will definitely be on the next.'

MCILROY'S BALLROOM
13 FEBRUARY 1969, SWINDON, UK

MARTIN VINCENT

I was Social Secretary at Swindon College between 1968 and '69. I booked Fairport Convention for a concert. The band's lineup was Sandy, Richard, Martin, Ashley and Simon. Sandy was lovely to talk to and discussed next steps and her love of traditional music. Richard Thompson was somewhat shy but had a weird tuning on his guitar which he showed me. Later that evening, John Peel turned up. He had been at his own gig in Swindon and was aware that Fairport were playing for the college at McIlroys ballroom.

I asked Sandy if she would be playing 'Who Knows Where The Time Goes?' and she said 'not really' but after some encouragement she agreed. The band played for an hour from about 9pm. John Peel on his show the following Sunday said that he had seen Fairport play that week and said it was the best gig he had attended. I've always thought that Sandy was the best female vocalist of her generation and a tragic loss so young. I carry the memory of this gig with me forever.

BROMLEY TECHNICAL COLLEGE
20 FEBRUARY 1969, BROMLEY, UK

MIKE PHILLIPS

I was 16 years old and in the fifth form at St Mary's Grammar School in Sidcup. Being the youngest of four children I had been influenced by my older siblings and consequently my tastes varied from Cliff Richard to Otis Redding and from The Small Faces to Chris Farlowe. But my tastes were changing fast in response to the unending wave of new bands and new music, and weekends were spent sitting with friends listening to the latest purchases or browsing through the record store for new names or new albums, most of which had amazing artwork.

I had been to a few gigs including Aretha Franklin, Free and The Jeff Beck Group (featuring Rod Stewart and Ronnie Wood). The one genre of music that I hadn't embraced was folk. It seemed a bit uncool for a guy. I'd vaguely heard of Fairport Convention but knew nothing about them until a school mate, Kevin Bell, asked if I wanted to go to their gig at Bromley Technical College. Kevin was a good authority on new music as he'd put me onto Pink Floyd and Van Morrison. I went along to the gig not knowing what to expect. It was sold out. It took me a while to appreciate what they were playing. It seemed all very pleasant and respectful but the place wasn't exactly rocking. I'd been used to more rock-based bands with lots of heavy guitar and drum solos. Richard Thompson didn't fit that mould! Then they played 'Jack O' Diamonds' and I thought, 'Here we go. This is more like it.' I started to get into it and notice how nice the girl singer looked and sounded.

Then they played a song that I'd never heard before. It was Leonard Cohen's 'Suzanne'. Sandy Denny was on the left of the stage and Ian Matthews was on the right side. Martin Lamble's initial soft drum roll and Ian's tom-tom beat created a great atmosphere and then Ian started singing with a slightly haunting voice which held my attention. And then… Oh my word this beautiful flaxen-haired angel started singing, 'And Jesus was a sailor and he walked across the water…' I had never heard a voice like it – so clear with such a beautiful tone and texture and from that moment I was hooked. I couldn't get it out of my head.

Browsing the racks at the local record shop in Welling, I found *What We Did On Our Holidays*. I read the track listing and was immediately disappointed to see that 'Suzanne' wasn't on it. Fortunately, in those days you could go into a booth and listen to an album before deciding whether to buy it. The first track on side one was 'Fotheringay' and Sandy's voice was everything that I remembered from the gig. I didn't need to listen to any more, and today that album remains like an old friend to me. It's a slightly odd album in many ways with a real mixed bag of musical styles, as if to illustrate that the band were still trying to find their way. The stand out tracks are those that highlight Sandy's voice and particularly her ability to flex her voice from soft and gentle to rousing. The Bob Dylan cover 'I'll Keep It With Mine' is a superb example of this, but also 'She Moves Through The Fair' and 'Eastern Rain'. Throughout the album, Ian Matthews' voice blends perfectly with Sandy's, and 'Meet On The Ledge' is another example of them alternating lead vocals to great effect as they did on 'Suzanne'. To this day I feel that the band lost some magic after Iain left – due to 'musical differences'.

IAIN MATTHEWS

Iain & Sandy (Iain Matthews)

It may sound like a strange thing to say, but I didn't really know Sandy very well at all. I worked on the same stage, in the same band for about a year, but outside of that we led completely separate lives. What I can say is that she was such a generous, gracious and egoless person. You'd think,coming into Fairport having written a song on a Judy Collins album, she'd be full of herself, but that wasn't Sandy. Always full of doubt and self-criticism. Always wanting to be better. When I first heard *Liege & Lief*, I could not believe my ears. An album that could never in a thousand years have happened without Sandy. A masterpiece, a musical statement never surpassed.

After my exit from the band, I asked her rather timidly if she'd consider coming in to the studio and play on a song for my first solo album and she had no hesitation in accepting my offer. The track she played and sang harmony on, 'Thro' My Eyes', became one of my favourite recordings to this day.

Thank you, Sandy, you beautiful soul, for allowing me to be part of your magical space in the time we called Fairport. A strong and super-talented woman in a predominantly man's world. My life might have been a whole other musical experience were it not for you and your presence. Much love and respect.

STUDENTS UNION BALL
25 FEBRUARY 1969, SHEFFIELD, UK

MICK MONK

I saw Sandy perform three times, twice with Fairport Convention and once with Fotheringhay. Each time hearing her sing was a revelation. The first time was the Isle of Wight Festival in 1968. The second time was in Sheffield University Students Union. Fairport Convention were on the bill of the Students Union Ball that was being organised by the Entertainments Committee (Ents). The bill also included The Hollies, The Moody Blues, Julie Driscoll, Brian Auger and the Trinity, Black Sabbath, Circus, The Spinners, Harmony Grass and The Wurzels.

Being a member of Ents, I was on duty and supervising the timing of artists performing in the Upper Refectory venue of the Students Union. The act before Fairport, Harmony Grass, were performing their last few songs. I was standing by the side of the stage. I turned around and Sandy Denny was standing just behind me. I am not sure how she knew I was part of the venue staff.

In a break between songs, she asked me how long it would be before Fairport were to go on. I said 15 minutes or so. We were running late! She thanked me with a smile and waited for another song to finish before she turned and left for the green room. I remember her having a shorter stature than I had thought before. The few words between us and the smile cheered me up. I had had a hectic evening up to that point, not only because we were running late but because there were some PA problems and I had got an electric shock when setting up!

Being a student ball with other acts performing, the Fairport set was shorter than it would have been otherwise, but I was transfixed throughout. Sandy was in fine form. Her voice was then (and remains) so distinctive from other singers. She always sang like she really meant it. As she held notes her voice, especially live, conveyed a kind of nostalgic yet relevant yearning of the soul.

There are so many adjectives to describe her vocals – resonant, expressive, haunting, emotive, luminous. All these descriptives would be true. That evening, up close and, as at the Isle of Wight in 1968, her singing was crystal clear, powerful, haunting and as always mature beyond her years, evoking a pure perceptive timeless beauty.

ADAM & EVE CLUB
26 FEBRUARY 1969, SOUTHAMPTON, UK

DAVE HARRIS

My first Fairport encounter was in Southampton where they opened with 'A Sailor's Life' for the first time. I still have my diary with the note in it. I've seen many gigs over the years but I still say that is the best one I have ever seen. It was very unusual, if ever, that anybody opened their set with a long number like that. Particularly an unheard one. It seemed to go on forever and was absolutely brilliant, sensational.

My friend Brian Hinton and I were both big fans of the group already, largely from the regular John Peel sessions that they recorded.

Swarb wasn't there, so it was mainly Richard. I can remember looking at the stage and seeing that Richard was almost in the shadows, Sandy and Ian were at the front, and how terrific Martin Lamble was. Ian was playing bongos and was very much involved in the set, though he left very shortly after. He was subdued and only played with the band a few more times. The direction of the band had changed, and I don't know if he expected to leave the band at that point, but with hindsight it was on the cards.

I talked to Ashley Hutchings about it about a few years ago. He said that all he can remember is that 'A Sailor's Life' was the first number, and that opening with a twelve-to-fifteen-minute number wasn't something they would normally do, but in the tiny dressing room before

Adam and Eve go West

DEVOTEES of that sound which has been described as a mixture of surfing music and folk, and goes under the general title of American West Coast, lend me your ears, or rather lend Fairport Convention your ears.

The group are taking in Southampton's Adam and Eve club on Wednesday to offer local fans the opportunity to hear if they can stand up to the title of the British group who have got nearest to West Coast

And they come on a wave of success which has put their new LP "What We Did On Our Holidays" out of stock at the manufacturers.

The line-up is Richard Thompson (lead guitar), Tyger Hutchings (bass), Simon Nichol (rhythm guitar), Martin Lamble (drums) and Ian Matthews (vocals). The girl member, Sandy Denny, has two-fold talents. She plays piano and sings.

And they all confess a sneaking regard for the American group The Byrds, the Moby Grape and The Grateful Dead—pioneers of the West Coast Sound.

* * *

Radio One DJ John Peel says of them—having a go at the British scene at the same time—"if Fairport Convention lived in the States they would be internationally known."

So there you have it. They could be a group that are yet to acquire the recognition they deserve.

And the Adam and Eve are taking the plunge in a big way with their Sunday night modern jazz session tomorrow night. Joe Harriott is due in tomorrow as the first of what is hoped to be a line-up of big modern jazz names.

Joe's line-up includes drummer Phil Seamen, pianist Harry Smith, bassist Freddie Mogul and trumpeter Ian Hamer.

Fairport Convention

Adam & Eve advert & preview from February 1969 (Ian Burgess) they went on, all that was on their minds was this new number. He remembered Martin Lamble playing on some chairs in the dressing room, using them like bongos as they prepared for the gig.

I remember the band looking at each other as Richard played his solo, searing and delicate by turns, as it just went on. From plenty of room at the start, by the end of the song we were pushed up right to the front. I was closer to Iain Matthews than he probably liked. There were other songs unknown to us, including 'Bird On A Wire'.

The Adam & Eve Club was tiny. When the gig started there were probably about fifty to sixty people in the room, which doubled to pack the place out as the show went on.

The first set closed with 'Jack O'Diamonds', another twelve minute or so piece. I don't know if they normally did an intermission, but they halted proceedings when part of the PA was dislodged and fell on a lady in the audience (stage left, if anyone's interested). Sandy got off the stage and put her nursing skills to use. She took it very seriously. I remember thinking that might have been it for the night.

They started the second set with another long piece, as 'Reno, Nevada' was again around twelve minutes long. I'd say you only get that brilliance in a small room. With more space the intensity seems to dissipate, no matter what level the musicians are delivering. Sandy had so much personality and presence, yet physically was quite small. I can't remember if Richard spoke at all, though Ashley spoke of course.

That's my memories, diary assisted, of the Adam & Eve gig. Admission was ten shillings (50p). Around this time, I also saw Free for about five shillings (25p) and Yes for six shillings and sixpence (37 ½ pence).

FOLK MEETS POP, ROYAL FESTIVAL HALL
24 MARCH 1969, LONDON, UK

PAUL CHESTERMAN

As a Dylan fan I went to this festival to see Al Stewart who I followed doing Dylan songs (along with Hatch at Bunjies). I have no recollection of his performance on that night – I can't even remember who I was with – but in the same way that you never forget where you were when you heard about JFK's assassination, I'll never forget the impact Sandy made.

She was seated at a black piano on the left of the stage. She was knitting (with a ball of wool and knitting needles) and had a drink to hand – a G&T? At some point in the concert, she moved to the mic at the front of the stage and sang. I was blown away.

Memories get muddled over time and I've assumed that it was 'Who Knows Where The Time Goes?' that she sang but looking up the playlist online it must have been 'I'll Keep It With Mine'. But it's not the song that made such an impression on me. It was Sandy's performance.

ALEX DISCO CLUB
10 APRIL 1969, SALISBURY, UK

DAVE HARRIS

The second time I saw Fairport was at the Alex Disco Club in Salisbury. Admission that night was 8/6 (43p). After seeing them at the Adam & Eve I'd been raving about the band, and again my dear old dad came to the rescue, taking me and my two sisters, both older than me, to the gig. I'd offered my friend Brian a lift, but he declined. I think it's one of the greatest regrets of his life. It was a superb concert again, but not as great as that first one. No Iain now, and still no Swarb. (The first time I saw him with the band was in September at the Royal Festival Hall.)

First edition of *ZigZag* magazine, with Sandy on the cover

They did 'A Sailor's Life' again, now more polished than the debut, and also played 'Suzanne', Sandy taking over Iain's lead vocal. I remember the volume that she could project was extraordinary, and with such clarity.

I still have a press cutting from before the gig that was passed to me by one of my mother's friends. It wasn't advertised in Southampton, the distance being perceptibly bigger in those days than now. I also have a memory of arriving, and a white ambulance in the carpark, Fairport's tour van. I was desperate to see the band again and was very glad to do so. Then of course in May they had the accident.

The Alex Disco Club was much bigger that the Adam & Eve, a barn of a place that held 700-800 people. (I remember seeing Chicken Shack there. During the set I was getting a beer and turned to find Stan Webb standing next to me while he was playing. A very long guitar lead indeed!)

SANDY'S PARENTS' HOUSE
SPRING 1969, WIMBLEDON, LONDON, UK

ERIC HAYES, PHOTOGRAPHER

Of all the bands I photographed during my year-and-a-half in London, Fairport was my favourite. We shared a common relaxed vibe and got along really well. One of my favourite memories from my short stay at Farley Chamberlayne was waking to the sounds of Dave Swarbrick's fiddle wafting up the stairs in the morning.

It was Sandy who, as we were all piling into the band's van to go take photos for the cover of the album *Unhalfbricking*, suggested we go to her parents' home in Wimbledon. It turned out to be a brilliant idea, and the cover was a big success. Fans of Fairport and of the cover have asked me how I managed to get each band member's head in a different square hole in the fence. I wish I could take some credit, but I assure you it was an accident. Congratulations to the art director who chose that particular image for the cover.

Unhalfbricking, cover photo of Neil & Edna Denny, Sandy's parents (Eric Hayes)

The first idea for the photo shoot was to portray the band members enjoying tea on the lawn (in a very English fashion). I believe that Sandy asked her mom if that was possible and she lovingly provided a pot of tea with cups and biscuits. But when Sandy's mom and dad came out to watch the shoot, that's when I could see the possibility of featuring them in the foreground with the band members in the background on the lawn. (You can see a church steeple in the background on the right, and when I watch the Wimbledon tennis championships each year, I can sometimes see the same steeple.)

When *Unhalfbricking* was released in the USA, the American record executives didn't like the cover. They figured that record buyers would assume that it was a couple of old folks (Sandy's parents) who were the musicians. So they used a photo of a woman appearing to stand on some circus elephants. However, there is an inset shot of the band enjoying tea on the lawn, as was the original plan.

JOE BOYD

She'd forget the sugar or something, and everybody would have their tea, and you'd be sitting around on the floor, some people sitting in chairs, and she'd get up to go to the kitchen to get the sugar, rolling papers, whatever – and trip over somebody's cup and spill it. 'Oh, God! I'm so sorry!' And backing away from that, she'd trip over somebody else's and have this sort of domino effect of getting to the kitchen and knocking over three or four cups of tea. She just had this sort of air of physical chaos everywhere she went, along with this laughter all the time.

'THE CRASH'
11 MAY 1969

KINGSLEY ABBOTT

I knew Sandy reasonably well from when I was sometimes driving the band in the early days, though it wasn't long before Harvey took over and I faded into the background apart from my personal connection with Martin Lamble. Sandy was a bundle of laughs and great fun to be around, but the memory that has stuck with me is the last time I was with her, which was after the crash. I was with her and Simon and we went to the Beeb where Sandy and Si were due to talk about the future on the John Peel show. The interview was serious and loving as they spoke, and afterwards Simon went off and Sandy and I walked slowly down the short way to Oxford Circus. We parted there with a big cuddle before we went our separate ways to lives that took us to very different times.

UNHALFBRICKING
RELEASED 3 JULY 1969

MIKE PHILLIPS

The next album, *Unhalfbricking*, came out and joined my collection. It continued the mixed bag of musical styles, including the slightly random 'Si Tu Dois Partir' which featured on *Top Of The Pops* but gave a totally misleading impression of what Fairport were about. Without Ian Matthews, Sandy was the out-and-out vocal star and for me 'Autopsy', 'A Sailor's Life' and 'Who Knows Where The Time Goes?' are the stand out performances on the album. Despite my love for Fairport, I never really got into the purer traditional folk music that they played and so when *Liege & Lief* came out, I decided that it wasn't for me. In my opinion, with some notable exceptions, that style of music didn't properly showcase Sandy's voice.

JOHN CLARE

I landed a prized job at Henry's Records and had only been there a matter of weeks when *Unhalfbricking* was released. *Liege & Lief* was a pioneering album and probably the precursor of the folk-rock movement but *Unhalfbricking* is one of my top ten all-time favourite albums. 'A Sailor's Life' doesn't just have a mind-blowing guitar solo from Thompson, but also a riveting duel between him and violinist Dave Swarbrick. It has an amazing French language version of Bob Dylan's 'If You Gotta Go, Go Now' plus two other great Dylan interpretations. And it has two more beautiful Sandy Denny songs, 'Autopsy' and the greatest song written by anybody, anywhere: 'Who Knows Where The Time Goes?'

That song sends me into raptures every time I hear it. It will be played, as my wife Linda well knows, at my funeral.

ELSPETH COWIE, SINGER

Sandy's was already a voice for the ages when I was a teenager in the late sixties. It still is. Her pure tone, crystal-clear diction and achingly sensitive interpretations have inspired me ever since. Choosing 'Who Knows Where The Time Goes?' for the title track of my 2023 album paid homage to a performer and songwriter who has remained a towering influence on us women folk and traditional singers. I first heard it when Fairport Convention released Unhalfbricking in 1969.

As part of my repertoire since then, 'Who Knows Where The Time Goes?' resonates with audiences everywhere, and to all ages. We've all been on that lonely shore at gloaming watching that evening sky. For many, the metaphors resonate in aspects of their own lives and assert the power of love to support and heal. They encapsulate the passing of time and our own wonder at where it goes.

Sandy's gift of being able to live within a ballad like 'A Sailor's Life' or 'The Banks Of The Nile', bringing the story to life, makes her a masterful seannachie, a storyteller. When I listen to her, I am transported into the place, time, event and emotions she is singing of. This applies both to her truly unique interpretations of traditional song and to her own songwriting, which can take a simple happening or feeling and weave them into a compelling story.

Take 'Fotheringay', imagining the last hours of Mary, Queen of Scots, and which I covered in homage on my Naked Voice album in 2000. In a few short verses, Sandy embodies the despair, anguish and sense of a wasted life. It is tempting, as other have done, to credit the Scots, Irish and Welsh sides of her heritage with the marked feyness I hear in her ballad singing. Her versatility inspires too. Towering traddy, modern troubadour, rocker: she smashed artificial barriers and proved that if a song's got soul, it's worth the challenge for the singer who wants to move people and show them more possibilities than they perhaps could have imagined.

'WHO KNOWS WHERE THE TIME GOES?'

DAVE MONK

I wonder how many of us imagine ourselves on that desert island with our carefully chosen selection of songs to remind us of life before being cast adrift. What songs would you choose? Too many in my case, but many feature Fairport Convention and in particular Sandy Denny and Richard

Thompson. So having whittled down the list to eight you then have to decide which one would be the one you would save before the rest. For me this would have to be 'Who Knows Where The Time Goes?'.

Why is this? Well firstly there is the trademark Richard Thompson lead guitar played with complete sympathy to the story that Sandy is weaving, blending to create the colours and images the song potently invokes. Her voice is of course the most powerful instrument, the richness and beautiful tone that draws the listener into the song as it did me as a young teenager when I first heard *Unhalfbricking*. In a strange way, whilst the song always reminds me of those teenage years, most of the pictures Sandy paints would also apply on my desert island. Most movingly would be the 'sad, deserted shore'. But would I dwell on the sadness? Not really, because I would have no thought of leaving if there was no sail in sight to bring hope of rescue.

And like Sandy I would not count the time but hope that I would still be able to muse and let my mind drift and wander freely. We all need to do this. We all need to dream like she does as the birds leave the evening sky and the winter fire burns. Clearly the desert island would have seasons, and winter would require the comfort and warmth of a fire. Unlike Sandy, though, I would be alone on this desert island. There would be no love to comfort me apart from the memory of such love. But listening to 'Who Knows Where The Time Goes?' would itself provide profound companionship, linking both to the sights and sounds of the island but also drawing me back to why I fell in love with the song in the first place, its poetic and lyrical blend of imagery that evokes daydreaming in the countryside of my youth and the timeless spirit of the song itself.

'GENESIS HALL'

IVAN RUIZ

There is no better Fairport Convention than when Sandy and Richard were together in the band. Just listen to 'Genesis Hall' on *Unhalfbricking*. The composition and musical execution are sublime. The lyrics are melancholically introspective and make you travel to absolute reflection. Listening to Sandy can pull you from a deep depression or sadness. You can be sad, tired, unmotivated, on the verge of death, or even happy, and if you put Sandy on your record player, all the negative thoughts fade away and are replaced by peace, nostalgia and an unconditional attraction to her. If you feel happy, you'll be even happier listening to her music.

Alexandra Elene Maclean Denny is the lost princess of British folk.

BROOKSVILLE AVENUE
JULY 1969, QUEEN'S PARK, LONDON, UK

MICK DONOVAN

I remember being on my own, lying on a settee put-you-up at the back of a mate's house in Queen's Park, north London, in July 1969, listening to the first side of *Unhalfbricking*, the pink-labelled Island disc spinning at the customary 33-and-a-third rpm on his turntable, the last to be recorded with drummer Martin Lamble who had tragically died in the May. 'A Sailor's Life', the traditional song Sandy introduced to the band, began. Her vocal on the recording seized me immediately. It would have taken an earthquake to disturb me as I was taken over by her voice, interpreting the ballad with restrained power. Sensitive to the tale. Building in intensity. All with the expectation of flipping over the disc to listen to her signature song, the incomparable 'Who Knows Where The Time Goes?'.

I recently stumbled over an audio of Sandy performing 'A Sailor's Life' live at the Royal Festival Hall on 24 March 1969. Her unmistakable vocal crackled through the rough recording (and I could also make out her friendly manner chatting to the audience). As it did for 'Autopsy', 'She Moves Through The Fair' and 'I'll Keep It With Mine'.

FARLEY HOUSE
1969, FARLEY CHAMBERLAYNE, UK

SIMON NICOL, FAIRPORT CONVENTION

Sandy and I always had the front bench seat in the van travelling to and from gigs, and she frequently fell asleep on my shoulder or lap, which was always comfortable as heaters were not what we're used to today. But we only slept together once, and this is how that happened.

We'd been bandmates for just over a year when, subsequent to the devastation of the van crash, we decamped to the timeless isolation of Farley House near Romsey to see if we could rebuild a band on the foundations so recently shaken. Ashley, Richard, Sandy and I needed to discover or create common ground with the force of nature who was Swarb and the unknown watchful Dave Mattacks (who had the hardest job, getting to know five total strangers at

DISC and MUSIC ECHO 1s

SEPTEMBER 13, 1969 EVERY THURSDAY

Wilson Pickett show here next week TURN TO PAGE 7

Johnny Cash, quiet man at the top TURN TO PAGE 13

FAIRPORT CONVENTION pictured in the garden of the house they've had to quit. From left: Simon Nicol, Dave Swarbrick, Richard Thompson, Sandy Denny, Dave Mattacks and Tyger Hutchings who owns the Collie dog.

FAIRPORT BACK ON THE ROAD!

AFTER AN absence from stage work of five months since the road crash death of their drummer Martin Lamble, Fairport Convention take to the road again next Saturday (September 20).

Fairport on the cover of *Disc and Music Echo*

Fairport (above & opposite) at Farley (Eric Hayes)

once.) As history has proved, we succeeded and the band not only gelled, we created *Liege & Lief*, and with that a small but important sub-genre of music for our generation.

It was midsummer and on rolling Hampshire downland: all was bucolic and calm. Sheep in the fields, occasional tractors the only traffic in the lanes. The darkest of skies when the moon was below the

horizon (although a few weeks later, all eyes, hearts and thoughts were focused thereon as Neil Armstrong came down his ladder – as cautious as he was bold) and it was a total change from our noisy city lives up to that point. Interruptions were pretty much zero, and Joe Boyd had found us the ideal nest and workshop.

ROLLING STONE

FAIRPORT CONVENTION: BEGINNING TO CONTINUE

Fairport on the cover of the UK edition of *Rolling Stone*

None of us had seen the house until we all came through the door and now I can't remember if we had a guide to show us round or if we all explored the accommodation freestyle, but there were many rooms in the Queen Anne farmhouse and a whole corridor of bedrooms, on whose beds bags were territorially tossed. Somehow or other, Sandy took possession of the end room, what must have originally been the master bedroom – huge, chintzy and with, of all things, an en-suite sunken bath – an unexpected extravagance and one of the very few I've ever seen. It was in a gorgeous shade of jade green (definitely not avocado, which was a fruit still a few months in my future).

Simon Nicol & wife Debs with Georgia, 2025

When we'd finished the day's business and heaped the washing up into a student-digs mess for attention in the morning (hopefully by someone else, we all thought), we retired to our first night in our new home, full of hopes for the music we'd start to make in the living room where we'd spent the evening setting up our gear. Lights began going out and the noise of movement grew less and eventually ceased.

But old houses, especially ones which have been resting vacant and are then descended upon by a largish group of people, can creak and crack a little. And Sandy felt uprooted from her always-noisy, brightly-lit Fulham a little too much. Sometime after I'd conked out in the next room, she crept in to wake me and almost tearfully, in a little-girl-lost way, asked me if I'd come in with her as she was spooked by the aloneness of it all. She was no longer the powerful singer who could draw every eye and silence every sound in a hall or theatre, who could enter and exit a stage and thrill the audience. She was scared and vulnerable to the point of not being able to sleep.

So we went back to her bed, and perhaps oddly (because it was after all, the sixties) there was never the slightest hint of 'romance', nor had it ever seemed even remotely on the cards between us: a sibling was as close as I ever felt to her. She was between the sheets and I rolled myself into her eiderdown (this was so long ago it preceded the universal uptake of the duvet into British life!) and she went out like a light. After a fitful couple of hours when my cold bare feet sticking out of the end of my makeshift bedding woke me up, I slipped back to my own crib. And thereafter she seemed untroubled, having had a proper first night at last.

Sorry to disappoint those hoping for something more salacious.

A PARK BENCH
AUGUST 1969, BOURNEMOUTH, UK

STEPHEN STATHERS

Stephen Stathers, then a 13-year-old boy, was visiting his grandmother Elizabeth in Bournemouth. Word was out that there were some hippies in town causing a nuisance. Elizabeth told her grandson 'not to listen to what people say about the hippies'. She had met one and had a lovely chat with

Sandy & Elizabeth Stathers on a park bench in Bournemouth, August 1969 (Sandy Denny Archive - photographer unknown)

her on a park bench – it was Sandy! A picture of the two of them was taken by a local photographer. Stephen's grandmother, who had been a fashionable young woman herself in her younger days, called the photo, 'Two ladies together: the flapper girl and the hippy.'

ROYAL FESTIVAL HALL
24 SEPTEMBER 1969, SOUTH BANK, LONDON, UK

JERRY GILBERT, JOURNALIST

I can't recall when I first met Sandy Denny. Probably in December 1969 when she agreed to participate in *Melody Maker's* 'Blind Date'. This was a series in which musicians were played some of the week's latest releases and had to guess the artist. I served up an eclectic mix ranging from British revivalist folksong to American full-on blues / rock. Her recognition was generally instantaneous – whether it was the High Level Ranters from Tyneside, Young Tradition or John Mayall. Only Johnny Cash and June Carter's 'If I Were A Carpenter' did she demand to be removed immediately from the turntable. 'I really don't like it,' she complained, 'please take it off, it's been so overdone.'

I never knew her in her Soho days, when she was hanging with the likes of Jackson C Frank, or her brief time with The Strawbs, though leader of the band, David Cousins and I spoke often about her and her brief time with the band.

Having been exposed to the plaintive female voice, in its many forms, through my time in folk clubs, my appreciation of Sandy's remarkable vocal control came when Fairport Convention played their 1969 breakthrough album *Liege & Lief* at the Royal Festival Hall. I think it was the week I joined the paper, when I also reviewed the album itself. It was a poignant event as it was their first concert since the tragic accident that had killed drummer Martin Lamble several months earlier. Her

Fairport at the Festival Hall (Rob Whitmarsh)

vocal timbre was different than anything I'd heard in the folk idiom… such a level of control, with so much under the bonnet, as the new line-up moved in a direction that would henceforth become known as folk rock.

Thereafter I met Sandy on many occasions, sometimes at the flat she shared with husband Trevor Lucas in Parsons Green, and Tim Sharman, who managed the band, Daddy Longlegs. I always found her playful, even flirtatious, but vulnerable. When I interviewed her in the spring of 1971, prior to her appearance at the Lincoln Folk Festival (after the breakup of Fotheringay and release of her first solo album, *The North Star Grassman And The Ravens*), she was in a good deal of pain following a dental operation, which copious amounts of wine failed to ease. She told me, 'There was nothing in my mind when Fotheringay split up, it was like a chemical reaction.'

It's no secret that Sandy loved a drink, and in my experience didn't hold it well. We occasionally met up socially with other members of the folk and jazz community at The Capricorn Club in Soho's Greek Street, run by Dave Bilk, brother of Acker. Here I would partner her on the darts board (not the safest of occupations), sometimes against Bert Jansch and Danny Thompson of Pentangle, while huge amounts of alcohol were consumed.

As for her output, easily her most memorable and moving performance was her intimate acoustic gig at the tiny Howff Folk Club in Primrose Hill on 4 September 1973. From memory she played solo at the piano in a gig promoted by Roy Guest, who had been her manager (although possibly Danny Thompson accompanied her on double bass). The show utterly vindicated Sandy's decision to pursue songwriting more avidly after leaving Fairport; and if Fotheringay had been a mistake, then this recital ensured that her astonishing 'Who Knows Where The Time Goes?' – written years earlier, in much more innocent times – would not be perceived as a one-off.

She had been at her most playful in November 1970 when I met her at Fotheringay's country retreat in Chichester. She was in no mood for being interviewed so we played an interview-type game instead and set drummer Gerry Conway as the referee.

Her final comment that day spoke volumes about her. 'I'm basically a simple musician – a singer who writes songs. I never plan ahead but rather do things spontaneously. My whole approach to life is that if I can't do something in the next five minutes then I won't do it at all. My influences? Alcohol [no, not really, she corrected]. I tried to model myself on Twiggy but that didn't work.

'I'm basically a coward and people are very important to me. I really like to be with people and if I find myself in the flat, I won't stay there. I'll go out and visit someone.'

'I've got no plans for the future but I hope the future has some plans for me".' There was a dreadful sense of foreboding in that final phrase which gave *Sounds* its headline. Unfortunately, the future did not.

She became a victim of what became known as the '*Melody Maker* curse' for the number of untimely deaths that followed winning the 'Top Female Singer' award – Sandy Denny in 1971 and Maggie Bell in '72.

DAVE HARRIS

The third time I saw the band was the comeback gig at the Royal Festival Hall, though I believe they did a few low key warm ups, starting at the Van Dike Club in Plymouth. At the Hall, Fairport of course headlined, with Nick Drake and John Martyn also on the bill. Martin Carthy was sat two rows in front of me. Great though it was, the space and size of the venue took the raw excitement out of it.

It was the last time I saw Sandy, Ashley and Richard with Fairport. I'm being picky of course, because it was one of the best things I have seen in my life, but for me the Adam & Eve gig topped it.

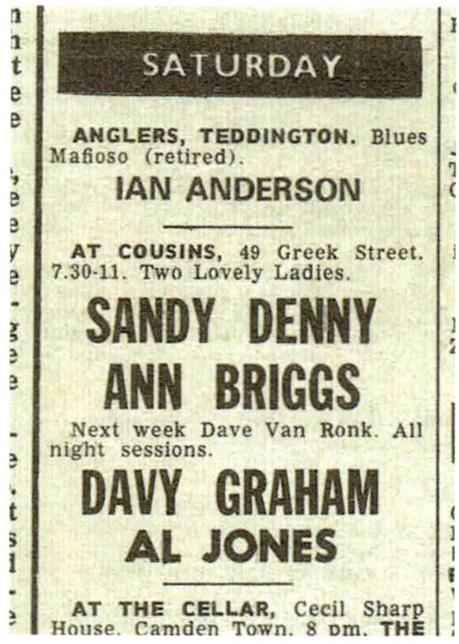

Les Cousins advert from September 1969 for 'two lovely ladies'

MANCHESTER UNIVERSITY
8 OCTOBER 1969, MANCHESTER, UK

JOHN WHITING

I'd first heard of Sandy Denny in her brief spell with The Strawbs, although I'm not sure whether I had actually *heard* her at that stage.

But then she joined Fairport, a group that had already registered with me, and I managed to hear some songs by them. Even on my crackly transistor radio, the quality of her voice shone out.

I saw one of Fairport's *Liege & Lief* concerts at Manchester University in October 1969. I went back to my lodgings in awe of the voice I'd been listening to (and the playing of the rest of the group, but that's another story). I managed to see Sandy again with Fairport, but was mortified at the announcement she was leaving.

Mollified somewhat by the establishment of Fotheringay, that was a group immediately on my wish list and I saw them when they too hit Manchester. Great singing and playing, and their LP absorbed more of my limited funds and joined the Fairport LPs I was accumulating.

I didn't manage to see Sandy solo but a session that remains firmly in my memory 50 years on is an appearance on a BBC2 *In Concert* programme; just Sandy, at a grand piano, playing and singing a few songs, although there was a guitarist with her and when she finished, the lights went up and there was Richard Thompson. His playing complemented Sandy's playing and singing so well, but it was really all about Sandy's songs and singing.

Things seemed to take a distinct upturn with her rejoining Fairport and the excellent *Rising For The Moon* LP. Sadly, that didn't last and things went downhill. And it was almost a 'Kennedy moment' when I heard that The Lady had died. What a loss…

However well Fairport do their regular 'Sandy slot' at Cropredy, however well their guest vocalists sing Sandy's songs, it would be so wonderful if Sandy could really be there, still singing 'across the evening sky…'.

FAIRFIELD HALLS
10 OCTOBER 1969, CROYDON, UK

DAVID ALLAWAY

I remember the first time I ever heard the voice of Sandy Denny as clearly as if it were yesterday. I was still at school. I was at my friend Mike's house, and he had just bought the Fairport Convention album, *What We Did On Our Holidays*, on the strength of having heard the single, 'Meet On The Ledge', a few days earlier. He put the record on and side one opened with Sandy's wonderful song, 'Fotheringay'. I was simply amazed by what I was hearing.

A lovely song, wonderfully accompanied by a couple of acoustic guitars, a gentle bass and some heavenly backing vocals. But it was Sandy's voice soaring above it all that really grabbed my attention – I'd never heard a voice quite like it.

Alas, I never had the opportunity to see that particular line up of Fairport live, and after their tragic M1 motorway crash in 1969, I thought it unlikely I'd ever get the chance to see them on stage. But after their recuperation and a few months rehearsing new material in a big house in the Wessex countryside, they were ready to start gigging again.

The first time I saw Sandy and the 'new' Fairport Convention was at the Fairfield Halls in Croydon, with my friend Mike. I had just turned 17, and it was the best musical event I'd ever been to, and still ranks very highly in all the Fairport performances I've been to since (there have been a heck of a lot).

We were very lucky to have seats in the choir section, immediately behind the stage. Dave Mattacks, their new drummer, was sitting right in front of us, and always having been interested in drums, this was a real bonus for me. (He is a bit of a genius in my humble opinion.) The set that night mainly consisted of new material from their latest album, *Liege & Lief*. I was a little disappointed that they didn't include any songs from their earlier albums. I recall Sandy wandering around the stage when she wasn't singing, making the audience chuckle with one or two silly jokes between songs.

And that voice? That voice was incredible. It was the voice of an angel, or perhaps an angel with a slightly broken heart.

MOTHERS
2 NOVEMBER 1969, ERDINGTON, BIRMINGHAM, UK

GERALD HULL

It's said that Sandy was self-conscious about her weight and her looks and somewhat jealous of Joni Mitchell. But Sandy's timing was impeccable – as was her diction – and she could hold soft notes well and show you she meant her lyrics. The songs on *Unhalfbricking* were all done as on record. I heard 'A Sailor's Life' at The Country Club (without Swarbrick) but not the 'French Dylan' – which they mimed on *Top Of The Pops.* We saw them at Mothers in Birmingham and at NW Polytechnic in Kentish Town – pretty samey performances, although I did not like the echo idea generally, especially on 'Mr Lacey'.

I saw them with a bunch of friends a few weeks before the M1 crash – at City of London University, Moorgate. They were on with a black reggae soul band called High Tension – an odd contrast. Sandy did the Cohen songs and 'Time Goes?' on the typical small stage they all had then. Tyger and one other had small bandages on their arms from jabs prior to a forthcoming US tour. This was the gig where Jennie the Taylor 'picked up' Thompson.

The crash occurred in May. The disaster left a void. We went to the Pink Floyd-organised relief concert at The Roundhouse, Chalk Farm. The whole of London was talking about it. I thought it was inevitable they would reform and we went down to Plymouth for the Van Dike Club 'reunion', mc-eed by John Peel. It was brilliant. They did all the *Liege & Lief* stuff (on the tiny stage) plus 'Joys Of Brotherhood' and 'A Whole Lot More Of Jesus'.

The Festival Hall show followed in September – a full crowd. I remember an idiotic drunken Scotsman ranting, 'I came here for folk music!' They were loud and when Thompson and Swarbrick did extended solos, Sandy left the stage – a very effective ploy. Further sets there, at the Fairfield Hall in Croydon and at Mothers in Birmingham were brilliant. I came away from the Birmingham concert and talked to Simon Nicol in the carriage down to Euston – about a move to Cricklewood. As I prepared to sleep on the station concourse whilst awaiting the Tube trains, I saw Thompson in his Levi's and with his Les Paul moving to the taxi rank. The band were due in Denmark next day, but famously Sandy would stay behind.

She was badly missing Trevor, did not like flying and, I think, was having trouble getting her material accepted by a group now exploring traditional folk-rock very loudly, and where instrumentals were driving the crowds crazy. This would cause Richard to leave within 14 months too – it was becoming Swarbrick's group, and everything was being played too fast. This said, we travelled everywhere to see the five-man

Fairport and I adored them, especially Richard's songs like 'Poor Will And The Jolly Hangman'. I always thought Tyger a better swing player than Pegg, but the Brummie certainly knew all the notes and in the right order, so he was perfect for the instrumentals.

ROGER GOULD

I only saw her once at Mothers in Erdington, Birmingham with Fairport. They performed the *Liege & Lief* album. It was the last time the six from that album played together. She was brilliant. She had such a powerful voice when she sang 'The Deserter'. I was right at the front.

It was Dave Pegg's 22nd birthday and he was in the audience that night. He joined the band shortly afterwards as Ashley Hutchings and Sandy Denny had left. It was the first time I'd seen an electric fiddle. Swarbs was superb. I bought the album a few weeks later from Beatties in Solihull.

I bought the album she did with The Strawbs, *All Our Own Work*, recorded in 1968 but not released till 1973. I bought it in Woolworths, Kings Heath. 'Stay Awhile With Me' shows her brilliant voice and 'Who Knows Where The Time Goes?' is on there, which is her most famous recording. Sandy is the greatest female singer I've seen, and I've also seen Dusty, Hazel O'Connor and Heather Small.

LIEGE & LIEF
RELEASED DECEMBER 1969

BONNY HOLDER

It was 1970, and I was just twenty years old, living in a funky apartment in Urbana, Illinois. We had moved there for my new husband's new job. Bill took the care to work and I stayed home all day. I knew no one in town. I couldn't drive around and explore. I would have felt sad and depressed, but the University of Illinois had a terrific FM student-run radio station to listen to. I knew all the timely hits. And there was a new trend taking hold of the rock scene – women singers like Grace Slick and Janis Joplin fronting new bands. I admired them, but being an old folkie, their bands didn't latch onto me.

One warm spring morning, the college DJ played 'Tam Lin' and everything changed. The lead singer was Sandy Denny, belting out the ancient song in her sincere, keening British voice. I fell in love, and I realised from the git-go that it wouldn't be a short affair.

The very next day, I drove my husband to work and then hit the record stores. It wasn't hard to find *Liege & Lief*. I learned that the producer, an American named Joe Boyd, was highly regarded by people who know such things.

Liege & Lief advert in *ZigZag* magazine

I couldn't wait for Bill to go to work the next day. I played that record all day long, and all the next day, and the day after that. It became my summer album. I loved the first song, which introduces the band. I wondered how old 'little Mattie Groves' was. I laughed at 'The Deserter''s predicament, and of course, 'O come and go as I please, and ask no leave of thee.' The ballad of brave young Janet... and Tam Lin.

I loved Sandy. I loved her occasional off-key note. I loved her romantic sensibility, in what was an insensitive world. When I saw the cover of *The North Star Grassman And The Ravens*, with Sandy sitting in an alchemist's chair, surrounded by herbs in beautiful jars, in the amber light of late November, I longed to *be* Sandy. To sit for just a minute in that amazing room is still a dream of mine.

Bonny Holder's life was changed by hearing 'Tam Lin'

I learned a month later, in May of 1978, that she had died. For a while, I couldn't listen to her music. Time passed and I missed her, and began to play her records again. My affection for Sandy is real, and has lasted for a half century, And becoming friends with her daughter Georgia Rose? Icing on the angel cake.

'REYNARDINE'

DAVE BUDGE

I first heard Sandy on CHUM-FM radio in Toronto in 1970. 'Tam Lin' sounded like nothing else in the post-psychedelic era and snared me wholly on first listen. I bought *Liege & Lief* the next day and loved the whole thing, start to finish. But the real magic was 'Reynardine'. The band's shimmering atmosphere behind Sandy's voice and storytelling took me centuries and a galaxy away.

When I'm walking a dog in a forest among the leaves so green, I have tried to sing the tale. I have none of the beauty of Sandy's voice – few do – but hundreds of repetitions have given me some control over the phrasing, and let me tap into my northern Scottish heritage for a feel I can't bring to any other song. Thousands of squirrels had heard my version but nobody else, until one night in a pub, after 25 years of forest practice, I had drunk enough to be persuaded to sing something. It had to be 'Reynardine'. It was near closing time; just me, two friends and one barmaid. When I finished, the server told my friends to leave and asked me to stay. Discretion prevents me from sharing any more…

VIKKI CLAYTON, SINGER SONGWRITER

I think I first heard the beautiful, extraordinary voice of Sandy Denny when a school friend played a copy of the album *Liege & Lief* to me. I was stunned. That astonishing voice!

I was a horribly precocious child from day one, much to the chagrin of my businesslike parents who, upon learning from my school teacher of my musicality, asked, 'Do you think she'll grow out of it?' I loved the English folk songs that I learned from that rather dotty junior school teacher. I played several instruments, and sang and played the guitar, but I was maybe thirteen or fourteen when I first heard 'folk rock'. I already had one foot in English folk song and the other in prog rock and that pink-covered album (*Liege & Lief*) hit me like lightning and I say again, that voice! It was thrilling, exciting, so beautiful. I knew then what I wanted to do when I 'grew up'. Luck and timing were with me.

Vikki Clayton (centre) with Ric Sanders & Georgia, Cropredy 2023

As I went down the musical path of life I started to perform in local folk clubs. People started to comment on how much I sounded like Sandy. I was astonished and surprised (and secretly delighted). However, being young and ambitious I was determined to *not* sound like anyone else. I wanted to sound like ME. And fearing that I was subconsciously being influenced by her voice, I stubbornly refused to listen to her exquisite voice and music throughout my teens – although I did go to see a live performance by Fotheringay when I was seventeen. I was blown away. I was the only time I ever saw her perform live and I have never met her.

No matter how I sang, people would remark that I sounded much like her and so in the end I gave in and started to listen to her albums. I had denied myself the joy and pleasure of her music for too long. I decided even if I was soaking up her influence I didn't care and I revelled in her music and her voice. I never once tried to emulate her and to this day I can't hear any resemblance between our voices or talent. She has an exquisite strength and huskiness to her voice that I have never had. But there you go. People said it and I accepted the compliment.

Later in my career, I was invited to sing her songs with the people who knew her well. It's not easy being a ghost, and it wasn't easy to get my head around some of the songs we sang either. I had to learn, dissect and understand the musicality she delivered so easily. I came to respect her as a great songwriter and superb singer. It became an honour for me to sing her songs. I would sit at the piano or pick up my guitar and take apart the lines of the music. Many a time I would wonder where a lyric came from or which note came next. She had ideas and expression that I marvelled at and, yes, I was humbled. She had more musicality in her little finger than I could ever dream of.

I remember hearing the sad news of her death on the radio. I had my baby son on my knee when the news came on the radio. After the shock came the tears. I thought of the music we loved, and that voice we might not hear again. I thought of the baby she had left behind. Her daughter was more or less the same age as my son. The sense of loss has never left and I often think of what she might have gone on to write had fate been kinder.

But despite her passing she *does* live on for so many of us. Such music as hers can never die. She is now just as alive for me today as she was in my youth. Her recordings stand up against time, her songs are timeless and her voice is unique; 'The Lady', 'John The Gun', 'Old-Fashioned Waltz' and, of course, 'Who Knows Where The Time Goes?'. So many more and all are wonderful. She has left us a legacy of music that will be sung and heard for centuries to come. We are so lucky to have had her.

MELODY MAKER
20 DECEMBER 1969

JERRY GILBERT

A cloak of mystery has been hanging over the Fairport Convention since their reported split a month ago. The Fairports have undergone a constant buffeting, culminating in the departure of Sandy Denny and Ashley Hutchings last month.

But with the power of resurgence reserved for the great groups only, the Fairport Convention have again got themselves together. A spokesman for Witchseason Productions, the management, announced this week: 'The group will go on.'

This time there will be no replacement for Sandy, the girl who stepped in for original member Judy Dyble. Dave Pegg, formerly of the Ian Campbell Folk Group, replaces 'Tyger' Hutchings, the bass player who has joined up with Terry Woods of Sweeney's Men to form an all-British traditional folk group, which is likely to be 'one step on' from what the Fairports are currently doing.

'The Fairports will be moving into a converted 18th century pub on the Herts-Essex border, and begin rehearsing seriously next week,' say Witchseason. 'We hope to have them back on the road as soon as we can. They have a tour of America planned for mid-January, and we want them to be ready considerably before then. When they're ready for recording, they will be straight back into the studios.'

The Fairport Convention's new album *Liege & Lief* is released on Island next week. As the title hints, it represents the most ambitious interpretation of British traditional folk music yet attempted.

But how will the absence of a girl singer affect the group's overall sound?

'We weren't really sure what to do. To replace Sandy would be a difficult job. It would be really difficult for the replacement, as she would continually be subjected to comparison with Sandy; so the boys thought they'd have a crack by themselves. With the traditional stuff, they really got together for the one album as a singular project only. But I expect they'll expand on that. We're all very happy with the way things have progressed,' say Witchseason…

Meanwhile, Sandy Denny is back pursuing a solo career. But she is unlikely to be recognisable as the folk singer of pre-Fairport days. She has advanced to a major extent and has clearly developed an individual style which she hopes will take her into concert appearances next year. She is already actively rehearsing a new album, which will be recorded in early 1970, but the extra spare time will enable her to write more songs, and thus fulfil another of Sandy's ambitions.

FOTHERINGAY FORM
JANUARY 1970

ALBERT LEE, MUSICIAN

My connection with Sandy is relatively short but I was very happy to work with her. I was recommended by Richard Thompson when she was looking for a guitarist and I was very happy to suggest my dear friend Pat Donaldson for bass. We rehearsed for a week or so but I was looking for something else at that time so I joined Tony Colton and Ray Smith in a project they were involved in. Pat suggested Jerry Donahue who we all knew and they ended up being part of Fotheringay.

I was onstage with Sandy just one time, it was at the Troubadour in Los Angeles. I played the piano! Sandy was such a great talent and a huge loss to music.

Fotheringay with Albert Lee in the line up (Linda Fitzgerald Moore)

CHIPSTEAD STREET
JANUARY 1970, LONDON, UK

JERRY DONAHUE, FOTHERINGAY & FAIRPORT CONVENTION

She was a character. I thought she was great the first day I saw her. She was so sweet, very bubbly. That's when I came along and did a sort of a trial… Pat Donaldson was the guy who roped me in. Pat said, 'Come on, you've got to come. You'll just love the music. So I said 'all right.' This is after Albert Lee didn't work out, of course.

I arrived with Pat at the Tube station, before either one of us drove, and just walked up to their place when they lived at Chipstead Street. Trevor was outside and I met him first and walked in and Sandy was upstairs. And it was all, 'Hello, how are you doing?' After we'd had a cup of tea she said, 'Well, shall we get started?' It was just very casual like that. The music was so great and Sandy was absolutely wonderful. When she was up, she was really up. She was an absolute delight to be around, absolutely fantastic.

Fotheringay at Sandy & Trevor's flat in Chipstead Street, 1970 (Barrie Wentzell)

I didn't see the down-side until much later. Actually, I didn't see it very much at all in Fotheringay. It seemed to be a very 'up' time in her life. Very, very few times were there any tears or anything like that… She was great, a great person, there was a lot more ups than downs during the time we were together.

The only time I heard Sandy, or anyone, raise their voice it was an argument with Gerry Conway about who was going to have the last cheese sandwich. There was just enough cheese for one sandwich. I couldn't believe how petty it was. We were all sitting there in disbelief at these two at each other's throats arguing over a cheese sandwich, you know? Who won? Gerry! He ate it! That's the only cross word that ever came up the whole time. It really was a family.

She used to get very nervous when we would go on stage, but once she was there and playing the piano she'd get absolutely lost in the song, drown in the music. It was just wonderful. She'd be absolutely fantastic, and then when she'd stop singing, she'd realise there was an audience there and she'd sort of get a bit awkward when she was announcing the next song, or get silly. She was like a little girl in between songs. She's broken my foot pedal more than once… She'd trip over a lead or something like that, knock a guitar down… very clumsy just like a little kid. But when she'd actually be doing the song there was nothing like it.

The (*Fotheringay*) album got to 14 in the *Melody Maker* charts and that was at the beginning. That was solely on Sandy's strength, but after we'd toured, we were accepted too. The next album would have done better, I think.

THE COUNTRY CLUB
29 JANUARY 1970, HAMPSTEAD, LONDON, UK

JERRY GILBERT

Dave Swarbrick recovered from a neck operation three days earlier to fiddle the audience literally off their feet, when Fairport Convention celebrated a triumphant return at the Hampstead Country Club on Thursday. And without being detrimental to Sandy Denny, who seemed to be leading the cheers, I believe Fairport Convention are now tighter, more exciting and more flexible. They have successfully overcome the prodigious vocal problem created by Sandy's departure, with Richard Thompson, Dave Pegg and Simon Nicol joining in a three-part harmony over Swarbrick's lead. Pegg has fitted into the set-up admirably, providing some very solid bass, and doubling up on mandolin along with Swarbrick. Dave Mattacks' drumming was superbly direct and when Richard Thompson got into full swing, his lead guitar work highlighted the difference between the group's country-rock style, and their straight traditional repertoire.

Page 16—MELODY MAKER, February 14, 1970

SANDY DENNY

on new sounds in Blind Date

SIMON & GARFUNKEL: "Bridge Over Troubled Water" (CBS).

That's Paul Simon and it's a great record. I don't believe Art comes in until right at the end. Are you going to give me these records afterwards? I didn't know he had so much power in his voice (Sandy sings along). The record has been fantastically produced like all their more recent records. Oh! Art didn't come in at the end.

STRAWBS: "Josephine For Better Or For Worse" (from the A&M LP "Dragonfly").

It's the Strawbs, and the record's called "Josephine For Better Or For Worse." I wish them all the best of luck as they never seem to have much luck. It's a great record which I'm sure will give a lot of people a lot of enjoyment. Dave Cousens sings very well on this track.

DIONNE WARWICK: "I'll Never Fall In Love Again" (Wand).

It sounds like Dionne Warwick. I prefer this to the Bobby Gentry version, it's much better. She's great—I love her voice but I wouldn't buy the record. It's a superb version though.

HIGH LEVEL RANTERS: "The Golden Eagle" (from the Trailer LP "The Lads Of Northumbria").

Is it Tom Gilfellon? Yes, and that's Johnny Handle playing in the High Level Ranters. They're absolutely incredible. One night we were sitting around in Newcastle and they played for absolutely hours. I like Gilfellon's little bass runs.

JOHNNY CASH & JUNE CARTER: "If I Were A Carpenter" (CBS).

Johnny Cash, and that's June Carter. I really don't like it. Please take it off. The song's been so overdone.

JOHN MAYALL: "Walking On Sunset" (from the Decca LP "The World Of John Mayall").

What label's it on? I'm very confused by this but I think it's John Mayall. Is it a new record? Oh, it's a reissue, that's a bit of a nasty trick. He really sticks to it, doesn't he? He sings well on this track, too.

JOHNNY WINTER: "Johnny B. Goode" (CBS).

I like the song very much. Is it an American? It could even be Chuck Berry. I don't know Johnny Winter and I can't see the point of doing this. I guess the bloke really enjoyed recording this, though.

YOUNG TRADITION: "Byker Hill" (from the Transatlantic LP "Young Tradition Sampler").

I can't say anything except the Young Tradition were absolutely superb and it's a dreadful shame they've broken up. I went to their farewell performance at Cecil Sharpe House which was a knockout. I believe Pete Bellamy's doing a solo thing now. This really is super.

SLY AND THE FAMILY STONE: "Thank You Falettinme Be Mice Elf Agin (Direction).

It's really incredibly like a machine; I'm just waiting for the steam to come out. It really makes me nervous listening to it. It's not got much tune has it? Sly? Yes, I don't mind them. A lot of work must have gone into this, and I can't say I'm keen. But I think there'll be an awful lot of people who'll buy it.

STEAMHAMMER: "Turn Around" (from the CBS LP "Mk II").

Is it the Liverpool Scene? I thought that was Adrian Henri talking. Don't tell me, I must try and guess this. I'm trying to think of the flute player. Steamhammer? It's quite pleasant but I'm not particularly impressed by this track. In fact it's becoming monotonously boring.

Sandy reviews the singles in *Melody Maker*, February 1970 (Stephen Royston)

TOWN HALL
16 MARCH 1970, BIRMINGHAM, UK

JOHN TWIGGER

I was very lucky to see the wonderful Sandy perform with Fotheringay on what was their debut gig and my 21st birthday. I went with some friends from Sutton Coldfield College and myself and my mate Andy Everett hung around after the concert and were lucky to interview her for the college magazine. She was a lovely lady and invited us into the bar, where we were able to have a couple of brandies with her and the group. I first met my wife Bernadette at a Fairport concert at the Belfry in Sutton Coldfield in 1971. We go to Cropredy every year and we feel privileged to have met Georgia there a few times. Her exhibition at The Brasenose on Cropredy weekend was such a lovely tribute to her lovely mum. It brought me to tears.

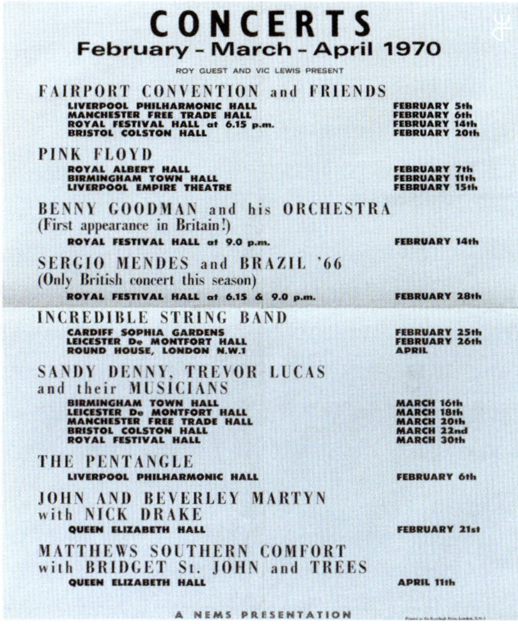

Sandy & Trevor in the gig listings (Pasquale Di Resta)

SALLY MAYBURY

In March 1970 my boyfriend's parents got us two tickets to see 'Fairport Convention' at Birmingham Town Hall. I was not familiar with the group but thoroughly enjoyed seeing Sandy at the forefront, playing her piano. It was many years later that I realised I had actually seen an early performance of Fotheringay! I instantly fell in love with the *Liege & Lief* album, which I then bought as a birthday present for my boyfriend. Some weeks later, he left it on a bus. I then bought it again, just for my personal enjoyment, and over the years I got the album signed by various Fairport members. It was a wonderful surprise to get Georgia to sign it at Cropredy.

COLSTON HALL
22 MARCH 1970, BRISTOL, UK

NO'AM NEWMAN

Growing up as a provincial grammar schoolboy, I first heard – or more accurately, read – the name Sandy Denny in the *NME*, in a speculative article entitled 'Sounds of the Seventies' (published in December 1969). The paragraphs about Fairport led me to see them in February 1970, although too late to see them with Sandy. On 22 March 1970, I was privileged to see a triple bill of Fotheringay, John and Beverly Martyn, and Nick Drake.

Shortly after, the eponymous *Fotheringay* record was released (and bought by me), and by the end of August 1970, I had purchased all three Fairport albums with Sandy. I especially loved *Unhalfbricking*, some of the vocal duets on *What We Did* and her songs on *Fotheringay*. When she went solo, I was probably the first person in my city to buy *North Star Grassman*. I used to call this her 'prog album' as several of the songs featured idiosyncratic chord sequences not from a folk background.

The next time I saw Sandy was when she popped up for a fleeting encore with Richard and Linda Thompson in April 1975. Then it was with Fairport at the Royal Albert Hall in June 1975, promoting *Rising For The Moon*, where the excellent ('One More Chance') rubbed shoulders with the dire. The final time that I saw Sandy was in November 1977, although not the concert that was recorded and eventually released.

I remember speaking about her death to some of my fellow university students a few days after reading about it in *Melody Maker*; one of them said that I spoke as if I knew her.

In the mid-1990s, in computing circles, the idea of hypertext was gaining traction; I thought that I could use this idea along with my love of Sandy's songs to create a database of those songs, showing when and where each song appeared on vinyl/CD along with notes. This database reached the Sandy fan base and was later converted into an internet website. I was lucky to have seen Sandy perform four times, when many of her fanbase never had the opportunity to do so. Her songs and voice will live on forever.

ROUNDHOUSE
23 APRIL 1970, CHALK FARM, LONDON, UK

DAVID ALLAWAY

This show consisted of three acts. First up was Matthews Southern Comfort. Then on came Sandy and her new band Fotheringay, who played a lovely selection of songs, mainly written by Sandy. The final act was Fairport Convention playing material from their *Full House* album. I feel very privileged to have seen this wonderful selection of bands and musicians all on the same day.

I saw Fotheringay once more before they disbanded, and lucky to have attended Sandy's very last concert at the Royalty Theatre on Drury Lane on 27 November 1977. Needless to say, it was simply unforgettable. Thank you, Sandy, for all the music.

GRAHAM HOWARD

I saw Sandy play with Fotheringay at the Round House, London, on a triple bill with Fairport and Matthews Southern Comfort. I was also at the Albert Hall for the concert with Fotheringay when Elton John brought the house down after the release of *Tumbleweed Connection*. But the nights I remember most were at the Coach and Horses in Farringdon, when Richard and Linda Thompson were playing acoustic gigs with friends such as Barry Dransfield – and Sandy – in an effort to recreate the simplicity of pub gigs after their sell out concert halls. 'Come on Sandy, give us a song.' It might have been 'Let's Jump The Broomstick'. There were only about 20 or 30 people there.

MICK DONOVAN

Fotheringay fed my addiction. I saw them at the fabled London Roundhouse in Chalk Farm before the release of their eponymous debut album at the end of the following month. I recall being backstage with Gerry Conway sitting with his drums on a riser, although sadly I did not spot Sandy. But the subsequent performance guided me into my nirvana. The songs were unfamiliar but so beautiful and mostly written by Sandy. I bought the album on release and the songs confirmed my first impression, especially 'Banks Of The Nile'.

HULL UNIVERSITY
9 MAY 1970, HULL, UK

DAVE HARRIS

The next time I saw Sandy was in the west refectory of the university on Saturday 9 May with Fotheringay. It was five shillings to get in. The room held around a thousand but there were probably 200 – 300 in there. I remember feeling so elated that this tour was coming to Hull. It was poorly advertised, possibly a late addition as none of the tour advertising, music papers and so on that I saw included the Hull details.

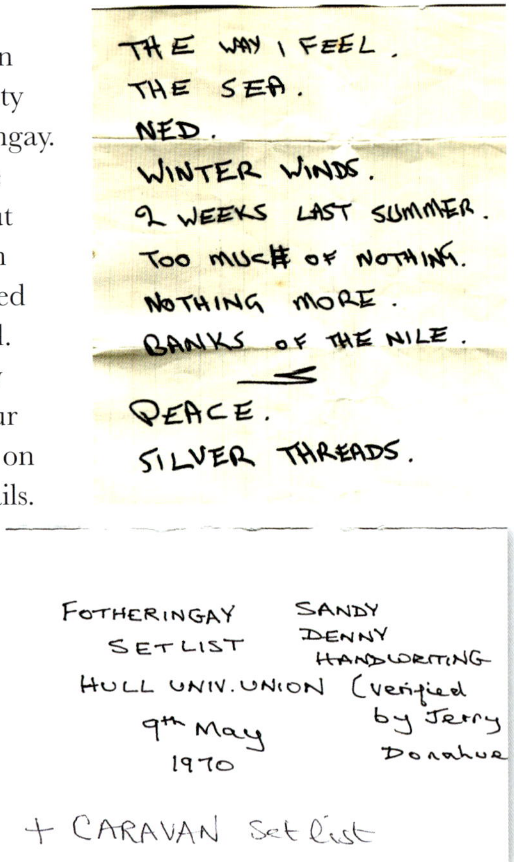

Sandy's handwritten setlist from Hull University

In those days they had nice tickets with a printed edge. The guy on the door ripped it in half of course, but I still have my half! I'm fairly certain that there wasn't a support act. It was a standing gig, and I managed to get as close to Sandy as possible, right in front of her vocal mic, slightly to stage left. Trevor was slightly stage right. I was so biased in favour of Richard Thompson, but Jerry Donahue was a fine guitarist.

I remember Fotheringay's debut John Peel session and the way that Jerry played those delicate notes on 'The Way I Feel'. He did so again on the night. It was an absolutely special evening. There was a stage, though it was only low. There was still a feeling of intimacy, despite the room size.

At the end of the gig there was a set list on the stage by Sandy's mic. It was the first set list that I ever nicked. I waited until they had finished the set and the two encores before doing so, of course. It wasn't a typed list, but handwritten. When I saw the reborn Fotheringay a few years back, I had a chat to Jerry. He said the band had never played 'Peace In The End' live. I knew they had, and being fascinated to know if the list was in Sandy's writing, had it with me. Jerry confirmed that it was her handwriting. I'm not aware of any others that she wrote. Some years back I put a copy up online. I was deluged by people asking for it. I've kept it lovingly for 55 years.

TOWN HALL
19 MAY 1970, OXFORD, UK

NIGEL SCHOFIELD

I saw Fotheringay at Oxford Town Hall, supported by a band led by another Fairport refugee, Matthews Southern Comfort. I noted at the time: 'Sandy Denny's new band works really well. Strong songs – nothing carried over from Fairport, but a couple of great electric trad songs as well as Sandy's own.' Those 'strong songs' were the basis of Fotheringay's album – 'The Pond And The Stream', 'Nothing More', 'Peace In The End' and 'Winter Winds'.

DAVE COUSINS

(Our album) *Dragonfly* had been released in February 1970 to mixed reviews. Tony Hooper's then girlfriend, Philippa Clare Hodgkinson, had taken the windswept photograph on the back of the sleeve. She was a close friend of Sandy Denny and Trevor Lucas, who had moved in together, and I went to visit them. Sandy had already left Fairport Convention after making three albums in two years. She enthused about her new band, Fotheringay, which she had formed with Trevor. They were recording the band's first album, and Sandy wanted to include my song, 'Two Weeks Last Summer', that we had recorded together in Copenhagen. She asked me to write an extra verse, which I did. As it happened 'Two Weeks Last Summer' did not appear on the first Fotheringay album, but it did finally make an appearance on Fotheringay 2, released in 2008. Sandy was excited about the upcoming Fotheringay show at the Royal Festival Hall, and invited me along. She had her hair styled for the show and told me she had sat next to Elton John in the salon. She was incandescent about him.

FOTHERINGAY RELEASED JUNE 1970

GERRY CONWAY, FOTHERINGAY & FAIRPORT CONVENTION

Gerry Conway in 1970 Fotheringay promo photo (Linda Fitzgerald Moore)

Sandy Denny was a very special person in lots of different ways. She not only had phenomenal musicality but also a rare demeanour that everyone loved. People in the music business saw her potential and tried to direct her in the way that they thought. She was not afraid of success but I think she had goals that took precedence over ambition.

Forming Fotheringay after leaving Fairport Convention was not a popular move with the music business. Sandy was very grounded in traditional folk music but she wanted a vehicle for her song writing and Fotheringay was initially formed for that. By this time she had partnered with Trevor Lucas and rehearsals for the first album were in the music room of their flat in Chipstead Street, Fulham.

I don't remember Sandy ever criticising our approach to her songs. She seemed quite happy to let the playing unfold organically and we gained a lot of confidence that way. She also had very broad taste musically and would listen to everything from folk, Crosby, Stills & Nash, The Band, Bob Dylan, Randy Newman and Stevie Wonder to Miles Davis. We had all become very good friends by the time that the first Fotheringay album was finished so we decided to rent a farm house near Chichester to 'get it together in the country'.

We started the second album at Sound Techniques but Sandy was under a lot of pressure to pursue a solo career and one morning in tears she told us that she had to leave. Sandy was very loyal to her friends, and content with people that she knew and trusted, so she really didn't want to do this.

On her subsequent solo albums with Island Records, she hired Pat Donaldson, Jerry Donahue, Trevor Lucas and myself from Fotheringay to play on them. It makes me smile every time I think of it!

(Gerry sadly passed away in March 2024. Georgia set up an annual raffle at Cropredy for the Motor Neurone Disease (MND) charity in Gerry's name. It has raised £1,361 so far.)

ATHENE ROBERTS, FIDDLE PLAYER, 3 DAFT MONKEYS

Sandy Denny is the voice of my early childhood. It gives me goosebumps to hear her earthy tones, and transports me back to the beginnings of my own musical journey. It reminds me of the times when I was about four years old and my folk music-loving parents would settle me and my brother down at bedtime. To help us go to sleep they would play music on the record player downstairs, and Fairport Convention was an absolute favourite. I remember many evenings happily dozing off as Sandy Denny inadvertently sang us a lullaby from the room below. It was about this time in my life that I decided I absolutely had to play the violin, and started to learn to play on a tiny sixteenth fiddle. I have no doubt that this decision was inspired by the music I had heard filtering up the stairs.

I also remember as a youngster being beguiled by the song 'Gypsy Davey', performed by Fotheringay and Sandy Denny. The trills and beautiful long notes of the song drew me in as I was transfixed by the romantic images of a travelling rogue. There is an honesty and clarity in Sandy's singing that brings the stories she tells to life in a colourful yet haunting way. Gentle and powerful, with her personality clearly shining through, Sandy Denny's style has inspired me to have the confidence to sing my own music in my own voice.

PENNY DAVIES, SINGER SONGWRITER

I was 17 the first time I heard the voice of Sandy Denny. It was 1970, and I was immediately captivated by that voice, by the songs, and by the beautiful cover art on the cover of *Fotheringay*, which was on the record player at a friend's house. I went on to discover more of the music she made, with Fairport Convention, with The Strawbs, and as a solo artist. Sandy became, and continues to be, my favourite singer. I mourned her when she left us, with so much yet unsung. I became a folksinger and songwriter myself, and owe a great deal to Sandy for inspiration and for being a shining light in times of darkness.

In 1986, after my young brother died, I threw myself into creating a radio documentary about Sandy. I lived in Sydney at the time and was able to interview visiting musicians who had known her. I spoke to Richard Thompson, Pat Donaldson, Gerry Conway and Jerry Donahue backstage at various venues; and Trevor Lucas was kind enough to allow me to talk to him at his home. I had the boxed set on LP (which I still treasure!), and was able to create an hour-long programme which was broadcast on Sydney radio stations 2MBS-FM and 2 SER-FM. Immersing myself in the songs she wrote and sang helped me through that hard first year of loss.

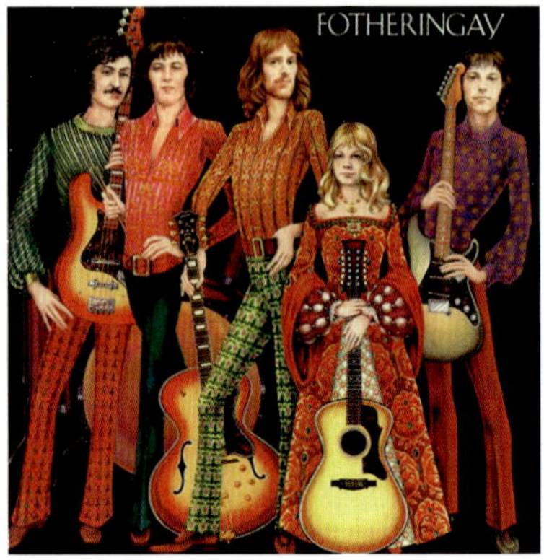

The *Fotheringay* album, with a cover illustration by Marion Appleton, Trevor Lucas's sister

Thank you, Sandy. All these years later I still feel that frisson of joy when I hear your voice.

ROSIE MCDONALD, SINGER SONGWRITER

When I first heard Sandy Denny, it was her interpretation of 'Banks Of The Nile' that drew me in. That classic folk song trope, 'women dresses as a man to follow/find her lover' had many varieties, but this one stood out. That voice and power in delivery, the jangly guitar, iconic bass line and building rhythm section. I was there in the zone, emotions raw as I imagined the pain of separation, the horrors of war, the desire to remain together so strong that the young woman would cut off her hair, dress in soldiers' clothes and go to war too. The women robbed of their sweethearts – a song so powerful that it evoked deep contemplation of the horrors of war yet the beauty of their love shone through, all carried by Sandy's ethereal delivery. As a teenage guitarist singer, I immediately sat down and learned the song and tried to summon that same depth of feeling, and that song led me on a journey of discovery of Sandy's brief yet luminous musical career. I eventually sang 'Banks Of The Nile' at London's iconic Cecil Sharpe

House singing session, taking it back to the city where Sandy had sung so many gigs.

In the time since, I have greatly enjoyed learning and singing many of Sandy's songs, trying to translate her beautiful piano arrangements to my finger style guitar playing, my voice not as effortlessly flowing and high as Sandy's but still my own interpretation of her complex and intricate songs. During Covid, when we all went online and connected across the planet, I started following Carla Fuchs and her interpretations of Sandy's songs and followed her collaboration with Sandy's daughter Georgia through social media. I played a whole Zoom folk club concert singing Sandy songs, with my partner Nigel Lever accompanying me on mandolin.

In 2023 I had the dubious pleasure of being Artistic Director of the first Bundanoon Folk Festival. I wanted to hold a special feature concert and decided that we would showcase a Sandy Denny concert. I reached out to Georgia who enthusiastically came on board as we had a line-up of performers each choose a song. Georgia delighted us with stories of her mother and answered our questions. The diverse array of musicians in the concert, some who had not yet discovered Sandy's music, were invited to find a song and interpret and then present it in a round-robin style concert. We finished with an all-in 'Who Knows Where The Time Goes?'. Young and more experienced performers alike enthusiastically embraced the challenge and the interpretations were spell binding.

Sadly, my partner recently passed away unexpectedly and Georgia has been a huge support, gifting me a beautiful sketch portrait of Nigel that I treasure. I had hoped that Nigel and I would work together on my dream of putting together a band and presenting the songs of Sandy and Trevor Lucas in concert so that a whole new generation of people could appreciate the songs. I still intend to follow through with that dream.

Georgia Rose was less than one when she lost her mother and eleven when her father passed away. I feel for the grief her younger self endured and marvel at her courage through her life and the legacy that she now honours. That is a great source of inspiration to me and I feel blessed to have had the opportunities that have brought us together.

THE EMERGENCY
31 MAY-4 JUNE 1970, WASHINGTON DC

DUGGAN FLANAKIN

I once won tickets to see Judy Collins because I knew who wrote 'Who Knows Where The Time Goes?'. One of my great disappointments was that Sandy had left Fairport when I saw them at Emergency, an all-ages venue run by a young Emmylou Harris in the Georgetown section of Washington DC. Richard Thompson was already a big favourite of mine and I was writing for the *Washington Free Press* at the time.

ROUNDHOUSE
7 JUNE 1970, LONDON, UK

BRIAN CULLMAN

I just finished the recent Sandy Denny biography. I was very disappointed by it. In the end, she dies. In the bio that I want to read, she's now living in a cottage in Wales and only drinking on Thursdays.

When Sandy joined Fairport Convention she upped their game exponentially, not just with a voice that could stop time with a whisper, but with original songs as rich and strong as the traditional ballads the band were exploring. The three albums she recorded with them in 1968 and 1969 are breathtakingly beautiful and mysterious, digging deep into British traditions and dragging them into an ecstatic and electric future. When she left to go off on her own in late 1969, first with her own group, Fotheringay, then solo, she was at the top of her game and she was lost.

One of the first concerts I saw when I got to London was Fotheringay at the Roundhouse. They were the headliners. Elton John opened, then Argent, and only then did Fotheringay come on. They sounded terrific but were a bit of a comedown after Elton John, who wasn't a known quantity yet and who hadn't turned into a genius goofball. He was on fire, fronting a power trio, playing 'Take Me To The Pilot' and 'Burn Down The Mission'. Fotheringay seemed quite sedate after all that, not stiff so much as studious, as if they were taking exams. I had seen The Band at the Felt Forum in New York a few months before, and they exuded the same quiet gravity. It was like watching scientists in a laboratory. I mentioned that to Sandy Denny after the concert. 'Oh, I wish I'd been there,' she sighed. She invited me over for tea.

Sandy was living in South London. All the other musicians I'd met were in the North. The house was dark, but there were candles and records all over the floor and cats who eyed me suspiciously from behind the couch. Sandy was drinking white wine. Or she was drinking gin. Or she was drinking brandy. It was hard to keep track. There were glasses everywhere.

And there were test pressings of Bob Dylan doing songs for others to record. She played me his version of 'I'll Keep It With Mine', then played me a version that Judy Collins had done a few years before. Judy Collins's version wasn't very good. Dylan's was good until you put it next to Sandy's version with Fairport Convention. Then all bets were off. Dylan's song is furiously tender, without a trace of irony. It's a song about wanting to take on someone else's troubles and shelter them from inevitable loss and heartbreak. Sandy's version takes it several steps further into the realm of sin-eating and sacrifice. It goes so far beyond romantic love that it comes out the other side, into the love of a parent for their child, into the need for a saviour and the need to be that saviour, to give more than you have and expect nothing in return. You come away from her version totally broken and totally restored. *Sanctified* is not too strong a word.

Sandy knew she was extraordinary, but she wasn't sure she was any good. Like most great singers, her voice knew far more than she did and kept waiting for her to catch up. The ghosts and spirits she sang about were real and holy and terrifying, and when she sang about Matty Groves, it wasn't an old folk song anymore but was fresh gossip, dirty news from the street. It was as if she'd just been drinking with Matty's sister at the pub and on the way back had torn her skirt. Oh, her skirt was always torn or was always a couple sizes too small. In the world of Twiggy and wispy girls in gossamer gowns, she always wanted to lose a few pounds or grow a few inches taller. And after she'd been drinking, growing a few more inches seemed the most sensible option.

Anyone who's been around drink or drinkers knows that there's a certain place you arrive at somewhere between the third and the eleventh drink, a crossroads, a calm in the middle of a storm, a place of clarity and quiet and weightlessness, between light and dark, between the promise of God's grace and the certainty of failure, where you hold the knowledge that however sweet the song, the record will end, and just before the end, the needle will skip. That's the place where Sandy lived full-time.

10TH NATIONAL JAZZ, BLUES & POP FESTIVAL
8 AUGUST 1970, PLUMPTON, UK

STAFFAN WENNERLUND

From the moment I dropped the needle on the first track on the A-side of *Liege & Lief*, I was mesmerised by Sandy Denny's voice and by Fairport Convention. That cold winter (1969-70), I bought the two preceding albums, clearly noting that Sandy was the vocalist. I loved her voice and music and became a fan. I was horrified when I then learned that she had left the band. Living in Sweden, information about the future of both Fairport and Sandy was hard to come by and she disappeared from my horizons.

Staying in London that summer, my then fiancée and I decided to go down and visit the Plumpton Festival on the Saturday. Opening the festival programme, I couldn't believe my eyes when I saw a black-and-white photo of Fotheringay, Sandy Denny's new group, on the first page and realised that we had arrived just in time for their 1.30pm slot. We sat down just beneath the stage, on the stubble and in the heat, and enjoyed a set that ended with 'Two Weeks Last Summer', 'The Way I Feel' and 'John The Gun', which I heard for the first time. Back in London, I bought the band's self-titled album which quickly became a favourite.

I followed Sandy's musical tracks through her album releases, and in the summer of 1974 I bought *Like An Old Fashioned Waltz*. By then she was back in the Fairport ranks and I got to hear her and the band when the *Live* line up came to my hometown of Gothenburg and played a blistering set on a sunny afternoon on the open stage of our outdoor amusement park at Liseberg (24 August 1974).

A year later, Fairport were back in Gothenburg, playing the Concert Hall on 14 December 1975. It was the *Rising For The Moon* tour and my expectations were high. I had intended to take a camera with me but didn't. 'I can take photos next time they come here,' was my thought, but it was never to be… Nevertheless, I was sitting in the front row and loved every minute of the concert, especially Sandy's singing.

From then on, I followed her recorded output as closely as I could, playing her solo albums as much as the ones she made with Fairport.

YORKSHIRE FOLK, BLUES & JAZZ FESTIVAL 1970
14 – 16 AUGUST 1970, KRUMLIN, UK

ED WALLAGE

Back in 1970 music festivals were in their infancy, and the influence of Woodstock was high, but trying to recreate Woodstock in the Pennines was, with hindsight, optimism over reality. This was however the first time I saw Sandy.

Ed Wallage's Krumlin Festival programme

I had just finished my 'O' levels and, rather worrying in retrospect, I was allowed to go along to this festival by myself. I had no tent, no proper sleeping bag, just an old quilt sewn up, carried in my school haversack. (Times were different, and I don't know whether to be pleased or disappointed with my parents.)

The line-up for the festival was a who's who of the time; Pink Floyd, The Who, etc were scheduled to play. But for me the big draw were Fairport and Fotheringay.

All went roughly to plan on Friday. Elton John was a particular highlight, just sitting and playing piano along with bass and drums. That night I was offered the use of a tent (without groundsheet) by some lads from Liverpool, who also provided beans for breakfast.

Saturday started, but the promised acts were not all forthcoming. Rumours began to circulate that the organisers were running out of money and/or bands were not turning up. There were still some excellent performances by some top acts. As the day wore on, the weather started to deteriorate and by early evening it started to rain. With no shelter I took the big decision to spend five shillings on a survival bag. The festival ticket was two pounds and ten shillings (£2.50), so it was a big expenditure but it lived up to its name!

Fairport went down a storm and I eagerly awaited Fotheringay. Chaos seemed however to be growing, and the rumour that bands were not willing to play until they had been paid continued. It was therefore with great excitement that I predicted the arrival of Fotheringay. Nothing had been said, and there was no programme as such. The main reason for my anticipation was the arrival of a bass drum on stage which I recognised from the centrefold photograph of the *Fotheringay* album. (Back then album covers were studied closely and were all part of the album experience). The band followed the bass drum onto stage and they proceeded to perform most of the album along with some standards.

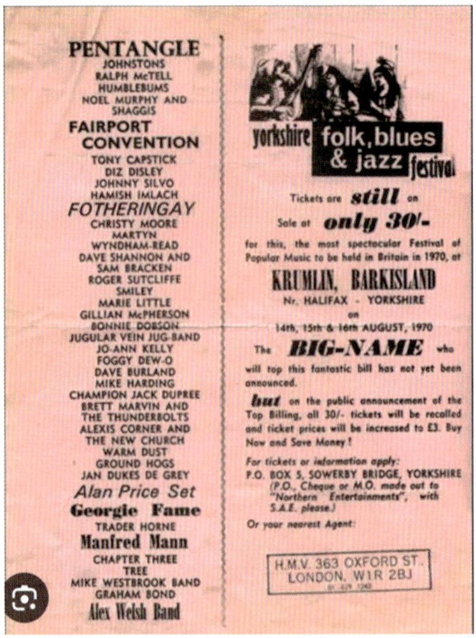
PENTANGLE
JOHNSTONS
RALPH McTELL
HUMBLEBUMS
NOEL MURPHY AND SHAGGIS
FAIRPORT CONVENTION
TONY CAPSTICK
DIZ DISLEY
JOHNNY SILVO
HAMISH IMLACH
FOTHERINGAY
CHRISTY MOORE
MARTYN WYNDHAM-READ
DAVE SHANNON AND SAM BRACKEN
ROGER SUTCLIFFE
SMILEY
MARIE LITTLE
GILLIAN McPHERSON
BONNIE DOBSON
JUGULAR VEIN JUG-BAND
JO-ANN KELLY
FOGGY DEW-O
DAVE BURLAND
MIKE HARDING
CHAMPION JACK DUPREE
BRETT MARVIN AND THE THUNDERBOLTS
ALEXIS CORNER AND THE NEW CHURCH
WARM DUST
GROUND HOGS
JAN DUKES DE GREY
Alan Price Set
Georgie Fame
TRADER HORNE
Manfred Mann
CHAPTER THREE
TREE
MIKE WESTBROOK BAND
GRAHAM BOND
Alex Welsh Band

yorkshire folk, blues & jazz festival

Tickets are **still** on Sale at **only 30/-**
for this, the most spectacular Festival of Popular Music to be held in Britain in 1970, at
KRUMLIN, BARKISLAND
Nr. HALIFAX - YORKSHIRE
on
14th, 15th & 16th AUGUST, 1970

The **BIG-NAME** who will top this fantastic bill has not yet been announced.

but on the public announcement of the Top Billing, all 30/- tickets will be recalled and ticket prices will be increased to £3. Buy Now and Save Money!

For tickets or information apply:
P.O. BOX 5, SOWERBY BRIDGE, YORKSHIRE
(P.O., Cheque or M.O. made out to "Northern Entertainments", with S.A.E. please.)

Or your nearest Agent:

H.M.V. 363 OXFORD ST.
LONDON, W1R 2BJ

Krumlin running order (John Armstrong)

Sandy was a diminutive figure alongside Trevor but she still commanded attention. There was a grand piano at the side of the stage which she used for some songs. The sound was remarkably good given the constraints of the equipment. As they played, the weather took a turn for the worse and I sheltered from the rain in my survival bag. I recall peering out of a gap in a rolled-up top trying not to miss anything.

Ed Wallage's Krumlin Festival ticket

The rest of the evening was spent in my orange cocoon. Thereafter the festival is a bit of a blur, probably because I had retreated into my survival bag. I remained there until the following morning. Around 5am, the police were walking around the field and gently kicking survival bags to see if there was anyone in them! There was an announcement from the stage via a megaphone that the festival was called off. (The PA could not be used given the danger of water versus electricity.) Rather meekly and without any fuss, people started to shuffle off site. I caught a bus back to Halifax, but my memory has either blocked out details, or I was suffering from lack of food, as the only thing I can remember eating all weekend was those beans for breakfast the previous day!

JOHN ARMSTRONG (& TONY JAGGER RIP)

As a 16-year-old I attended the Krumlin Festival on the hills above Halifax. I was a big fan of Fotheringay. Unfortunately, when they played on the Saturday night the rain came down, but it didn't stop them. My cousin Tony and I lay in our tent, legs outside in the open, listening to Sandy's voice drifting over the damp moorland. I have told many people over the years that it is the most beautiful thing I've ever heard in my life, and I can still hear it in my head now. There was just something about her voice... plaintive, pure, emotive, the very essence of English folk music... that no-one else came near to matching.

When Sandy Denny of Fotheringay talks, she talks to Melody Maker...

...a very good reason to buy it.

Personalities who adorn today's music scene have a lot to say about themselves and about their music. And they say it to Melody Maker. Because they know we're involved. Week after week we make our pages echo with pop, jazz, folk and progressive–plenty of good reasons to buy Melody Maker.
If you need any more, this week sees the first part of a competition that could win you a new M.G. Midget equipped with full stereo cassette playback!

Melody Maker

Out today. One shilling.

HEADMASTER BANS FOURTEEN BOYS WITH LONG HAIR

YOUR STARS

Sent home .. four boys whose hair is too short

When Sandy talks... (*Daily Mirror*)

FAIRFIELD HALLS
13 SEPTEMBER 1970, CROYDON, UK

COLIN HOUGHTON

I saw Fotheringay at the Fairfield Halls in Croydon. They were excellent but they made several false starts to numbers and I recall Sandy getting quite cross as they had clearly rehearsed intros which were going wrong.

MELODY MAKER POLL WINNERS PARTY SAVOY HOTEL
24 SEPTEMBER 1970, LONDON, UK

CHRIS CHARLESWORTH, JOURNALIST & AUTHOR

They were a 'hot little quartet', according to Chris Welch who reported on the event in *Melody Maker*'s September 26 issue. He was referring to Sandy, Robert Plant, Jimmy Page and John Bonham, the former present to collect her award as Top UK female singer, the latter three as Top UK group, toppling The Beatles who had won that category for as long as anyone could remember.

'She is a small but heavily built young lady, with a noticeably large bosom and a face that defies any suggestion of showbiz glamour,' wrote Michael Watts in a profile of Sandy that appeared in the previous week's *MM*, alongside the news that she had won the poll, beating last year's winner, Christine Perfect, soon to be Christine McVie, into second place. 'It's a real honest-to-God English folksinger's face; there is no trace of that saintly purity of feature that American girl singers, like Joan Baez and Judy Collins, always have. It belongs to the small, bare upstairs rooms of English pubs, where everyone is downing pints and the person in the seat at your elbow suddenly gets up and sings unaccompanied a 20-verse traditional ballad. It's a wholesome country barmaid's face that makes you feel at home.

Sandy with Led Zeppelin at the Melody Maker awards, September 1970 (Sandy Denny Archive - photographer unknown)

'She was pleased she had won the *MM* poll, but not in personal terms. She knows she is not the most conventional idea of a female singer, so she figures her success is a victory for music.'

Sandy on the cover of *Melody Maker* (Barrie Wentzell)

Back in 1970 winning the *MM* poll was a bit like winning the Brits, so much so that national newspapers carried the results and the winning acts took the trouble to turn up to collect their awards, this year presented by Jimmy Savile. The three members of Led Zeppelin flew back from a US tour to attend – John Paul Jones was holidaying in Hawaii – and a host of others were on hand, whether they won anything or not, including Ian Anderson, Jack Bruce, Ginger Baker, Keith Emerson, Greg Lake, Carl Palmer, members of Free and Mungo Jerry and Top DJ John Peel.

Sandy had her photograph taken with the members of Led Zeppelin by the Thames at the rear of the hotel and there's a likelihood that it was here that she was invited to sing on 'Battle Of Evermore', the song on Led Zep's untitled fourth LP that was released the following year. Although Sandy had left Fairport Convention to form Fotheringay with her partner Trevor Lucas, her old band's bass player Dave Pegg was a lifelong friend of fellow-Midlanders Plant and Bonham, and the following month Page and Plant went to see Fotheringay supporting Elton John at the Albert Hall. Inclusion of the song on their next LP gave Sandy the singular distinction of being the only outside musician ever to be credited as having sang on a Led Zeppelin album.

It also seems likely that in keeping with her reputation for enjoying herself at parties, she helped herself to a few glasses of complimentary wine. 'Sandy Denny terrified Jiving K Boots by attacking him in the lobby,' reported Chris Welch in reference to the fictitious rock star who made regular appearances in *MM*'s 'Raver' gossip column. 'She revealed she was upset because Boots had been graceless in his observance of proprieties,' he added mysteriously.

ROYAL ALBERT HALL
2 OCTOBER 1970, KENSINGTON, LONDON, UK

JERRY GILBERT

Even at the Albert Hall, home of the automatic encore, it is dangerous to reserve the showpiece for the curtain call. Fortheringay discovered this on Friday night when audience reaction scarcely invited a return at the end of their set. But Sandy Denny insisted on singing her beautiful 'Banks Of The Nile', still the best number in the band's repertoire.

Not that Fotheringay were bad. Sandy's voice was clear and powerful yet remarkably controlled, and the sound balance was perfect despite the presence of electric and acoustic guitars. Good solid rock drumming from Gerry Conway and precise country-style riffs from Jerry Donahue wove together a tight sound spearheaded by Sandy Denny, now featured far more on piano, and Trevor Lucas. Paradoxically Sandy's penchant for piano meant the lack of an hilarious moment usually provided when she starts grappling with her guitar. Friday's concert could have done with such a lift as for the most part Fotheringay were subdued, and the best numbers like 'The Sea', 'Ned Kelly' and 'The Way I Feel' all appeared early on in their set, after which entertainment came a poor second behind sheer professionalism.

MICK DONOVAN

I saw the short-lived line-up which also included Sandy's husband Trevor Lucas (guitar/vocals), Jerry Donahue (guitar) and Pat Donaldson (bass) at the Royal Albert Hall. Legend has it that Elton John, then an up-and-comer, stole the show in his sparkly jacket and flamboyant performance. Not in my book. No one ever put Sandy Denny in second place. Myself and my mate Tony were in 'the gods', the top balcony of the cavernous hall looking way down on the performers. If I close my eyes, I can picture a brilliant band with brilliant songs and a singer capable of making time stand still.

SOUTHAMPTON UNIVERSITY
17 OCTOBER 1970, SOUTHAMPTON, UK

SAM GARRETT-JONES

I fell in love with Sandy and her music as a first-year undergraduate. I had already heard and liked Fairport pre-Sandy – 'If I Had A Ribbon Bow' (in February 1968) and the first album (June 1968) – but not bought these records as cash was short!

When I arrived at Southampton University in October 1969, 'Meet On The Ledge' was on the jukebox in the coffee bar. I forget where I first heard *Unhalfbricking*. Possibly a friend had a copy, or more likely it was played to the suitably relaxed patrons in the dim lounge and where the Progressive Music Society met (no-one called it 'prog rock'). I was immediately struck by the songs by Denny and Richard Thompson – of course 'Who Knows Where The Time Goes?' – and by the epic 'Sailor's Life'. I'd heard nothing like that before. I loved the pulsating bass (which my mum detested) and Swarb's fiddle. But Sandy's voice with its power, range and breathy emotion was what truly captivated me.

When *Liege & Lief* came out at the end of the year I bought it almost unheard (apart from a few snatches in a 'soundproof' cubicle in the record shop in Southampton with friends). *Liege & Lief* remains one of my all-time favourite records.

We were studying geography, and one afternoon's practical exercise was to draw a realistic map of an imaginary island. Fairport seemed a good name for a fishing village, and of course it had to have a Sandy Bay. Maybe I was unoriginal, but I couldn't get the connection between Fairport and Island (Records) out of my head.

It was autumn term 1970 when Sandy visited Southampton with her new group, Fotheringay. They had a tighter, sparser sound than Fairport, which worked superbly on the magnificently atmospheric 'Banks Of The Nile'. Her live performance of that song is something I shall never forget. It was absolutely spine-tingling and demanded our total engagement: the audience was hushed for the full nine minutes.

On the other hand, we sallow English students didn't quite know how to take the tall brash Aussie, Trevor. His guitar was clearly integral to the Fotheringay sound but his voice was from another world. Little did I know then that I would in time become a brash Aussie (but never tall). I wore out my UK copy of *Fotheringay*, but picked up another in the US years later. It was released on A&M, but by that stage I was past drawing imaginary islands.

When Sandy returned to Southampton in autumn 1971 it was as 'Sandy Denny And Her Band'. But it was 'Fairport lite' – Richard Thompson played, and I'm sure I recall Swarb too. The set list drew on *Liege & Lief* as well as *The North Star Grassman And The Ravens*, which had just been released. Her performances of the two epic ballads, 'Matty Groves' and 'Tam Lin', were mesmerising, more so than her then unfamiliar solo songs.

Large concerts at the university were held in the Old Refectory. We all sat on the floor and the artists had to pass through whatever gap in the audience they could find to reach the stage. At one of these concerts – I think 1971 – I was sitting on the edge of the nominal 'aisle' with my left arm outstretched in support. I remember turning around to see the band members entering and being excited that Richard Thompson was there. As the band glided past, Sandy's long dress brushed my arm and her right foot either grazed or stepped on my fingers (I've no doubt embellished the story over the years). 'I'll never wash this hand again!', I cried. My admiration for her music has lasted a lot longer than that promise.

In about late 1981 or 1982 I saw Trevor again, at a gig with Eric Bogle at the Australian National University. He never mentioned Sandy, but towards the end of the set he said, 'Here's a song written by my best friend…' and played 'Who Knows Where the Time Goes?'. It brought tears to my eyes.

A few years ago, Swarb, who looked quite sick, gave a house concert for the Illawarra Folk Club at Mairie Peterson's house on Shellharbour beach. As an encore, he played the 'Lark In The Morning' set of jigs from *Liege & Lief* absolutely note perfect. The small audience didn't seem to appreciate its crucial historical significance in the annals of English folk rock, so I jumped up to applaud, almost falling over on the 'dry and sandy' ground.

CITY HALL
14 NOVEMBER 1970, NEWCASTLE-UPON-TYNE, UK

HENRY RACE

I only saw Sandy Denny once. I'd taken my *Fotheringay* album cover with me to the City Hall, and after the gig I was running around outside trying to get all the members of the group to sign it. I'd nabbed Pat

Donaldson, Jerry Donahue and Trevor Lucas but the cars had started to arrive to whisk them away to their rock star accommodation for the evening.

Gerry Conway and Sandy were heading in separate directions to separate cars and I figured I only had time to get one of them to sign my album cover so I went to Sandy. I presented her with the (gatefold) cover and a pen and asked her to sign it. With a straight face but with a twinkle in her eye, she asked me, 'Do you want it inside or outside?'

'Inside please, Sandy,' replied the 16-year-old me, blushing slightly. She duly signed it inside but I realised that Gerry Conway had driven off while I was talking to her.

The sleeve stayed Gerry-less for decades and it continued to bug my happiness! A few years ago, I noticed that Fairport – with Gerry Conway drumming – were playing at Dumfries Theatre Royal, not far from me, and even though I wasn't going to the gig, I cheekily went over beforehand at soundcheck time, found Gerry and, after telling him the story of how I'd spurned the chance to have him sign my *Fotheringay* sleeve all those years ago, he laughed out loud and happily signed it for me.

Fotheringay at Manchester's Free Trade Hall

Fotheringay at Sheffield Uni (Mick Monk)

After decades, I finally had the full set of autographs and my happiness was no longer bugged. RIP to Sandy, and Gerry.

UNIVERSITY OF BRADFORD
28 NOVEMBER 1970, BRADFORD, UK

TERRY HAYES

I didn't know who she or the group were. They were meant to be the support act to Fairport Convention (who I had gone to see). That didn't happen though, as another group I hadn't heard of called The Strawbs replaced Fairport. I remember the concert was amazing and I bought the *Fotheringay* LP on Island soon after. I also had to get The Strawbs' albums. I love Sandy's vocals on their 1968 LP.

THE DOME
5 DECEMBER 1970, BRIGHTON, UK

STEPHEN ROYSTON

In the summer of 1969, I bought Fairport's single 'Si Tu Dois Partir', having seen them perform it on *Top Of The Pops*. It was the B-side, Richard Thompson's 'Genesis Hall', which particularly impressed me, and still does to this day. That track was the beginning of my lifelong devotion to Fairport and to Sandy.

I was fortunate enough to see Sandy in concert six times, between 1970 and 1977, at various venues around England. Both the first and last times I saw her were at The Dome in Brighton. The December 1970 concert was great value at 50p a ticket and the only time I saw Sandy with Fotheringay. The way the ticket is printed makes it look as though Fotheringay was the name of the singer with Colosseum; in fact, they were the support act.

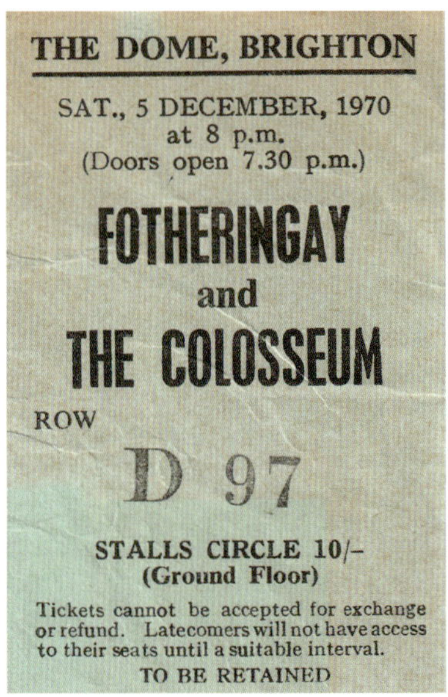

Stephen Royston saw Sandy six times altogether

I next saw Sandy in October 1971, performing at Brighton College with a band that included Richard Thompson. I noted in my diary that it started very late but was 'superb; an excellent concert'. I recall Sandy sitting at the piano performing The Beatles' 'Let It Be'.

A year later, I went with my girlfriend Frances to Sandy's solo concert at the Queen Elizabeth Hall on London's South Bank, with John Martyn as her support act. Among the songs she performed were new ones from her second solo album, *Sandy*, which had just been released. Dave Swarbrick crept in from the wings to play a fiddle solo at the end of Sandy's performance of 'The Quiet Joys Of Brotherhood'. I didn't enjoy the concert as much as the 1971 one, missing the band. I have since read that Sandy was very nervous during this particular show. I recall that the new album, plus the EP *Pass Of Arms*, containing two songs by Sandy (neither written by her) which were not available elsewhere, were displayed in the foyer.

Stephen Royston & wife Frances (left) with Georgia Rose Lucas, Brasenose Arms, Cropredy, 2025

In June 1974, Frances and I saw Sandy with the *Fairport Nine* lineup for the first time, at the Greyhound in Croydon. I noted in my diary:

They played excellently, all the old Fairport/Sandy/Fotheringay favourites, although for me I think that some of the magic has gone.

In November 1975 I went with Frances (who was my wife by this time) to see Sandy with Fairport once again, at UMIST in Manchester. By this time, Dave Mattacks had left the band for the second time and been replaced on drums by Bruce Rowland. I wrote in my diary:

The band weren't on stage until nearly 11.00pm. Appalling conditions, with far too many people crammed into the hall, all standing up, sweat dripping all over the place. The band were very disappointing; all humourless and tired. All rather depressing for me. I really don't want to see them again.

(I have seen Fairport many, many times since!)

The very last time I saw Sandy was on her final tour, back at Brighton

Dome, in November 1977. I noted in my diary:

Sandy was very sweet and radiant after the birth of her child, and sang well despite a bad cold. A good band too, including Trevor Lucas, Dave Mattacks and Pat Donaldson. The Dome was only a third full though, which reflects changes in people's musical tastes, post-punk. Danny Thompson was the support act, and John and Beverley Martyn were in the audience.

I remember that she mentioned baby Georgia quite a lot.

At Cropredy in 2025, fifty years on from when we last saw Sandy together, Frances and I were delighted to meet Sandy and Trevor's daughter Georgia Rose Lucas at her wonderful exhibition of Sandy's treasures and memorabilia at The Brasenose pub. Georgia was kind enough to let us be photographed with her, with images of Sandy looking over our shoulders.

TRAFALGAR SQUARE
31 DECEMBER 1970, LONDON, UK

MANDY SYLVESTER

I worked behind the coffee bar at Les Cousins folk club. My boyfriend Gordon used to roadie for Sandy and had a Transit van which only had two front seats. On New Years Eve (I think it was 1970) we had celebrated at the club with Sandy and Trevor and others, and Gordon offered to drive them home. They had to sit in the back of the van and I was in the front seat. It had been snowing, and as we passed through Trafalgar Square, a very merry Sandy leant forward and wound down my window in order to shout greetings to the revellers, at which point one of the revellers threw a huge snowball through the window which hit me squarely in the face. Much hilarity and laughter (at my expense) ensued.

SOUNDS
16 JANUARY 1971

JERRY GILBERT

Sandy Denny admitted this week that Fotheringay's producer and recording manager Joe Boyd had precipitated the breakup of the group. And Roy Guest, manager of Britain's top female vocalist, added: 'We were about halfway through the album and Joe just wasn't satisfied, so he stopped it and brought the whole thing to an end. It was a traumatic shock because Fotheringay were a very successful group; but once the decision was made, Sandy, Trevor Lucas and I were quite happy with the result.'

So after spells with The Strawbs, Fairport Convention and Fotheringay, Sandy Denny again faces an uncertain future. And at present she has no plans to start work again.

Fotheringay's plight is not unique by any means. For they were working a necessary three or four gigs a week to earn a living, and that was more than either Sandy or Trevor were keen to play, according to Roy Guest. 'The three other musicians in the group really liked gigging as often as possible, but Sandy and Trevor only liked it if it was a good gig, and it was this pressure that led to the break up.'

'The trouble is it's a vicious circle because on two gigs a week you are only breaking even – it's the third and fourth you are making money on. The genuine expenses of the group were tremendous, but I think Sandy and Trevor would have preferred to do only two gigs a week.'

January 16, 1971 SOUNDS Page 9

Sandy Denny talking to Jerry Gilbert

FOTHERINGAY –THE TRUTH

SANDY DENNY admitted this week that Fotheringay's producer and recording manager Joe Boyd had precipitated the break up of the group.

And Roy Guest, manager of Britain's top female vocalist, added: "We were about half-way through the album and Joe just wasn't satisfied, so he stopped it and brought the whole thing to an end. It was a traumatic shock because Fotheringay were a very successful group; but once the decision was made Sandy, Trevor Lucas and I were quite happy with the result."

So after spells with the Strawbs, Fairport Convention and Fotheringay, Sandy Denny again faces an uncertain future. And at present she has no plans to start work again.

□ □ □

Fotheringay's plight is not unique by any means. For they were working a necessary three or four gigs a week to earn a living, and that was more than either Sandy or Trevor were keen to play, according to Roy Guest. "The three other musicians in the group really liked gigging as often as possible, but Sandy and Trevor only liked it if it was a good gig, and it was this pressure that led to the break-up.

"The trouble is it's a vicious circle because on two gigs a week you are only breaking even — it's the third and fourth you are making money on. The genuine expenses of the group were tremendous, but I think Sandy and Trevor would have preferred to do only two gigs a week."

"Actually doing the gigs didn't get me down", Sandy retorted, "but it was the time involved in doing a gig. I just wish the day was five hours longer so that when you arrive back late from a gig you can go to sleep and then wake up with a whole day ahead of you instead of thinking like 'there's only an hour before the bank shuts' or something.

"I never had the time to just sit down; and when I did I'd just lie and look at the ceiling.

"The point is that we were well into three gigs a week and sometimes four, and all the time I felt very responsible to the group for finding songs and writing songs; I was conscious that a lot of pressure was on me.

"I like thinking a lot, and I hardly ever had time to be on my own; as it is I shall now have the amount of time I really want. I feel that everyone should have the time to just sit and think about things, and you're not doing yourself justice if you don't give your brain a chance."

□ □ □

Time is the one thing that Sandy Denny will find in large supply now she is free from group commitments. Although I believe it will not be very long before she is feeling sufficiently restless to form another band.

Sandy is not looking into the future with any conviction, although she hopes to get a solo album under way. "I don't know what I'll do, although I reckon that in three months' time I shall be unbearable because I shall want to be on the road again.

"I just want time to stand still really, but in three months' time, if I'm not in America making a record I would probably be very nervous and tense, and wanting to do something. I shan't definitely be forming a group, although when I let Fairports it was driving me mad not having a group before Fotheringay formed.

□ □ □

"I shall deinitely be making an album, and I think I'll have to work with someone on the album that I know and respect musically. I've got a few songs written for it but I'll have to think about it carefully; I shall think about the conception of the album for at least a month or two, and I'd like to get a really detached place like a house in the middle of Wimbledon or something."

Would Sandy be moving right away from London in order to facilitate and expedite her songwriting? "Yes, it might be best to get right away from London, but it's necessary to keep a place going in London as well."

Said Roy Guest: "The thing is I don't want to work too hard and I have a feeling Sandy doesn't want to either; that's why I'm her manager."

"But", concluded Sandy, "I've a feeling that this year is going to be very exciting."

Sandy talked to Jerry about the Fotheringay split

'Actually doing the gigs didn't get me down,' Sandy retorted, 'but it was the time involved in doing a gig. I just wish the day was five hours longer so that when you arrive back late from a gig you can go to sleep and then wake up with a whole day ahead of you instead of thinking like 'there's only an hour before the bank shuts' or something. I never had the time to just sit down; and when I did, I'd just lie and look at the ceiling. The point is that we were well into three gigs a week and sometimes four, and all the time I felt very responsible to the group for finding songs and writing songs; I was conscious that a lot of pressure was on me.

'I like thinking a lot, and I hardly ever had time to be on my own; as it is, I shall now have the amount of time I really want. I feel that everyone should have the time to just sit and think about things, and you're not doing yourself justice if you don't give your brain a chance.'

Time is the one thing that Sandy Denny will find in large supply now she's free from group commitments. Although I believe it will not be very long before she's feeling sufficiently restless to form another band. Sandy is not looking into the future with any conviction, although she hopes to get a solo album underway.

'I don't know what I'll do, although I reckon that in three months' time, I shall be unbearable because I shall want to be on the road again. I just want time to stand still really, but in three months' time, if I'm not in America making a record, I would probably be very nervous and tense, and wanting to do something. I shan't definitely be forming a group, although when I left Fairports, it was driving me mad not having a group before Fotheringay formed. I shall definitely be making an album, and I think I'll have to work with someone on the album that I know and respect musically. I've got a few songs written for it, but I'll have to think about it carefully; I shall think about the conception of the album for at least a month or two, and I'd like to get a really detached place like a house in the middle of Wimbledon or something.'

Would Sandy be moving right away from London in order to facilitate and expedite her songwriting? 'Yes, it might be best to get right away from London, but it's necessary to keep a place going in London as well.'

Said Roy Guest: 'The thing is I don't want to work too hard and I have a feeling Sandy doesn't want to either; that's why I'm her manager.'

'But,' concluded Sandy, 'I have a feeling that this year is going to be very exciting.'

QUEEN ELIZABETH HALL
30 JANUARY 1971, SOUTH BANK, LONDON, UK

GERRY CONWAY

Fotheringay was a very happy band. It was very nice working with Sandy. Everyone in the band adored her. I loved to play her songs. I think had the band not been forced to quit, it would have continued for quite a long time. Sandy was the type of person who once she felt comfortable with her musicians, would stick with them. It was a very difficult decision she had to make. Even when she made the decision to be a solo singer, the first thing she did was employ the musicians from the band to play on the solo album. That speaks for itself.

Melody Maker announces the Fotheringay split

Every so often, someone will come up to me with a Fotheringay album to sign. Every time that happens, I get a very nice feeling. I have a real soft spot for that album and period. It was a very nice thing. Musically, the album's not perfect, but a lot of people tell me how much they enjoy it. It still happens quite often. It's like you suddenly have a bond with that person. It's a weird thing.

The break up was very upsetting at the time. We had a meeting with the band after we learned Sandy wasn't going to be in it anymore. We were deciding whether or not to continue without her. I'm usually the last person to say 'let's stop', but I recall in that situation I said, 'No, Sandy equals no band for me.' I was pretty clear cut on that. So, that's it. It folded.

Had we decided to stick together, we would have had to undoubtedly find another singer. Whether breaking up was a misguided emotional decision done on the spur of the moment in terms of, 'If Sandy's not doing it, then I don't want to do it,' I can't really say. All I know is when she went, I didn't want to continue.

Without a rehearsal, we'd play something and it was mostly an intuition thing. You could always see if she was happy or not. When you got it right and it sounded right, she would let you know she was really happy. She was no taskmaster. With Sandy, it was about a kind of feeling from her when you had it right. She would never say, 'It would be nice if you'd play the fiddle here or do that.' It was never that. It was always up to me to construct my own parts and when it was right, it was right. It also had to do with the fact that you had to first gain her acceptance as a musician, but once you did, she really trusted you to do the right thing and you were left to do that.

Rhythmically, Sandy was pretty laid back. We didn't play anything frenetic. As a drummer, I learned how to play slowly which is possibly twice as hard as learning to play fast! Chordally and lyrically speaking, she was fantastic. When I started working with her, it was the first time as a drummer that I was aware of the song. The songs she wrote grabbed me. They did something for me. Suddenly, I found myself wanting to play the best possible thing for the music. That's often quite difficult. The creative process, no matter which instrument you play, is quite a painful thing when you're going from square one to bring something to fruition. It was quite a big learning curve for me to learn how to do the best thing for those songs.

We had all become very good friends by the time that the first Fotheringay album was finished so we decided to rent a farm house near Chichester to 'get it together in the country'. We started the second album at Sound Techniques but Sandy was under a lot of pressure to pursue a solo career and one morning in tears she told us that she had to leave. Sandy was very loyal to her

Fotheringay at the QEH (Steve Free)

friends, and content with people that she knew and trusted, so she really didn't want to do this. On her subsequent solo albums with Island Records, she hired Pat Donaldson, Jerry Donahue, Trevor Lucas and myself from Fotheringay to play on them. It makes me smile every time I think of it!

JOE BOYD, PRODUCER

A&M loved Sandy and agreed a very large advance for the American rights to her solo recordings after she left Fairport. She refused to make a solo album and ploughed the money into supporting a democratic partnership with Trevor and the others in Fotheringay, which both A&M and I were always against. She felt she needed to make Trevor her 'equal' in order to save the relationship. Trevor spent money like water – Bentley, Stonehenge PA system, etc. – and Sandy's A&M money was evaporating fast.

While working on the second album after I had agreed to join Warner Bros and leave London, the atmosphere was bad and the music uninspiring. Sandy knew it and asked me if I would produce her solo album if she scrapped the group. I said yes, meaning I would take time off from my new job to do it. We had both had a few drinks. She understood me to say that I would stay in London and not go to LA, and felt betrayed when I told her I was going the next day. The morning after that talk, she broke up the group and three of them took jobs with high-paying singers (Cat Stevens for two of them). I believe she understood the financial peril she was in and was relieved to find a reason to end Fotheringay, but for the sake of relationships with Trevor and the others, blamed me for it.

January 9, 1971

SANDY DENNY TO SOLO AS FOTHERINGAY SPLIT

FOTHERINGAY, THE group spearheaded by singer Sandy Denny, have broken up, and the five members will all be going separate ways.

Sandy, herself, is currently unsure of the future, although she will definitely pursue a solo career and will be recording her own album in due course. Said Sandy: "I'd like to do more writing, but I'm not able to do this as part of a group when we're doing gigs all the time."

□ □ □

Sandy and boyfriend Trevor Lucas formed Fotheringay after the breakup of Eclection. Sandy left Fairport Convention, and Gerry Conway, Jerry Donahue and Pat Donaldson all joined the new band at the beginning of 1970.

Now Gerry Conway and Pat Donaldson plan to do free-lance session work, and Trevor Lucas aims to learn record production and engineering. Jerry Donahue will free-lance for a time, and then he hopes to join another band.

Fotheringay play a special farewell concert at London's Queen Elizabeth Hall on January 30, when they will be inviting friends to come along and play with them.

● TREVOR LUCAS: formed Fotheringay with Sandy Denny after Eclection broke up

Joe Boyd to join Warner Brothers in States

JOE BOYD is leaving England at the end of January to take up a post as Director of Music Services at Warner Brothers studios in Burbank, California. Joe said this week that he will be in charge of the music for Warner films — "I've always been a film freak" — and in a statement, John Caley, executive vice-president in charge of production said: "His production and managerial strength make Joe Boyd unique in this vitally important position in a film company. Warner Brothers will be relying heavily on Boyd's taste and experience in first quality music."

Joe will be leaving behind his Witchseason, Warlock and Werewolf companies, which will continue, he said, mainly as music publishers and agents. No one will be taking Joe's place, as such, and many of the Witchseason bands will produce

CHARISMA

CHARISMA RECORDS are planning two tours for their bands, the first featuring Van Der Graaf Generator, Genesis and Lindisfarne. This opens at London's Lyceum on

The Right Road" on January 22, this will be followed by an album, "Extraction".

Dates for Gary include Hampstead Country Club (February 12), Cooks Ferry, Edmonton (15), 1832 Windsor (16), Leeds University (20), Romford (22), Sisters,

Sounds had the Fotheringay split exclusive

Sandy was a very confident

musician but lacked confidence as a person. She was insecure about her looks and worried that she couldn't keep Trevor by her side without giving him power and responsibility over her career, first in Fotheringay and then as producer. Trevor was not a bad guy, just a bit out of his depth with Sandy's talent. Every record he produced had some great tracks, but there was no one album that lifted her to another level. I always believed Sandy could have been a great international star. I have no reason to doubt that now, looking back. Her legacy is as yet unrealised.

CECIL SHARP HOUSE
1971, PRIMROSE HILL, LONDON, UK

ROYSTON WOOD

I used to work down in Cecil Sharp House, then the headquarters of the English Folk Dance and Song Society, in the cellar of this organisation, taping things and editing tapes for Chapel Recording Company. It was a little organisation that existed independently almost of this society. And Sandy with her band, Fotheringay, used to come and practice in the room next door, because they had practice rooms all over the place. I heard them playing 'John The Gun' through the wall of the studio, which I'm not supposed to be able to do in a soundproof studio – but I did. And I fell in love with the song.

And about a year after I first heard it, Sandy said, 'Do you want to be on the session of an album I'm making?' and I said, 'Yes please! Can I make a request? If I'm going to sing on your album, can I be on one particular song if you're gonna do it?'

She said, 'What is it?' and I said, 'John The Gun'. She said, 'That's what I had you in mind for!' So 'John The Gun' it was.

It was a terrific song. We were drinking Foster's Australian lager and got really tanked up, blasted out of our minds, including Barry Dransfield the violinist. Barry didn't know what he was doing, but if you just listen to his violin break, he even comes in on key at the end of it.

SOUND TECHNIQUES STUDIO
1971, LONDON, UK

JOHN WOOD, SOUND ENGINEER

I think Sandy probably visited us, on her own in Suffolk, much more than Nick (Drake) did. This was before they (she and Trevor Lucas) were married. For *North Star* it was her idea to bring Richard (Thompson) in. Both of us to an extent, but she'd always had a really strong bond with Richard. She had enormous respect for Richard. Actually, I can't think of any other musician she had that level of respect for. So, for this, it was the three of us who chose who played on it and how it went whereas by, say, the time we're doing *Old Fashioned Waltz*, Trevor is choosing the band. For this, he wasn't really around. She was certainly emotionally involved but not musically.

Relaxed? I think the nearest she got to it was the *North Star Grassman* album, she didn't feel pressured. She was very herself… just chilled, really relaxed. It was pretty easy. No tantrums, no nothing. 'John The Gun', that's one of the most under-appreciated songs, I'm amazed that no one is playing it at the moment. It's a phenomenal song. Those highlights, they're just great. When we did 'John The Gun', I think it's the best song on the record, especially Richard's playing. Electric. I saw her do it live years later at Sydney Opera House with Fairport… just incredibly powerful. I'm amazed that nobody is doing it as a contemporary song, the way the world is at the moment. I mean… you could do 'John The Gun' with a full-blown classical choir.

For 'Jump The Broomstick' we had the bloke out of Mighty Baby, Roger Powell on drums, the rest was Gerry Conway. 'Crazy Lady Blues', that's quite a fun little song, I remember sending Joe the tape of that to get Buddy Emmons on it. There weren't many pedal steel players who were up to that standard. 'Crazy Lady Blues' – she always said that was about Linda (Thompson).

Was Sandy a first take? No… not that many takes and singing, you don't want to do too many takes, certainly not Sandy because she wouldn't be able to keep going. How long did her voice last? In the studio? I don't think we'd ever attempt more than a couple of songs at a time. Well, 'Quiet Joys Of Brotherhood' I know we did that in one evening over at Basing Street. And she got the idea for that from Norma

Waterson's husband, Martin Carthy. She played this Martin thing… he's very straightforward, very traditional, an on-off singer and I thought, 'God, what are you going to do with this?' It's a Richard Farina song. But she really made it work. Voices and the fiddle at the end. There are these high spots in her career, always. 'The Quiet Joys Of Brotherhood' – that's Sandy for me. Every record she made, there are one or two gems.

Sneaky Pete just happened to be in the country. That was accidental, pure happenstance. He'd gone to play on something of (Marc) Ellington's, so we co-opted him and he showed up at Basing Street and overdubbed. He was phenomenal, not flamboyant at all. Turned up with his instrument. All pedal steel players set their own instruments up differently. I learned that from Bill Keith when I was working with him years before. We did the overdub in the control room at Basing Street, plugged him in and we played him the track once and the next was the take. Then he said he'd put another part down and he just did it. Listen carefully and you can hear the two parts. It was me, Sandy, Trevor, the tape op and Sneaky Pete. One should have been surprised but, by this time, I'd worked with some of these extraordinary players and… you just watched in awe. Jaw dropping.

Sandy really liked Harry (Robinson)… If she didn't she wouldn't have gone on using him. I don't believe this took more than six or eight weeks. We weren't waiting for material, all the material was pretty much there. Generally, you'd go in during the afternoon and since you weren't dealing with unions, you'd crack a couple of tracks and then go back to something you'd already been working on. Sandy hardly ever did live vocals. The only ones I really remember were when we did the big sessions at Island for *Rendezvous*. I used to have to talk her in to things like that – the whole concept of recording that way because she wasn't used to it. She was very nervous when we did that. But then so was Pat Donaldson, because he'd never sat with an orchestra before.

How would she hide her nerves? Interestingly enough and unless you knew her, you wouldn't have seen it, you had to know her to know she was a bit unsettled. She'd avoid too much attention if she was nervous or insecure by being jokey. And, of course, the more you know someone, the more you can see them do it.

MURIEL'S
1971, SOHO, LONDON, UK

LINDA THOMPSON, SINGER SONGWRITER

Sandy and I were belting the Crosby Stills & Nash song 'Change Partners' out. We were singing 'James Barker'. Swarb said, 'I think you'll find that lyric is 'so we change partners again'.' Sandy and I were Miss and Miss Malaprop. I still sing 'James Barker' to remember her.

I was at Sound Techniques studio, singing some jingles, and Sandy was in of an afternoon recording some Fairport stuff. Woody (the legendary John Wood) was getting drum sounds and guitar sounds. Sometimes that took forever, so Sandy and I scarpered, and caught a cab. She cabbed everywhere, and headed for Muriel's, a famous drinking establishment in Soho. In those days licensing laws were draconian. No daytime drinking. There were, however, private clubs where you could drink your liver out. Muriel's was the louchest of those places.

Francis Bacon was always there. I didn't even know who he was at that time. I'm sure Sandy did. Muriel the proprietress hated everyone, except a chosen few, and she loved loved Sandy, because Sandy was so funny and clever, and she could also drink a navvy under the table. I didn't drink and Muriel felt very sorry for me just for that reason alone, and always patted me on the head, and said 'there, there'. We got to the club around 4pm. We were going to stay for an hour. Needless to say, we were still there at 10pm when Swarb waltzed in, announcing that Sandy had to go with him to do a vocal.

'How did you know I was here?' said Sandy.

He just raised an eyebrow and shlepped her out of there. They were honestly such memorable days.

Linda Thompson, Sandy & Richard Thompson, c1971

A ONE DAY FESTIVAL OF TRADITIONAL & CONTEMPORARY FOLK MUSIC TUPHOLME MANOR PARK
24 JULY 1971, LINCOLN, UK

GERALD HULL

I saw Fotheringay at the Festival Hall in summer 1970. For me, they never came alive. All Sandy's songs sounded similar, even in the imagery. She did not swing or rock and it was hard to get excited. She did a slow version of 'Silver Threads And Golden Needles' which was wonderful and 'Banks Of The Nile' is still, for me, the best thing she's ever done. But Jerry Donahue was no Thompson, could not push or surprise.

I saw her again at the Queen Elizabeth Hall in 1971 or '72 (John Martyn was on that bill, stoned). She performed some stuff from *The North Star Grassman* which is a favourite LP, essentially

Lincoln Festival poster

Lincoln Festival, with Richard Thompson (Sandy Denny Archive)

for the variety. (She was okay on *The Bunch* LP. 'Hand Jive' was nicely arranged as was 'When Will I Be Loved', but she was no Linda Rondstadt.)

Sandy was better at the Lincoln Folk Festival. Here, with Thompson in his Rupert Bear t-shirt, with Fairport plus Gerry Conway and no Swarb, fully electric, outside on an early evening, the band was relaxed, interesting. 'Blackwaterside' was terrific and unusual.

WYN WRIGHT

I first discovered Sandy's music when attending a party thrown by a school chum when I was just 15 years old. He had recently purchased two albums, *What We Did On Our Holidays* and *Unhalfbricking*. Despite being a big contemporary folk music fan, I had not heard of Fairport. Sitting in his conservatory and listening to the two albums, I was really impressed with 'Meet On The Ledge' and the first intimation of Sandy's singing prowess. But when I heard 'Who Knows Where The Time Goes?', I was utterly blown away by the power and soulful beauty of her rendition (and by the song itself). All thoughts of drinking and chasing girls (my normal MO at such events) were completely forgotten as I replayed this music over and over. Who was this vocal goddess? And where could I see her live?

It wasn't until a couple of years later that I got the chance. Myself and three friends travelled down to Lincoln from Leeds and, after numerous drinks in a local pub, set off (in the dark) to walk the eleven miles or so to Tupholme Manor Park to see the festival beginning the next day.

This was when I finally got to see Sandy Denny live, with Richard Thompson, and I was not disappointed. I have remained a fan for the rest of my life, and her music and her incomparable singing voice, still move me just as much today as they did all those years ago. I am sorry that she did not apparently find fulfilment in her life, and in whatever she was seeking. But I am so grateful to have been alive during the same time period as she.

God bless you Sandy, and thank you so much for sharing your wonderful gift and music. You are loved by many!

CRYSTAL PALACE BOWL GARDEN PARTY
31 JULY 1971, CRYSTAL PALACE, LONDON, UK

JONATHAN JOY

I became aware of Fairport Convention in 1969 when I went to St Martin's School of Art, on Charing Cross Road. I got talking to the handyman-caretaker. I think his name was Ron and his surname was Dyble. He was the father of Judy, Fairport's first singer. I decided to follow them then and there. I loved their music and knew then how folk music would never be the same again!

I saw Sandy live twice, both times with Fairport. The first time was at Crystal Palace Bowl. Elton John was topping the bill. He was so bad that the audience were throwing tins and cans at him. Luckily, he and the band were on an island and not many reached him!

Jonathan Joy first saw Sandy at the Crystal Palace Bowl Garden Party

I love Sandy's voice on 'Who Knows Where The Time Goes?' and on the classic Fairport songs 'Tam Lin', 'Matty Groves', etc. There's too many to choose from.

THE NORTH STAR GRASSMAN AND THE RAVENS
RELEASED SEPTEMBER 1971

NIGEL SCHOFIELD

Sandy must have had high hopes with the launch of her solo career and the release of her debut solo album, the somewhat cumbersomely entitled *The North Star Grassman And The Ravens* in September 1971. Maybe the album looked too dark and folkie… Maybe the title was too obscure… Maybe the timing was wrong… Maybe there was just too much folk rock around to lay claim to your hard-earned cash. Whatever the reason, it was the first instance of success simply eluding Sandy. It still baffled her towards the end of her life, as she told me in my last interview with her:

'I can't explain it, the lack of commercial success. I made it in other ways… fan polls, great reviews from critics, respect from fellow musicians. I had, generally, support from the record company. I even followed, sometimes against my better judgement, the advice of those supposed to know about such things. But I haven't yet achieved that thing that makes all the difference in this business – a hit record.'

Advert in *Sounds* magazine for Sandy's solo debut

CHARLOTTE LE BLOND

I've been a fan of Sandy Denny for decades. She is simply a part of who I am. When I was 20 a friend of mine played *Led Zeppelin IV* and I heard 'The Battle Of Evermore'. I was immediately mesmerised. I wanted to know who she was and everything about her. I listened to the song over and over. Sometime later, I got the money to buy *The Northstar Grassman And The Ravens*. Each song feels like the soundtrack to my heart. I know every word and every sound. The sound of the sea rushing in moves me to yearn for the sea even more. The ship's bell is so atmospheric. I love all the images and references in her work.

When I hear 'Next Time Around' I want to enter the song. It's my mind that I hear in the lyrics. Like all ardent fans, I feel it's written for me.

When Apple Music made all the older songs accessible, I couldn't believe some of them. 'She Moved Through The Fair' is such a wonderful song. I love it. Plus I really love 'Milk And Honey'. Such a raw sound. This song is so important to me that it's taken over me wanting it at my funeral from 'Who Knows Where The Time Goes?'. I love Sandy's voice. It's a voice I wish to have had. She's my spiritual mother, I like to think. (I also suffered from self esteem issues and weight anxiety in life.)

I love to listen to all of her songs on my earphones or loud in my house.

The North Star Grassman And The Ravens, 1971

I know every melody, every lyric of my favourites. My life would be so much less poetic, rich or pagan for having not known her work. Every sound moves me. I've been listening to her music for decades and I never tire of the unique timbre of her voice. It calls me.

I've read books about her but they tell me nothing that helps to truly have known her soul. She was so special and like an angel. I've a few artists, Celtic ones, whom I love but no one comes close to her.

RON LINDEBOOM

I bought every album and box set that Sandy Denny ever made, first as LPs and then the CDs. I love them all but my favourite will always be the truly remarkable 'The Northstar Grassman And The Ravens'. It holds such beauty and emotion, which have never waned over the many decades since its release.

QUEEN ELIZABETH HALL
10 SEPTEMBER 1971, LONDON, UK

DAVE HARRIS

I saw Sandy solo twice, firstly at the Queen Elizabeth Hall in London, which I believe was her first solo gig. I remember getting the train from Southampton to London and reading in the paper about the upcoming gig. I assumed that she would have a band behind her but she didn't. It was completely solo.

There were two support acts, Duncan Browne, a very quiet man, but I remember really enjoying his set. Then we had John Martyn, and Sandy would have done an hour plus. Compared to the previous gigs I had seen this was so different. Voice, with piano or guitar only. So gentle, pastoral, magnificent. I have it in my memory that she was quite nervous. But solo, a big venue and the start of the tour… who wouldn't be?

DINO

Back in 1969, I'd not long left school and like many youngsters of my age I never missed *Top Of The Pops.* It was Fairport's one and only appearance on the show. I first started work in August and, with my first pay packet in my pocket, I went to the local record shop in my lunch break to buy the album that had featured 'Si Tu Dois Partir', by a band I had never heard of, but who had a lead singer who had the voice of an angel. Little did I know what that was the beginning of!

I have seen Fairport live 42 times. The first time was at the Garden Party in Crystal Palace Park in July 1971. By then, Sandy had left the band but I had seen her with Fotheringay in March 1970 at the Royal Festival Hall, and again in May and then October, and then in January the following year and finally in September for a solo gig at the Queen Elizabeth Hall, where I witnessed her a little bit tipsy, but singing like an angel nonetheless. I never saw her live again.

I probably have more albums by Fairport that anyone else, plus every album Sandy has ever been associated with, including *Led Zeppelin IV*, where she is the only female to have ever sung on any of their albums. But you knew that!

Sometime in the future, one of many like me I am sure, 'Who Knows Where the Time Goes' will be played at my funeral, whenever that may be.

I only have to hear her voice and I am transfixed. The day I found out she had died was a very black day.

I've always said that once you hear Sandy sing, you will never forget that voice. I have one of those pictures that David Bailey took, on the wall as I type this, looking down on me. Oh Sandy!

Last year, I don't remember how, but I discovered where she is buried and visited her grave with flowers. Needless to say, I wasn't the only one. I will go again this year and try to make it on the day of the anniversary of her death, which I just missed last year.

Georgia, your mother will always be much loved the world over, because of that voice.

ROBIN DENSELOW, JOURNALIST

'Sandy Denny is the oddest and most important lady in the British music business.' Well, that's what I wrote in *The Guardian* when I interviewed her

Sandy wins *Melody Maker*'s 'Best British Female Singer' award, 1971

for the paper for the first time. It was an intriguing encounter with a singer I liked and admired enormously, but she proved far more complex and defensive than I had expected.

Her importance was already clear for everyone to see, back in 1971. After all, she had launched the British folk rock boom, then in very fine shape, thanks to her extraordinary work with Fairport Convention. She had quit and formed Fotheringay, but had now quit that band too to launch her solo career with *The North Star Grassman And The Ravens* album – and in the process providing another reminder that she was a formidable songwriter. There were female pop stars in Britain, and a few fine female folk and blues singers, but Sandy was unique, both for her range and her songs.

That's what I wanted to talk about, and I thought it would be straight forward. I had first met her two years earlier, when talking to Fairport Convention, and she had seemed jolly and easy-going, happy to have a laugh and chat about absolutely anything. She was, I reported, 'A cheerful girl of 23 who lives with a massive dog, an Australian (Trevor Lucas) and three cats in Fulham and looks as if she would be most at home making cups of tea.'

But once we started the interview, she admitted that she was going to be hard to talk to. She couldn't help it, she said. Things were like that. As soon as her music was mentioned she began to tense up, became defensive and admitted she was playing for time, not wanting to give anything away. She wouldn't discuss why she left Fairport, why she split up Fotheringay, and certainly wouldn't talk about the often bleak and brooding lyrics to her new songs.

'They are biographical,' she said. 'About ten people can understand them. I just take a story and whittle it down to essentials. I wouldn't write songs if they didn't mean something to me, but I'm not prepared to tell everybody about my private life, like Joni Mitchell does. I like to be a bit more elusive than that.' She went on to attack John Lennon for being too explicit. 'He certainly blew his cool when he explained exactly why he wrote 'Lucy In The Sky With Diamonds'.'

On the day the article appeared she was giving her first London solo concert at the Queen Elizabeth Hall, and it seemed she would be without some of the musicians who played on the album (Richard Thompson was touring in the States and Gerry Conway was working with Cat Stevens). Members of the current Fairport line-up would apparently be helping out, but they hadn't had much time to rehearse. Sandy didn't seem too worried. And when asked if she was ambitious, she said, 'No. Yes. Well, I just plod. It just happens.'

Once the interview was over, she was instantly relaxed, as chatty, friendly and funny as ever. Those often dark and mysterious songs she would be singing at the QEH were a reminder that appearances can be deceptive. Sandy was a brilliant, intriguing lady.

BARRIE WENTZELL, MELODY MAKER PHOTOGRAPHER

Sunday afternoons were spent in one of the many folk clubs around London recovering from late night Saturday rock, blues and trad jazz venues and parties. Over an espresso coffee we could hear and see the likes of Wizz Jones, Ralph McTell, The Strawbs, Noel Murphy, John Martin and Sandy Denny. Fairport Convention's first album took acoustic guitars into a more electrified sound and had interesting versions of songs like Joni Mitchell's 'Chelsea Morning'. When Sandy joined, the band moved towards a more rock 'n' roll sound. *Liege & Lief*, with Sandy singing 'Matty Groves' and traditional English folk music played with such power and gusto raised it up a notch or two, with Sandy's voice strong and full of soul and sweetness.

At the *Melody Maker* Readers Poll Awards, Rod Stewart won best male singer and Sandy Denny best female vocalist for 1971. I managed to persuade Rod and Sandy to pose for a 'happy snap' which was used on the cover of the *Melody Maker*.

The photo shoot I did at the Fotheringay flat in Chipstead Street (page 93) was a really casual and relaxed one. The band were just lying around after a late night. I did some group photos and then Sandy alone by the window, looking beautiful. I ran into Sandy and Trevor a week or so later and Sandy told me she loved the photos we did. It was always a pleasure to see her. Her music and art endure and will be ever new. Bless you, Sandy.

SOUTHAMPTON UNIVERSITY
12 OCTOBER 1971, SOUTHAMPTON, UK

JON FOSTER

My interest was sparked by an article by Karl Dallas in *Melody Maker* in the summer of 1971 about the recording sessions of the *North Star Grassman* album, and in particular of 'John The Gun'. I was going to the Lincoln Folk and Blues Festival in July, and looked forward very much to seeing Sandy and her new band there. The only song I specifically remember her singing was 'Down In The Flood'. A much more vivid memory from later on that day is of feeling totally caught up in 'Meet On The Ledge', played over the PA between sets.

North Star Grassman was released in September, and I played it avidly. In early October I started life as a student at Southampton University, and one of the first things I did was to buy a ticket for Sandy's concert there in the first week of term.

My abiding image is of Sandy in a floral dress singing closely into the microphone, with Richard Thompson an ever-watchful, concentrating presence behind her. Sandy played acoustic guitar throughout – I don't recall there being a piano on stage – and she seemed really happy and relaxed.

I assume the set was primarily songs from *North Star* – I'm pretty sure they didn't perform any Fairport songs. I remember an audience member calling out for 'Meet On The Ledge' and Sandy replying with the rather lame pun that, 'Richard doesn't eat meat anymore!'

SWANSEA UNIVERSITY FOLK CLUB
15 OCTOBER 1971, SWANSEA, UK

BOB WOOD

I was lucky enough to see Sandy Denny solo in a small room with around 60 other people. The entrance fee was 50 or 60 pence. Decimalisation had taken place that February and students like myself were outraged that beer had shot up from one shilling and eight pence a pint (eight new pennies) to ten new pence!

Sandy played and sang, just her and her guitar. I had been a fan for quite a while and her voice was stunning. I remember Simon Nicol from Fairport saying how her voice was like a crystal glass in a sink of dirty dishes and that was so true. We sat mesmerised at this voice. When she did 'Who Knows Where The Time Goes?' the reaction was amazing.

ASTON UNIVERSITY
21 OCTOBER 1971, BIRMINGHAM, UK

ALED LEWIS

I only saw Sandy once and that was at Aston University, Birmingham in October 1971 when I was a student at West Midlands College, Walsall. Age plays tricks with the memory but I think she was billed as 'Sandy Denny and Friends'. I cannot remember any of the songs but I can still see the band onstage in my mind's eye. I seem to think Tir Na Nog were also on the same night. A few weeks later I saw Fairport for the first and only time at Birmingham Town Hall, on 19 November 1971. It cost all of 75 pence and they performed *Babbacombe Lee*, which was released that month.

Ticket for Aston University (Rob Whitmarsh)

LED ZEPPELIN IV
RELEASED 8 NOVEMBER 1971

CHRISTOPHER L SMITH

My introduction to Sandy Denny was probably similar to that of a lot of other people, her beautiful voice singing counterpoint to Robert Plant on Led Zeppelin's 'The Battle Of Evermore' from Zeppelin's fourth album. I discovered her in 1982 and, pretty much a rock and metal guy, it was a while before I started to really appreciate a lot of other forms of music. But I had always thought there was something unique about her voice on 'Evermore'. Shortly after that, I was saddened to find out she had passed away back in 1978. Around the early 2000s, I started getting into folk. It opened up a whole new music world, with Nick Drake and Sandy leading the way. I discovered Fairport Convention's *Liege & Lief* and the *Fotheringay* album, as well as Sandy's solo work. 'Who Knows Where The Time Goes?' gains more introspection for me as the years go by. Even though Sandy has been gone for 48 years, her music and spirit will be with us till the end of time. I really love her versions of 'Two Weeks Last Summer' with The Strawbs and Fotheringay.

GERT NISSEN

As a 13-year-old boy, I first heard the Led Zeppelin song 'The Battle Of Evermore' and wondered, 'Which woman is singing in this song?' It wasn't until several years later that I became interested in English folk music, and that's how I discovered Sandy Denny. Her music immediately touched my heart – which made her early death all the more devastating! With the later spread of her music videos, I saw the first film footage of Sandy Denny – this made her songs even more powerful. And a few years ago, I came across the Dutch folk singer Linde Nijland, and I've been able to see her live several times. That's how Sandy Denny came to life for me. Linde and I plan to meet at Sandy's grave in London – it will certainly be an emotional moment.

LES LAB4

I first encountered Sandy's beautiful voice when I bought *Led Zeppelin IV*. I remember the day like it was yesterday. I was 16 at the time and it was the end of school term in December leading up to Christmas. I got home from the record shop, made a coffee, took the brand new vinyl out of its sleeve and put the needle on the disc. The moment 'The Battle Of Evermore' started playing, I realised it was snowing outside. It just seemed to be such a magical moment and Sandy's voice was like an ethereal, otherworldly element that lifted not only that song but gave another dimension to that album entirely.

What an amazing vocal duet. Imagine being sat in on that session at

Headley Grange seeing history being made. I was so fortunate meeting Georgia in Sydney Australia, when she mentioned who she was and her family history I was lost for words, first time ever. I know so many people who have said 'The Battle Of Evermore' is their favourite Led Zeppelin track. What an incredible legacy Sandy left for us.

MARK MOERMAN

I can quite reasonably draw a line from the first time I heard Sandy to the time I met the love of my life, 22 or 23 years later. My family is American, but we lived in England (Derby) for two years in the early seventies. I had never heard of Fairport or Sandy at that time, but I did become very fond of Lindisfarne and The Strawbs, who were at their peaks of popularity and having hit records. This helped instil in me a lifelong love of British folk music.

My favourite Led Zeppelin song has always been 'The Battle Of Evermore' and, in later years, people who knew I was into Fairport and such would sometimes react: 'Oh, you just say that because Sandy Denny is on it.' But it's exactly the other way around!

I first heard *Led Zeppelin IV* sometime around 1973 or '74, after my family was back living in California. I was immediately captivated by the female voice on 'The Battle Of Evermore' and I looked at the LP credits and noted who it was. I don't think I had heard Sandy's name before.

Jump ahead a few years to my first year in college in San Jose, California. One day I was at the main city library downtown near the campus. They had a great record selection and borrowing from the library was how I satisfied my insatiable hunger for music. One day I came across the US two-LP compilation *Fairport Chronicles* on A&M. By this time, I had at least heard of Fairport Convention and was curious enough to pick up the album and peruse it. And what did I see but that name: Sandy Denny!

That record went home with me that day, and in short order I was hooked. Over the next few years, I began to gather as many Fairport and Sandy records as I could. So many wonderful records had gone under the radar, particularly the *Sandy* LP. The niche nature of Fairport's and Sandy's music, particularly in the US and in years subsequent to the release of these albums, was such that one could easily overlook it.

When I began to hear about the annual Fairport festivals some years later, I resolved to go. That took a while, but finally I reached a point where I was successful enough in life to attend the Cropredy Festival in 1990, 1991 and 1992. I also went on Nancy Covey's Festival Tours all three years, which involved two or three weeks of music events with a group of like-minded people.

I was always a bit of a misfit, overweight and rejected by the 'cool kids' in school, and I had great social anxiety. I was a hardcore record collector and sci-fi nerd, and as a young adult my only friends were other hardcore record and sci-fi guys. I was a failure at relationships and could barely even speak to women on more than a superficial level.

Those Fairport tours literally changed my life. Being in close company with those other folks for two or three weeks at a stretch helped (to employ Pink Floyd terminology) to tear down the wall, and I began to have a concept of what it meant to relate to people on an adult level. I made enduring friendships, some of whom were reasonably local and who helped me plug into the northern California scene of small venues where the touring British folk acts performed. Over the next few years, I went to as many shows as I could and met lots of wonderful people and for the first time ever had an actual social life.

Just over four years after the last of my three times on the Fairport tour, I met the love of my life, Barbara, just after Christmas 1996. We moved in together on Valentine's Day 1998, and we have been together ever since.

I can definitively state that I would not have been the person she fell in love with – or been capable of properly returning her love – without the experiences and growth spurred on by my time on the Fairport tours for those three years.

And, of course, all of that dates back to that time when I first heard 'The Battle Of Evermore' and was so captivated by that female voice singing along with Robert Plant.

MARVIN ALLEN

It started with 'The Battle Of Evermore' for me. Because of that song, I was always predisposed to love the sound of Sandy's voice. Several years ago, I began to discover the rest of her amazing work and was just so moved by her beautiful voice and the quality of the writing that I kept following the thread. There is such an incredible wealth of beautiful music in that scene that she came from. Sandy led me to Fairport, Fotheringay, Richard and Linda Thompson, Nick Drake and Pentangle and I have spent hours wondering over the beauty that was her musical gift. I love the way she played the piano and guitar and the way she connected with, and channelled her musical muse. She was a beautiful artist who could resonate in the heart in a way that no one else could.

TRACEY CAMERON

I was a Led Zeppelin fan from my early teens. They were my 'go to' music. On hearing 'The Battle Of Evermore', I made a point of finding out who the 'other voice' belonged to. The only way of finding out anything was through music mags or friends. This led me to Fairport Convention and everything changed! I became a folk-rock fan. Nothing felt quite like listening to Sandy though. Her music just belonged wherever I went.

Tracey & Georgia, 2019

As a Cropredy attendee since the mid-eighties, I would always wonder why Sandy's daughter Georgia was never there. Australia couldn't keep her away, surely? Maybe she just didn't grow up wanting connection? However, every Cropredy Georgia would be in my thoughts. One day whilst scrolling through the Fairporters' site her name cropped up. I just knew I would know her one day.

Within days Georgia sent me a private message and we started chatting about life, music, family, health… and Sandy. We had become good chums. I suggested she come to Cropredy that summer, and in July 2019 Georgia arrived at Liverpool Lime Street station. I felt like I had known her forever.

We spent the next week having a UK holiday together. Georgia sat sketching beautiful portraits of Sandy in my kitchen. I felt so privileged and yet it seemed so familiar. Then Cropredy followed. I was thrilled to see Georgia surrounded by love, hearing stories about her mum and listening to Fairport sing Sandy songs.

I hope I played a small part in encouraging Georgia to come back to Cropredy. Thanks, Sandy, for bringing Georgia to me!

VAN DIKE CLUB
25 NOVEMBER 1971, PLYMOUTH, UK

JULIA GOODE, DENNY FAMILY FRIEND

I grew up on the outskirts of Plymouth, just on the edge of Dartmoor. Sandy's aunt (Dorothy) was married to Sandy's dad's brother, Bill. Bill and Dorothy lived in a place called Newton St Cyres in Devon. They had three boys – David, Robin and Peter – and my mother was friendly with Dorothy. I was in my very early teens, and I spent a lot of time with Bill and Dorothy and the boys. Of course, they were immensely proud of Sandy. When Sandy was on tour she'd visit. I can remember her featuring on Westward TV and she invited us along to be part of the audience.

My mother was involved with a quite well-known Plymouth club called the Van Dike Club. Sometimes the band would walk through the club to get backstage, but super famous acts would leave the dressing room area, go out of the building and around and come in at the backstage door. And even though I shouldn't even have been on those 'licensed' premises, I looked older than I was and I used to have the backstage key, so I'd let them all in.

I can remember at a really young age seeing a bottle of what I thought was Coca-Cola on the side of the stage as Derek and the Dominoes were playing. I took a swig and – oh my God, it must have been practically neat rum with the tiniest splash of Coke in there.

I was backstage the night of the infamous Fairport Convention police raid, and my mother ended up being a witness for Swarb at the ensuing trial. I can't remember if the police were the Flying Squad or the Drug Squad from Scotland Yard but they were such a rum bunch. A lot of things got smoked back in the day, but you have to have 'beyond reasonable doubt'. The magistrates were persuaded that the drugs that Swarb was accused of possessing had been planted on Swarb.

When I was 16, I broke my leg and was in plaster from toe-a-hip. Fairport were playing a gig in Torquay and staying at the Imperial Hotel and Peggy pushed me around in my wheelchair. We went for a pre-gig dinner at the Imperial and they ordered whitebait. To the maître d's alarm Peggy ordered brown sauce with it and the maître d' didn't want to bring it. And I just thought, these boys are paying these charges – and they were earning good money back then – and they can have what the fuck they want!

Sandy was just such a sweet, sweet soul but quite a tortured soul as well, which I think a lot of truly artistic people are. Sandy died, and her brother David died in a road traffic accident in the US a couple of years later, and then Bill got cancer and died. Edna died not long after, probably of a broken heart.

I met Neil, her dad. He used to come down and spend quite a lot of time with his sister-in-law. And as I sit here, I am looking at a beige sofa with two matching chairs that Bill kindly gave us that had been part of the Denny home. I really think one day they ought to be returned to Sandy's daughter.

Was Sandy destined to go early? You sort of get a sense about some people. And the great irony is that *the* song that she wrote is about the passing of the time and, for somebody so talented to go so young, it's just so bittersweet, isn't it?

We saw her at Bristol Colston Hall, which is a fantastic venue, and I can remember the Marquis of Bath coming along. He was that crazy, long-haired, very flamboyant chap with his 'wifelets'. He walked up onto the stage in a long fur coat and just enveloped Sandy. But, by God, the acoustics were fantastic and it was one of those places where her voice would just soar. She was so young when she wrote some of those songs. I'm baffled as to how she found the emotional maturity to write them.

She was hell-bent on self-destruction, and I know people like Linda Thompson tried really hard to help her. And Trevor tried to help her, but he'd reached rock bottom because he could see that she couldn't be helped until somebody is ready to help themselves. It was a real shock when I learned that Trevor had died so young as well.

Sandy was a sweet soul. She needn't have bothered with her aunt and uncle because she was working, but she always took the time out.

I think her parents blamed Trevor for her death. But Neil lived for quite a time and he could have known his granddaughter. But he was very Scottish and being part of that very proud generation, he'd formed an opinion and nothing was going to change it.

FAIRFIELD HALLS
28 NOVEMBER 1971, CROYDON, UK

BOB BATTERSBY

For some reason I was at home in Surrey rather than at my boarding school in Kent. It must have been one of the long weekends we sometimes had mid-term, when we were allowed to see if we still recognised our parents. Like so many people, I had been captivated by *Liege & Lief* and had been more than a little disappointed to learn that Sandy Denny had left the band by the time I 'discovered' Fairport Convention (although *Full House* is probably my second favourite album).

I must have seen the solo tour advertised in the *Melody Maker*, which was essential reading for us high-brow types rather than the trashy *NME*, and saw that Sandy was playing the Fairfield Halls, just up the road from me.

This was the first gig I had ever been to and, both nervous and excited, I took the 405 bus up the A23 to Croydon. Being an impoverished schoolboy, I bought the cheapest ticket, right at the back of the auditorium, and took my place. I have no recollection if there was a support act, and if there was, if I saw them, but the lights came up and Sandy walked on stage, alone.

She opened with 'The Lowlands Of Holland', a cappella and – I think – without a microphone and every hair on the back of my neck stood up! The voice, the phrasing, the sound echoing around the hall – I was mesmerised. I can't recall anything else about the gig – except it was wonderful. Her band that night was Timi Donald on drums, Pat Donaldson on bass and Richard Thompson on guitar. I didn't manage to stay for the encore (or encores) as I had to catch the last bus home.

I went out and bought *The North Star Grassman And The Ravens* the following week – and still have my vinyl copy. I subsequently saw her during the *Rising For The Moon* tour at the Fairfield Halls on 8 December 1974 where she tripped over a mic lead on her way to her piano and measured her length on the stage – only to get up with a laugh and carry on! I finally saw her, with Fairport Convention, at the Portsmouth Guildhall in 1975.

CHIPSTEAD STREET
JANUARY 1972, FULHAM, LONDON, UK

DENYSE ANGER, POET

I worked for Sandy and Trevor, cleaning their flat, from January to June 1972. I was working for London Domestics who sent me to the home of Linda Fitzgerald-Moore, a photographer living on Chipstead Street in west London. She mentioned that her upstairs tenant (and friends) were also looking for 'someone'. 'They're musicians,' she said. I popped upstairs to meet Trevor, who was warm and gracious, and Watson, their sweet and funny Airedale. I felt at home and we made arrangements for me to start weekly house cleaning for them.

On the first day I started cleaning they were sleeping. Their friend and landlady let me in. After clearing a massive pile of dishes, I entered a room insulated with heavy, maroon theatrical curtains, and carefully placed guitars. On the shelf, something caught my eye… *The North Star Grassman And The Ravens* cover photograph, so familiar to me as an admirer and fan of Sandy.

When I realised whose flat I was in, I was a little panicked. While they slept, I familiarised myself with the surroundings… and began to clean. I remember an Alphonse Mucha print and large vintage jacaranda vases in the front room, and a letter with a fan request for 'Banks Of The Nile' to be included in the setlist at an upcoming show.

Sandy and Trevor were wonderful, full of great stories, always making me feel welcome. Prior to my arrival, they'd had a house cleaner who called herself 'The Wednesday Woman'. Sandy described how every Wednesday she would pull spiders off of the hedges and keep them in a glass jar where they would fight to the death. One morning I recall Sandy, accompanying herself on piano in the next room, singing Carole

King's 'You Make Me Feel Like A Natural Woman.'

Months later, at my parents' home in Virginia, I wrote to Sandy and told her the things that I wanted to tell her back in her Chipstead Street flat. Like how I worried that I would hum 'Who Knows Where The Time Goes,' as was customary when I cleaned, while I was literally in the presence of the very singer-songwriter whose creation accompanied me throughout the day. Or how I was dumbstruck in Kensington Market on first hearing *Liege & Lief*.

Sandy was the real thing. Not only did she embody the songs she wrote and sang with the utmost beauty, authenticity, and sometimes startling force, she captured the essence and went beyond it in covers from Bob Dylan to Child ballads. And her bright, open, easy manner and conversation always made me feel at home and in the company of friends.

RECORDING STUDIO
1972, LONDON, UK

JOHN FORD, THE STRAWBS

During the recording of the Strawbs album *Bursting At The Seams* in London around 1972, I was approached by our lead singer Dave Cousins to tell me he had a message from Sandy Denny asking if he knew of a bass player to play on her album. He obviously recommended me because I had previously done a lot of sessions for other artists. How the date was arranged I can't recall, but I trundled off to Island recording studios in awe, because I was a great admirer of Sandy's voice and was excited to meet her.

I was sort of thrown in at the deep end without having any idea what I was to play or rehearse, but it turned out to be 'John The Gun', a composition of Sandy's. I struggled through verses which were odd timings with no charts to read, but eventually nailed it. We all went up to the control room to listen and I was introduced to Sandy. I nervously said something about what a great voice she had and she graciously said something about The Strawbs of which I can't recall. It's ironical that on the Strawbs previous album, her husband Trevor Lucas, sang on the song 'Benedictus'.

THE BITTER END
5 FEBRUARY 1972, NEW YORK, NEW YORK

BRIAN CULLMAN

Sandy played in New York at The Bitter End. Jackson Browne opened for her. Solo. His first album had just come out, and he performed most of the songs from it. He was a warm and generous performer, and he seemed comfortable on stage. He seemed to know his audience and seemed like one of them. Or that was the illusion.

Sandy was stiff and awkward in comparison, and she couldn't make eye contact with the crowd. I can't remember what she played. I remember what she didn't play. She didn't play 'Who Knows Where The Time Goes?' or 'Farewell, Farewell' or 'I'll Keep It With Mine'. She didn't play 'Tam Lin' or 'A Sailor's Life'. She played songs from a new album that was just out in the States. Very few people at The Bitter End were familiar with them. That included Sandy, who was still working her way through the music as if it was a menu in a Hungarian restaurant. Richard Thompson was playing guitar for her. I watched him. He was studiously counting the number of bricks on the wall behind the bar.

EDWARD HABER

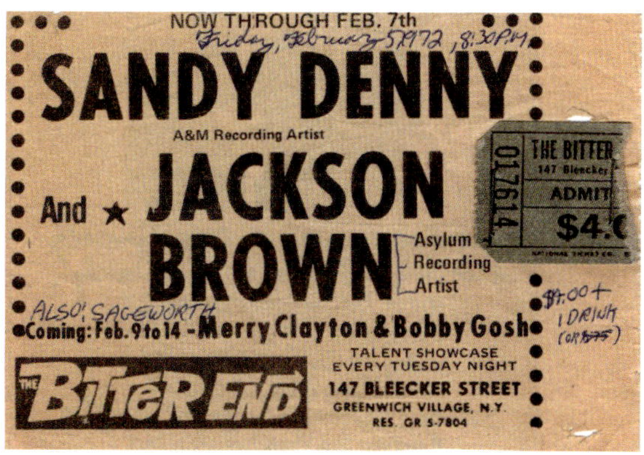

Sandy at The Bitter End, NY (Edward Haber)

I can still picture, as if it were yesterday, Sandy Denny at the piano at The Bitter End in New York, singing 'the methods of madness, the pathos and the sadness' (the song, 'Late November'). It was February 1972 and I was just 16 years old, a senior in high school. I had heard earlier recordings with Fairport – probably from my older brother, but also on the local NY progressive rock station WNEW-FM. But to hear her live in a small club was another thing entirely. The songs and her voice and her on-stage personality made a deep impression on me. And it didn't hurt having Richard Thompson, Pat Donaldson and Timi

Donald as her band! I can also picture her standing stage centre singing an unaccompanied traditional song (though I don't remember which). The one song I knew from her earlier recordings was 'Matty Groves', though without the instrumental playout at the end. An initial band, Sageworth, made no impression on me but the advertised opening act was Jackson Browne, whose first LP was just coming out. He did a lovely set and David Lindley may have sat in on fiddle for a song. But Sandy was the deserved star of the night. (*Village Voice* misspelt Jackson Browne's last name in the ad!)

This was the first of five US tours Sandy did, the last three with Fairport. I had the fortune to see her six times. The second time was solo the following year in Boston at Symphony Hall on a triple bill with Martin Mull and Randy Newman.

LISSA MURPHY

In 1972 I was blessed to meet Sandy Denny and Richard Thompson at The Bitter End in Greenwich Village. After my parents' divorce, Dad would sneak us in and out of bars to hear music and meet his friends (something Mom would have hated if she found out).

Dad is the one who introduced me to the music of Sandy and Fairport Convention after his British girlfriend, Janet, gave him that amazing album *Liege & Lief*! The next time I saw Sandy was in 1973 at the old Hollywood Sportatorium in Florida, opening for Loggins and Messina. The last time I got to see Sandy was in 1974 or 1975, when Fairport Convention were appearing at the Brooklyn Academy of Music with Renaissance. I have tried unsuccessfully to find the fantastic photographs that my dad took that night, but all of my life I have cherished these wonderful memories!

RICHARD

You didn't have to be in Britain to have seen Sandy in person. She made several tours of the US. I first saw her at the Bitter End club in New York's Greenwich Village in early 1972. Richard Thompson was touring with her and Gerry Conway. She sang mostly songs from the *Northstar Grassman* album that had been released in the US a few months before.

I went to the second of two shows at the Bitter End and I remember that Sandy and her entourage walked right by me on their way out the front door for a break after the first show. However, I was too shy to speak to her as she passed by. I really wished that I said something.

I remember that she was doing more than a one-night stand but I don't remember it being for an entire week. I wouldn't think that there would be that much fan interest at that time to support a week's worth of gigs. Before the show began, there was someone fixing up the equipment on stage who I took to be a roadie. It turned out to be Richard Thompson, who I didn't recognise until he came out to play with Sandy.

I also saw her with Fairport at the Academy of Music in New York a couple of years later. Finally, I saw her as the opening act for Genesis at Avery Fisher Hall in New York. She performed unaccompanied and just worked with a piano. It was depressing to see her there because the audience was filled with young boys who had no interest in her and who had come to see Genesis with their amplified sound and laser light show.

TROUBADOUR
16 & 20 FEBRUARY 1972, WEST HOLLYWOOD, CALIFORNIA

JIM BICKHART, A&M RECORDS

Back in 1969, while Fairport Convention were recovering from the tragic motorway accident, Sandy Denny, Richard Thompson and Simon Nicol travelled to the US accompanied by Witchseason Productions' 'minder' Anthea Josephs, for a short, presumably recuperative, non-performing visit. Unfortunately, my college studies prevented me from getting to meet them during their brief time in Los Angeles. But it was the beginning of my journey with all three of them over many ensuing years.

In 1972, Sandy, with Richard Thompson in tow to accompany her on guitar, did a short American tour supporting her *The Northstar Grassman And The Ravens* album. I got to see her perform at The Troubadour opening for then-notable comedian Robert Klein.

My hazy recollection is that Sandy, Island engineer John Wood and perhaps Anthea and Richard were staying at the Tropicana Motor Lodge on Santa Monica Boulevard in West Hollywood, a legendary music stop-off in Southern California. On a sunny Sunday afternoon, they were hanging out by the pool and, somehow, I was invited to join them for a while. It was the first time I got to chat with Sandy and the only time I met the venerable Mr Wood. I wasn't sure why he was part of the entourage and don't remember if I asked him. To the best of my knowledge, no live recordings were being made of Sandy on that tour. Too bad.

(I could be completely off on the timing of the poolside hang-out. If it didn't coincide with Sandy's gig at The Troubadour, I don't remember why the lot of them were in LA and lounging by the pool that weekend!)

I was doing a lot of independent work for A&M Records (both Fairport and Sandy's American label at the time) and had worked with the company's artist-friendly PR/Artist Relations maven, the late, lamented Bob Garcia, on trying to promote Sandy, Fairport, Procol Harum, Free, Gene Clark and the Flying Burrito Brothers, among others. For *Northstar* we homed in on 'Crazy Lady Blues' and pushed A&M to work it as a single. Obviously enough, while it was released, it was not successful.

Sandy next surfaced in '72 with her *Sandy* album and once again visited LA. I don't remember if she performed during that visit, but she held court in a room at the Chateau Marmont to do a series of press interviews to promote the album. Inexplicably, she requested that I be there along with A&M's press rep to chaperone, because I presumably was a comforting presence. The only thing I can think of is that she saw me as being as tall as her husband, Trevor Lucas, and thus a familiar-looking presence, despite my hair not being red. But it was a pleasant afternoon and I was happy to help.

Garcia and I once again championed a Sandy single, this time 'Listen, Listen', which seemed to have chart possibilities until we ran up against the American radio tradition of adding the record of only one female solo performer during any given short period of time. They were choosing Judy Collins' 'Cook With Honey' instead of what may have been Sandy's best shot at widespread airplay, so we struck out again.

ALEXANDRA PALACE
7 MAY 1972, LONDON, UK

MICK MONK

I saw Sandy for a final time, after she had launched her solo career, at the Alexandra Palace with Richard Thompson, Pat Donaldson and drummer and Fairport associate Timi Donald. The Ally Pally was another cavernous structure, built for entertainment and sport. (My dad played darts on television there.) Songs from her debut solo The *North Star Grassman And The Ravens f*eatured as the light filtered through the windows on a sunny afternoon. Sandy was as captivating as ever to this devotee.

CITY HALL
10 MAY 1972, NEWCASTLE-UPON-TYNE, UK

ED WALLAGE

The Doors (post Jim Morrison) were the headline act, with Sandy in support. I wasn't interested in The Doors, but I must have queued for tickets as I was sat in the centre of the front few rows. I had previously seen Sandy with Fotheringay but this was to be the first time in her own right. The evening began… and on came Hawkwind. This shouldn't be happening! Off I went to the box office to demand my money back.

As it happened, Hawkwind were an extra act. (Apparently, they had had some equipment stolen and this was a fundraiser for them.) I was assured that Sandy would still be appearing. She was not alone; the backing musicians were to be Pat Donaldson on bass, Timi Donald drums and Richard Thompson on guitar. Not a bad line-up, especially as they had all featured on her solo recordings. It didn't quite go as planned. Timi Donald had broken his arm, so no drums, and Richard appeared on stage with his Strat but no lead (easily sorted). They had only played a short while when Pat Donldson broke a bass string (I've never seen that happen before or since). All in all, it was a bit chaotic. That said, the music was still great with Sandy playing grand piano and guitar, and it was a bonus not to have drums, as it allowed Richard's guitar to come through clearly. I don't think they played a long set and I blamed Hawkwind for restricting the time they had.

I didn't get to see much of The Doors, partly because I wasn't that bothered, but mainly because I had to leg it back to the station to catch the last train home!

DAVID WRAITH

I remember a couple of solo Sandy concerts when she had obviously over-indulged and was very giggly. However, her voice was like an angel. The one where she supported Hawkwind and a three-piece Doors in 1972 was something else. Stacia danced and then on came Sandy. She did about 40 minutes and then The Doors. For one concert, Sandy had Richard Thompson with her and for the other, she supported John Martyn. I think it was shortly after the release of *Solid Air*.

PETER SMITH

It's not often you attend a gig for one band and come away having witnessed something altogether more lasting. That was the case for me in 1972, when I went along to Newcastle City Hall to see The Doors on their post-Morrison *Other Voices* tour. Supporting them that night was Sandy Denny, a name I already knew from Fairport Convention, but it was the first and only time I saw her perform live. It's a memory I still treasure.

To say it was a diverse bill is an understatement. Hawkwind opened the evening unexpectedly – they weren't even advertised – and put on a full psychedelic assault complete with joss sticks, strobes and Stacia's mesmerising dancing. Then came Sandy, walking out alone and sitting at a grand piano centre stage, the atmosphere shifting entirely. What followed was something far more intimate, and quite beautiful.

I can't recall her full setlist that night, but I believe she was performing songs from her second solo album *Sandy*, released that same year. Tracks like 'It'll Take A Long Time' and 'Listen, Listen' were likely candidates – songs full of poise and emotional depth. I remember being struck by the sheer purity of her voice. In a night otherwise dominated by electric guitars, synthesisers and spectacle, Sandy's performance stood out for its simplicity and sincerity.

There was something incredibly grounding about her presence. She had this calm, steady confidence – no theatrics, just the strength of her songs and that extraordinary voice. Even in a noisy rock crowd, she held our attention.

At the time, I probably didn't fully grasp the significance of what I was witnessing. Sandy Denny was already something of a legend in the folk rock world, having written 'Who Knows Where The Time Goes?' and shared the stage with the likes of Richard Thompson and Led Zeppelin. But in that moment, she felt like a brand new discovery.

It was the only time I saw Sandy live, and I often wish I'd had the chance to see her again. But perhaps that's what makes the memory so special. Among the noise and chaos of the early seventies music scene, she offered something rare: stillness, simplicity, and songs that have lingered in my mind ever since.

CHIPSTEAD STREET
SUMMER 1972, LONDON, UK

DIANA MATHEOU, LES COUSINS

When I became part of running Les Cousins in 1969, Sandy had already moved on. I know she dated Bert Jansch in the early days of the club – he too had moved on. My only meeting with Sandy wasn't easy. It was some years later. Andy and I were together and by then Sandy was with Trevor. They were living in a flat, and Andy and I went to visit one morning time. It was light and warm so it must have been summer. I was wearing a full-sleeved broderie anglaise blouse and a long, flowered skirt which I'd made myself. I was pretty and slim plus writing my own songs and singing on the London circuit. Little did I realise then that these three things about me were like litmus paper for Sandy.

She was boorish and challenging with me. I must have appeared competition, although she was already famous and I was far from being an assertive kinda girl. Trevor was there and friendly, and everyone liked Andy and he probably didn't notice Sandy's manner. I'd already found other women on the circuit being competitive with me, but it just wasn't in my nature.

THE HOWFF
SUMMER 1972, PRIMROSE HILL, LONDON, UK

ANDREW BATT

It was Anthea Joseph of Witchseason who introduced Bambi Ballard to Sandy Denny in the sixties and that friendship became one of the most important of her life. Bambi had a successful career as a costumier, and she designed theatrical costumes before rising to prominence as one of Britain's leading rock designers. After designing stage outfits for Elkie Brooks in her Vinegar Joe days, Bambi went on to create outfits for an illustrious group of stars that included Sammy Davis, The Bay City Rollers, Procol Harum, The Sweet, Alex Harvey, Steeleye Span and of course Sandy Denny. Bambi marvelled at how she could miss someone so much so many years after she died, but Sandy she said, was just one of those people, never to be forgotten. Sadly, Bambi passed away in November 2025, but she had many wonderful stories to tell about Sandy, and I had encouraged her to write some of her recollections down.

BAMBI BALLARD

In 1972 David Bailey photographed her (Sandy) for the cover of the *Sandy* album. The shoot was a hoot – a last-minute dash to Marks & Spencer to get a black top to wear and me lying on the floor behind her with a hairdryer which created this incredible effect you can see in the final photos. I lived two doors away from Bailey, so Sandy came to stay the night after the session. We finished a bottle of Southern Comfort and then, around 11-12 pm, Sandy suddenly said to me: 'Would you like to hear my new album? Is there anywhere we can go that has a piano?'

Well yes! Just round the corner there was The Howff, a folk club run by Roy Guest. We got there just as Roy was leaving; first we persuaded him to sell us a drink, then we persuaded him to let Sandy use the piano. He knew us both, of course, so he decided to leave anyway, saying, 'Just lock the door after you when you go.' He appeared more worried about the piano: 'He thinks I'm going to break it!' Sandy quipped. Then she sat down and played all those wonderful songs to me: 'The Lady', 'It'll Take A Long Time', 'The Music Weaver' – the entire album, privately, at The Howff.

But even with just me for an audience, she was unsure of herself. She kept stopping in the middle of a song and saying, 'Shall I go on? Are you enjoying it?' 'Do you really want to hear any more?' I had to encourage her to carry on and of course it was wonderful, I was in tears. She really needed the praise although she was not just seeking praise. She knew that she was good but she didn't know how good she was, and there's a subtle difference. She needed a lot of reassurance and she had that kind of nervousness and fear that rather than holding her back, could in the right moment bring out creative greatness.

Sandy was someone who was very stimulated by books, by music of course, by poetry, painting, by sculpture. She wasn't at all snobbish in what she liked. For example, I despised Queen but Sandy loved them. 'Queen,' she said, 'you're wrong. This is a fabulous band.' She was someone who had really wide-ranging taste, and although she had a very singular style it did all filter into her work. She was very private about her song-writing. There's a process whereby there's a part of yourself, a pocket of yourself that, however much it's battered by the world, you keep it aside and you know you've got it to draw on, and Sandy had that.

I don't think it was always a comfortable process because it's very easy not to do the hardest thing in the world which is to do something creative. There's nothing harder than that hard climb up to God, as Thomas de Quincy said, but nothing replaces it either and that is something Sandy and I talked about – the hard climb up to God.

In that sense she did need the deadline, but she wasn't writing to order. Writing to a deadline and writing to order are two very different things. She would often say, 'I have to go home now' – this was on a Sunday afternoon after an all-nighter – 'I've got to do some bread-and-butter work because Island are expecting five songs.' She was very conscientious. That's why she had all those notebooks. She would make notes all the time and then find the time later to flick though her notebooks. She copied them out.

Her notebooks could be very scrappy but then she would go through her sketches and poems and songs and think, 'Do I want to keep this? Do I want to keep that?' She would write it out in very beautiful handwriting but, even then, loosely enough so she could change words if she wanted to. Despite fluctuations in confidence, Sandy did have the capacity of knowing that when she finally produced a song it was always good.

I think she took herself for granted as much as we all took her talent for granted. Even though we all thought she was brilliant, none of us really knew how good she was as a singer and songwriter until later. She belonged to that golden period when there was so much going on, and we were all so young. We just assumed that every decade would produce many great artists and it was only after she had gone that we realised she was in fact the best of the best.

CAMBRIDGE UNIVERSITY
10 JUNE 1972, CAMBRIDGE, UK

ROYSTON WOOD

It must have been the summer of 1972. Sandy fell over things. I was in a 'let's-sing-traditional-songs-with-a-rock-and-roll-background' band called the Albion Country Band for a while, and we opened for Sandy one day at Cambridge University. I still have the college rugby shirt I bought in a snooty university outfitters' the afternoon of the gig to wear on stage. We did our opening hour and the stage was then set up for Sandy – the piano here, a guitar there, mic on booms and mic leads and PA cables all over the stage – and she hit or tripped over every one of them. Laugh? I could have died.

WINTER GARDENS
24 JUNE 1972, EASTBOURNE, UK

KEVAN TAPLIN

I booked Sandy for a gig supported by Hookfoot (Caleb Quaye's band). I asked Terry King (Sandy's management) if Sandy was going to be solo or with some sort of band. He didn't get back but Sandy rang me and said not to worry as there would be a backing band. As the gig got closer and I focused on advertising the gig, I again phoned Terry to find out who might be in the backing band and I received a letter back from him saying that in the backing band would be Richard Thompson, and what had been the rhythm section for her band Fotheringay.

He also included some posters which were going to be the original cover for her forthcoming album. I gather Sandy didn't like the cover and so it was later changed.

On the day of the gig, I asked Sandy if she would consider doing 'Let's

Jump The Broomstick', which she'd covered on her first solo album, as an encore. She simply said 'no' (and one didn't argue with Sandy), but 'we have got something planned.' The gig was well attended, and probably full beyond what the fire regulations would allow. When it came to the encore, I watched about 650 people sit on the floor and witness Sandy singing 'Banks Of The Nile'. I think it was the first time she performed it, and with Richard's infills it was stunning.

About eighteen months later, I applied for VSO (Voluntary Service Overseas) and was posted to the Sudan. In those days I had a little Phillips cassette player and one tape contained my favourite tracks, including 'Banks Of The Nile'. When I went through a bad patch (such as when I caught malaria) or when I actually sat on the banks of the Nile, I played it to lift my spirits.

Kevan Taplin booked 'Sandy Denny & Friends'

SANDY
RELEASED SEPTEMBER 1972

DAVID JACKS

Gary, my best friend back in 1972, had invited me over to his house one Saturday afternoon. It was fall – my favourite season; the air had cooled and the leaves were already turning in combinations of reds and golds. He knew what a music fanatic I was and as we sprawled in his bedroom, he reached into his cedar chest where he kept his albums. 'I ordered this album by mistake,' he said, pulling a disc out of its cover and placing it on his turntable; I believe he was a member of a record club of some sort. 'I thought you'd like it,' he continued as he handed me the cover.

Its photo was striking. *Sandy*, it said at the top. Living in the United

States, I was unfamiliar with her name and reputation in UK music circles. My sister owned Judy Collins' *Who Knows Where The Time Goes* album and I had heard its lovely title track, but I had no idea who'd written it. And Fairport Convention had made nary a ripple in the States, so I truly had no expectations.

David Jacks recalls the first time he heard the album *Sandy*

It began with a gentle acoustic rhythm, and after 30 seconds came the voice: 'Oh, it's like a storm at sea / And everything is lost...' I was immediately transfixed. And as she continued there was such lovely precision in her notes as she weaved this yearning tale – simply gorgeous singing; emotional honey being poured into my ears. 'Who IS this?' Even the photo of her (and it was hard not to stare at it) fit the colours of the season perfectly: creamy reds and golds...

With 'Listen, Listen', side two's opener, I thought, 'Damn, this should be a hit!' Then came the unusual chord changes and lush arrangement of 'The Lady' – what a magical composition. Gary and I were both quite taken with the lyrics of 'It Suits Me Well'; 'And they ain't no lies' became a catch phrase between us. And all along was this magnificent voice.

'Listen, Listen' was released as a single

This was long before you could search the internet for info, so it took me a while to find more information on Miss Denny and her history. But this first introduction to British folk-rock led me up a 'Primrose Hill' toward discovering so many other great artists – Richard and Linda Thompson, Steeleye Span, Nick Drake, John and Beverly Martyn, Shirley Collins, along with Sandy's earlier bands

Fairport and Fotheringay – and all of these artists' albums I bought in the next few years as I moved away to college and record stores with more eclectic inventories became available to me.

Sandy was such an 'ear-opener' for me – introducing both a world of music I was missing and an artist of such incredible talent. And I never did find out what album my friend Gary was originally going for – something by Sandy Posey, perhaps? Sandy Bull? Sandy Nelson?... Hmmm…

SIMON EVANS

When I was a kid, about 12 years old, I used to stay with my cousin Barbara in the valleys in Yorkshire, England. On weekends, she would invite her friends over and listen to music, and that's where I discovered the voice of an angel… The album *Sandy* became an album I just about wore out, and its cover became etched in my memory.

Years later, I was looking through some folk CDs in a music store in Chatsworth, California and I found her again, on CD. I bought it and listened to it over and over and it took me back to those days, years ago and thousands of miles away in Yorkshire, and good times.

When I returned to the UK 15 years ago, I was in London visiting my cousin Barbara and we talked about the old days, the seventies, and that vinyl album came up. I remembered all the joy that album bought to me. It inspired me to go to Sandy's resting place in Putney and I left roses and thanked her for the memories.

Sandy is listened to often, and she is loved.

JOHN CLARE

I was heartbroken when Sandy quit Fairport Convention. What I hadn't figured on was that we were now bound to get more Sandy vocal. The *Fotheringay* album was okay and sold well at my shop, Henry's Records, but it was not a patch on what Sandy had done with Fairport.

Enter the magnificent *The North Star Grassman And The Ravens*. Sadly, this album didn't really sell a huge amount (at Henry's Records anyway) despite my recommending it to every one of my regular customers who I considered to have an impeccable taste in music and despite Karl Dallas in *Melody Maker* saying, 'We always knew that Sandy had the capacity to make a brilliant record and we were right.'

If I was peeved at the lack of sales of *Ravens* at Henry's, the lack of sales of the follow up, *Sandy*, in 1972 upset me even more. The definitive Sandy album, it failed to take her to the heights of contemporaries Joni Mitchell, Carole King or even Joan Armatrading despite containing four of the greatest songs she ever wrote in 'Listen, Listen', 'It Suits Me Well', 'It'll Take A Long Time' and 'The Lady'. It was all downhill from there.

The end of Mick Houghton's book, *I've Always Kept A Unicorn*, is one of the saddest things I've ever read. The disappointment of her solo career, Joe Boyd leaving, her record label Island Records having no idea how to market her, her womanising husband, the drugs and the booze… absolutely heartbreaking.

To me, she'll always be the most magnificent female voice in popular music of all time.

NEIL ATHERTON

Sandy Denny's solo albums can frustrate to a degree, as does her work with Fotheringay. There is this sense that others are adding too much of their ideas to a project rather than Sandy being allowed to own the work. Maybe that's why I love her gorgeous demos so much. Sometimes it is the song choice being patchy, or it can be over-blown arrangements or just too many musical influences on one album. With Fotheringay the musicians are so good, so used to the rhythm of a 'Fairport'-type session, they sometimes give the feeling that it is just an easy session in the studio, a day at the office for them. But in all of Sandy's albums, solo or with Fairport, there are absolute world class gems. She is *the* English female vocalist of the twentieth century – I do not engage in arguments over that one.

Sandy is her most fully realised album. On this album it comes together, with fine songs and cover versions that complement her own writing, and fabulous musicians that do not overpower her glorious vocals. This is highlighted by some gorgeous contributions from Richard Thompson on guitar and mandolin, so sympathetic to Sandy's writing and vocals. Her voice is at the peak of its powers – tender with also perfectly directed power, and Trevor Lucas applies just the right amount of direction as producer. Despite their often-tumultuous relationship, at this point they are working in complete unison.

This album should have been the one that took her through the critical acclaim barrier and into superstardom. It had to be, as although she had been producing fine songs and performances, she was just treading water as regards popular acclaim. She was the darling of the critics but that does not pay the wages. She was certainly, in her own mind, running out of time. While not quite a case of drinking in the last chance saloon, this album had high expectations surrounding it.

The intent of the album is there from the cover alone. A photo by David Bailey of the beautiful Sandy. By all accounts, the session with him was tortuous and there seems to be a hint of a look that says 'just take the picture and be done with it' about the cover shot. It is still a gorgeous photo. Sandy writes down all the lyrics herself in the centre fold. It is a professional package and designed to impress – it says she has arrived in the mainstream. But had she?

If she had not, then this was certainly a fine attempt at 'making it'. If you need any proof of her status as a great vocalist, then the stunning a cappella 'Quiet Joys Of Brotherhood' showcases her talent, with Dave Swarbrick coming in at the end with his haunting violin solo the icing on the cake. On 'Listen, Listen' she effortlessly soars and swoops around the complex melody. Mention 'The Lady' to anyone of a certain age who loves this era and music and it will be translated into 'Sandy Denny'. On the track itself, she is tender and sings a delightful knowing vocal around some simple but atmospheric piano work and sympathetic arrangement. It sounds autobiographical now from this distance – and sad.

On 'It Suits Me Well' she goes into a young lady and poor wayfaring traveller mode, her voice going into character. It is a remarkable piece of contemporary 'traditional' folk song writing and the vocal is another example of her diverse vocal range.

The cover of Dylan's 'Tomorrow Is A Long Time' sits perfectly on the album and, dare I say it, is better than the original.

'Bushes And Briars' conjures up an Englishness that she returns to again and again in her writing. She seems on this, and on the whole album, to be completely at ease with her talent. She sounds confident and that must be down to a large degree to Lucas's sympathetic production. She does not always exude this confidence in her recordings and arguably she never really would again.

It is a wonderful album. It should have been the one that made her a national treasure. Sadly, it did not even chart despite some generous radio play support. It is one of life's great conundrums; why is Sandy Denny so revered today over forty years after her death but still so little known in most circles?

A lot of this is down to her not keeping to a fixed path long enough for people to discover what she was all about. The variety of styles and song choices was often just too much for a single album. She lacked full confidence in her talents and was consistently unsettled in her personal life.

The album was not a success. Her follow up which was not long in coming was not as good. It was not without merit, but it never stood a chance. Her solo work became too over blown in production and her song choice was not as good as on *Sandy*, despite some lasting and much-loved gems of her own songwriting.

She rejoined Fairport Convention for *their* 'last chance saloon' album. It should have been a triumph but again the songwriting was not as strong as it needed to be, the dynamics of the previous band having been lost. The reunion was short lived.

Only one more album came before her tragic death in 1978. Lucas produced her final album, *Rendezvous*, but their relationship had deteriorated dreadfully and the almost pop production on this album did the songs no favours. Looking back now some of her songs on *Rendezvous* are amongst her finest works and much loved. There were also some inexplicable song choices on the album.

Sandy died a few months later. I still vividly recall popping out from work to collect my *Melody Maker* at the newsagents only to see the headline, 'Sandy Denny Dead.' Work or conversation were hard to accomplish for the rest of that day, my thoughts being elsewhere, of loss and of what should have been.

I never saw her live in concert, something I truly regret. Her legacy is a relatively small body of work compared to most artists. But it does show that she was indeed 'The Lady' – the finest female talent England produced.

TED IAROCCI

I am a 72-year-old male who has lived in the NYC Metro area my whole life. In 2010 I had heard Sandy's name but was totally unfamiliar with her work and Fairport's, but I started to get into British folk rock, primarily via Richard Thompson. I loved what I heard. I was in a local record store and looking for artists I might like that I missed first time around when I came across the *Sandy* album. Somehow, I had a great feeling about it although I had never heard it. On first listen, I was instantly enchanted and in love with it. Rarely have I been so enamoured with a record. Sandy's music takes you to another world with its lyrical imagery, gorgeous melodies and the voice of an angel. I soon considered her the greatest female singer-songwriter ever.

I was soon collecting her complete discography, mostly on vinyl. I was late knowing about the big 19 CD box set. It would have been an instant buy. However, I obtained an unofficial FLAC download of it, including all the books and artwork (PDF). I would happily purchase a reissue if it ever comes to be.

I consider myself an audiophile. My system is great but relatively modest. I love all Sandy's recordings but still the *Sandy* album is my favourite and it would be in my top ten Desert Island Discs along with my favourite Beatles, Dylan and Stones records. For that reason, I've been determined to find the finest-sounding vinyl copy. I obtained several copies of near mint original first press US pressings as well as a recent repress/remaster. They sounded great, but I believed that a UK original would surpass them and so the search continued. Finally, I found a reputable UK Discogs seller who listed a first press UK copy in near mint condition for $100.

On first listen, it was immediately apparent that my search was over. The record had minimal background noise. The sonics soared above the US copies. I was in heaven. I play it often. All the songs are fabulous. My favorites are 'Bushes And Briars' (one of the most beautiful songs ever recorded!) and 'It Suits Me Well'.

One of my great regrets in life is not knowing of Sandy during her lifetime. I would have bought all the records and attended as many of her live shows as I could.

'IT SUITS ME WELL'

JONNY WAH WAH

Punk rock propelled me from a lost, directionless adolescent to a person with meaning, a belonging to a family that I didn't really need to know, along with a strange understanding that there are magical things in this world waiting to be uncovered. I had the Sex Pistols, the Damned, The Clash… People telling stories of everyday life, normal, real people, real folk, stories of folk...

Folk and punk are very similar. Punk gives a tip to the past, it's rock 'n' roll. It's anti-establishment but it's traditional rebellion, in a room, a story, a feeling, many feelings....

Fairport Convention came into my life after things started to cross over; the Pogues, who were Irish trad with a hint of punk, and bands like Flogging Molly from the USA, who I supported on tour, and The Levellers with their drunken raucous English peasants revolting. All beautiful songs... Folk-punk was a thing, and I delved into the British sixties and seventies folk scene and came almost immediately to Fairport.

And there it was... that voice, that sound, the sound, the voice.... It encompassed so many emotions; it was effortless yet had precision and a perfection that straight away I had to get to know the person behind it.

So my love affair with Sandy Denny began. My first viewing of her on film, on TV, was exciting: the BBC sessions of 'Late November' and 'The North Star Grassman And The Ravens'. There were the Fairport albums, Fotheringay, the solo albums, and then *Gold Dust* (a live album with some talking in between songs), box sets, books, rare interviews, etc.

It wasn't an obsession. It was a connection, many connections. The personality traits were uncanny: Wimbledon (my spiritual home); the battles with addiction; untreated trauma. But I don't want to get dark because it never does. Sandy and her music lifted – and continues to lift – me out and away from such binds…

The love story with Trevor, her amazing daughter Georgia (who I have met and bought artwork of Sandy from, and by whose Cropredy exhibition I was blown away), and Sandyfest, where you hear first-hand accounts of Sandy and think... I wish I'd known her, been her friend, her lover, written songs with her… And I wish I'd seen her perform in real life.

Sandy is omnipresent in the book I just wrote. I've toured the various places she lived and performed, and I've visited her resting place at Putney Vale. I sang a Sandy song live just recently – 'It Suits Me Well' – at a pagan convention where I explained how I feel spirits can be with you at times of need.

Sandy is up there for me... The music, the songs, the life. The spirit will be with me forever and it only brings eternal joy.

ROYSTON WOOD

This is one of Sandy's songs which I sang a long time ago because I really liked it in the way it expressed what I think Sandy was. I think this is what Sandy was up to. And in a way what she was trying to say was: 'We (musicians and artists) are all gypsies of one sort or another, and we are really looking out for ourselves, and journey along a kind of odyssey and there is no guarantee that we're gonna come out particularly right.' But I think the philosophy of the song was, 'Whatever we're doing, then we gotta be into it and we gotta get something out of it.' The song is called 'My Own Man' or 'It Suits Me Well'. I don't know what she called it, actually. Now, three characters appear in the song, and there are three absolutely separate verses. And it's almost as if there was one character stepped up to the front, it's a bit like a sort of mystery play thing: one character comes forward and sings a little explanatory verse about who they are and what they do, and then steps back and another character comes forward and sings the same thing. And there are three characters. The song has no story, no sort of plot, just these three little characters, each one of which gives you a verse about what they are and what they do. A fellow called John the Gypsy is one of 'em.

WELL HALL OPEN THEATRE
5 AUGUST 1972, ELTHAM, LONDON, UK

ANONYMOUS

This was a spur of the moment recording. I was on vacation in Manchester, visiting relatives who I had not seen since we emigrated to the USA in 1960. I saw an advertisement for a series of folk-orientated concerts taking place throughout the summer at the Well Hall Open Theatre. Fortunately, I was going to be in England for the one in the series that I most wanted to see –

the Sandy Denny concert. Even better, Richard Thompson was in the band. Well Hall Open Theatre was an open-air bandshell kind of a set up with a small stage with fold up chairs for the audience. The opening act, Cobb, never showed up for some reason so Sandy played early, which was fortunate because it started raining just after she had finished.

I had decided to record the concert on the only recorder I had available, a Radio Shack $20 mono cassette recorder with a built-in condenser mic that we had brought from the USA as a birthday present for my cousin. The PA was a typical seventies set up, not too clear with a bad resonance around 120Hz or so. This caused the vocal and piano in particular to be very muddy. Anyway, Sandy did a great set and Linda Peters joined in on one tune and it was a great evening.

I remember taking some pictures with a Kodak Instamatic. I have looked for them many times without success. Around 1975, I transferred the recording from a Boots the Chemist cheapo cassette to a reel-to-reel tape and, later, to DAT. Then, when CDRs came along, I transferred it to CDR. Whilst not up to today's audio standards I find it very listenable, and it is a great part of Sandy history. I believe this is the only recording to turn up with 'Rigs Of Time'.

STEINWAY & SONS
SEPTEMBER 1972, LONDON, UK

MIRANDA WARD

When Sandy went to choose a piano, the gentleman serving her was pretty disdainful at first. Young sort of hippy chicks were not known for buying grand pianos, especially expensive ones. He showed her a couple of cheaper ones, but I think she only played a couple of bars. He then took her through to the large area where the top grand pianos were. Another customer was there trying a piano, and Sandy went still and listened intently. When the pianist finished, the man indicated she should go in. She declined –

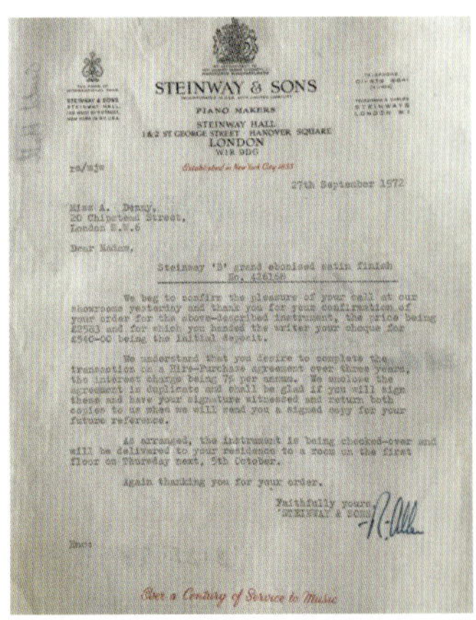
STEINWAY & SONS
PIANO MAKERS
STEINWAY HALL
1&2 ST GEORGE STREET HANOVER SQUARE
LONDON
W1R 9DG
Established in New York City 1853

27th September 1972

Miss A. Denny,
20 Chipstead Street,
London S.W.6

Dear Madam,

Steinway 'B' grand ebonised satin finish
No. 426158

We beg to confirm the pleasure of your call at our showrooms yesterday and thank you for your confirmation of your order for the above-described instrument, the price being £2583 and for which you handed the writer your cheque for £540-00 being the initial deposit.

We understand that you desire to complete the transaction on a Hire-Purchase agreement over three years, the interest charge being 7% per annum. We enclose the agreement in duplicate and shall be glad if you will sign these and have your signature witnessed and return both copies to us when we will send you a signed copy for your future reference.

As arranged, the instrument is being checked-over and will be delivered to your residence to a room on the first floor on Thursday next, 5th October.

Again thanking you for your order.

Faithfully yours,
STEINWAY & SONS

Encs

Over a Century of Service to Music

Sandy's receipt from Steinway & Sons for her piano

she was not going to even try to follow the previous playing, saying, 'It was Moura Lympany, wasn't it?' The guy was taken aback. He had not expected Sandy to recognise the person from the playing. Sandy said she would return the next day. She did, and the guy was really helpful, having realised she was serious about wanting a grand.

CONNECTICUT RIVER VALLEY
FALL 1972, CONNECTICUT, USA

JIM COHN

The first time I did mescaline was with friends at Hampshire College in Amherst, Massachusetts. I didn't have a car and was hitchhiking back to my apartment in Northampton. The sun was going down on a beautiful day as a VW bug pulled over to give me a ride. As I walked over to the car, I could hear a woman singing and immediately I was engaged in the quality of her voice, how it seemed from another time, another world. They were playing Fairport Convention's cover of 'Percy's Song', a ballad by Bob Dylan performed at Carnegie Hall on 26 October 1963, but not released by Columbia Records until 2013. The song, about a car crash in which four people were killed, and which has the hauntingly recognisable chorus refrain, 'Turn, turn to the rain and the wind,' was the first track recorded by Fairport for their *Unhalfbricking* album.

As my fellow travellers and I crossed the wide tobacco fields that grew in the Connecticut River Valley between towns, and as night was falling, I was stunned by the emotional intimacy of the song, performed in the then still new folk rock genre, and which I was hearing in a very heightened state of mind.

What was most stunning of all was the empathic and otherworldly power of Sandy Denny's voice, her emotionally intimate treatment of the lyrics, in the song's telling. From that moment to this, Sandy Denny has held a special and immoveable place in my spirit's life, and perhaps lies at its core.

No less overpowering on my ride from Amherst to Northampton that evening was the last song I heard from *Unhalfbricking*, one I'd already heard and learned, 'Who Knows Where the Time Goes?'. The song, much like Dylan's work of his youth, conveys a paradoxical and timeless sense of mystery that should only come with experiencing age, and feels similar to Dylan's own 'My Back Pages', where he juxtaposes youth with age in the refrain: 'I was so much older then, I'm younger than that now.'

The kind people in the VW dropped me off on Route 9 next to a Northampton graveyard lit up by the moon. I was 19, renting a room for $75 a month on Graves Avenue. In that room was a mattress, a box of records and a record player. I remember getting out of the car and wandering among the tombstones, enraptured by the music I'd just heard, and the singer I heard that evening to whom I have felt bonded ever since. Throughout my next decade, I collected Sandy Denny records, wherever I could find them, especially the solo recordings.

In 1980, I was a student at the Naropa Institute's Jack Kerouac School of Disembodied Poetics, in Boulder, Colorado, where I became a teaching assistant to poet Allen Ginsberg and a mentee of Anne Waldman, the school's poet-founders. Among my cohort of students at the Kerouac School, I met the American poet Denyse Anger (née King, aka du Roi), whose work I admired most among my peers. We were at an after-reading party one night in Boulder when we got to talking, really for the first time, and learned that we both had our own love affairs with the music of Sandy Denny. I learned that Denyse had *worked* for Sandy and Trevor Lucas, with whom Denny was married, and with whom she collaborated in forming Fotheringay and in producing her solo recordings, in England, on assignment from a cleaning service.

It was later that year that Denyse suggested the idea of writing a masque, a short allegorical dramatic entertainment originating in the 16th and 17th centuries and performed by masked actors. This led to Denyse writing *The Masque of Sandy Denny*, an unpublished piece to this day that we wanted to collaborate on, but that I failed to find the right language to do so. What that experience working on *The Masque of Sandy Denny* showed me was that my own passion for Sandy Denny's music was more inexpressible than otherwise.

At 50, in 2003, I became the father of a fourth generation Aries girl. I made it a point to share Sandy Denny's music with my daughter, Isabella Grace Cohn, and gifted her the solo recording albums. One day, she will receive the 2010 *Sandy Denny* box set which comprises on 19 discs all the studio material and recordings made during Sandy Denny's time both as a solo artist and as a member of Fortheringay, Fairport Convention and the other groups she was a part of, together with home demos and live recordings.

BIRMINGHAM UNIVERSITY
1972/'73, BIRMINGHAM, UK

PETER HOCKENHULL

I've been a fan since seeing Sandy perform a solo gig at Mason Hall, my hall of residence at Birmingham University, in late '72 or early '73. She was flu ridden but croaked her way through the whole gig. What a trouper. I watched standing on a partition between dining hall and kitchen

She also did a gig with her band in the students' union of the uni in maybe late '73. I was floor manager for the Ents Committee and smitten. My role was to 'satisfy' the rider, which meant I responded to her personal request for a bottle of white wine. I requested 'Matty Groves' which she did with a personal shout out. I was trebly smitten.

I was away working in Glasgow when I spotted a *Melody Maker* on a rainy street with the front page of 'Sandy Denny dies' or similar. I was shocked.

GUILDHALL
12 OCTOBER 1972, NEWCASTLE-UPON-TYNE, UK

NICK PILLEY

It's October 1972 and I'm a 19-year-old first year student at a college in Durham. Somehow, I find out that Sandy is playing in Newcastle on the 12th. Hmmm, that's a must if I can manage it. After all, I've been to Newcastle shopping on the train before and the venue isn't far from the station. There's a snag though – the last train back is likely to be before the end of the concert and my onl y transport is a very elderly three-speed bicycle. Still, I can take the bike up on the train and cycle back. It's only just under 20 miles...

So that's what I do. The concert is at the Guildhall on the quayside and both Sandy and Martin Carthy are on the bill. Two musical heroes in one concert!

Unfortunately, Martin has a bad throat and, although he's there, he's not able to perform. Never mind, I know I'll see him (with Richard and Linda) in a few weeks and it's Sandy that I'm really there to see. One of my earliest purchases with my student grant has been a secondhand battery cassette recorder. It's a basic Phillips mono model with a cheap microphone but it works. I'm sat on the floor at the front of a rather noisy audience – the bar at the back is open all night – and there's no-one between me and Sandy, about 20 feet away.

Nick Pilley got Sandy's autograph on his freshly-made bootleg of the Guildhall show

The concert is wonderful and afterwards she goes off into an adjacent room which is being used for the artists. There are windows from waist high and I can see her there with Trevor. He goes off to get her a drink and, on his return, I have the cheek to ask him to get the cassette autographed by Sandy, which she does.

And so it's time to go home and there's a snag. Although I've cycled that distance a few times before, the weather has changed and the temperature has dropped noticeably. I'm certainly not dressed for it and with about three miles to go I can barely ride the bike. Fortunately, at that point the road starts to go down and I'm back in the dorm by 3.30am. A memorable night in many ways.

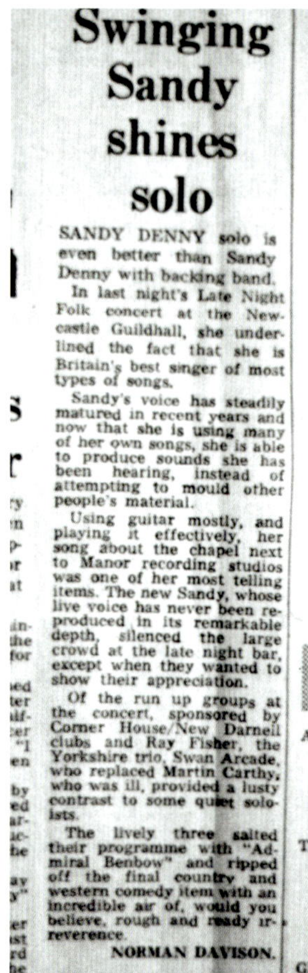

Swinging Sandy shines solo

SANDY DENNY solo is even better than Sandy Denny with backing band.

In last night's Late Night Folk concert at the Newcastle Guildhall, she underlined the fact that she is Britain's best singer of most types of songs.

Sandy's voice has steadily matured in recent years and now that she is using many of her own songs, she is able to produce sounds she has been hearing, instead of attempting to mould other people's material.

Using guitar mostly, and playing it effectively, her song about the chapel next to Manor recording studios was one of her most telling items. The new Sandy, whose live voice has never been reproduced in its remarkable depth, silenced the large crowd at the late night bar, except when they wanted to show their appreciation.

Of the run up groups at the concert, sponsored by Corner House/New Darnell clubs and Ray Fisher, the Yorkshire trio, Swan Arcade, who replaced Martin Carthy, who was ill, provided a lusty contrast to some quiet soloists.

The lively three salted their programme with "Admiral Benbow" and ripped off the final country and western comedy item with an incredible air of, would you believe, rough and ready irreverence.

NORMAN DAVISON.

Newcastle Journal review of the Guildhall show

YORK UNIVERSITY
14 OCTOBER 1972, YORK, UK

DOOMANDGLOOMFROMTHETOMB

The audience tape from this night captures her touring in support of her first two LPs, *The Northstar Grassman And The Ravens* and *Sandy*. Alone onstage, the performance is charming and intimate, as she offers stripped-down selections from both albums.

UNIVERSITY OF MANCHESTER
17 OCTOBER 1972, MANCHESTER, UK

ALIX DEARING

Mine and John's first date was as new students at Sandy's solo concert at Manchester University students' union. We were both big fans of Fairport already. We were impressed with her cool composure and relaxed style even though she wasn't playing Fairport favourites. She was beautiful, and her singing was mesmerising. We go to Cropredy every other year when we're not in France and always love it when Sandy songs are sung by a woman singer. John and I married in 1977 and Sandy is a big presence in our lives. I can't believe she didn't have any particular training. It just shows you that talent will out.

TOWN HALL
23 OCTOBER 1972, OXFORD, UK

NIGEL BANKS

I first saw Fairport Convention play live in November 1970. Sandy had already left the band so my familiarisation with her vocal and songwriting talents came from listening to Fairport's earlier albums. Her versions of traditional ballads such as 'A Sailor's Life', 'Matty Groves' and 'Tam Lin' became staples of my listening as a student, along with her own original compositions and covers of Dylan songs.

I first saw her in the flesh as a guest audience member at a charity gig at Cecil Sharp House in December 1971. She was there along with Trevor Lucas to support Fairport, who were headlining the concert. Trevor was invited onstage at one point by Dave Swarbrick to sing a couple of Aussie folk songs, plus some rock 'n' roll standards. Sandy did not sing that day, but I did hear her voice later, when I happened to pass by the makeshift artists' dressing room. She was clearly not at all happy about something or someone, and was clearly not someone to get on the wrong side of. Richard Thompson's description of her being occasionally 'grumpy' was clearly the case here!

I eventually got to see her perform live in October 1972 at Oxford Town Hall when she was appearing with John Martyn. He was supposed to play first, but had been delayed for some reason, and so Sandy came on early. Her second solo album, *Sandy*, been released earlier in the year, so she showcased several songs from it, as well as previous favourites. Her voice was as pure and soaring as it sounded on records. Unfortunately, because the concert had started late, I had to leave before the end to catch the last bus back to my student digs, and so missed Sandy and John Martyn doing a duet as part of the encore.

NIGEL SCHOFIELD

The concert was arranged by The Guitar Society of the University, who also booked John Martyn as support. Use of the Town Hall permitted Sandy on stage access to a piano (about which some in the Society complained). The album *Sandy* had just been released and her set featured songs from that, as well as some classic material. 'Bushes And Briars' had a memorable intro when Sandy explained its inspiration in a traditional song collected by Vaughan Williams and then talked about the church nearby which, as she said, 'was only attended on high days and holidays' – nonetheless the vicar held service on schedule each week. Sandy talked at some length about the songs, and with good reason. John Martyn has missed his Oxford train and had not yet arrived by the time the concert was due to start (which was later than normal at 8.00pm).

After a while the audience was growing restive and Sandy volunteered to go on and fill in until John arrived. She started with a couple of things she hadn't planned on playing, before (with a nod to the time and John's non-arrival) moving on to her setlist. Eventually he turned up. Sandy finished her current song and there was an unscheduled interval while John set up his various pedals and gadgets – most of the audience stayed to watch. He played his set, which seemed a little long for a support act!

Then Sandy returned. She had barely got into her set when the management came on to announce we had passed the time booked for the event; they would consequently be shutting off power to the stage after the next song. This they did, obviously and abruptly. John came back on, signifying half apology, half support for a clearly confused Sandy. He grabbed his guitar, whispered to Sandy, and the two sat on the edge of the stage to play an acoustic set, until 'total lights out' was threatened. I didn't note down the whole set, but I recall they started with 'May You Never', which John had not found time to play, 'Learning The Game' and Free's 'A Little Bit Of Love'.

I also saw her play at Oxford Polytechnic. After Virgin's recording complex, The Manor, opened in Shipton-on-Cherwell (ten miles north of Oxford – if you're following the canal out of Oxford, you're a quarter of the way to Cropredy!), it was not unusual for artists who were residing there to turn up unannounced and play at the Poly. On one such occasion, Sandy played an informal solo set for the slowly gathering audience (word had got round). At one stage, she announced a song from a poem by Richard Farina, 'Quiet Joys Of Brotherhood'. Eyes closed, she sang a cappella and, as the song ended, we heard the drone of a fiddle, stage right… Dave Swarbrick, playing unplugged, emerged and walked across the back of the stage, not acknowledging Sandy or the audience, but exiting stage left with perfect timing. The audience erupted, Sandy murmured, 'Thanks, Swarb,' picked up her guitar and began the next song.

LANCASTER UNIVERSITY
21 NOVEMBER 1972, LANCASTER, UK

BARRIE FROST

In 1971/72 I ran the Folk and Blues Club at Lancaster University and welcomed Richard and Linda Thompson on one memorable night and Sandy Denny on another. Richard and Linda turned up in a big old Mercedes and Richard used foot pedals to provide bass, which added to his excellent guitar playing. At the end of the gig, they came up to the small kitchen in Lonsdale College residential block for coffee before setting off, much to the surprise of other students. They were lovely people.

Sandy was also great and performed a sell-out show in the theatre. I had to buy in a grand piano for her which reduced the profit on the gig but was money well spent. I still have the Sandy Denny contract for that night signed by Trevor Lucas.

TRENT POLYTECHNIC
25 NOVEMBER 1972, NOTTINGHAM, UK

STEVE SHELDON

I was late to the party as far as live Fairport shows were concerned, so I missed the Sandy years and her subsequent time in Fotheringay. Nevertheless, her music had been the soundtrack to my late teens, and by late November 1972 I was the Social Secretary at Trent Polytechnic Students' Union in Nottingham, where we'd booked Sandy 'and Friends' with John Martyn as support. My job on the night was what we would now call 'artists' liaison'. As a big fan of Sandy, I was slightly nervous about meeting her, but I opened with my usual question, 'What would you like to drink?' We were heavily geared up for artists' alcoholic consumption in those days, so I was astounded when she said, 'Could I have a cup of tea please, Steve?'

Despite the gig being held in the union refectory, we had no tea and coffee-making facilities available, but a quick trip to an adjoining hall of residence produced a kettle, tea bags and milk. Job done. Sandy was so grateful, and my impression of her as a kind and thoughtful soul has not diminished with the passing years. I consider myself fortunate to have been there and to have exchanged pleasantries with someone who I admired so much.

The rest of the gig is a little hazy, but I do remember a blistering version of 'John The Gun' and the band's large PA system, inherited from Fotheringay. I believe it had 'Fotheringport Confusion' stencilled on the cabinets.

KINGSTON POLYTECHNIC
DECEMBER 1972, KINGSTON-UPON-THAMES, UK

CHRIS BUSSICOTT

I was fifteen years old, attending my very first concert. This was after Sandy had officially left Fairport but I had recently discovered Witchseason and the many amazing artists on the roster, so seeing Fairport (even without Sandy) was a mind-blowing experience! As was the bottle of Watney's Pale Ale I was thrilled to have been able to buy without anyone questioning my obvious youth…

In fact, the ale was having another urgent effect on me and I had to dash out for a pee. I was in such a hurry that as I ran through the doors at the back of the hall, I ran straight into a woman who had been peeking in from outside while smoking a cigarette.

'Oh, sorry!' says I.

'That's fine, no harm done,' says she, 'but I hope you're not leaving now?'

'No, err, just the gents.'

'Oh good,' says she, 'then I'll see you later...'.

By the time I got back she had gone, so imagine my surprise then when Sandy Denny – for it was she – joined the band for the encore. I know lots of people talk about their life-changing first live music experiences, but I think mine must come pretty high on anyone's list!

(I was delighted to find that this wasn't an adolescent fantasy when, years after the event, a portion of the gig featuring Sandy appeared on Fairport's *The Airing Cupboard Tapes*.)

GREAT NGĀRUAWĀHIA MUSIC FESTIVAL
6 – 8 JANUARY 1973, HAMILTON, NEW ZEALAND

EWAN MCDONALD, JOURNALIST

1973, and Fairport Convention came to Hamilton, New Zealand (or Kirikiriroa, Aotearoa) as joint headliners for the country's first major festival, attracting 20,000 to a riverside farm a few miles north of the city. Fairport were joint headliners with… um, Black Sabbath, but it turned out well on the weekend.

My best mate Murray and I were FC nuts and turned up at the local motor hotel to welcome them to town with a tray or possibly two of Newcastle Brown. I remember DM asking at reception for a vegetarian salad and being told, 'We could take the steak off the lettuce.' This was NZ in the seventies, after all.

Seduced by the beer and a stinking hot afternoon, everyone repaired to the hotel pool, led by Trevor Lucas. Swarb insisted that Murray hand over his 18-month-old daughter Willa and spent most of the afternoon swimming up and down the pool and taking care of her.

At some stage, there was a lull. Which was broken by Sandy – not previously seen all afternoon – entering stage left from her poolside unit. I believe FC had been recording at the studios in LA shared by Island, A&M, Motown, etc. and she had somehow persuaded / uplifted / borrowed raw tapes of Stevie Wonder's *Innervisions* album.

Ewan McDonald remembers Sandy accompanying Stevie Wonder

She was wearing a yellow bikini and carrying one of those huge seventies battery-powered ghetto-blaster cassette players over one shoulder. It was playing the lead-off track, 'Higher Ground', at full volume – remember no one had ever heard it, it wouldn't be released for another few months – and she was dancing around the pool, duetting and BV-ing and jamming with Stevie Wonder.

Sandy pictured in the 1973 AUS/NZ tour programme (Ian Burgess)

Sandy had some kind of a voice – Robert Plant struggled to keep up with her. All I can say is, until you've heard the raw, vamping, Sandy Denny going a cappella with and against Stevie Wonder on 'Higher Ground' and other tracks, going off into scat-singing riffs that even he couldn't imagine, you have never heard one of the great soul (not only folk) singers at the peak of her powers. Stevie really should have hired her for his backing vocals.

For that afternoon, I am eternally, and blessedly, thankful. It was quite some experience for a young Kiwi journalist who went on to write for a bunch of music publications in Aotearoa, Australia and the UK.

We heard Fairport once again in Hamilton, when they played the Hamilton Founders. The highlight of that night was 'Sloth', with Swarb's fiddle and Sandy's voice. It was great – but it wasn't 'Higher Ground'.

LADY SPENCER CHURCHILL COLLEGE
16 FEBRUARY 1973, WHEATLEY, OXFORD, UK

CLIVE PHILLIPS

The only time I saw Fairport live. I can't remember a thing about it except that Dave Swarbrick was excellent. I have only one of their albums – *Rosie* – on vinyl, which I bought a year after the gig. I still love listening to them, especially Sandy Denny.

ZIGZAG
APRIL 1973, LONDON, UK

ELTON JOHN

I'm really into bands like Fairport and Lindisfarne – the English people don't know what they've got in their own backyard. It's the same with Americans, of course, but people like Fairport are so fucking good, any of the lineups, but particularly with Sandy Denny and Dave Swarbrick – *Liege & Lief* – but I still love the other albums they've made.

SYMPHONY HALL
1 APRIL 1973, BOSTON, MASSACHUSETTS

WILD BILL

Sandy was sharing a bill with Martin Mull and Randy Newman. It was almost a full house. By the back stage door I met a guy with a light blue Ford. I gave him a dozen roses to give to his sister(?) Sandy. Sandy came on first, a wise move as Martin Mull's first LP was just released, an impossible act to follow. She wore a long black dress and stocking feet.

She played a seven-song set including 'Willie O'Winsbury', maybe 'Late November', and 'John The Gun' at the piano. (Randy Newman said it was a Baldwin and sounded 'muddy'; it did.) She forgot the lyrics.

She did 'Quiet Joys' a cappella and said something like, 'This is a song by Richard Farina set to a traditional Irish tune. I really like Richard Farina's lyrics… and Irish traditional tunes.' The audience laughed. Then she couldn't find the key. She walked to the piano, hit one note, skipped back to the mic and sang it note perfect. She also introduced her two 12-string guitars – 'Gilbert', a blond Gibson J45, and 'Mabel', a Martin D28.

The audience asked for one more. Someone asked for 'Who Knows Where The Time Goes?' and Sandy obliged. She seemed happy and maybe a bit surprised. Then the stagehands began bringing out Martin Mull's furniture.

I asked two people with cameras if they could make me copies of the photos they had taken that night. One didn't call. The other did and said 'they didn't come out'.

Fairport played at Sanders Theatre at Harvard twice in '74. One night Sandy wasn't looking too good. She made it through part of the show, spoke with Trevor and left the stage. He played two more songs and left the four-piece Fairport to carry on. Sandy checked into Mount Auburn Hospital a few blocks away for a couple of days. The first time Fairport played there, Trevor stood on the stage, looked around the hall and said, 'This place is really nice – reminds me of home.' There were a few laughs from the sell-out crowd. 'Not *my* home!'

ELTING GYMNASIUM, SUNY
7 APRIL 1973, NEW PALTZ, NEW YORK

RICHARD SINGLETON

Sandy was on a triple bill with Randy Newman and John Prine and I was a big fan of all three. Sandy played piano and the song that sticks out in my memory is 'Solo'. She was wonderful. John Prine and Randy Newman's performances were also terrific. John's 'Dear Abby' from that concert is on his *Sweet Revenge* album.

FRANCES MARION PLATT

I saw her a couple of times with the *Nine/Rising For The Moon* Fairport line-up, but the one time I caught her performing solo was as the opening act in an extraordinary trifecta in the Elting Gymnasium at the State University of New York at New Paltz, my alma mater.

Randy & Sandy, April 1973 (Edward Haber)

I vividly remember Sandy seated at a grand piano, singing 'Solo' with such an air of defiance and determination. It pierced my young feminist heart, especially as I'd just recently exited a toxic romantic relationship. She was in splendid voice and came across as a powerful, indomitable force of nature, someone who wasn't about to take any crap from boyfriends, bandmates or record companies. Inspiring.

The second act was John Prine, whose work was new to me at the time. His crew was recording his set that evening, and the tape of 'Dear Abby' from that set ended up being included on his third album, *Sweet Revenge*, because he wasn't satisfied with the studio version.

The headliner that night was Randy Newman, touring in support of his 1972 *Sail Away* album and introducing a few cuts that would appear on *Good Old Boys* the following year. Altogether a brilliant evening of music from three of the greatest singer/songwriters of the era.

It's peculiar how the seventies are thought of as the heyday of disco, or the formative years of punk/new wave. Everyone seems to forget that the decade was also the absolute golden age of the singer/songwriter. It was a great joy to hear Sandy in such glorious company!

GRANADA THEATRE
25 APRIL 1973, CHICAGO, ILLINOIS

PATTY SANDERS

The first time I ever heard Sandy sing was when I listened to Fairport Convention's *Liege & Lief* LP. My older brother Michael had purchased the LP and brought it home. I was particularly intrigued by the combination of Sandy Denny's voice and Dave Swarbrick's violin work. It made me want to hear more. Before listening to Sandy and Fairport Convention, my music tastes as a child leaned towards Big Band, Peter Paul and Mary and The Kingston Trio. In my teens, it was rock, British rock. There was just something about Sandy that made me dig deeper into British folk rock. I then picked up Fairport's *What We Did On Our Holidays*. Hearing the track 'Listen, Listen' hooked me even further. Beyond that I had found Sandy's *Fotheringay* LP and *The North Star Grassman and the Ravens*. I then found a four-LP set of Sandy's songs.

In the US, Sandy was described as being the Judy Collins of England. In my days of playing the coffee house scene in Boston, Chicago, I would always put a couple of Sandy's songs in the mix: 'Like An Old Fashioned Waltz', 'It Suits Me Well', 'Donkey Ride', etc. Whenever I hear 'Old-Fashioned Waltz', I envision my mum and dad in heaven, in a castle ballroom dancing together with 'no one else there'. Sandy's music helped me embrace my British ancestry. It simply gives me a sense of home. She came to Chicago in 1973 to play at the Granada Theatre. I wish I could have gone to see and meet her. Sadly, I had to work that night.

SOUNDS
9 MAY 1973

PAUL SIMON

I remember Bert Jansch when he first came to London from Glasgow, Davy Graham was there and Sandy Denny – we all used to live in the same house, me and Artie (Garfunkel), Judith Piepe, Sandy Denny and this other guy Jackson Frank. Al Stewart was sort of a couple of years later but he was coming on, John Renbourn, Ian Campbell Folk Group were real popular when I first came. That period taught me a lot about performing too because I did a lot of performing by myself. I really learnt a lot about being on the stage.

FOOT OF JANSS STEPS
10 MAY 1973, LOS ANGELES, CALIFORNIA

JIM BICKHART

I next encountered Sandy when she accompanied the *Fairport Nine* ensemble to the US as a non-performer. While they were in LA, we arranged a free noon concert for them at UCLA (a follow-on to a successful such event I'd arranged for Fairport in 1970, when they toured in support of *Full House*). Steeleye Span were in town playing at The Troubadour or Roxy Theater, so we invited them to come over to the campus for the concert, vainly hoping that they might participate. They all showed up and Sandy sat with them on the lawn, chatting and watching the show on a sunny afternoon.

A&M also staged an invitation-only performance by Fairport in one of their immaculate recording studios. Joni Mitchell showed up for that one. After the band's excellent performance, Joni took Sandy and a few of us into another, smaller studio (she regularly used A&M to record her albums because she typically wanted to work with engineer Henry Lewy), sat at a grand piano and played several of the songs (with no vocals) she was preparing for *Court And Spark*. It was a gesture of respect for Sandy on Joni's part.

Fairport then undertook the rest of their around-the-world tour, during which Sandy rejoined the band and recorded *Live At The Sydney Opera House* (released as *A Movable Feast* in the US). They eventually wound up back at The Troubadour for several nights of shows. It was already obvious that they were struggling to reintegrate her into the presentation. She recorded *Like An Old Fashioned Waltz* some time in that '73-'74 period and seemed more interested in playing songs such as 'Solo' on the piano than rocking out with the lads.

That became even more apparent when next she visited LA with Fairport in 1975, in support of *Rising For The Moon*. The band's reputation had grown sufficiently that they could play larger venues than The Troubadour, but the album stiffed and, upon their return to England, Sandy left.

I encountered guitarist Jerry Donahue at Island Records' short-lived offices in LA who told me he had grown frustrated with Sandy's attitude and had departed the band just before she did. He had moved back to

LA, where he'd lived before going to England, and maintained a bit of a trans-Atlantic existence for decades to come until a serious stroke disabled him and forced his untimely retirement.

He retained a strong affection for Sandy's artistry, however, leading him to play on her subsequent *Rendezvous* album and play a big role in preparng her posthumous *Gold Dust* live album, as well as the *Fotheringay 2* album.

Sadly, I didn't have any contact with Ms Denny after the *Rising* tour and, I'm sure like all of us, I was saddened to learn of her passing in 1978.

The Sandy I knew and observed was a complex mixture of effervescence, brooding and intellect, along with being a fine musician and songwriter deserving of considerably more appreciation than she received in life (despite that which she did manage to earn in her time). Her marriage to Trevor was troubled and, ultimately, tragic for both parties.

STATE THEATRE
20 MAY 1973, SYDNEY, AUSTRALIA

IAN JONES

Fairport were touring the *Rosie* album (Ian Jones)

As an avid reader of *Melody Maker* from the late 1960s, I discovered Fairport Convention and Sandy Denny. I purchased the local version of the *Unhalfbricking* LP and was hooked. Then I purchased *What We Did On Our Holidays* and the classic *Liege & Lief*. Sandy had become my favourite female singer and remains so to this day.

After Sandy left Fairport in 1969, I purchased the Fotheringay LP and in 1971 got an import copy of *The North Star Grassman And The Ravens*. I continued to buy all her LPs and, later, her CDs.

Fairport finally started to tour Australia and I saw them at Sydney's ornate State Theatre in May 1973. The band was touring the *Rosie* album and, luckily, the special guest was Sandy. It was such a thrill to finally see her live in concert..

Then I went to the magical concert at Sydney Opera House Concert

Hall on 26 January 1974. Sandy was in the band and her performance was breathtaking. The concert was subsequently released as *Fairport Live Convention*.

Fairport returned to Sydney on 6 August 1975 and the Hordern Pavilion, at the Sydney Showground. Once again, Sandy was in Fairport. It was another great concert with Sandy a real star.

Trevor and Sandy left the band in late 1975 and never toured Australia again. After a Ralph McTell concert at Sydney's City Recital Hall on 5 March 2019, I met up with old Fairporter John Penhallow, who introduced me to Trevor and Sandy's daughter Georgia. It was so delightful to be able to tell Georgia how much I'd enjoyed her parents' music and about the wonderful 1974 concert at the Opera House.

I'm so pleased that there have been so many releases since Sandy's early passing. Her music is timeless and there is now so much to enjoy. My life has been enriched by all this wonderful music.

Ian Jones saw Sandy with Fairport in Sydney

CHIPSTEAD STREET
1973, FULHAM, LONDON, UK

ANDY PAY

It was 1973. I was with a friend of Sandy and he wanted to call round to her flat. When we arrived, Danny Thompson was also visiting. I don't know why, but Danny took an instant dislike to me. He said, 'Do you want me to thump him, Sandy?' Back came the reply, 'No, just leave him alone Danny.' I've always felt grateful to Sandy for that!

ALL OUR OWN WORK
RELEASED 1973

THOMAS LOTTI

All Our Own Work was recorded in 1967 but not released until 1973

At 15 I was turned onto Yes by my older brother. Genesis, ELP, Renaissance, etc. followed and I became a big-time prog guy. I got into Zeppelin and was amazed by 'The Battle Of Evermore', and when I heard Sandy's voice it was just incredible.

I had been listening to Tull and Ian Anderson when they went heavily folk, so I started listening to Fairport, The Strawbs, Steeleye Span, etc. and just fell in love with that genre. It was a little confusing at the beginning, keeping track of the different bands and solo stuff that Sandy had done. I think I am one of the very few who really likes the first Strawbs album. It is the epitome of folk, and when I listen to Sandy on that album and the early albums with Fairport there is just such a warmth and an old timey feeling. My mind can drift back to a time other than the twentieth and twenty-first centuries and there is a calming and relaxing effect that takes one away from the hard metal world. It's very similar to reading Tolkien or some of the other great fantasy writers.

Sandy is one of my three favourite singers along with Maddy Prior and Annie Haslam. I guess my favourite song of Sandy's is 'Listen, Listen'. I can't listen to that without crumbling and melting a bit. 'Farewell, Farewell' has a similar effect and impact.

FOLK FESTIVAL
2 JUNE 1973, ENSCHEDE, THE NETHERLANDS

FRITS WIELENS

Sandy's performance was the second last of the festival, at about 11pm on the Saturday night. The Albion Country Band closed the festival. I remember thinking how nice it would have been had Sandy appeared with them as a guest for a few songs. Years later in Dublin, I saw Frank Quinlan busking. He also appeared at that festival, and he said that he played snooker with Sandy in Enschede.

CAMBRIDGE FOLK FESTIVAL
28 JULY 1973, CAMBRIDGE, UK

CHRIS BOLAND

John Prine was playing on the main stage. He said something about having a guest come up. Sandy walked on and Prine left the stage to her. I think she played maybe three or four songs. She said she was nervous about playing a six-string guitar. She'd mostly been playing twelve-string for a while.

GREAT WINDMILL STREET
AUGUST 1973, SOHO LONDON, UK

GERED MANKOWITZ FRPS, PHOTOGRAPHER

In the summer of 1973, I was asked by my good friend, the art director Fabio Nicoli, to meet with him and discuss a forthcoming album by Sandy Denny to be called *Like An Old Fashioned Waltz*. Fabio wanted a portrait of Sandy that would reflect the title, and I proposed that we create a Victorian type of portrait situation in my studio, using daylight and shooting on large format Polaroid colour that I thought might impart an old-fashioned texture to the portrait – it was the first time that we made a cover directly from a Polaroid print.

Gered Mankowitz recalls working with Sandy (Dawn Kemp)

Sandy came to my studio at 41 Great Windmill Street in London's Soho in mid-August for the shoot. I had set up a background of a suitable Victorian-looking wallpaper under the skylight at the edge of the studio, and with the help of some reflectors created a very soft natural looking lighting that

Sandy at the Enschede Folk Festival
(Paul Neuray)

I felt was in keeping with the brief. I had brought in a make-up artist and Sandy spent a while in the dressing room, choosing her outfit and getting a look that felt natural and had the simplicity that we all wanted.

When she emerged, she looked lovely and was very patient with the slightly cumbersome and slow large-format camera, but we all agreed that this process itself contributed to the old-fashioned feel that we wanted to achieve. We shot about 20 sheets of Polaroid before we got one that everybody felt captured the right mood, and that was that. Fabio left with the Polaroids in his bag and Sandy went home!

The finished album looked great, and Fabio had placed a floral motif around the portrait, and had it embossed which worked beautifully, but this wasn't reproduced on most versions as it was too expensive. At one point, we discussed the idea of printing the portrait on an inner sleeve and cutting out the frame on the cover like a picture frame, but I believe that was thrown out as being too costly and complicated!

Everybody seemed delighted with the finished cover and the rest is history. Sadly, I never met or worked with Sandy again…

THE HOWFF
4 SEPTEMBER 1973, PRIMROSE HILL, LONDON, UK

ROBIN DENSELOW

These days, Regent's Park Road is one of the more cool, swanky locations in north London, boasting a collection of coffee shops and restaurants catering for those in need of refreshment after a stroll up Primrose Hill, or for the tourists checking the house where some of the Paddington films were shot.

Back in the mid-seventies, when it was slightly less upmarket, it was also the location of a small music venue, The Howff, named by the promoter Roy Guest after the sixteenth century Scots word for a meeting place where one could enjoy songs and good company. And it was here that Sandy gave a solo show that was one of the finest events I have been lucky enough to attend.

It was all the more extraordinary because no-one knew quite what to expect. We hadn't seen Sandy for a while, for she had been off in the States earlier in the year, and had been recording a new album, *Like An Old*

Fashioned Waltz. Now she was previewing some of these songs in a tiny club, and was playing solo, accompanying herself on a Steinway piano.

I was told afterwards that she had been suffering from stage fright before coming on, but that was not reflected in her performance. It was a hot night, she was wearing a green dress, and she was in remarkable form. There were no traditional songs, for she concentrated on her own compositions. There were some that her audience knew – from 'Late November' to a powerful treatment of 'John The Gun' – and then there was the new material, from the title track of the new album to the exquisite 'Solo'. This was a song where the lyrics needed no explanation, for it was a powerful, emotional, and perhaps autobiographical story of individual isolation. She ended with a change of mood and style, with a song made famous by Fats Waller, 'Until The Real Thing Comes Along'.

This was a night when Sandy proved she really was the real deal. For me, it was up there with watching a solo and acoustic Bob Dylan at the Albert Hall, or Bob Marley at the Lyceum.

CHIPSTEAD STREET
8 SEPTEMBER 1973, FULHAM, LONDON, UK

JERRY GILBERT

Sandy Denny and Trevor Lucas were at their Fulham flat watching the test match when I arrived to tape 'The Talk-In'. England's terrible plight was temporarily averted as the TV was switched off and the tape recorder, blaring the skeleton of Sandy's new album (produced by Trevor), was turned on. Pat Donaldson, Gerry Conway, Dave Pegg, Dave Mattacks, Danny Thompson, Jerry Donahue, Richard Thompson, Alan Skidmore, Diz Disley – the featured musicians on the new album – are a fairly typical assembly for Sandy, but there was evidence of at least a few surprises.

We retired to the front room, talked about America and then debated how Sandy could possibly have got her giant grand piano into the house. 'They must have built the house around it,' I challenged, but Sandy proved with the aid of geometry and a vivid imagination that this was not necessarily the case.

We haven't seen much of you in this country – do you still enjoy gigging?

Yeah, I do – I enjoy actually doing concerts, and when I'm at home installed in my house I quite miss not being on the road but being on the road is actually a lot more strenuous than you remember, though in fact I like doing gigs. That to me is probably the nicest part of any work like that – it's worth going to America and Australia and stuff just to work.

Do you find it difficult in organising situations with other musicians for touring or recording?

Ideally – and this is the truth – I'd like to be in a band so that I didn't carry all the responsibility. It's not that I'm shirking, it's just that when you do have a band that's literally working for you, it's quite a responsibility especially if you're using musicians that you really respect, like telling them what to play and everything. I think the ideal situation is being in a band and everybody having their own ideas and calling it something else. Like for the past two years I've been 'Sandy Denny' or it has been 'The Sandy Denny Band' or something and I kind of miss the slight anonymity of just being a member of a group.

Even with Fotheringay it tended to be the Sandy Denny/Trevor Lucas band, though.

Yeah but at least it was all spread out over everybody. It was nice in that band, I think.

Why didn't things work out in Fotheringay?

Oh, I dunno. I'm easily swayed by people with strong opinions. It was a funny band and when I think of it now, I wish we'd kept it up, though it's silly to say that, because when I think back, I've learnt an awful lot and I've written a lot too, and I think that my writing's getting better. You forfeit one thing for another, and musically I suppose I've developed along a certain line though whether it's the right one or not is irrelevant to the amount of knowledge I've gained in the last couple of years.

Do you feel now that some of the pressure has been taken off you? I mean there was a time when so much was expected of you after topping polls and so on.

Oh, right – but all that was really weird. I'm constantly feeling the pressure because I've got to keep at it, and even though I haven't worked in England for a long time I've still been working a lot and really it's all happening, it's just that one doesn't hear about it always over here. As far as I am concerned the pressure has never really been off, and if it completely disappeared I don't know what I'd do with myself. I mean, if there really wasn't any pressure for me to do anything I'd think, 'Oh God something terrible's just happened and I've become totally talentless and nobody wants to hear anything anymore.'

But I shall be working a lot more here – I shall be starting to work in October, and I'm really looking forward to it. I really am. I'm going to be playing with Pat (Donaldson) and Gerry (Conway) – just them to start with until we get something else happening. We just think it's fine as it is, just as a trio to start with. I don't know whether it'll be a band or me with Pat and Gerry backing me, it's all in the air at the moment.

Will it be in the form of a tour?

Yeah, because I think that's what we need to do – we really need to do a lot of work before we go back to the States. I mean, I went over to the States last year with Pat playing and Timi (Donald) and Richard (Thompson) and we did fairly well, but we hadn't rehearsed enough and the pressure is so much more over there to be really tight and professional, otherwise it's just not on, and I'd like to work around all the places here and then we'll go again to America. I'm not putting America first by any stretch of the imagination, but I feel it's easier because the pressure is less and we'll be able to relax more over here.

I don't know if you're able to draw parallels, but how has your music been accepted by American audiences in comparison with the reaction here?

This time I went over on my own, and I think the reaction was extremely favourable. But I still feel that I work better with musicians and a lot of people in their reviews were quite favourable about what I was doing and a few said it would be nice to hear me with a band. And actually, when I was at The Troubadour, Fairport were in town (Los Angeles) and they got up on stage with me and did five or six of my songs and we did some looning about and stuff and I felt a sudden sense of relief when they started playing. It was just really nice to have them all behind me – you can't play that many bum notes when you're on your own. I'm not looking for excuses for playing bum notes, but if you do play a rotten note there's no one behind you – so you've got to be good in every way.

Do you tend to be bound to the piano these days?

It's just that I love playing the piano much more than I like playing the guitar.

And presumably you write far more on piano.

Well, as a matter of fact, that one thing you just heard, 'The Carnival',

I wrote on guitar. But there's one I really like on this next LP that was written on piano and there are quite a few on piano. But the trouble with me is that I tend to use the same chords re-arranged and with the tempo a bit different. But I really do like playing the piano.

If the piano situation was such that it could be possible, would you like to be back in a band with Trevor? I know he's been producing your new album, but his life has been changing musically since you went back on the road with Fairport.

Yeah, well I would, I really would because obviously we're away from each other an awful lot – I mean, he's off on the road again for a couple of months at the end of September, then he's off again after that, so it's obviously a bit of a strain. But he's really got into it – he really likes to be up on the stage and it's good for him, I think. But if he wants to get another band together after a while, I think we might do it. I miss that really warm feeling we used to have with Fotheringay. We've all got a soft spot for Fotheringay.

You've always been fairly close, too, to Fairport and the musicians involved through the respective bands.

Well, right, but it's a very peculiar thing because everyone always uses the same musicians and...

Let me ask you how you've seen the development of Fairport since you left.

It's a difficult question for me to answer because I'm obviously going to be slightly biased in favour at the moment and I think that since they've become more solid – I mean this particular lineup has been together for about a year now – and at the beginning of that year when *Rosie* came out there was this element of them not staying together and it was all on the brink of disaster. But since then they've stuck together and had this one goal to stay together, really work hard and try and do it properly instead of looning around all over the place. And I think because of their tenacity they'll probably be a good band again. I think up until now they've had slight material problems because of elements like everyone's going to leave and you can't write songs because you're so uptight and their sets have been really thrown together because they've just had to work to live; I think you'll notice the difference now anyway.

People still talk about Liege & Lief *as being the pinnacle of Fairport's achievements, which of course you were featured on...*

I don't think it was the best record at all, of the ones I was on. If you're going to do an all round thing... there are numbers on every album that I like and ones that I really don't, but in general the one I like most of all, except for the recording of it which wasn't as good as it should be, was *Unhalfbricking*, I think that was the nicest one... and next to that I like *Full House*. Then it started to crumble around a bit and everyone was being schizophrenic and one even wondered whether Fairport would continue at all.

How have you managed to keep sane through it all?

I really don't know. I think I have this mechanism which just clicks off when it's really like disaster. I don't believe it really would be. I know it is but I won't admit it and I think that's how you get through any heavy traumas or changes. You have to think things are going to look up tomorrow.

Since we're talking about your past, are there any songs you've written over the years that still hold a very dear place in your heart – going back to the period of 'Who Knows Where The Time Goes?' for instance?

I like that one sometimes, and there are occasions when I'm really in the mood to sing it and audiences quite like it if I do – but I can't get it together to do it a lot. It was one of my first songs, and I just wish people would listen to some of the other ones, although some people still maintain it's the best song I've ever written. They can't all be wrong, although I don't agree with them – I've written lots more songs that I and they too prefer, but at the moment I'm too into the album to think which ones they are. I think I've done my best stuff on this record that's going to come out.

On your earlier solo albums you seem to have had a preoccupation with sea...

Everyone's asked me that question. I dunno. I just love things like that. When I write songs I often picture myself standing on a beach or standing on a rock or a promenade or something. I just put myself there sometimes and without even realising it I find myself describing what I'm looking at and often it's the sea. I keep promising myself I'll put myself somewhere else when I'm writing songs but I really can't think of anywhere that's nicer than that.

Have you tended to write this album in one burst or has it come together over a long period?

What's tended to happen, funnily enough in the last couple of months, is that I've written a song in my head and I've written the tune down and I've known what the song is about, but I haven't written the actual words until recently. Not that I don't do that every time I go into the studio – I'm usually writing the words as I run up the street to the studio but I've really worked on a lot of the songs more than I normally do. I've really thrown out things I don't like very much and started again. I've used up reams of paper on this album just because I don't want to waste record space.

I mean, are there any songs that are out of your head the minute they're down on wax?

No, it's not fair to say that because the songs are about things... a lot of my songs are really about specific circumstances and people that I know but whether I've put it better is the thing.

Is there any sort of definition you can give in words to describe the new album? I mean, you've recorded a Fats Waller song for instance.

No, and I'll tell you why – because it hasn't got its fur coat on yet, it's still very basic. I say this every time, but it's more positive than the last record – I just feel it's stronger in some ways, but we haven't gone through the dramas of mixing it and adding things on like orchestras yet.

When's it due out?

October 12, but it's really going to be a rush getting it out by then.

So who've you heard recently that you've really dug?

Interesting question. Well recently the person who I've been most knocked out with is Randy Newman... you see, I haven't been to all that many places in England and I haven't heard very many people, which is a drag. But I worked a lot with Randy Newman and I just couldn't believe it; he was so amazing and so incredibly pertinent in his songs. He's so cynical about the whole thing and I really got amazed – that was one of the nicest parts about being in America, the fact that I did five or six gigs with him. Then there's Dick Gaughan on the folk scene. I mean, he's always been great, but I've only just realised it. I met him at the Cambridge Festival this year...

You turned up and did a surprise spot during John Prine's set...

Yeah. Well, I did a gig with him in the States and I met him and his manager and everybody and I was looking forward to them coming over. So I had to go along and see them anyway... and Steve Goodman as well, all from the stable. It was the first time I'd been to the Cambridge Festival ever and John just asked me if I wanted to, and I said, 'I only came to see you', and he said, 'You can play my guitar' and I said, 'I haven't got any picks,' so someone rushed off and got me some picks... so I got up and did a couple of songs but I was pretty nervous. They were really nice, actually, the audience.

Aside from the folky people you use on your albums, the folk revival as such appears to have disintegrated somewhat, don't you agree?

Yes, it has a bit. Everyone seems to be gradually retiring or disappearing into oblivion. I should think worth hearing would be John Martyn and Danny Thompson. There don't seem to be any folk clubs like they used to be. Since the Cousins closed down it was almost like a nucleus was taken away for some reason, for one part of it. In those days there was always a John Snow for the tradition people and then Cousins for the folkies with the harmonicas and it was always buzzing around, the trads against the contemporaries. It's still going on, but it's such a sophisticated feud now and one doesn't enter into blatant ignoring of people. But there are these staunch ones left like Pete Bellamy.

Do you get bored?

Yes, I can't think of anyone I want to go and see and there isn't anywhere to go and see them – not like a folk club with the same kind of feeling. The Chieftains I like, but who doesn't, really?

So what are your fondest remembrances?

I suppose when everybody used to go down the Cousins when it was open all night and everyone would be on – Martin (Carthy) and Swarb and all kinds of people like Alexis Korner would do an overnight thing and Bert Jansch and John Renbourn would be there and the Watersons and Les Bridger. Davy Graham would do the all-nighters as well and those were really good days. John Martyn used to do it too, and Jackson Frank. There were so many visiting American people, Paul Simon used to go down there; then there was Mike Seeger, Tom Paxton.

Do you think that the placidity of your music is a sign of the general laid back feel that seems to have taken over since the days you're talking about?

Yes, a lot of the things I write are slow, because I find it difficult to play the piano fast and I think that restricts me a bit, but even so I don't mind that very much because I really don't like to be disturbed by my music – I like to take it easy. I suppose I'm quite influenced by the folk songs I've sung in the past, and I suppose I sing a bit in that way so you'd always call me a kind of a folk singer because the way I sing is a bit folky – it's a style rather than an actual definition of what folk music is. I love some folk tunes but there are people who spend most of their time getting the traditional stuff out and reviving it in a really pleasant way and while people are doing that I quite like writing my own stuff. I like doing it because I think I do it well and a lot of other people are into a lot of different aspects of folk music and like to do it authentically and properly. And why not?

Do you collaborate very much with Trevor during the writing stages?

No, not at all. I'm a very peculiar writer. I don't like writing with anyone around at all. I have to be on my own. I am quite secretive about it all, because I don't like anybody to hear anything until I think it's really good. So consequently Trevor gets used to the idea that he can only go on what he can hear, which is usually just the backing track. It's very tense but it works out alright in the end and I don't know what I'd do in the studio without him.

Did you ever miss Joe Boyd in an artistic role when he went to the States?

I dunno. I just kind of plodded on, really. I don't remember it specifically, but yes, it was a bit higgedly-piggedly after he left, but it sorted itself out. I mean afterwards, Richard (Thompson) and John (Wood) and I just said, let's have a bash at doing this record and it was a very laidback album to say the least. But at least it was a try.

READING UNIVERSITY
19 OCTOBER 1973, READING, UK

DAVE CHICK

I feel very privileged to have seen Sandy in concert four times. The first time was at Reading University on 9 October 1971, with Osibisa as support. Sandy's singing was superb and I remember Richard Thompson doing a stunning guitar solo on 'John The Gun'. I saw her again at Reading University in October 1973, with Batti Mamzelle supporting. Quite often the Students Union banned non-students from attending events, so I was glad that people from the town had not been causing any trouble around the time of Sandy's gigs! Many of the songs were from *Like An Old Fashioned Waltz*, which would not be released until the following June. I don't recall which song it was, but Sandy was sitting at the piano playing the intro and cried out, 'Help! I don't know how to get out of this!' She then joked that, 'This is avant garde. I 'aven't garde a clue what I'm doing!' It was, of course, another wonderful performance. For the encore Trevor Lucas, whom Sandy had married the previous month, joined the band and performed some Fotheringay songs. The line-up on stage was Fotheringay but with a different drummer – I can't remember who.

IMPERIAL COLLEGE
16 NOVEMBER 1973, KENSINGTON, LONDON, UK

SIMON HART

I saw Sandy twice with Fairport Convention, the first time at Imperial College in London with the classic *Nine* line up of Sandy, 'new boys' Jerry Donahue and Trevor Lucas plus the three Daves – Swarbrick, Pegg and Mattacks. The second time was the following November at the Rainbow Theatre in Finsbury Park, with the same line up. I was also at her last solo concert which took place at the Royalty Theatre in November 1977, subsequently released as the CD and album *Gold Dust – Live At The Royalty*.

Around the early 1980s my mother lived in a block of flats in Hampton, Surrey. She had recently remarried and her new husband, a keen outdoor/indoor bowls player, persuaded her to join the local bowls club. She did, and while a member of the club she met Neil Denny, Sandy's father, and they became neighbourly friends.

Knowing I was a fan of Fairport and Sandy, she was quick to tell me her news. Neil asked my mother if she and I wanted to visit for tea and to look at some of the memorabilia that he had of his daughter. Of course, I said yes and got to see the treasure trove of goodies and pictures that were on display in his apartment: Sandy at art college; early gigs with Dave Cousins and Fairport; Sandy and Richard (Thompson) at a piano; in the garden at the house in Wimbledon, plus notebooks with drawings, lyrics and musings. There were also some boxed open reel-to-reel tapes with recordings of Sandy solo and some with Richard as a duo. Sadly, we could not play them as Neil did not have a suitable tape machine. It was a wonderful archive of some of her personal artefacts. Sadly, Neil passed away in 1999 but we did spend a few afternoons taking about Sandy and her wonderful music, both as a solo artist and as a member of The Strawbs and Fairport.

OPERA HOUSE
26 JANUARY 1974, SYDNEY, AUSTRALIA

RHONDA MAWER

I fondly remember seeing Sandy, Dave Swarbrick and Trevor Lucas with Fairport play in an afternoon concert at Sydney Opera House. There was Sandy with her bare feet, dancing around the stage. I absolutely loved her voice and her songs. I was very much a part of the folk scene, being a singer myself. Sandy will always be alive through her music. She is sadly missed but never forgotten.

Rhonda Mawer remembers Sandy performing barefoot

Sandy was back in Australia less than a year after her previous visit (Ian Jones)

ROGER ILOTT

Along with fellow band members Joe Cannon and Peter Garrety from Meadowband (later Rusty Dusty Bros), I arrived at the Sydney Opera House to see Fairport Convention. Though I was quite familiar with Fairport, Joe and Peter had got me more interested in their music as we were performing a few of their songs.

Shortly after the support act – John Currie and band – had left the stage, Dave Swarbrick, Trevor Lucas, Jerry Donahue, Dave Pegg and Dave Mattacks bounded on stage and launched straight into a ripping version of 'Hexhamshire Lass', followed by 'Polly On The Shore'. Both were from the recent album, *Nine*, which I'd had for a few weeks.

Fairport in Sydney, 1974
(photographer unknown)

The poster for the concert featured that line-up, so nobody had any inkling what was about to happen next. Though Sandy had left Fairport in 1969, we all knew she had recently married Trevor Lucas. The band started a familiar riff, and suddenly on walked Sandy to a tumultuous reception. 'Matty Groves' brought the Opera House down!

The rest of the concert comprised quite a few Sandy songs, including a few she performed on piano. She had a very serene stage presence. The band played old and new tracks from their slightly strange history – the current line up featured no original members – and Swarbrick led the band through lots of jigs and reels, which had the place absolutely rocking.

Trevor Lucas exuded calmness even though some of the music was absolutely frantic, and his Ovation semi-acoustic was as clear as a bell. In some of the instrumentals, when Dave Pegg changed to mandolin, Dave Mattacks played Pegg's bass while still sitting at the drum kit playing kick drum and tambourine.

As a Byrds aficionado, I was particularly interested in Jerry Donahue's playing. He was using a Fender Telecaster like the Byrds' Clarence White, bending the strings and using a volume pedal to take the attack out of some chords and notes. A few days after the concert I went down to the Salvation Army Guitar Store in Pitt Street, Sydney, and ordered a Fender Custom Telecaster, set it up with Bigsby Palm Pedals, and added a volume pedal. I've played it like that ever since.

I couldn't help but notice that during their rendition of 'The Brilliancy Medley' and 'Cherokee Shuffle' – in the key of A – though he'd played it on an acoustic guitar in the G position capoed on the 2nd fret, Gerry played the tearaway melodies in A on the Telecaster. No capo. Incredible playing!

UNKNOWN VENUE
JANUARY / FEBRUARY 1974

JERRY PRYKE
I spent a huge amount of my pocket money in the sixth form and then uni seeing Sandy in various guises: the seminal line-up of Fairport Convention, with Fotheringay, and as a solo artist. I recall a gig during the Three Day Week in 1974 when the power and lights went out. Someone brought a candelabra out and Sandy bashed out 'Nothing More' on the piano. It may have been the Albert Hall, or it could have been the Fairfield Halls in Croydon. My memory is a bit sepia now, but Sandy's voice is eternal.

LET IT ROCK
MARCH 1974

CLIVE JAMES, JOURNALIST & BROADCASTER
Alexandra Elene MacLean Denny, you are charged that in the years between 1968 and 1974 you did, whether wilfully or out of plain carelessness, content yourself with merely becoming a British rock queen, instead of nurturing a world-class songwriting talent into the revolutionary force it once bade fair to be. How do you sing to that?

Well, we know how Sandy Denny sings. Joining Fairport Convention for their exquisite second album, *What We Did On Our Holidays*, she introduced a rock vocal style that kept power in reserve while energising the melody with precisely focused dynamics. The Denny singing characteristics were put on display all at once, as if no period of development were needed. Notes were hit dead centre with a white-hot needle and held while they burned and faded. It was an open space, low-volume, high-intensity vocal style that left room in its interstices for the Witchseason/Island constellation's spellbinding electro-folk sound to develop into a new rock idiom – the idiom in which, among others, the earlier and later Fairports, Fotheringay and Steeleye Span have at one time or another all operated.

If that special rock idiom now shows signs of regressing, of once again becoming solely a folk style – if, that is, Steeleye Span now look like becoming its true heirs and exemplars – the reason can be sought in the material on which the idiom attempted to build. With the important exception of Richard Thompson, the one person within the style capable of writing a contemporary language was Sandy Denny. And her gift for writing such a language was the very gift which she decided – for one reason or another – not to exploit.

Somebody who can sing so beautifully has little need to be adventurous in her writing as well. It is wise, then, to be grateful for the adventurousness she did show in her early songs – wise to be grateful for that, and wise to accept her later reliance on the well-worked folk vocabulary as inevitable. On *What We Did On Our Holidays*, her song 'Fotheringay' gave concrete evidence of the potential for innovation in the mind behind the voice:

The evening hour is fading
Within the dwindling sun
And in a lonely moment
Those embers will be gone
And the last
Of all the young birds flown.

Already she was singing with an effortless legato line reminiscent of the famous story about Elizabeth Schumann at the height of her lieder-singing powers: it's said that Schumann could sing full force into a candle flame without making it so much as waver. Such lavish delicacy of sound, however, tends to deafen us to the quality of the world/music combination itself, which would be interesting even if Bruce Forsyth sang it. Words like 'dwindling' and 'moment' are partly chosen for the way their grouped consonants resist her tendency to flow unimpeded from vowel to vowel – her temptation to sing English the way Joan Sutherland sings Italian. At this stage Denny is still intent on keeping some Germanic roughage in the text, thereby providing her melodic sweetness with something to bite against.

Equally interesting is her ability to use a literary tense – 'And the last / Of all the young birds flown' – without slipping into archaism. This is modern grammar and syntax: complex, but contemporary. It was a path along which British rock sorely needed to advance, for there was no escaping from the fact that our most creative rock bands were hampered in their songwriting by lyricists who rarely know the difference between the subjective and objective case. If we were to add a literate element to our store of written material – something comparable to the college-educated rock-writing tradition which in America had airily come up with John Sebastian and Randy Newman – then this was the kind of attention to detail that needed desperately to be encouraged.

On *Unhalfbricking* (1969) Sandy Denny finally recorded her own version of the song airily made well-known by Judy Collins. One of the two or three dozen crucial songs in rock, 'Who Knows Were The Time Goes?' showed the full power – for the one and only time – of the gift its author so unselfconsciously possessed.

Across the evening sky
All the birds are leaving
But how can they know
It's time for them to go...

Those terminal vowel sounds (sustained unaltering in the first stanza, intensified and withdrawn in the second, and so on through as many variations as required) were placed at the ideal points for her voice, yet were by no means the most important musical features of a given line. Just as important were the packed consonants, as in:

Sad deserted shore
Your fickle friends are leaving..

It's a strophic song, but short enough – and with enough minor variety from stanza to stanza – not to be in danger from predictability. And here, for once, the loose structure made sense: two stanzas about the birds leaving, and a third about a loved one being away, with no logical connection between the first two and the third, but an emotional unity that needed no interlining. The diction was open to arbitrariness (Collins sang 'morning' instead of 'evening' and it was hard to see that the difference mattered) but in this case the neutrality of vocabulary helped the song seem timeless by draining it of context – it was just camped elegantly in the void. A superb song, with a forward flow that the Fairport musicians decorated with fastidiously schooled guitar-lines and copybook stick-work on the rim of the snare.

MASSEY HALL
25 APRIL 1974, TORONTO, CANADA

TOM COXWORTH

I saw Fairport twice in Toronto. The first show was at the famed Massey Hall and while it was only half full it was a great show – especially the solo Sandy part of the programme. The highlight was the singing of 'Rising For The Moon'.

Six months later, at the smaller University of Toronto's Convocation Hall (27 October 1974), was very different. I was excited to see them again and bought tickets for my friends. The opening act was the very fine Stringband and they went over a storm with a great and engaged set. Then Fairport wandered on stage. Sandy's clothes had not arrived and their equipment had not arrived so they had to borrow some and it appeared that none of them were getting along. Sandy and Trevor were very cold to each other. They struggled to get the energy together and Swarb started dancing around like a demon fiddler only to be flattened by the head stock from Peggy's bass. Swarb wobbled and went down. It didn't get much better after that.

IRVINE AUDITORIUM
26 APRIL 1974, PHILADELPHIA, PENNSYLVANIA

SUSAN TOBIAS

I first heard Sandy Denny on my local 'underground' radio station (as they were called in Philadelphia, PA). It was 1970 and I was 16 years old. I don't recall the song, but it would have probably been on *Liege & Lief*. From the moment I heard that music and Sandy's voice, I became obsessed with British folk rock and Fairport. We all know how quickly those years flew by, and I followed Sandy all the way. I purchased an import copy of *Fotheringay* which was a big deal to find. I spent hours of every day listening to albums: *Sandy*, *The Northstar Grassman And The Ravens*, *Like An Old Fashioned Waltz*. I saw Sandy with Fairport at a large venue in Philadelphia early on. I was standing on the floor in front of the stage. A memory forever.

And one day I was in my car on Horsham Road, in a suburb of Philly, when I heard that she had died. It is truly possible to grieve forever for someone you never met.

Sandy has been a part of me and my life always. I named my cat Tamlin, although I'm not sure Sandy loved having to sing that song over and over when on tour.

I am now seventy. I have shared her with anyone who would listen and many of my friends have, but many times I had her all to myself.

I 'met' Georgia in 2013 on Facebook. Georgia has allowed me to be in her Sandy groups and I learn so much from her. What I have learnt from Georgia most is the enduring love she holds for her mother and father. The gift of love.

UCONN SPRING CARNIVAL
27 APRIL 1974, STORRS, CONNECTICUT

ALAN BERSHAW

It was a free afternoon concert that went down in the parking lot behind the ice hockey arena in Storrs as part of the UCONN Spring Carnival. Bruce Springsteen and the yet-to-be-named E-Street Band opened, followed by the funk band Fatback and then Aerosmith. The event was closed out with a set by headliners Fairport Convention featuring my favourite musician of all time, Sandy Denny. I was literally an hour away, but 15-year-old me was blissfully unaware, and as far as I know, it's the only time Sandy Denny ever performed in Connecticut. Bruce and the Fairports

Sandy at the UCONN Carnival Conneticut, April 1974 (Mike Rosenberg)

must have made a beeline out of there after their respective sets, as both played other shows later the same day, Bruce at the University of Hartford and Fairport at Clark University in Worcester, MA.

I was able to catch Sandy on that tour several weeks later (the one and only time I saw her live) when a friend called and offered me a place to crash and a ticket for the second of two nights at My Father's Place in Roslyn, Long Island. There I got to briefly meet Sandy and Trevor, who got a kick out of the fact that I had hitchhiked to the show. It was before I had a driver's license or car. When Trevor asked how old I was, I told them, despite being too young to be in a bar. Thankfully, nobody was checking IDs.

THE JOINT INN THE WOODS
4 MAY 1974, PARSIPPANY, NEW JERSEY

BOB KANOUSE

In the late 1960s, FM radio started to air more diverse musical groups and styles and not limiting themselves to Top 40 music. One station, WNEW-FM, had a show each Friday afternoon called the 'English Hour' which played more deep cuts from albums, many of which were not available in the US. One Friday afternoon sometime in late 1970 I experienced the most interesting sounds ('A holiday, a holiday, and the first one of the year…') and I could not wait to find out the name of this band and album. That Saturday I went to the record store to buy *Liege & Lief* but the only Fairport album that they had was *Full House*, so I bought that. It was a great album, but – hey – where was the female singer? Shortly afterwards, I was able to find the earlier Fairport albums and so began my lifelong love of English electric folk rock.

In the pre-Internet era, it was harder to track down information about music and bands, but we did have *Rolling Stone*, *Creem* and *Melody Maker* magazines. I would buy new Fairport albums as they became available, as well as solo albums from members of the band.

In 1974 I finally got to see the band live three times. Sandy had rejoined. The first concert was at the brilliantly-named The Joint Inn The Woods in Parsippany, New Jersey, about five miles from my house. I got there real early and was first in line. While waiting, I got to meet Dave Pegg and

Dave Mattacks, who were very friendly. I was able to position myself front row centre and I waited for the band to begin. The house lights went down and there in front of me stood Swarb, Trevor, the Daves (M and P) and Jerry! They started playing and out came Sandy, with beautiful blonde hair and a bemused smile. She started to sing: 'A holiday, A holiday, and the first one of the year…' and I was entranced. I was struck by the power of her voice and the playing of the band.

Sometime later that year the band was playing at the same venue. I was first in line again. Before the show we were informed that Sandy was sick and would not be performing with the band that night but that the rest of the group was still going on. We were offered refunds but I still wanted to see the show. They played a lot of different material to make up for the absence of Sandy.

Lastly, in October of 1974 I saw the band in Carnegie Hall in NYC. This was quite a step up from The Joint Inn The Woods! I had a seat in one of the boxes just to the side of the stage. The group's equipment was at the centre of a very large stage. The house lights went out and there were jack-o-lanterns lit as it was Hallowe'en. The band took the stage and opened with 'Rising For The Moon'. They were once again awesome and really on top form. This was the last time that I would see Sandy live.

Since then, I have probably seen Fairport Convention over forty times and always enjoy their shows. I often listen to Sandy's music as I enjoy her powerful voice and the way she paints musical pictures and evokes time and place. It fills me with joy when I am at a concert and get to talk with the people around me about the different concerts that we have attended over the years. If the talk turns to Fairport and Sandy, they really want to know about her, as if living vicariously through my experiences. We are fortunate to have her records to keep her music alive.

SANDERS THEATRE
10 MAY 1974, CAMBRIDGE, MASSACHUSETTS

ANDY NAGY

I was thirteen or fourteen when I fell in love with Sandy Denny. An older friend had recommended several records to me, one of them being *Unhalfbricking*. The first time I heard 'Genesis Hall' I was hooked. I can still remember finding that album and *Basket Of Light* by Pentangle, another my friend had recommended, and pulling those records out of the bin, ready to take them to the cashier.

A small group of friends and I became enormous fans. As young teenagers we talked about who we liked better, Sandy or Jacqui McShee, and told fanciful tales about Dave Swarbrick, the amazing fiddler who had won a competition by playing three fiddle tunes at once. In my young mind I never doubted Swarb being able to play three different tunes all at once. It wasn't until years later that I realised it meant a medley of three tunes, not three tunes played all at once!

Fairport with Sandy Denny, Sanders Theatre, May 1974 (Edward Haber)

I was excited when *Fairport Live Convention* appeared in my record shop. I couldn't believe how great Sandy sounded singing back with Fairport. 'Matty Groves' seemed to have gained even more depth and intensity. After school the next day, I tucked the record under my arm and walked the mile to my friend Erica's house. Once there, we played the whole album three times over.

Later that year Fairport and Sandy were playing at Sanders Theatre, a beautiful old concert hall on the campus of Harvard University. I went with my friend Aram. Aram's aunt had been married to Dave Van Ronk, and Aram had been given his old guitar. We used to jam on songs like 'John Barleycorn', 'Cold Haily Windy Night' 'Sea Of Joy', with me playing bass and flute.

Fairport were only a few songs into the set when Sandy left the stage. There was some shuffling around (and I forget if they had started to play anything) but shortly after one of them (Trevor?) announced that Sandy was ill and had gone to the hospital, but that they would continue without her. And continue they did. Their set was absolutely wonderful, and I remember being so incredibly impressed that they could do so well when so much of that night's concert would have been featuring Sandy and songs that she sang.

I was in such a high after the show as we walked back across the lawns to the bus station, but all my friend could say with a grimace was, 'They were so loud.' I got annoyed, and chose to not even talk about it and stay in my high.

FRED JEFFERY

I saw Fairport at the Boston Tea Party on the *Full House* tour opening for Traffic, who had just put out the *John Barleycorn* album. Fairport were great! I was a big fan from the *Unhalfbricking* album forward, and the song off *Full House*, 'Walk Awhile', was of many favourites they played that night. I saw them again at the Sanders Theatre in Cambridge, MA when Sandy Denny was back with the Trevor Lucas version of the band. They were very good, but a very different band than what I had seen at the Tea Party.

ACADEMY OF MUSIC
17 MAY 1974, NEW YORK, NEW YORK

ANNIE HASLAM, RENAISSANCE

Renaissance were booked to perform our very first concert with an orchestra in NYC with 'special guests' Fairport Convention featuring Sandy Denny!

As the sound checks were echoing through the building I walked out into the foyer for some quiet time. I can picture so clearly standing in the foyer of the Academy of Music, meeting and talking with Sandy for the very first time. A lovely gentle soul, yet strong, friendly and honest in her conversation, her calming speaking voice sounding like she was singing – a timeless ethereal 'voice' now eternally present in the universe and beyond.

She will always be the 'Queen of Folk Rock'. There are great folk singers all over the globe but none to touch Sandy's exquisite voice and her undeniable pristine yet sometimes dramatic quality in her songwriting. This meeting with Sandy and hearing and seeing her lift the spirits of the audience that night (from the side of the stage) was to be my only time with her. I wouldn't have missed that for the world.

Many years passed and on a cold winter's day in early 2018 I had been listening to Sandy as someone had mentioned her in conversation, so I played 'Who Knows Where the Time Goes?'. Then a couple of months after that, just before twilight, I went outside for some fresh air. Lo and behold, about 20 feet away from my front porch where there is the stump of a maple tree that has a small statue of an owl sitting on it, there was a red fox foraging for food.

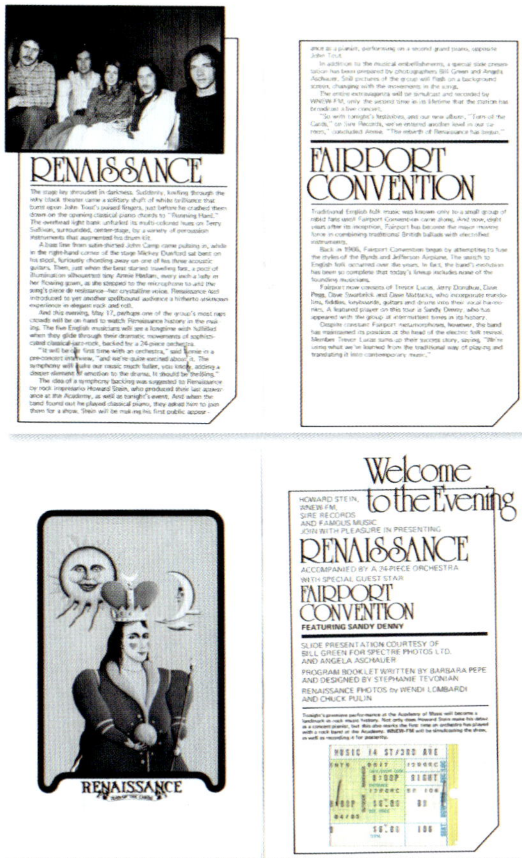

Renaissance & Fairport shared the bill in NYC (Edward Haber)

Not unusual, as I am in a rural area. But to the left of the fox was what looked like a 'spirit' floating about ten feet high, on this side of the road. It was vertical and almost see through. I ran indoors for my iPhone to take a photo but when I got outside it was dissipating. I did get an image and it looks like the head with a face in it… That's what I see anyway… a magical experience!

A couple of months later, I received an email from Ray Coles, manager and promoter of the The Strand Theatre in Lakewood, New Jersey and collaborator with Dave Cousins from The Strawbs. I called Ray and he said the Strawbs' fiftieth anniversary was coming up in 2019 and Dave Cousins wanted me to be part of the concerts (over two days). He wanted me to sing 'Who Knows Where the Time Goes?', with a 34-piece orchestra conducted by Tony Visconti. I was so elated, I couldn't believe that I would be singing my all-time favourite song of Sandy's. What an honour.

The Strawbs' fiftieth anniversary weekend in the spring of 2019 was a resounding success. Sandy most definitely was there!

When this all happened, I looked back at the day I saw the 'spirit' in my garden. After all, it appeared not too long after I was listening to Sandy singing 'Who Knows Where The Time Goes?' in my den. I also totally believe she was the 'spirit' in my garden and that she had a hand in what was to come.

Love and gratitude to you, Sandy. I will see you on the other side of morning.

Annie had a spiritual visitation

EDWARD HABER

In May of 1974 Sandy had rejoined Fairport, and I got to see them for the first time with the dynamic *Nine* lineup at the Sanders Theatre in Cambridge, Massachusetts. It was a fantastic show. The following week they were at the Academy of Music in New York opening for Renaissance, who were accompanied by a 24-piece orchestra. I might have been disappointed at the shorter set for Fairport, but having seen them do a full show the week before, myself and some friends from my college radio station, WBRS, were sitting in the second row of the orchestra and made sure that we acted as a cheering section for Sandy and Fairport.

In October of 1974 Fairport were back in the US and back at Sanders Theatre. Sandy was clearly ill, and it impacted her singing – apparent when she was singing quieter passages which seemed a struggle for her. But she pushed through the soft passages and still managed to sound great on louder passages. My memory is that she did her best for about two-thirds of the show and then left the stage.

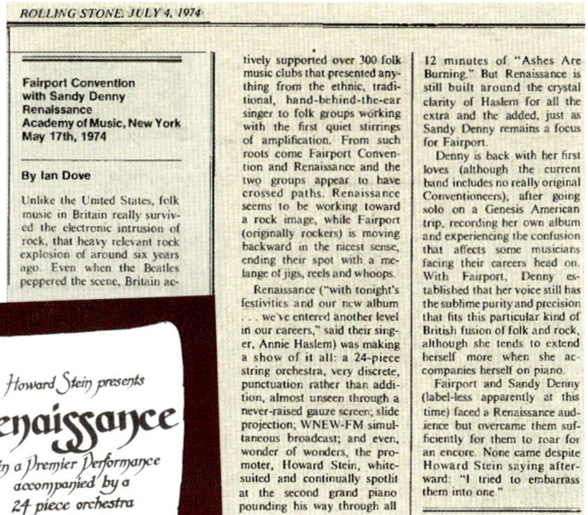

ROLLING STONE, JULY 4, 1974

Fairport Convention with Sandy Denny
Renaissance
Academy of Music, New York
May 17th, 1974

By Ian Dove

Unlike the United States, folk music in Britain really survived the electronic intrusion of rock, that heavy relevant rock explosion of around six years ago. Even when the Beatles peppered the scene, Britain actively supported over 300 folk music clubs that presented anything from the ethnic, traditional, hand-behind-the-ear singer to folk groups working with the first quiet stirrings of amplification. From such roots come Fairport Convention and Renaissance and the two groups appear to have crossed paths. Renaissance seems to be working toward a rock image, while Fairport (originally rockers) is moving backward in the nicest sense, ending their spot with a melange of jigs, reels and whoops.

Renaissance ("with tonight's festivities and our new album . . . we've entered another level in our careers," said their singer, Annie Haslem) was making a show of it all: a 24-piece string orchestra, very discrete, punctuation rather than addition, almost unseen through a never-raised gauze screen; slide projection; WNEW-FM simultaneous broadcast; and even, wonder of wonders, the promoter, Howard Stein, white-suited and continually spotlit at the second grand piano pounding his way through all 12 minutes of "Ashes Are Burning." But Renaissance is still built around the crystal clarity of Haslem for all the extra and the added, just as Sandy Denny remains a focus for Fairport.

Denny is back with her first loves (although the current band includes no really original Conventioneers), after going solo on a Genesis American trip, recording her own album and experiencing the confusion that affects some musicians facing their careers head on. With Fairport, Denny established that her voice still has the sublime purity and precision that fits this particular kind of British fusion of folk and rock, although she tends to extend herself more when she accompanies herself on piano.

Fairport and Sandy Denny (label-less apparently at this time) faced a Renaissance audience but overcame them sufficiently for them to roar for an encore. None came despite Howard Stein saying afterward: "I tried to embarrass them into one."

Above: Rolling Stone's review of the NYC show

Left: Renaissance & Fairport at NY's Academy of Music (Edward Haber)

The rest of the band continued as a five-piece, so we got to hear some of the Fairport *Nine* (and maybe *Fotheringay*) songs that might not have typically been done on that tour, after which Trevor Lucas said that Sandy had gone to the hospital and he was leaving to follow, and a four-piece Fairport concluded the show with a brace of reels. Sandy was a true road warrior that night, and a complete professional, a trouper giving her best to the audience for as long as she could.

I last saw Sandy on her last US tour with Fairport, supporting *Rising For The Moon*, at the Harvard Square Theatre in Cambridge, Massachusetts, with Jean-Luc Ponty as the opening act. The acoustics were somewhat brittle compared to the much warmer sound at Sanders Theatre, but Fairport and Sandy were in great form, with some wonderful songs by Sandy from the new record. They even unexpectedly did 'Tam Lin'.

While I never did have an opportunity to meet Sandy, it was a privilege to hear her so many times on all those US tours.

KEN ROSEMAN, JOURNALIST

I met Sandy Denny twice – after concerts in Cambridge, Massachusetts and Washington, DC. I was just starting out as a music journalist and Sandy was gracious and kind to me. I will never forget her.

LISNER AUDITORIUM
18 MAY 1974, WASHINGTON DC

DENNIS HOESCHLER

A friend turned me onto *Unhalfbricking* in 1969. It changed the musical course of my life, and by 1970 Fairport had become a favourite. I was frustrated as I had missed the infrequent shows Fairport or any associated acts had made to the Virginia / Washington DC area, except that Richard Thompson and Iain Matthews in 1971 played a show billed as Plainsong. I so wanted to see Fotheringay.

Spring 1974 came around with word that Fairport with Sandy Denny were finally going to play in Washington DC at the Lisner Auditorium, which was associated with George Washington University. I had friends who worked there.

Fairport played their first set and were ending with two lengthy instrumentals. Sandy had left the stage and I could see her moving to the music, just off the stage. I went to see if I could get backstage and it was no problem. I was nervous but went over and introduced myself. She was so gracious and friendly that I was immediately put at ease. She even offered me a beer and we talked for about five minutes.

After talking to me, she went back out on stage and played (beautifully) 'Like An Old Fashioned Waltz' (a favourite of mine) and 'Rising For The Moon'.

Dennis Hoeschler saw 'The Fairport Convention with Sandy Denny'

The band took a break and, not wanting to intrude, I excused myself but not before asking her if she wanted a joint. She smiled and said 'thank you' and gave me a hug. I was so excited meeting Sandy, who meant so much to me – and still does. This was one of the high points of my life and I still can't believe that I had the good fortune to meet her.

I have heard many other great artists but none as memorable as Sandy was to me and so many others. My ticket cost $5.50 for Fairport with Sandy Denny. What a great time to be alive and grooving to the music!

DENYSE ANGER

The last time I saw Sandy and Trevor was in May 1974 at the Lisner Auditorium during Fairport's US tour that year. Sandy recognised me immediately, calling to me when they arrived, although we hadn't seen one another since June 1972. Visiting with her backstage after the show, she wrote her address and made a quick sketch of their beloved Airedale, Watson, on a scrap of paper before we said goodbye. 'Isn't she beautiful?' Sandy said to Trevor. 'She looks sunny and healthy,' said Trevor. In my optimistic state of mind, I felt that seeing her again in her Northamptonshire abode was a real possibility.

LIKE AN OLD FASHIONED WALTZ RELEASED JUNE 1974

NEVILLE FICKLING

In 1971 I left my home town of King's Lynn for Brighton to do an HND in Applied Biology. Students lent LPs to each other and that is how I got to hear of Fairport. *Unhalfbricking* was the album I borrowed first, then *Liege & Lief*. I didn't notice Sandy much other than her remarkable voice. Fairport vocals were shared between other members of the band, in particular Dave Swarbrick. I became a Fairport fan rather than a Sandy fan. Sandy left and I ended up seeing Fairport around the time of their *Nine* album.

Old Fashioned Waltz promotional photo

Then I went back to Lynn. I borrowed a tape from the library, *Like An Old Fashioned Waltz*. I nearly wore the tape out. Over the years, I obtained all her other LPs and enjoyed them all, including *Fotheringay*. I always think of Sandy when I pass near the village of Fotheringhay. I never got the chance to see Sandy before she died. Later, living in Leicester, the girl sharing the house with my wife-to-be had a friend who was the girlfriend or partner of Trevor Lucas. That is my sole claim to fame.

I still listen to Sandy's music. My favourites are 'I Am A Dreamer', 'Solo' and 'Rising For The Moon'. No-one has ever duplicated her voice. 'Who Knows Where the Time Goes?' is one of my funeral service songs.

'SOLO'

FABIO ROSSI, WRITER

I recall a day shrouded in sadness, when I sought solace by placing a record upon my turntable. I knew nothing of the artist; the album was a gift of a moment, lent to me by a classmate during our high school years. It was *Like An Old Fashioned Waltz*. As the haunting, poignant notes of 'Solo' began to drift, Sandy's angelic voice cast a spell, enveloping my very soul. I found myself breathless, transfixed by such ethereal beauty. From that day forward, I gathered every fragment of her music, and when my path led me to become a writer, I dedicated a book to her in Italian an endeavour that received the profound honour of being cherished by her daughter, Georgia. I love you, Sandy; you shall remain, forevermore, the voice closest to my heart.

KATHRYN ROBERTS, MUSICIAN

Growing up in a folk household I had been introduced to Sandy's singing through Fairport Convention and, as I recognised her name, I bought myself a copy of the CD *The Best of Sandy Denny* around the age of 14. My entire approach to music changed. Suddenly unaccompanied folk song wasn't enough for me. I wanted to do more!

Having only played woodwind up to that point I was inspired to take up the piano as an accompanying instrument. I learned every Sandy song I could get my hands on but the one that spoke to me most of all was the song 'Solo' – the perfect combination of lyric, melody and piano lines. I was hooked.

It was a song that stayed with me through the decades of being a professional musician, performing it on a regular basis with my husband, Sean Lakeman.

Then in 2015, when asked by Jerry Donahue to join the reformed Fotheringay, I had the opportunity to sing all those wonderful songs with Sandy's friends and bandmates. The thrill and honour of performing all those pieces which were such a huge formative part of my development as a musician was enormous for me. Every night, singing 'Solo', glancing over at Pat Donaldson, Gerry Conway and Jerry Donahue, gave me such an emotional chill, hoping I could do the song and Sandy proud.

Her legacy as a songwriter can never be appreciated enough. I still find now, after years of listening, that I can get something new from her music; the subtlety and nuance, the layers of emotion. Sandy's music will continue to be an inspiration to me and many others for years to come.

PETER ROE

I first heard Sandy's music when I bought the double album *The History Of Fairport Convention* in 1972. From first hearing her voice I knew she was special. She didn't just sing a song – she inhabited it, drawing you in to the world of that song. You were there in that castle with Mary the day before her execution. You were there with that couple facing the separation of war. Sadly, I never met her or got to see her perform live either solo or with Fairport, so the very limited video material available is really treasured.

One way she directly affected me though was as follows: I had always enjoyed painting and drawing since I was a child and would have liked to have pursued this as a career. For various reasons this was not possible and, by my mid-twenties, I had set art aside as not having much point.

I bought the *Like An Old Fashioned Waltz* album when it was released and when I listened to the song 'No End', I heard the verse that started with, 'Why don't you have no brushes any more, I used to like your style?', it made a connection. I knew she was not singing about me personally but it made me think – and I got those brushes out again and restarted my hobby and have continued with it to this day.

BOROUGH HALL
21 JUNE 1974, GREENWICH, LONDON, UK

DAVE CHICK

I was very fortunate to see Sandy solo a couple of times, and also twice with Fairport after she rejoined. In June 1974 I was in Borough Hall at Greenwich. Amongst the audience was a couple with a very young child. The person in the next seat to mine mentioned that they were local councillors. Sandy started to sing: 'Good morning, good afternoon, and what have you got to say?' With absolutely perfect timing, the baby let out a loud cry!

Fairport Live Convention was released in July 1974

CARNEGIE HALL
25 OCTOBER 1974, NEW YORK, NEW YORK

THOM LUKAS

It was a Friday night at Carnegie Hall. I was 22 when I took these photos and super lucky to have gotten tickets. It was the second time I'd seen Fairport. (Sandy had just left when I saw them for the first time in 1970

at the Fillmore East opening for Traffic.) Finally, I was able to hear her gorgeous ethereal voice live onstage performing the songs from *Liege & Lief* and *Full House* that I'd listened to dozens of times on my headphones. However, the majority of material performed that evening was new to me. I feel privileged to have been part of that exclusive audience.

Above & bottom left opposite: Fairport in action at New York's Carnegie Hall (Thom Lukas)

CONVOCATION HALL
27 OCTOBER 1974, TORONTO, CANADA

GREG TORRINGTON

I became a Fairport devotee back in my high school days in Ottawa, Canada when *Liege & Lief* was released. It was a music epiphany for me that has lasted to this day. I never got to experience that album's band configuration live; they never toured Canada in that era. I was saddened when Sandy left the band after that album but I followed them – and Sandy's solo career - religiously. I did get to see the *Rising for The Moon* tour in Toronto, which line up included Sandy's husband, Trevor Lucas. Myself and five other Ottawa Fairport devotees crammed into a van to make the five-hour drive specifically for the concert.

The opening act was Canadian folk trio, Stringband, whose violin player was Ben Mink who later became the songwriting partner of kd lang. Sadly, Sandy was enduring a bout of laryngitis that night and could barely speak. But she still managed to sing beautifully!

BERKELEY COMMUNITY THEATRE
10 NOVEMBER 1974, BERKELEY, CALIFORNIA

DAVID MILLER

I was thrilled to learn that Sandy was reuniting with members of Fotheringay and Fairport. The Berkeley Community Theatre is a great place. I once read that it was Bill Graham's favorite theatre. Large enough, but not too large to enjoy an act from any seat. We were lucky to get front row seats for Fairport Convention.

I remember how polished the band was. They didn't look like the scruffy hippies from the early days. Dave Swarbrick put on a powerful performance. He seemed to be the leader of the band. Trevor Lucas took front stage for his vocals. Jerry Donahue played rock riffs on his electric guitar, while Trevor Lucas filled in with acoustic guitar.

Sandy Denny played piano and added vocals. She was to my left, but I could not see her at all behind her piano. I was disappointed and worried that I might never get a chance to see her properly. Toward the end of the concert, she came out from behind the piano and took front stage with a tambourine. I took photos of her until I ran out of film. In one shot she is looking at me and smiling. In another shot she and her husband, Trevor Lucas, are looking into each other's eyes. The look on her face is very poignant. She sang 'Who Knows Where the Time Goes?' The beauty of that song, with her voice and the mournful look on her face, was breathtaking. I think they ended with a rousing version of 'Matty Groves'.

After the concert we walked behind the auditorium. We saw the band's truck being backed up to load their equipment. To my amazement, Sandy Denny was standing there, giving instructions to the driver. She was calling out to the driver and laughing, with some comment like, 'Where did you learn to drive a truck?' I was standing right next to her as she chided the truck driver, and she patted me on the stomach with the back of her hand, as if to say, 'Watch me give this guy a hard time!' I remember looking down at my stomach and thinking, 'Wow! Sandy Denny is hitting me on the stomach!' She signed my paper pad, but never took her eyes off the truck backing up, so her signature is almost illegible. Dave Mattacks and Dave Swarbrick (with cigarette hanging from his lips) also signed for me. It was a great concert, and all the more memorable due to the wonderful Sandy Denny.

ABERYSTWYTH UNIVERSITY
17 NOVEMBER 1974, ABERYSTWYTH, UK

ROBIN WHITTAKER

I only saw Sandy perform live once but it remains a very special memory to me. She had rejoined Fairport and the tour took them to Aberystwyth where I was studying at the time for my archive qualification. The music was superb but what stands out in my memory over 50 years later is her standing mid-stage and holding the whole audience in the palm of her hand – the still centre of all that was going on. Her charisma endures over the years in between.

UNIVERSITY OF SALFORD
22 NOVEMBER 1974, SALFORD, UK

JOHN BARLASS

I bought my first Fairport album, *Live Convention*, in August 1974 and just a couple of months later I attended my first Fairport gig. The band's lineup that evening was the same one featured on the *Live Convention* album – Sandy, Trevor, Peggy, Swarb, Jerry D and DM. The vast Maxwell Hall at the university was packed; this was Fairport's first UK tour with Sandy back in the ranks and she was a big star. But this evening things went a bit off course…

Some bonehead in the audience thought it would be a jolly jape to throw a plastic beer glass at the stage, just as the band were making their entry, and the glass hit Sandy on her head. Trevor Lucas, her husband, was furious and threatened to deck the culprit, a sentiment that was clearly understandable, although still rather shocking to my gentle, non-violent, teenage self. There's no doubt that this incident cast a shadow over the rest of the evening's events, and there were a few further disappointments to come.

I, and – I suspect – many others in that packed hall had been drawn to Fairport by their good-time, fast-paced approach to their music, but here was a new Fairport on show. The set list was dominated by Sandy's solo material and by songs more associated with Fotheringay than with Fairport. That's all material that I love dearly and deeply now but, in November 1974 it was all totally new to me. There was some familiar

Fairport in action in Berkeley, California, November 1974 (David Miller)

stuff in the set – 'The Hexamshire Lass', 'The Hen's March', 'Who Knows Where the Time Goes?' and 'Matty' – but all in all, I was a bit underwhelmed.

UNIVERSITY OF LEEDS
23 NOVEMBER 1974, LEEDS, UK

DAVID POLLARD

Leeds University was the first and alas the only time I heard Sandy sing live. (Although I saw her walking with Trevor at the Cambridge Folk Festival a couple of years after.) Some fifty years later I can remember standing in the refectory but not what was played. I think Sandy was wearing a white dress but that's possibly my imagination linked to the song.

How did I come to listen to Sandy? I'd heard Richard and Linda's 'I Want To See The Bright Lights Tonight' being played at a concert as music over the PA and asked what it was and bought it. I worked back from that to Fairport Convention and started collecting their albums, as well as solo albums by ex-members (though Sandy had of course rejoined by then). This became an expensive hobby.

David Pollard was in Byfield when the blue plaque to Sandy was unveiled

Sandy had such a beautiful voice and was a wonderful songwriter. I was very upset when she died and a few tears were shed when the piper played 'Flowers Of The Forest' one year at Cropredy, a tune which had been played at Sandy's funeral.

For BBC Music Day in 2017, a plaque was unveiled on the outside of Byfield Village Hall to mark the spot where Sandy played her last gig. I was interviewed live by Radio 6 Music because I'd driven down from Yorkshire just for the day.

MARTIN ASHE

Martin Ashe was captivated by 'Who Knows Where The Time Goes?

I first heard Sandy when I bought Fairport's *Unhalfbricking* and was captivated by 'Who Knows Where the Time Goes?'. I even bought the budget-priced Sandy Denny and The Strawbs LP, *All Our Own Work*, to get another version of that song. But it was the 1971 Island sampler *El Pea* that introduced me to 'Late November' and the magic of Sandy's solo music.

At university I worked on the Student Union stage crew. That generally involved giving up your Saturday afternoon to help the band's roadies unload the trucks and haul equipment onto the stage. After the concert, we'd help the crew reload the trucks. A side benefit was that we might get to meet the performers. On one occasion I was able to meet Sandy Denny.

I had seen Sandy perform solo at the university the previous year – an outstanding show – but on this night she was performing as a member of Fairport Convention, the 'classic' line up that was in the process of recording *Rising For The Moon*. After the concert, while carting equipment off the stage, I noticed Sandy alone at the rear of the stage, resting against some scaffolding and drinking Liebfraumilch from a paper cup. I introduced myself and told her how much her music had influenced me. Without a word she picked up the bottle of wine, filled another paper cup & offered it to me. We drank quietly and chatted about the evening's performance. I asked her to sign the stage crew badge on my t-shirt. She was concerned that her signature would wash off. I assured her that it wouldn't. I still have it today.

It is over 50 years since that encounter. I remember it like yesterday. Few people leave such lasting impressions.

UNIVERSITY OF NOTTINGHAM
27 NOVEMBER 1974, NOTTINGHAM, UK

GRAHAME BAUMBER

I first saw Fairport at the time of the *Rosie* album. Dave Swarbrick had his leg in a cast and was singing harmonies and smoking simultaneously. When DM walked up to his drum kit, he paused at a microphone and said, 'Guess the line up and win a prize!' They were back in Nottingham a couple of years later. Sandy was back with them and not in the best of moods. She stomped on to the stage saying 'let's get this song over with' as the band launched into 'Matty Groves'. I have not seen them open a set with this since…

FAIRFIELD HALLS
8 DECEMBER 1974, CROYDON, UK

STEVE GERCKE

I first heard Sandy's voice when my brother bought the first Fairport Convention album she sang on. I would also hear her on John Peel's Sunday afternoon programme on Radio 1. I was bowled over by her delivery and songwriting. I followed her career through Fotheringay and her solo albums, but only got to see her once, at the Fairfield Halls in Croydon, when she joined Fairport Convention on stage for a couple of numbers at the end of their concert. This was just prior to her rejoining Fairport.

Many years later, my wife and I brought a new canal boat and called it Who Knows Where The Time Goes.

KONINKLIJK THEATER CARRÉ
JANUARY 1975, AMSTERDAM, NETHERLANDS

TON SCHURINGA

It was January 1975 and they played in Carré, a theatre with almost 2,000 seats. At the start of the concert, we were informed of some changes in the line-up. They had a temporary drummer (Paul Warren) and the female singer of some years ago had returned to the fold. This was the first time I ever heard Sandy's voice.

It was an unforgettable experience. When she was not singing (which was about half the time, as I remember it) she was sitting on a chair at the side of the stage, knitting. And when it was her turn, she stood up, opened her mouth and filled the entire theatre, seemingly effortless like she was having a conversation. The band was great. I remember Swarb being totally unable to stop making music; when he had no part, he grabbed a tambourine from an amplifier and just kept on going. But when Sandy sung, nothing else mattered.

CHATEAU NEUF
5 FEBRUARY 1975, OSLO, NORWAY

JACOB ERSTAD

The first time I ever heard Sandy was in 1971, when I bought *Led Zeppelin IV*. I fell in love with her voice at once. And I still love her. 'The Battle Of Evermore' included the two best voices ever in rock music. Of that there can be no doubt.

Fairport Convention played in Oslo twice in six months. The first time, in the summer of 1974, they appeared at the Isle of Calf Festival on a small island near Oslo called Kalvøya. I was there with my fiancée, some friends and a cousin of mine. There was no Sandy. In February 1975 they showed up at Chateau Neuf. Tickets were sold out. The concert itself was only okay – the sound was too loud – but Sandy was still the queen.

When I'm out on my daily walks in the forest around Oslo, I always bring Sandy with me and never a day goes by without 'Who Knows Where

Fairport in Oslo (Jacob Erstad)

The Time Goes?'. I have told my oldest granddaughter that this song, Zep's 'Ramble On' and maybe a Neil Young song are the only songs to be played at my funeral.

HORDERN PAVILION
9 APRIL 1975, SYDNEY, AUSTRALIA

THERESE DILLON

For Therese Dillon, pictured here with her brother David, Sandy will be 'forever young'

I was at school in Dublin in the seventies and our favourite place was The Gods (St John of God) where the best rock bands played. My favourite band was The Reform, a brilliant band from Limerick who always finished the night with an absolute cracker of a number which wasn't exactly their genre. One night I got the courage to go and ask what the song was. The band were a lovely bunch of guys and they told me the song was 'Matty Groves' and they filled me in on Sandy Denny and Fairport Convention. That was the beginning of my lifelong journey.

I left school in 1972 and in 1974 moved to Sydney, Australia where I found the best folk record shop in Paddington called Folkways. They had everything Sandy. In April 1975, Sandy and Fairport played at the Hordern Pavilion. I couldn't believe I was there but sadly I had no camera to take photos.

John Penhalllow with Fairport Convention c1975

In the seventies in

Sydney, a group of us regularly had great music sessions, with lots of great singers and musicians. One of the best was my friend's sister-in-law, Shaylee Wild, who ended up playing at the Mercantile Hotel for over 30 years. Back then you might have thought it was Sandy singing!

We found out about Sandy's passing when my brother Ben emigrated to Australia and read about it in *Time* magazine on the plane over. My husband Alan practically lived in Folkways and was always on the lookout for anything Sandy / Fairport. He had to check for himself as he couldn't believe it was true. None of us wanted it to be true. We were all fans and we were all devastated.

Our sessions faded as we got older, but Sandy would be forever young and always in our hearts.

MAYNE HALL, UNIVERSITY OF QUEENSLAND
11 APRIL 1975, BRISBANE, AUSTRALIA

IAN DEARDEN

I saw Fairport, with Sandy and Trevor, at the University of Queensland. It was an extraordinary concert and I got to dance on stage with Sandy. There was no security in those days!

Fairport promotional photo, 1975

RISING FOR THE MOON
RELEASED JUNE 1975

NIGEL SCHOFIELD

Rising For The Moon was dominated by Sandy. She wrote seven of its eleven songs and sang lead vocals on eight. There were no traditional songs. There were no instrumental tracks (which Fairport had made a *de rigeur* element of anything wishing to call itself a folk rock album). It was produced by Glyn Johns who aimed for a smoother radio-friendly sound. For Sandy, it was another attempt to achieve the commercial success that reflected the esteem in which she was held. Fairport fans were disappointed that it didn't sound like a Fairport album. Colin Irwin gave the album such a slating (among other things describing it as a Sandy Denny album with Fairport backing her) that she stormed out ahead of a scheduled interview when she read it.

Rising For The Moon's cover was illustrated by Marion Appleton, Trevor Lucas's sister

18 months later, she told me, 'Just because it was different doesn't mean it's not a Fairport album. Personally, I think it's a great Fairport album, one of their best. For me, it was a personal album because my songs dealt honestly with a lot of things I was going through at the time. Did it matter that there were no flash instrumentals, no epic ancient ballads, no fake folk songs? Condemning the LP for that is like those people who have a go at Dylan because he's not writing 'Blowing In The Wind' anymore!'

KEITH FUDGE

As a teen in the mid-1970s, I was working at a local radio station in a small town in Arkansas. For the most part, it was uninspiring work, monitoring broadcasts of live sporting events, and enduring a format of country and western music on the AM side, and easy listening (instrumentals) on the FM dial. In other words, this was not the Top 40 music or underground album-oriented rock that dominated my portable transistor or car radio.

One weekend at work, I noticed a storage room door was open, and peeking in saw rows upon rows of albums, new and unopened. Upon further inspection, I noticed that the records were copies of demo albums from record companies that were sent to hundreds of small stations like this one, all across the country. What I found that day opened a door to music that would stay with me for a lifetime.

On my next shift, I asked the owner about the albums in the storage room. He replied something to the effect, 'We don't play that stuff. You can have what you want.' Making that offer to a 16-year-old was like giving me my own private record store, and for the next few weekends I went to work early to begin my search inside a musical goldmine. And it was in those stacks that I first discovered the music of Fairport Convention and Sandy Denny.

As I flipped through the rows and shelves of albums on those cool fall afternoons, one of the first albums that caught my attention was Sandy's latest release with Fairport Convention, *Rising For The Moon.* The artwork on the cover immediately captivated me, and from there it only got better after listening to the record. Even today, when the cool winds of autumn begin and the leaves change their hues to reds and golds, *Rising For The Moon* always finds its way to my turntable, or to my playlist. Another find that weekend was the self-entitled *Sandy*, and from the moment I first heard 'The Quiet Joys Of Brotherhood' and 'It'll Take A Long Time', I knew that this voice, and these songs, would always be with me.

In my early days of learning about Sandy and the band, I rarely shared the music with anyone. I had found Sandy and this music on my own, and these songs were mine alone. In the privacy of my room, or in my car, I would listen to 'Matty Groves' 'Farewell, Farewell', 'White Dress', 'One More Chance', 'Autopsy' and others, with a focus that I did not devote to the other music of my era. Sandy's voice and the emotions found within those songs cultivated something in me difficult to understand then, and still hard to convey today. They stirred complex emotions deep within me.

I graduated from high school and went to college. Life became busy with new friends and diverse interests, and without realising it, many of my past priorities, including my previous tastes in music, faded away. But, while those songs were gone, they were not completely forgotten.

I rediscovered Sandy's music approximately 15 years ago while teaching an upper-level class on The Beatles at a local university. While the students were thrilled enough to be in such a class, one day they asked who were some other iconic artists from the UK during the late sixties, and without hesitation I said, 'Sandy Denny.'

A hush fell across the room. No one knew of her, nor had they ever heard her voice. Immediately, I began to play her songs for the remainder of the class time. After the first few moments, I looked at the class. Students were spellbound. One student said something to the effect of, 'Her voice…' but that was all she could manage. I recognised right away that Sandy's magic had touched them as well, all these years later.

It was during these times, talking with students, that I finally realised just how personal Sandy's music was to me, and how it had always been with me, even when I wasn't hearing it. I have always avoided saying that a particular work or artist is timeless, but Sandy is different. She was more than just a singer with a special voice, singing what might become a favourite song. It is the essence of her work, her craft and her life that resonates and transcends generations. Now, being able to come full circle with her and feeling compelled to share her remarkable gift with others who don't know her, gives her another meaning in my life. While writing this piece, I realised that it has been more than fifty years since I first heard her the day that I walked into that storage room and took those records home. Who knows where the time goes?

'WHITE DRESS'

MARTIN CUNNING

The *Rising For The Moon* album holds fond memories for my wife Anne and me. Not long after buying the LP, Anne picked 'White Dress' as one she really liked. (It's Sandy on vocals.) I had the pleasure of meeting Dave Swarbrick and telling him this. He was so kind as to sign the album sleeve, 'Dave Swarbrick, the bloke who wrote 'White Dress'.'

ROYAL ALBERT HALL
10 JUNE 1975, KENSINGTON, LONDON, UK

DAVE CHICK

The last time that I saw Sandy was the Fairport gig at the Royal Albert Hall in June1975. I remember Sandy standing alone on stage for 'The

Quiet Joys Of Brotherhood'. She sang beautifully but was visibly, and not surprisingly, very nervous. It felt like everybody in the Albert Hall was holding their breath and willing her on. As the song finished the tension was broken by Swarb walking on to play the coda.

TIM EDMONDS

It is one of my lifetime regrets that I did not witness Sandy Denny performing live more than a handful of times, all of them with Fairport Convention during her two spells with the band. The first was at the Corn Exchange in Cambridge, when the support band was Eclection, of which Trevor Lucas was a member. The others were in 1974-75, and perhaps the most memorable was at the Royal Albert Hall in June 1975, when the set included a haunting performance of 'Quiet Joys Of Brotherhood' and several other Sandy gems from her solo albums, such as 'Listen, Listen' and 'It'll Take a Long Time'. There was also what I think was a first outing for 'No More Sad Refrains'.

NEIL STOREY, ISLAND RECORDS

I first heard Sandy when I was sixteen. It was when I bought *What We Did On Our Holidays* just before Christmas 1968. It'd only been out a few days and, with pocket money burning a hole in my trousers, on the first day of the Christmas holidays I high-tailed it to Reading (my mother was going shopping there anyway) and made my way to Hickies on Friar Street. It was, even then, a very old-fashioned shop – more pre- than post-war, with an overriding smell of floor polish and with sales assistants dressed just so with shoes polished to a fine sheen. Maybe one or two wore a button-hole; it was that kind of a shop.

The ground floor housed a large array of pianos, from Steinway concert- and Bechstein baby-grands to pub-style uprights; those lesser instruments were always stored to the side. There were a few home-organs (very popular at the time), a handful of gut-strung Spanish and acoustic guitars alongside the obligatory recorders and other instruments on which young children were schooled in at the time. The first floor via a wide staircase was my destination – it housed their admirably well-stocked record department and, had I been a betting teenager, I reckoned it'd be as near odds on as made no difference they'd have the

Fairport's new album in stock. They did.

To be honest, I knew precious little about the group. I'd read bits and pieces in my weekly musical bible of the time, *Melody Maker*. And I was intrigued by the *MM* advert for the album, a strange, almost fairytale-like pen and ink drawing by someone I'd never heard of. It was though on Island and there were no other Island releases that week. Even at this young age, I'd started collecting Island albums. Therefore, despite the fact I'd never heard a note of music, this would be my purchase. I remember pulling it out of the rack and reckoning the sleeve looked pretty cool, as if someone had assaulted a blackboard. That appealed to me almost as much as the back cover picture, which showed a dog asleep on a stage as the band played; this band must sound as good as they look. Only one way to find out.

Cash handed over and, by mid-afternoon, I'm curled up beside the family Dansette (red, in case you were wondering) and listening to the first Island pink-label Fairport Convention album in mono.

The first three minutes of the album bewitch. For my teenage self it is a complete double-whammy. Sandy's voice and the subject matter of her song, 'Fotheringay', as it drifts into silence I reach across and replace the needle, this has to be heard again. And again. It takes a good hour before I get anywhere near side two. The voice is like nothing I've heard in my life before. Yes, haunting but there's something else – a poignant beauty in the storytelling. I imagine it as a calming voice when you're lying in a hospital bed, the voice which soothes, the one which makes the hurting go away. (Little did I know). And, albeit misspelled, there's no doubt in my mind this opening song has to revolve around the last hours of the Queen of Scots as Mary prepares for her execution. Wrestling with as terrifying a thought as that can't have been much helped by it being the bleak cold of a February 1587 morning in a damp, dank castle. The river Nene flows just below the castle and, at that time of year, the post-dawn mist coming off the river would have completely enshrouded Fotheringhay, set deep in the north Northamptonshire countryside as it is. I shudder.

Decades later, I'm living a few miles south of Fotheringhay; it is a simple afternoon drive past Oundle before taking the Peterborough road to Warmington and then a left by an old, broken down and long-abandoned diner before traversing a narrow mud-splattered lane and then taking a right turn which will lead over the small hump-back bridge into the village itself.

Having been besotted by the life of Mary and her death at Fotheringhay, I've built this moment up in my mind to such a degree since first reading about her as a pre-teen at school that it is inevitable I'll be disappointed. I am. The castle is no more than a mound of stones. As if stuck in time, the river flows slowly by while the village itself is no more than a single street flanked by (mainly) very lovely, genteel homes.

The soundtrack however is exactly right; Sandy's voice and those plaintive words which open the final verse… 'Tomorrow at this hour she will be far away…'. It, too, is on repeat in my head as I walk to where the old great hall once stood before the castle fell into disrepair, only to be pulled down, its stone to be used in the village houses I've just driven past.

Over the following few years, travelling to Fotheringhay became a little bit of a pilgrimage. Always accompanied by Sandy's voice, always that song. By now, of course, I knew that Sandy had lived in Byfield but that was the other side of Northamptonshire, a good hour plus away. Had she, I mused, ever visited? To walk that pile of stones, to reflect on a captive queen and, perhaps, feel the things I felt? Did she, way back when, go to Fotheringhay, and was that where that magical song was conjured up?

I first saw Sandy at… now, here is a confession. I simply cannot remember. But I was there on 10 June 1975. A Tuesday. Venue – the Royal Albert Hall. The London stop on the *Rising For The Moon* tour. Centre stalls. Took my dad. They opened with 'Walk Awhile', 'Sloth', 'Tam Lin' but inexplicably not 'Matty Groves' before some of the real Sandy set-pieces – 'It'll Take A Long Time' (missing Sneaky Pete), before we headed into the end game: 'Listen, Listen', Quiet Joys…', an absolutely staggering version of 'John The Gun' before 'One More Chance', the song I'd been waiting all evening for. The piano intro… the pleading 'Is it too late…', then the near four-minute piano-underpinned instrumental coda – Donahue's clipped Telecaster solo, Swarbrick hovering in the wings before his violin cuts in, Mattacks precision drumming with its extraordinary choked cymbals, and Sandy's voice soaring.

The roar of approval and the standing ovation as the song climaxed was something else entirely. I'm not ashamed to say I was in tears. Sandy may not have hit every single note as cleanly as when it was recorded at Olympic but that was of no matter – the sheer emotion within her voice carried the whole. It was a real privilege to have witnessed that.

I met Sandy at a party in North London. It was after a gig I'd been to at the Rainbow. I'd been bidden to an address just off the North Circular, somewhere in Southgate.

Park up, its dark and leafy and rainy – odd how details like that stick. I can hear rather than see there's a party going on not far away; bass-heavy dub splits the nearby air. Stride manfully up to the front door and press the buzzer. Within a few moments the silhouette framed in the glow behind the door turns the handle. The door swings inwards. Standing there, cigarette in one hand, glass of wine in the other, is Sandy. She looks me up and down rather sternly.

Clearly, she hasn't a clue who I am. 'OK, and who might you be?' I got that one right, it's not so much a question as a statement. We stare at one another. She cuts quite a dramatic figure, a floor-length figure-hugging Edwardian-style dress, auburn hair pulled back. She's smaller than in any publicity picture but far, far prettier.

I explain this is my boss's house and I'm invited. A raised eyebrow. She suggests I'd better come in. The house is absolutely jam packed. I see an elphin-like Swarbrick holding court in one corner. Pegg smiles a greeting – he and I have recently spent time together shooting the breeze until all hours at a Shepherd's Bush hotel. People are generally milling about. The din of the music coming from the sitting room precludes any small talk until Sandy grabs me by the wrist and steers me deftly into the kitchen, 'Come and have a drink and tell me what you do at Island?'

THE PEACOCK PUBLIC HOUSE
SUMMER 1975, NORTHAMPTON, UK

CHRIS COLES

I knew Sandy on a personal level during the last few years of her life after her relocation to Byfield. I first met her one lunchtime in the summer of 1975 in a new underground pub called The Peacock near the Grosvenor Shopping Centre in Northampton. Sandy was sitting on a stool at the virtually empty bar wearing neatly pressed trousers with a crease down the front, a fur jacket and a t-shirt. I ordered myself a drink as I looked at her. This was unintentional but I was so taken by her beauty that I made it obvious I was looking at her.

Sandy by Castle Ashby Lake, based on a photo by Chris Coles

'What are you looking at?' she asked. I said, 'I just thought how gorgeous and beautiful you looked.' I asked if I could buy her a drink, which she accepted. We sat together exchanging details. I asked her name and she said it was Alexandra Elene Maclean Denny. 'Alexandra' was the name she always asked me to call her. She said later, 'My grandmother calls me Sandy for short and a few of my friends also called me that, but not my parents.'

She said she lived at 'The Twistle' and I said, 'The only 'twizzle' I know is a TV programme I watched as a kid.' She said she played the piano and wrote

Chris Coles assembling Sandy Memorial Bench, Brasenose, Cropredy, 2025

music for a living and that she was on her way home from playing in London the night before. She didn't tell me she was a well-known singer until after a few weeks.

She liked exploring and visiting places, especially ones of historical interest. She was a very intelligent, adventurous, caring and lovely person. She was also deeply psychic. As she once said, 'If I die, I will come back to you and prove all I say…' And she did.

She would show me loads of photos and tell me the story behind each one, making sure I knew all about her life, from when she was a baby right up to the present.

Whenever we went to music concerts, she would put on a long black wig to avoid being recognised. We went to a Fleetwood Mac concert once where the group had recognised her. They got her to stand up with the spotlights on her while the audience clapped. (I kept my head down…)

I would drive her to concerts she was meant to be performing at but she would be too nervous to go in. We would be in the car seeing the theatre doors close and hear the band starting. It would then take a while to persuade her to bang on the theatre doors to get them to let her in.

Sandy was the most incredible, beautiful, loving, caring woman. Jill Conway, Gerry Conway's wife, was one of Sandy's most trusted friends. Jill would often visit my work with Sandy and then later accompanied her and Georgia.

GRAMPIAN TV
17 JUNE 1975, ABERDEEN, UK

ALAN DAVIDSON

In 1975 I was going out with a girl who was at Aberdeen University and a member of the University Folk Club. I recall seeing Wizz Jones and Vin Garbutt there. We were very lucky when the local TV station, Grampian TV, invited the folk club members to be in the audience for their forthcoming series, *Marc Time*. This was fronted by the late Canadian musician Marc Ellington, who had recently relocated to the North East of Scotland. The main acts for each show were musicians with whom he was already friendly, and who had appeared on his own records. We attended two shows.

The second featured Richard and Linda Thompson, Loudon Wainwright and Sandra Kerr, whilst the first had Sandy Denny, Gallagher and Lyle and The Matthews Brothers. Studio One at Grampian wasn't very big, but a basic tiered seating area had been constructed, facing the performers on the studio floor. The format for both shows had us filing into the seats at quarter to seven in the evening, for a dress rehearsal/audience warm-up of the show, during which cameramen made notes on angles, close ups etc.

The floor manager encouraged us to applaud loudly at the end of songs, but there really was no need, as we were all thrilled to be there. Marc started with his intro piece, 'Marc Time', before introducing the first act, young Irish singers The Matthew Brothers, who sang a cheerful song in praise of Kilkenny. After the applause subsided, he welcomed Sandy with a few words about her winning the *Melody Maker* 'Best Female Singer' award.

It seemed quite strange to be almost within touching distance of Sandy. *The North Star Grassman And The Ravens* was already a favourite album of mine and I was in awe of her. Sandy's first

Alan saw Sandy recording a show for Grampian TV

song was the traditional 'Blackwaterside', accompanying herself on acoustic guitar. She sang and played beautifully and the floor manager must have been delighted at the volume of applause.

After Gallager and Lyle performed two songs, Marc brought back The Matthews Brothers for a number and then played his version of Gordon Lightfoot's 'Early Morning Rain', which set the mood nicely for Sandy to sit down at the piano for her second song. Marc jokingly mentioned that someone had said to him backstage that, 'Sandy sounds a great deal like the girl in Fairport Convention... She *is* the lead singer of Fairport Convention. Let's have another hand for a song she's just written... Ladies and gentlemen, Sandy Denny!'

Sandy's stunning version of 'No More Sad Refrains' followed, and was the high point of the evening, much discussed by us in the pub afterwards.

The show then ended with Marc thanking the other acts before being joined by Sandy for 'Pack Up Your Sorrows'. (On the broadcast version you can just hear Sandy at the start saying, 'You can do the verse.')

After our applause faded there was a fifteen-minute break for technical checks before the whole show was repeated for recording purposes. We were delighted to see everything again, and enjoy a second helping. Sandy, in full-on performance mode, sang even better than on the run-through versions, sending shivers through me.

A few weeks later, the programme was shown on TV. I had a small black and white portable set in my flat. It had a small output for a jack plug so I plugged in my little cassette recorder and pressed record. Looking back, I wish I'd had better equipment and a better quality tape, but it was only done as a souvenir of a fantastic evening.

Later that same year I did see Sandy sing again, with Fairport at Aberdeen Music Hall. I enlisted my girlfriend's help to smuggle in my cassette recorder in her bag and recorded the show, but the quality was muffled and it ran out near the end of 'Sloth'. It was still a great gig, although Sandy this time was much further away. Now, more than fifty years later, I wish I could be that teenager again, listening to that fabulous voice singing live, and, it seemed then, just for me.

THE ROYAL OAK
1975, EYDON, UK

CHRIS LESLIE, FAIRPORT CONVENTION

Chris Leslie with Georgia

It was such a long time ago now, but this is how I remember it.

It would have been around 1975 when, as a young music-besotted fiddle player, I would find myself on occasional Sunday lunchtimes being part of my dream session at a pub, The Royal Oak in the small Northamptonshire village of Eydon. Thanks to my brother John, who I was in a duo with at the time, I got to know Peggy, who was living in Cropredy. Peggy asked me to bring my fiddle over to this session, where he and Simon would sit in the window and play a bit of music.

One particular Sunday, Sandy and Trevor were there. After the session finished, various people were going back to their house in the nearby village of Byfield. I hadn't plucked up the courage to say hello to them, but they came over and invited myself and Linda to join everyone there. I remember a lovely afternoon. They were fab hosts and so welcoming to us.

Many years later I was so honoured to be asked by Jerry Donahue to add some backing vocals together with Simon Nicol to a live recording of Sandy's being released posthumously called 'Gold Dust', a very special day recording for me.

All these years later, having been in Fairport to date for thirty years, it is such a privilege to sing and play some of Sandy's songs. I particularly love 'Rising For The Moon' and 'Who Knows Where The Time Goes'. Thank you so much, Sandy, for all the music and inspiration you continue to give…

TØNDER FESTIVAL
AUGUST 1975, TØNDER, DENMARK

JENS DREWSEN

I first heard Sandy Denny in the mid-seventies at a folk festival in the town of Tønder in southern Denmark. She was there with Fairport Convention, but she also did a solo gig on a smaller stage during the festival. It was a spontaneous thing and not part of the official programme. It is the only time I heard her live, but I have been a devoted fan ever since. Her voice still calls out warmth. She was the foundation of my own musical career…

AMAZINGRACE
12 SEPTEMBER 1975, EVANSTON, ILLINOIS

TOM DELANEY

I saw Sandy once after she had rejoined Fairport Convention. Amazingrace was a small venue that had started out as a coffee house on the Northwestern University campus but which had moved shortly before this date to a building called The Main (on Main Street, of course), morphing into a small concert venue with maybe a couple hundred capacity at most. You sat on the carpeted floor and the stage was about five feet up from the floor. A friend of mine, Ken Bloom, was the opening act, so I was in the front row. They had rolled a grand piano out for Sandy so I was sitting right underneath it. What else can I say? It was glorious.

BEACON THEATRE
20 SEPTEMBER 1975, NEW YORK, NEW YORK

FRANK FORTUNAT

On the second anniversary of Sandy and Trevor's wedding day, Fairport Convention played the Beacon Theatre in NYC during the *Rising For The Moon* tour. After the show my cousin and friend looked to find the stage door to bring Sandy a bouquet of flowers, only to find Sandy already outside talking to herself about the time it was taking the bloody driver to come around with the car, saying she wanted to punch him in the nose! She then realised we were standing there and we all started to laugh! It was a moment I'll treasure forever.

HARVARD SQUARE THEATRE
2 OCTOBER 1975, CAMBRIDGE, MASSACHUSETTS

ANDY NAGY

The next year, *Rising For The Moon* came out. We loved what we heard. I was thinking that 'One More Chance' would be absolutely incredible in a concert hall, with the sound of Jerry's solos just wrapping all around us. It didn't take too long to find out. Fairport and Sandy returned to tour the US in the autumn, playing at a big old movie theatre in Harvard Square. Jean Luc Ponty opened up, giving a beautiful set of his own, but I was so eager to hear the main act. And what a magical concert it was! One incredibly exciting song after another, with 'Tam Lin' reintroduced into the set.

Fairport with Sandy Denny at Harvard Square Theatre, October 1975 (Edward Haber)

A few weeks earlier I had done a pencil drawing of Sandy, playing her guitar in a clearing in the forest watched all around by entranced animals. My portrait was based on the picture on the cover of the *Fotheringay* album.

I had brought the drawing to the concert with me, hoping to give it to Sandy. I had never tried to meet anyone at a concert before, and my friend urged me to go to the door at the side of the stage. There stood a stage hand. I told him what my mission was, and he showed me through.

One of the Fairports (I think it was Jerry) was relaxing in front of me and I asked if I could give Sandy my gift. He was very friendly and said he'd be happy to find her for me. But just then who should come walking over towards us but Sandy herself!

Jerry called to her and said here was someone who wanted to say hello. She was so lovely! She welcomed this bashful long-haired youth with a smile. I held out the flat box that contained the gift, and told her I had drawn a picture of her and wanted to give it to her. She accepted the package, took out the picture and smiled.

'Thank you,' she said. 'This is very nostalgic. I haven't been playing guitar for some time, you see, now I play the piano.'

I was too starstruck to remember what more was said. But she did then excuse herself and said, 'I have to go to the loo.' She went down the stairs that were beside where we were standing. And then she was gone. I walked out of the back of the stage area in a daze and rejoined my friends.

And that was my amazing meeting with Sandy. Fifty years later, I can say with certainty that I still love her just as much. Her voice moves me in ways few others can.

Sandy was absolutely one in a million. Maybe a billion.

DAVID EVPAK

I was fortunate to see Sandy once, with Fairport. My most vivid memory of the evening is that she spent a good portion of the concert with her hands planted firmly on her hips and glaring at Dave Swarbrick.

CARDIFF UNIVERSITY
6 OCTOBER 1975, CARDIFF, UK

BRIAN THOMAS PHILLIPS

I'd been absolutely besotted by Sandy since I first heard her voice some years, before when I'd bought the *Bumpers* sampler double LP from Island Records. I must have owned every recorded work of hers by the time of this gig, so it was not only Sandy's voice I was besotted by but her face. I was 17 at the time and in the full flush of teenage angst / infatuation / despair / love, etc.

The band were preparing to take the stage. I'd arrived late, and after a long journey I needed to visit the loo. I left the packed concert hall and entered a long corridor. I was dithering around wondering which way to go but there was no one at all there to ask. Then I saw Sandy, also entering the corridor about 20 or 30 yards away. Sandy approached me along the corridor, possibly thinking I was familiar with the University.

She stopped directly in front of me and asked whether I knew where the toilets were. I didn't reply apart from a strange sort of hesitant and garbled 'urrgghh!' It would have been better to be entirely speechless, but no, I was being blessed by the dribbling imbecile variety of speechlessness. I remained petrified and stuttering, drop-jawed, and wide-eyed with every emotion imaginable coursing through my teenage, temporarily mutated brain. She might have repeated her question before giving up and turning to go but all I can remember is the turmoil in my head and heart as the angel I had worshipped for years stood so close to me.

Sandy suddenly hesitated, turned back and kissed me very briefly on the cheek before gliding away down the corridor. My next memory is of being back in the audience with my hand on my cheek, utterly stupefied by my encounter and by the angelic voice I was now listening to as she performed the best version of 'Who Knows Where The Time Goes?' that I have ever heard.

I can't say for certain whether I have fully recovered my senses.

TOWN HALL
7 OCTOBER 1975, BIRMINGHAM, UK

GLEN COLEGATE

Like all teenagers in the mid-seventies, I read the *NME*. Sandy was twice voted UK female vocalist of the year and so I was intrigued. I had also read about Fairport Convention so I used my pocket money to buy the double album, *The History of Fairport Convention*. It was a bit of a life changer, filled with all those wonderful songs. And then Sandy rejoined and an album – *Rising For The Moon* – and tour were announced. That was an exciting prospect!

I couldn't afford the album but I could afford 75p to see them play at Birmingham Town Hall. It was Sandy, Trevor, Swarb, Jerry Donahue and Dave Mattacks. The gig was sensational. The next day I borrowed the money to buy *Liege & Lief*.

It was a couple of years later that I was lucky enough to see Sandy again, this time solo at the same venue. Support was no less than Danny Thompson.

These days I live in south west London. People local to me in Thames Ditton have told me she used to babysit the daughter of Alun Jones – Cat Stevens' guitarist during his glory years, who is also a local.

Sandy's voice and songs will live forever.

ST GEORGE'S HALL
9 OCTOBER 1975, BRADFORD, UK

NIGEL SCHOFIELD

I interviewed Sandy during the soundcheck. She was distracted by what her bandmates were doing: 'That doesn't sound right'; 'The drums are too loud'; 'Something's out of tune, can't they hear that?'. She said all the right things – how well the tour of America, which ended less than two weeks earlier had gone ('I think I'm still a bit jet-lagged'), how she appreciated the short hop between UK gigs, how pleased she was with the way the new album had turned out and with the new single: 'It's the band really as a unit. Swarb wrote it. I sing it. The rest of the band are great on it. The B-side is by Trevor, a song called 'Tears' which is not available anywhere else.' It all felt a bit pluggy; it didn't quite ring true. Something felt amiss.

The feeling persisted during the show (with some tape left, I clandestinely recorded some of it). Since 1970, I'd got used to Swarb being in charge: that night he felt sidelined. I was also used to both Fairport and Sandy moving on from their previous repertoire with each new release. That night the set darted all over the place (and curiously avoided all the songs on *Live Convention*). There were songs from the latest albums by both Fairport and Sandy, from Fairport's first two albums with Sandy (before Swarb joined) and from across Sandy's career. The standout instrumental was Jerry Donahue's version of Jerry Reed's 'The Claw', a guitar showcase rather than a fiddle extravaganza. In his solo slot, Trevor offered us a choice of a Dylan song or a Richard Thompson song (we ended up hearing 'Down Where The Drunkards Roll'. There were even a couple of unfamiliar songs. But the abiding memories are of 'Old Fashioned Waltz', 'It Takes A Long Time', 'Who Knows Where The Time Goes?' and 'Stranger To Himself'. The over-riding impression was that it was very much Sandy's gig. The seeds of implosion were sown.

Leeds Uni poster (David Pollard)

UMIST
11 OCTOBER 1975, MANCHESTER, UK

HOWARD BRINDLE

I was a student at the University of Manchester (UMIST) and in digs with an amazing family near Stockport. The children of the family were a little older than me and had a vinyl record collection which introduced a novice to Jethro Tull, King Crimson, Steeleye Span and of course Fairport Convention. I first heard Sandy on *Liege & Lief* on vinyl and a *History Of Fairport Convention*. I thought she was amazing. I was hooked.

The son of the family was really into Steeleye Span so I went to a lot of their gigs in Manchester. I became more of a fan of Fairport and collected all their albums and Sandy's I could get my hands on. It was fantastic when in 1975 Fairport with Sandy Denny came to do a gig at UMIST union bar. The concert blew me away and I briefly met Sandy Denny – a highlight of my music experience at that time!

I have always loved the album *Like An Old Fashioned Waltz* and still use the CD version as a reference CD. Many people have complained about the string section backing Sandy's vocals on the album. I think it is absolutely superb and goes perfectly with her performance. The original *Fotheringay* album is also incredible and also a reference.

Sandy's performance and writing on Fairport's *Rising For The Moon* album is very special. In recent times I contributed to the deluxe CD version and am mentioned on the credits of this re-release.

My record collection now only consists of CD and SACD albums, having abandoned vinyl many years ago. I think I have every album Sandy made, including her appearances on other artists' records. I have spent a large part of my life listening to Sandy Denny again and again and always love hearing her. She is the reference I use when listening to other female singers!

JOHN MAGEE

It must have been hard for bands touring those kinds of venues. They'd basked in the glamour of the Royal Albert Hall a few months before, but this was a gruelling trek around eleven universities dotted across England in 16 days, and not always in a logical order. At UMIST, everyone was crammed into quite a small hall sitting on the floor, beer at 17p a pint was spilling everywhere, and the acoustics were terrible. The band must sometimes have had to drag themselves onto those stages, and I guess they were often literally rising for the moon. For Sandy in particular, it might have been too much. Yet the commitment to the songs and the truly outstanding musical talent was there for all to see and hear. It's quite something that 50 years after the event, I can still hear Sandy's voice echoing through that concrete hall: 'Is it too late?'

What a gift it is to make someone's spine tingle decades after you've gone.

UNIVERSITY OF LIVERPOOL
15 OCTOBER 1975, LIVERPOOL, UK

GERALD HULL

I last saw Sandy with my wife when, back with a full Fairport, they played Liverpool University in November 1975. It was a typical Swarbrick fag-fest, noisy and full-on, and Sandy was drowned. The encore was 'Who Knows Where The Time Goes?': it was terribly sad. Her voice had gone, she was weak, forlorn – not even poignant. The good times had slipped away. Within three years she too had gone down with the ship. What many missed (and as far as I know was never recorded) was Richard playing residence with Sandy's electric band in 1972/73 at The Bottom Line in Greenwich Village, New York. What was in their set? Dylan (living round the corner) is believed to have been present. Richard says Sandy was so nervous at this that she gave a terrible performance.

NORM THOMAS

I was a fan of folk music back in the late sixties and early seventies. I used to go to a folk club in Brentwood, Essex, where I had moved from Liverpool. I'd bought some Strawbs and Fairport Convention albums, so I was quick to act when I saw that a planned trip back to Liverpool coincided with a Fairport concert. It was wonderful to hear Sandy sing and I can still recall that night with great clarity. It was part of the tour to promote *Rising For The Moon*, still my favourite Fairport album.

My brother, Richard, also liked folk music and has always been a big fan of Richard Thompson. He did some things that I did not, like going to the original Cavern Club in Liverpool, and seeing Pele and Eusebio appear at Goodison Park during the 1966 World Cup. But in later life, whenever I said I was envious of those things his immediate rejoinder would always be, 'Yes, but you got to see Sandy Denny perform live and I never did.'

YORK UNIVERSITY
24 OCTOBER 1975, YORK, UK

NIGEL BANKS

I saw Sandy perform live on two further occasions, both with Fairport when she had rejoined the band alongside her husband Trevor Lucas. The first time was at the De Montfort Hall, Leicester in the summer of 1974. I was so happy to see her reunited with Fairport and hoped it would lead to a long and fruitful collaboration of such talented musicians. Alas, it was not to be.

But I did manage to see that line-up one more time at York University in October 1975. My attendance at the gig was dependent on me passing my driving test the previous day. Luckily, I was able to throw away my L-plates and do my first proper solo drive to the venue. The band were supported by the folk singer Bryn Howarth and played several numbers from the *Rising For The Moon* album. Little did I realise then that it would be the last time I would ever see 'The Lady' and be able to hear that peerless voice live.

I've listened to her records countless times in the following years. I only have to hear her introductory hums to her version of Dylan's 'Knockin' On Heaven's Door' to feel the hairs standing up on the back of my neck and the tears begin to fall.

My favourite song of hers is 'One Way Donkey Ride', both for her singing and the poetic quality of her lyrics:

No one is given the map to their dreams
All we can do is to trace it
See where we go, know where we've been
Build up the courage to face it

While we fumble in the darkness, where once there was light
Roaming the land of the ancients
Oasis of love, sweet water of life
God bless the poor ones, whose patience never died

COLSTON HALL
28 OCTOBER 1975, BRISTOL, UK

MIKE MURPHY
I saw Sandy Denny just once. I was surprised that the band had expanded somewhat at that point. It consisted of Swarb, Peggy, Sandy, Trevor Lucas, Jerry Donahue with Bruce Rowland on drums. As they were promoting the album *Rising For The Moon*, Trevor Lucas was also lead vocal on a couple of songs. Trevor gave the sound more of a country flavour than we were used to at that stage. I still recall the really sharp lead guitar playing by Jerry Donahue, which added some depth to the band (as Richard Thompson had previously). The encore was 'Who Knows Where The Time Goes?'. Sandy was in fine voice and the musicianship of the band was, as ever, exuberant, powerful and memorable. That's about all I remember about the gig, but I've never forgotten it. Regrettably, Sandy left the band not long after the tour.

BRUNEL UNIVERSITY
31 OCTOBER 1975, UXBRIDGE, UK

PETER BROWN
I first discovered Sandy in 1973 at age 14, thanks to my sister-in-law's job at Island Records which gifted me the ability to build an eclectic and enviable record collection. Sandy's voice was a siren call that instantly captivated me, especially on *What We Did On Our Holidays*. *Like An Old Fashioned Waltz* stands out too – for its music, but mainly for the personal memories it conjures of a teenage lad navigating the twists and turns of relationships and growing up.

I was fortunate enough to see Sandy perform live twice, first with Fairport at Brunel University in October 1975 – an imperious presence amongst a stellar group of musicians – and then on her debut night at the Royalty Theatre in 1977. I thoroughly enjoyed the latter concert although this time she seemed more tentative, perhaps not fully at ease or lacking rehearsal time with her band.

I remember vividly the moment I learnt of Sandy's passing, at Hayes and Harlington station, via the front page of *Melody Maker*. It was the first time the death of a musical hero hit me on a personal level.

Since then, I've explored her career, trawling through her back catalogue and the subsequent 'rare' releases. Her more sombre tracks resonate with me, whilst 'By The Time It Gets Dark' has become a cherished tune for lifting my spirits.

I've read her biographies with her complexities and fragilities. I once had a brief social encounter with her friend, Linda Fitzgerald-Moore, who spoke a little of her memories but referenced Sandy's challenges with her own gifts. That inspired me to visit 'The Lady's' grave in Putney.

Sandy was a guiding light in my musical journey and, 50 years on, she remains someone I still find myself encouraging younger generations to discover for themselves. Who knows where the time goes?

SALFORD UNIVERSITY
NOVEMBER 1975, SALFORD, UK

MIKE JACKSON

I'd been a fan of Sandy's since 1968, but due to my age I was only able to see her sing once. She was five foot three inches tall with a full figure. She was a wonderful singer and sang with such passion.

THOMAS PLATH

In 1976, when I was 17 years old, I listened to Sandy's voice for the first time. 'Crazy Man Michael', written by RT and Swarb. What a singer! I fell in love with her voice immediately. My friend and bandmate, Rolf, who I was visiting in Eckernförde, Germany, noticed my reaction and suggested we play the entire *Liege & Lief* album again. From then on Sandy became part of my life.

As soon as possible I took a trip to the record store in the next village to find more music with Sandy and discover just what a wonderful songwriter she was. My favourite songs were 'One More Chance' and 'Who Knows Where The Time Goes?'

In April 1978 I heard Sandy had passed away and I had to cry. A part of me was not there anymore. I miss her. Her musical integrity, her soul, her talent, her beautiful voice, her passion, her love and much more are what made her a one of a kind, a genius.

I regret not going to England to see Sandy perform – but she's still in my heart.

Sandy Denny quits again

Fairport Convention have hit another crisis, with San Denny, Trevor Lucas and Jerry Donahue all quitting t band. The three remaining members — Dave Pegg (bas Dave Swarbrick (fiddle) and Bruce Rowlands (drums) are planning a new, five-piece, Fairport Convention wi the addition of a keyboards player and a guitarist. It w be the band's eleventh different line-up since 1967.

Sandy Denny has left the band to resume her solo care She re-joined Fairport in 1974, after four years away from t band. Denny was featured on Fairport's last album, "Rising For The Moon," released last year.

Trevor Lucas is planning to return to record production — it was while he was producing Fairport's eighth album that Lucas was asked to join the band. One of his first projects will be Denny's solo album.

Jerry Donahue, the son of American swing musician, Sam Donahue, has returned to Los Angeles where he has become a session guitarist. Donahue, however, is expected to work on Denny's album in Britain later this year.

The remaining members of Fairport have already recorded a new album using guest musicians in place of the departed trio. They will return to live performances at the end of April, coinciding with the release of the LP.

On Wednesday this w (February 11), Swarbrick Pegg played a one-off reun gig with former-Fairport C vention guitarist Simon Ni at Dingwalls, London. Br Maxine was the vocal Swarbrick, however, den that either of them were to members of the reconstitu Fairport.

'Sandy Denny quits again...'

FRIARS
26 JUNE 1976, AYLESBURY, UK

ALISTAIR THOMPSON

I saw Sandy on TV with the *Rising For The Moon* line up. I think they played 'White Dress'. I'd bought the 1972 *History Of Fairport Convention* double album and bought my ticket to see Fairport at Friars Aylesbury. The line-up I saw was the Fairport which toured the *Gottle O'Geer* album. It was a fun gig but just a mite disappointing as I only recognised Swarb and Peggy. I never had another opportunity to see Sandy perform, although I have bought pretty much everything she recorded.

ISLAND RECORDS
MAY 1977, CHISWICK, LONDON, UK

PATRICK HUMPHRIES

Of course she died too soon, but the fact she is still remembered nearly half a century on is a testament to what Sandy achieved in her all too short life. I never *knew* Sandy. I admired her, listened to her, saw her play and I was lucky enough to interview her. It was in May 1977, at the old Island office in Chiswick. She and Trevor were there to promote

Rendezvous. Ruefully reflecting, she knew this was a make-or-break effort. Island had been supportive during the Fairport, Fotheringay and solo years, but in the cut-throat music industry, sales were what mattered.

Like so many I was always baffled at how badly Sandy fared, to my mind at least two of her solo albums – *Sandy and Like An Old Fashioned Waltz* – should be in every record collection. But it never quite *happened*… 'Taxi drivers see me carrying a guitar,' she laughed when we met, 'they say 'What do you do for a living?' And I say 'I'm a singer' 'What's your name?' 'Sandy Denny' 'Never heard of you!''

There was also that sense of frustration the way that that Sandy was categorised: 'It's an odd trip for me to be labelled as a 'folk singer', which I always have for some unknown reason, but I somehow wish they would knock the 'folk' bit off as it's misleading… I'm not writing in the folk style, and haven't done for a long time.'

You can share her frustration. Sandy's songs were just so good, in whatever category you put them. But folk was only an ingredient, along with a lifelong love of country, pop and selections from the Great American Songbook.

Apart from the sheer quality of her work – I single out 'Solo', 'Like An Old Fashioned Waltz', 'Listen, Listen', 'One Way Donkey Ride' – she managed to cram an awful lot into her career: that under-rated LP with The Strawbs, fronting Fairport Convention and Fotheringay, getting a gold disc for the stage version of *Tommy*… bruising American tours opening for Randy Newman and Steve Miller among others… *Melody Maker* Female Singer Of The Year two years running… the only other singer ever featured on a Led Zeppelin LP… (she also recorded with Charlie Drake)…

It must have been so *frustrating*. She knew she was talented, she held her own in a man's man's world, but yet real success eluded her. To promote her records she had to tour, and end up 'like a spaced-out brain on legs'. Taken too soon, one can only speculate on Sandy's future had she lived: she had many influential friends and admirers in America, and a move there would have made commercial sense.

When I think of Sandy, and listen to her sing, I am always reminded of Simon Nicol's memory of her Fairport audition: 'She stood out like a clean glass in a sink full of dirty dishes.'

'RINGING DOWN THE YEARS'
JULY 1977/AUGUST 1998, CROPREDY, UK

DAVE COUSINS

It was in July 1977 that I had a call from Trevor Lucas to give me the best news I'd heard in years; Sandy Denny had given birth to a girl - Georgia Rose Lucas. Georgia was born two months prematurely, weighing barely two pounds.

Dave Cousins & Georgia, 2024

Skip forward twenty years... A call from Dave Pegg of Fairport Convention set it all in motion. Dave asked me if I would guest with them in August 1998 at the annual Fairport Cropredy Convention; he wanted me to sing 'Ringing Down The Years', my tribute to Sandy Denny. I had written the song on piano and the timing was unusual, but once we'd sorted out the count-in as 'one, two, three, four, one' it worked straight away. Fairport, and especially Ric Sanders, played it magnificently. I must say I choked up as I sang the chorus:

Every time I hear your name, my eyes moist up with tears
As every word you ever sang comes ringing down the years

I could sense Sandy smiling at me as I sang the song.

GEORGIA ROSE LUCAS

My mum's life is often measured in tours and recordings, but her story is also held in the quieter everyday spaces, with people who knew her as a friend, away from the world of music. Denise was one of those friends, and she looked after me as an infant:

We were close friends for over ten years; in the banal day-to-day world we sort of needed each other. My husband Doc Proctor (that's what they called him, for obvious reasons) was the techy and roadie all rolled into one. He took me to a gig one day and your mum swept in. She was in tears because some idiot said she was not as pretty as her album cover – equivalent to today's troll, especially just before going on stage – but she was late and had not made up. That was my first memory of her, so vulnerable and sensitive. She greeted me and I hit her with a wall of full-on worship. I adored her voice. Your mum and I would escape from anyone involved in making money from music to my home in the village of Greatworth, near Banbury. I was part of your mum's less star-studded life.

Your mum had a will of steel and I knew she would glue herself to you. That's why we were on tour with her; she would go nowhere without you. It was not a long time but it was very intense.

Top: Denise & Georgia, 1977
Above: Denise now

I used to sit and watch her draw for hours. She used to love to draw. Horses were interesting to her. I love that you draw so much like your mum. Your mum loved sketching with pencil. The way you portray your mum adds a spiritual dimension. Your drawings look ethereal, so beautiful, and bring her back for us. Your mum was really psychic too; we studied the Tarot together. I'd used cards since I was a student nurse and I taught her; she was a good student. I'm not surprised she's using the psychic route to get to you.

I bonded with you when you were three months old. That beautiful first smile, and my Manda was behaving like your big sister – she was four and you were at her fourth birthday celebration. I cried for weeks when you went. Your dad only allowed me a glimpse of a sleeping toddler in the dark at Dave Pegg's. You were two years old then, and it broke my heart to see you again, 'cause he was gone again the next day.

But you are doing such beautiful pictures of your mum; you can see the love, Georgia. She would be thrilled – if she isn't actually sitting there thrilled in heaven, I think she must be, 'cause she brought you back to me and that has healed a hole I have carried for 40 years.

PRESCOTE MANOR
23 JULY 1977, CROPREDY, UK

STAFFAN WENNERLUND

In the summer of 1977, I saw a small notice in an English music magazine saying that Fairport Convention were playing a garden fête at Prescote Manor in Cropredy to help raise funds for a new roof for the village hall. On a whim, I flew to London and then travelled on to Cropredy. Just finding my way to Cropredy was an adventure, but I soon found a couple of friends in the small crowd, who were having a pint or two.

In the evening light, I went down the path to the portaloos, which is when I saw Sandy getting out of a car and heading towards me on the path. She was wearing a long white dress, with Trevor in tow. We met on the path and I couldn't get a word out of my lips. I was starstruck. The moment passed and they continued up the path toward the backstage area. I so wanted to have told her what her singing and music had meant to me for so many years, but I was tongue-tied. I have regretted it ever since…

When I came back to my newfound friends in the crowd, I was very excited and told them that Sandy and Trevor were there and that I was positive that she would sing a song or two. But, alas, that was not to happen.

But it is a beautiful picture I have in my memory of Sandy coming towards me on the path, in the evening light, in her white dress.

FOX & HOUNDS
AUTUMN 1977, ALTHORPE, UK

DAVE CLEMO

In autumn 1977 I and my friends went to a folk club in a village pub a few miles to the west of Northampton (I think it was Althorp) to see Dave Pegg and Trevor Lucas in concert. The room was packed and, as the concert progressed, I became aware of a woman standing slightly behind and off to the side of me. She was drunk and heckling the duo on stage. I realised that it was Sandy, a lot the worse for wear. The venue was only a few miles from her and Trevor's home in Byfield, so I guess it was the closest thing to a home gig. It was the last time I saw her. Within a few months she was gone.

ROYALTY THEATRE
6 NOVEMBER 1977, LONDON, UK

LESLIE SMITH

I saw Sandy perform twice in 1975, first in June at the Royal Albert Hall and then later at the Drury Lane Theatre as part of the *Rising For The Moon* tour; both were great concerts. But, along with my friends, I was also in the audience for one of the two last concerts she did in London, at the Royalty Theatre.

Me and my friends Trevor and Alan were very excited to get tickets and be in the audience that night. The concert was wonderful and, as it ended, Sandy announced that if any of the audience wanted to stay behind, the band would be in the bar after the show. Well, we thought this was too good an opportunity to miss. The bar area was literally at the back of the auditorium, so we were there very quickly. We soon realised that there we were surrounded by lots of notable people from the folk world. Besides the wider Fairport family, I recognised Ralph McTell, Maddy Prior and Julie Covington to name a few.

Me and my friends were in our early twenties and feeling a little insignificant. Then someone said

Leslie Smith has lost his signed photo but friend Nick still has his

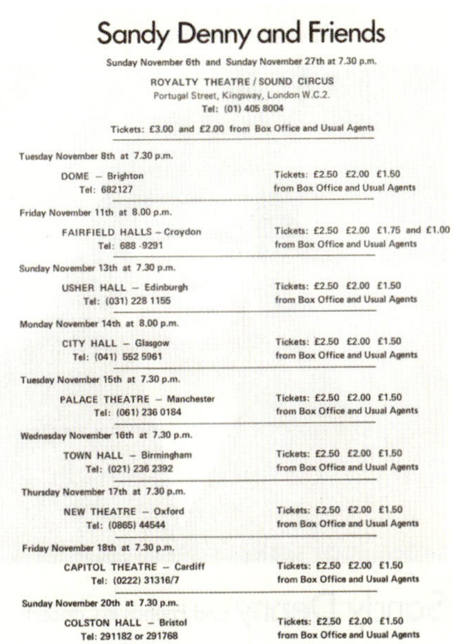

Sandy Denny and Friends

Sunday November 6th and Sunday November 27th at 7.30 p.m.

ROYALTY THEATRE / SOUND CIRCUS
Portugal Street, Kingsway, London W.C.2.
Tel: (01) 405 8004

Tickets: £3.00 and £2.00 from Box Office and Usual Agents

Tuesday November 8th at 7.30 p.m.	DOME – Brighton Tel: 682127	Tickets: £2.50 £2.00 £1.50 from Box Office and Usual Agents
Friday November 11th at 8.00 p.m.	FAIRFIELD HALLS – Croydon Tel: 688 -9291	Tickets: £2.50 £2.00 £1.75 and £1.00 from Box Office and Usual Agents
Sunday November 13th at 7.30 p.m.	USHER HALL – Edinburgh Tel: (031) 228 1155	Tickets: £2.50 £2.00 £1.50 from Box Office and Usual Agents
Monday November 14th at 8.00 p.m.	CITY HALL – Glasgow Tel: (041) 552 5961	Tickets: £2.50 £2.00 £1.50 from Box Office and Usual Agents
Tuesday November 15th at 7.30 p.m.	PALACE THEATRE – Manchester Tel: (061) 236 0184	Tickets: £2.50 £2.00 £1.50 from Box Office and Usual Agents
Wednesday November 16th at 7.30 p.m.	TOWN HALL – Birmingham Tel: (021) 236 2392	Tickets: £2.50 £2.00 £1.50 from Box Office and Usual Agents
Thursday November 17th at 7.30 p.m.	NEW THEATRE – Oxford Tel: (0865) 44544	Tickets: £2.50 £2.00 £1.50 from Box Office and Usual Agents
Friday November 18th at 7.30 p.m.	CAPITOL THEATRE – Cardiff Tel: (0222) 31316/7	Tickets: £2.50 £2.00 £1.50 from Box Office and Usual Agents
Sunday November 20th at 7.30 p.m.	COLSTON HALL – Bristol Tel: 291182 or 291768	Tickets: £2.50 £2.00 £1.50 from Box Office and Usual Agents

Sandy Denny & Friends tour dates, November 1977 (Stephen Royston)

'would we like to meet Sandy?' and of course we said yes. She came over to have a chat and asked if we enjoyed the show. She was very modest when we said how much we had enjoyed it. Not knowing quite what to say when you meet one of your idols, I mentioned a song she hadn't sung. To which she quite rightly replied, 'Well, you can't do them all!' Sandy then kindly signed a promotion flyer for the concert for each of us. Both my friends still have theirs but, regretfully, mine has got lost in the mists of time. This is a memory I treasure.

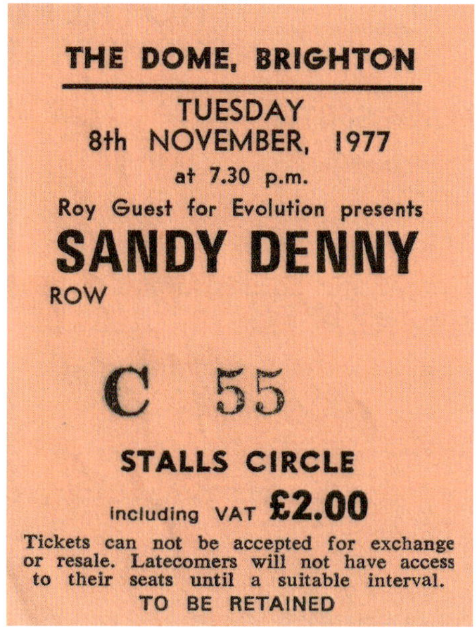
THE DOME, BRIGHTON
TUESDAY
8th NOVEMBER, 1977
at 7.30 p.m.
Roy Guest for Evolution presents
SANDY DENNY
ROW
C 55
STALLS CIRCLE
including VAT £2.00
Tickets can not be accepted for exchange or resale. Latecomers will not have access to their seats until a suitable interval.
TO BE RETAINED

Ticket for the Brighton 1977 show (Stephen Royston)

FAIRFIELD HALLS
10 NOVEMBER 1977, CROYDON, UK

GRAHAM WARREN

I recall seeing Sandy perform solo only the once. She had a cold and was a bit snuffly but that didn't stop her singing wonderfully. Memory is a strange thing as I thought it was a solo gig but I have since learned that Danny Thompson was part of it and perhaps a band of the usual suspects too. I wish I had taken some photos but they were very strict there about photographers – and about dancing!

Graham Warren saw Sandy once

CHRIS GROOM

The ex-Fairport vocalist turned in a strong performance, despite the inconvenience of a heavy cold and she spent most of the evening seated at the piano, atop which sat various cold cure remedies and some Vicks

Sinex! The material was strictly Sandy – any audience requests for old Fairport standards such as 'Matty Groves' or 'Tam Lin' were firmly refused. The support slot was filled by Danny Thompson, no easy task for a man alone with his double bass, but his amiable personality and humorous stories more than made up for the absence of extra musicians.

USHER HALL
12 NOVEMBER 1977, EDINBURGH, UK

DAWN KEMP

I have loved Sandy Denny since I was a teenager growing up in Edinburgh, Scotland in the seventies, listening to my brothers' Fairport albums and *All Our Own Work*, Sandy with the Strawbs, bought at our local Woolworths in 1973. My brother had a Fairport songbook and we would play our guitars and sing (sparing the ears of others) 'Sloth', 'Crazy Man Michael', 'White Dress', 'Meet On The Ledge' and 'John The Gun'. Sandy was the first British female singer I knew who played her own compositions – as genius as any of the American women singer-songwriters I loved.

Georgia at London's Royalty Theatre, July 2025

For my sixteenth birthday my best friend got us tickets to see Sandy at the Usher Hall in Edinburgh, on what was to be her final tour. Her stage presence was mesmerising, her voice sublime, magical, despite battling a dreadful cold. The tour ended at the Royalty Theatre in London later that month.

In July 2025, Sandy's daughter Georgia, our friend Vlad and I sat alone in the middle of the 999-seat Royalty (now the Peacock) Theatre in Portugal Street, London. For 90 minutes we listened on headphones to the recording of Sandy's last concert of her 1977 tour. The stage was empty but in my mind's eye I could see Sandy again at her piano on the left-hand side of the stage. I was transported back to that night in

Edinburgh 48 years before. I know now Georgia was in the wings – a babe in arms being looked after while her mum and dad were on stage performing.

Back to 2025. Sandy's voice, her spirit, transcending place and time, felt like a personal message of love and solace directed at Georgia, her 'beautiful, most precious child'. When our special private 'concert' ended, Georgia got up and walked to the front of the auditorium, climbed the stairs and stood centre stage. Looking out across the theatre and up to the gods, she said quietly 'thank you'.

CITY HALLS
13 NOVEMBER 1977, GLASGOW, UK

MOIRA THORBURN

In November 1972, Sandy Denny was playing at Glasgow University Union. I was 18 and loved her voice, so managed to get in to see her. I accidentally ran into her backstage and got chatting. She was really friendly and interesting. I told her some friends and I were jamming together and were hoping to form a decent folk/rock band. She wished us all the best and even gave me a couple of plectrums and her autograph on my ticket stub, which I treasured.

Sandy at Birmingham Town Hall, 15 November 1977 Jones/Birmingham Music Archive)

Five years later, my then partner and I were going to see her at the Glasgow City Halls. Whilst looking for a parking space, I spotted her and another band member going into a wee pub in the Candleriggs. Once parked, we went in and there she was. I mentioned that we were looking forward to her gig and that I had met her before, at Glasgow Uni. She remembered.

During our conversation she asked me my favourite song of hers and I said, 'The North Star Grassman And The Ravens'. She asked my name and I told her 'Moira'. She said she had a friend called Moira who hadn't been well and that when she thought of her, she would think of me. She also mentioned having her baby (Georgia) in July. It was a happy time for her. It became time for her to head to the nearby City Halls. Then she explained that 'The North Star' wasn't on her list.

Nearing the end of the gig, to my surprise she announced that the next song was for 'Moira – that I met earlier tonight.' I couldn't believe she had mentioned me and had even dedicated a song to me. I was in tears. It was wonderful.

Sadly, her UK tour in 1977 was to be her last. She was the best female vocalist then – and still. Her haunting lyrics and voice will never be equalled in my eyes. I am so proud to have met her and often wonder what beautiful songs she would have written had she not passed away so young. She was such a talented woman.

CAPITOL THEATRE
18 NOVEMBER 1977, CARDIFF, UK

JANE HOUGHTON

It wasn't long before she died. I was 21 or 22 and I really don't remember much except she was seriously worse for drink or drugs and I had to semi-carry her from the stage to the dressing room. I just got her there and left her with people. It was no surprise to hear of her death.

ROYALTY THEATRE
27 NOVEMBER 1977, LONDON, UK

IAIN RACE

I had moved down to London from Middlesbrough and had always been a huge fan of Sandy, Fairport and Richard Thompson. I used to listen to Sandy and Richard Thompson and try to transcribe the songs and sing and play them!

I saw in *NME* and *Melody Maker* that Sandy was doing a tour and I went to see her twice, firstly at Croydon Fairfield Halls on November 10th but also at what was to prove to be her very last gig at the Royalty Theatre in London.

I can remember the gig so well. Trevor Lucas was on guitar, and the brilliant Dave Mattacks was on drums. I was near to the front and it was just such a warm and friendly gig and that is how Sandy made you feel... very warm. I loved her. Her phrasing was quite unique, sometimes coming in slightly late which added more drama to the song. 'Solo' was a favourite, and 'No End'.

It was just a special gig and none of us knew of course that it would be her last.

MALCOLM HOLMES, TALKING ELEPHANT RECORDS

My first real introduction to Sandy was via Fairport but I recall owning a small cassette entitled *It's Sandy* which I treasured for many a year. It died through constant listening and then getting caught up in my old deck. *Live Convention* was what moved me to buy just about everything involving Sandy.

Little did I know that the first and last time I would see her live would be the final date of her solo tour back in November 1977. She kept apologising for the sound of her voice due to a cold, but to me she sounded just amazing and a true night to remember.

Malcolm Holmes only saw Sandy once

Who would have thought that, all these years later, I would end up working within the industry and more to the point with Fairport, members past and present? More recently, after being introduced to Georgia, we put out the wonderful *Songbird* album that is so beautifully crafted with music in the classic style of Sandy by Carla Fuchs and with the use of Sandy's own unreleased lyrics. It was a sheer joy to be involved in and something I will treasure all my life. And then in 2025 we released a special limited edition of *Like An Old Fashioned Waltz*, this time with Georgia's own beautiful artwork, which brings the whole release to a very personal point, for mother and daughter connected.

RICHARD GLEAVE

I was fortunate to be present at Sandy's last concert at The Sound Circus (in reality, the Royalty Theatre) in Kingsway, London. I have read some criticism of the sound quality and of Sandy's vocal performance, but that is not my recollection at all. I thought it was enchanting, especially when something went slightly wrong and there was a false start to one of the songs. It came to an abrupt halt with Sandy lowering her head as if to bang it on the piano and I had the impression that she was giggling rather than upset.

1977 tour programme cover (Dawn Kemp)

I knew that the concert was being recorded and eagerly anticipated its release on an album but the years passed and nothing appeared until 1998 when *Gold Dust* finally emerged on CD. Only then did I discover that the main reason was a problem with the recording process, mainly involving the electric guitar (Rob Hendry, I believe) which resulted in Jerry Donahue re-recording guitar parts on many of the tracks. That CD remains a favourite, partly because of the slight fragility of the performance and partly because it's a record of the last time I saw her perform.

CHRIS WHILE, SINGER SONGWRITER

I remember when I first discovered Sandy Denny. I was fifteen and had already been singing contemporary folk music in folk clubs for a couple of years, accompanying myself on guitar. I was a promising young singer searching for women I could look to, inspirational voices to guide me. When I first heard Fairport Convention, and particularly 'Who Knows Where The Time Goes?', I remember thinking, 'Wow, this woman has everything I love.' She could bend her voice, had a remarkable range and her songs were so singable.

There was soul in her singing too, and soul music had always been a huge part of my life alongside folk. Sandy was the first person I'd heard who truly brought those two worlds together. I listened to her constantly, learned some of her songs, and she became a huge inspiration to me.

VILLAGE HALL
1 APRIL 1978, BYFIELD, NORTHANTS, UK

LOU HART

I first came across Sandy Denny singing with Fairport Convention via the album *Liege & Lief*, released in 1969. I had been listening to bands like Jethro Tull. Folk rock was really new to me and I was completely awed by both her voice and song writing ability.

There was something about her writing which was always a bit wild and wistful – to do with the natural world, with nomads and travellers, and ravens and magic, with freedom and rebellion. Add this to her ability to vocalise intense emotions such as passion, sadness or joy, seemingly without effort, and the result was stunning.

Sandy's blue plaque

In 1978 my girlfriend was learning guitar with Dave Pegg, and told me that Sandy and he would be performing a small concert in the schoolhouse in Cropredy. She got us in and I saw Sandy performing live. There weren't that many in the audience, maybe 30 of us, and I think we sat on benches. But I still have a mental image of Sandy at the front, singing songs that I mostly recognised with that unique voice.

At the end of the concert, I was able to go up to her and tell her how much her singing meant to me and how beautiful her voice was. She just said 'thanks'.

I was devastated to hear of her death, just two weeks after this.

DAVE PEGG, FAIRPORT CONVENTION

In early January 1974, Fairport caught a plane at Heathrow and thirtynine and a half hours later, after various stops and, in my case, a transfer from economy seating to first class after a certain Ozzie Osbourne had 'parked the tiger' on the adjacent seat and passed out, we arrived in Sydney, Australia.

Sandy had been booked to play at New Zealand's first ever open-air festival and had spent the previous Christmas at Trevor Lucas's parents house in Melbourne. Trevor had wangled us onto the bill for the princely sum of £500 plus return airfares and hotels.

We were excited as we hadn't gigged in Oz or NZ before and we were big fans of Barry McKenzie, the cartoon character in *Private Eye* magazine. We celebrated being in Sydney by chundering off the Sydney Harbour Bridge as in the Bazza McKenzie cartoon and then met up with Trevor and Sandy to down a few pints of Fosters and see some Aussie night life. Sandy was not over pleased to be refused entry to the first three pubs we tried because of their 'men only' bars.

She was also not shy in complaining when under duress, as she proved on another occasion later that year at the Beacon Theatre in New York, when we were trying to enter via the stage door thirty minutes before we were due on stage and had not been given passes. She clocked a burly black security guy with her handbag and gave him a piece of her mind while us brave men sneaked into the gig!

It was not easy for Sandy touring with Fairport. We never made it big enough to get the limo treatment and had to stay in basic hotels. She put on a brave face and became one of the chaps most of the time.

She was never happy about her performances, which most nights were truly amazing. I got a slap once when she complained that she had played a bum note on the piano. To try and cheer her up, I suggested she should move the piano stool one inch to the left. Wrong!

I was at Sandy's final gig at Byfield Village Hall and remember how happy she was when Georgia was born.

She made so many people happy and I hope that this lovely book from Georgia helps keep alive the memory of one of England's greatest singer/songwriters.

NIGEL SCHOFIELD

There was a final concert, effectively a by-invitation-only low key event held in her local village hall. I was putting together a documentary about *Liege & Lief* and travelled down with the intention of interviewing Sandy before the concert. She was distracted and talked less about the making of the album than how it didn't turn out the way she thought it would and how as a songwriter she felt frustrated by Fairport's new direction. The evening performance was informal, among friends and showed if anything how she had somehow developed the ability to create an intimate rapport as she chatted between a selection of songs from her past. There were false starts, declined requests and tender, fragile versions of a few of her classics. I wrote on the train home next day, 'There was something otherworldly about it, a fragile Sandy spending time among friends with the ghosts of her past.'

Twenty days later, news came through of Sandy's death. Much has been written, most of it speculation, about the circumstances surrounding it. I recall something Sandy said when I attempted to analyse the background to one of her songs: 'Sometimes it's better not to know. There's a lot to be said for leaving things mysterious.'

And mysteriously, she was gone.

SIMON FITZPATRICK

I grew up in a village called Eydon, just a hop and a skip from Byfield. As teenagers we were all aware of the local 'celebrities' including Fairport and Sandy; when Fairport started their garden parties in 1976, we all blagged our way in to see them – I remember the *Bonny Bunch Of Roses* event with Bob Davenport and the Ian Campbell Folk Group. Anyway, Sandy was around Byfield at the time, usually careering around in an old VW Beetle.

The first time I saw her live was on the *Rendezvous* tour in 1977. I was at Oxford Poly so we went to our local gig at the New Theatre. It was a bit underwhelming, to be honest. It wasn't promoted very well and the theatre was only half full. The highlight was Danny Thompson as support; he played one tune and then told stories for half an hour. It was very funny but probably not for grandma!

I came home for Easter the following year and a neighbour mentioned the village hall gig. I went down early to watch Trevor Lucas setting up the sound 'system' and then watched the gig, all very relaxed and local. Sandy sat at a table with friends and family (…and smoked a load of fags). Peggy and Swarbrick turned up to help – dressed in suits and ties, as I recall – and they banged through a few tunes. 'John The Gun' was great but she forgot all the words to 'Matty Groves'. Fortunately, everyone in there knew them so it ended up being a cheery singalong!

And that was that. The next thing we knew she had died. All very sad.

Years later, a mate of mine came back from abroad and we went for a beer. It turns out that his mum and dad bought Sandy's cottage in Byfield so I did get to visit a couple of times.

We went to the Cropredy festival a few times and saw Richard Thompson on several occasions, plus the mighty Home Service, but Fairport went off the boil for me as the festival became more corporate.

ATKINSON MORLEY HOSPITAL
21 APRIL 1978, WIMBLEDON, LONDON, UK

JOHN O'REGAN, JOURNALIST

Sandy Denny's death robbed the music world of one of the greatest vocal and songwriting talents ever produced in Britain. While for me her demise was a tragedy beyond belief and one of the saddest events of that year, not everybody felt the same sense of loss and bereavement. When I relayed the news of her death to a classmate of mine who was a fellow music head, I wasn't prepared for the reaction: 'So what?'

Those words cut my teenage heart like a knife. They were like a searing scar running right through me. I couldn't understand my classmate's apathy and disinterest. But this was the year of disinterest, the year after 1977 and the ground zero period of music history, when Old England burned in a funeral pyre and its demise was greeted with apathy by the punks and new generational boomers who had engineered its dissemination. Many who had worn jeans and dungarees and whose hair tipped below their waists now joined the revolutionary brigade.

My Sandy Denny story began in April 1972 when I bought the *New Musical Express* for the free Rolling Stones flexidisc that came with that week's edition trailing their new album, *Exile On Main St*. I saw an advert for the new album, *Sandy*. The cover picture looked directly at me – a vision of beauty and forthrightness. I was enthralled, and I was only eleven years old.

Melody Maker
SANDY DENNY DEAD
APRIL 29, 1978 15p weekly USA 75 cents
by COLIN IRWIN
Marley's huge gig
KNEBWORTH: DEVO & BECK? SEE PAGE 4
INTERVIEW WITH NICO! ON PAGE 9
MEAT LOAF, ANDREW GOLD TALK ON PAGE 23

Sandy's death made the front page of *Melody Maker* magazine

In the nineties I began to write a book about Sandy. At the time there was very little in print about her. My journey led me to my spiritual home of Cropredy to meet members of Fairport Convention, and many trips to London to meet her friends and associates, including Linda Thompson, Dave Swarbrick, Karl Dallas and others as I sought to trace her story, visiting Wimbledon, her birthplace and where she worked, walked, played, toured and ended her days at Atkinson Morley Hospital in April 1978.

I got as far as writing a rough draft and sending sample chapters of the book to publishers who were indifferent or felt the manuscript just didn't cut the mustard. I still have bound copies of *Sandy – A Fan's Tribute* at home for my own use. Luckily, Clinton Heylin, Mick Houghton and Phillip Ward's excellent tomes fill the empty space and tell the story much more eloquently than I could.

I have visited her grave in Putney Vale Cemetery in London and paid my respects to 'The Lady', laying flowers on her grave. I have had imaginary conversations with her, and with her brother David and parents Neil and Edna, who rest close by. Hers is the voice that has blessed my ears and enriched my life in a way that no other voice or mind could. There is no voice quite like that of Sandy Denny.

To further address the question asked by that classmate of mine, with Sandy's passing we lost one of the greatest – if not *the* greatest – female vocal and compositional talent of all times. I am thankful to have access to her recordings, both public and private, and am also thankful for her generational influence in the musical world that grows daily. I hope that somewhere, somebody, while reading this is discovering Sandy's music for the first time and is getting hooked or at least intrigued as to her wonderful lyrical and interpretative gifts. Sandy Denny's talents are worth celebrating and investigating. Wherever you are on your musical journey, I believe that she will be as good an ally to you as she is to me.

JOHN PEEL SHOW
21 APRIL 1978, LONDON, UK

NIGEL SCHOFIELD

Tributes to Sandy were fulsome and plentiful (no one was repeating nasty rumours or planting stories in the press at this stage). John Peel, who was currently surfing the new wave and promoting post-punk, began his BBC Radio 1 show that night with a wordlessly eloquent tribute. In total contrast to what his new fans might have expected, he opened with three Fairport-era Sandy tracks played back to back, ending with a personal tribute to the passing of his friend Sandy Denny: 'Perhaps the greatest and certainly the most under-rated singer Britain has ever produced; I had the honour to be a friend and a fan from her earliest days in the music business, which were also my earliest days in British radio.'

PUTNEY VALE CEMETERY
27 APRIL 1978, LONDON, UK

SYLVIA PRYOR NICOL

Dear Georgia,

First of all, what a great name they gave you! I didn't know your lovely mum well, but I remember her vividly and with huge fondness.

The first time I met her, in the autumn of 1976, Simon and I were briefly staying in Eydon, Northants. We arranged to meet up with your

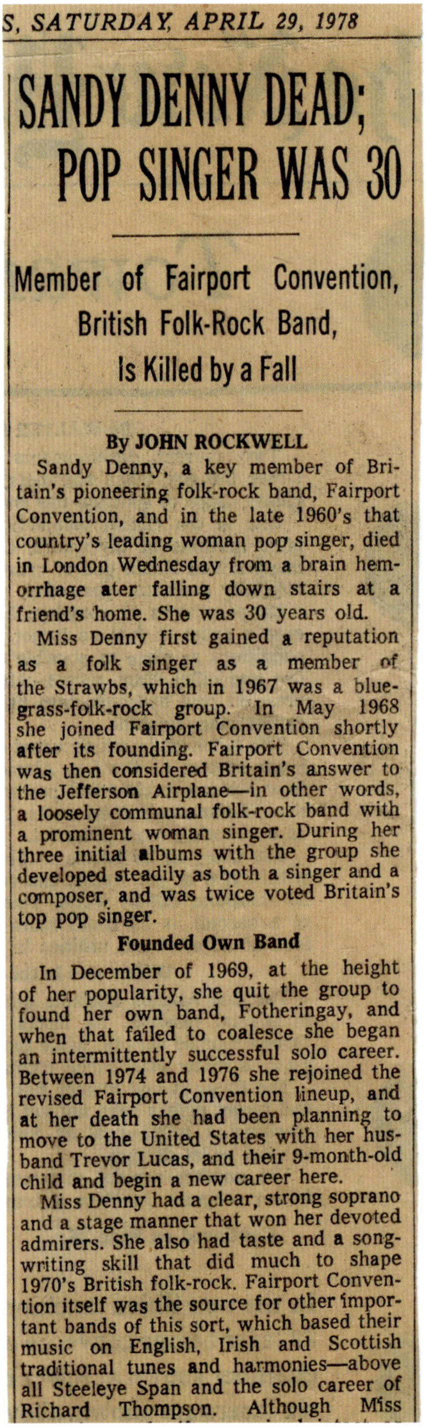

S, SATURDAY, APRIL 29, 1978

SANDY DENNY DEAD; POP SINGER WAS 30

Member of Fairport Convention, British Folk-Rock Band, Is Killed by a Fall

By JOHN ROCKWELL

Sandy Denny, a key member of Britain's pioneering folk-rock band, Fairport Convention, and in the late 1960's that country's leading woman pop singer, died in London Wednesday from a brain hemorrhage ater falling down stairs at a friend's home. She was 30 years old.

Miss Denny first gained a reputation as a folk singer as a member of the Strawbs, which in 1967 was a bluegrass-folk-rock group. In May 1968 she joined Fairport Convention shortly after its founding. Fairport Convention was then considered Britain's answer to the Jefferson Airplane—in other words, a loosely communal folk-rock band with a prominent woman singer. During her three initial albums with the group she developed steadily as both a singer and a composer, and was twice voted Britain's top pop singer.

Founded Own Band

In December of 1969, at the height of her popularity, she quit the group to found her own band, Fotheringay, and when that failed to coalesce she began an intermittently successful solo career. Between 1974 and 1976 she rejoined the revised Fairport Convention lineup, and at her death she had been planning to move to the United States with her husband Trevor Lucas, and their 9-month-old child and begin a new career here.

Miss Denny had a clear, strong soprano and a stage manner that won her devoted admirers. She also had taste and a songwriting skill that did much to shape 1970's British folk-rock. Fairport Convention itself was the source for other important bands of this sort, which based their music on English, Irish and Scottish traditional tunes and harmonies—above all Steeleye Span and the solo career of Richard Thompson. Although Miss

folks. Your mum and your handsome dad breezed into the pub, which I believe was the Royal Oak in Eydon. I remember your Mum being beautiful with lovely, long blonde-y hair. She was very stylishly, but casually, dressed. I think a Liberty print was involved, and a very cool jacket. She really did look like the star she was! And I must say, they both looked so happy and in love.

I guess we had a couple of drinks, not sure what, but I know we had a good time.

When I first saw Sandy sing live, later on, solo with piano, she had a bad cold, but her voice was perfection. That was the concert that Simon had to be 'theatre-row surfed' across our guest aisle due to staying too long in the Playhouse bar! Sandy thought it was hilarious later!

The funeral was so, so sad. I don't remember it clearly, but everyone was devastated. Linda T was clutching Simon's arm, stumbling, totally distraught and inconsolable. Swarb arrived wild and late by extravagant taxi from Byfield, but he made it to the service. He was also desperately sad.

The vicar hadn't really known Sandy but he had gleaned enough from her friends and family to perform a kind and glowing eulogy. Unfortunately, I can't remember if

THURS, 4/27/78, N.Y.T.

Sandy Denny, 31, British Singer, From Injuries Suffered in a Fall

LONDON, April 26 (AP)—Sandy Denny, one of Britain's leading popular singers, died last Friday after she suffered head injuries in a fall, a spokesman for Atkinson Morley's Hospital in Wimbledon said today.

Miss Denny, 31 years old, once a singer for the rock group Fairport Convention, was in a coma for four days after falling down the stairs at a friend's house, the spokesman said.

She had been planning to move to the United States with her husband, Trevor Lucas, a musician, and their 9-month-old daughter, Georgia.

SANDY DENNY, 30 4/29/78

Sandy Denny, British folk singer and rock star, died Wednesday in London from a brain hemorrhage after falling down stairs in a friend's home. She was 30.

Miss Denny gained recognition as a folk singer in 1967 with the Strawbs, a bluegrass and folk rock group. In 1968 she joined Fairport Convention, a British acid rock group. A year later she embarked on a solo career, rejoining Fairport from 1974 to 1976.

Survivors include her husband, Trevor Lucas.

US obituaries for Sandy (Edward Haber)

others spoke; someone will know.

There was a piper. Pretty much everyone was sobbing or tearful. I don't know if there was a wake. The funeral, for me, was a haze.

The day I met your mum was much clearer and obviously a happy one. She had such a wonderful smile. That first meeting is the main memory I have of her and I prefer to remember her that way: radiant, happy and just the best fun.

STRATHCLYDE STUDENTS UNION
11 MAY 1978, GLASGOW, UK

KENNY KEMP

In 1978 I was Vice President of Strathclyde Students Union and I instructed the Ents Officer, who was into punk by then, to book Fairport. I was 21 and I remember being very nervous. I went backstage to give my condolences to the band about the passing of Sandy a few weeks earlier. It went down like a lead balloon. The guys all signed my Fairport music book, but they were all still in shock. For several years after I was quite traumatised. It sticks with me to this day.

Sandy at the Enschede Folk Festival (Paul Neuray)

Sandy's Legacy

CHRISTINE COLLISTER, SINGER SONGWRITER

The first time I heard of Sandy was in the eighties. I was in RT's touring band at the time and we did 'For Shame Of Doing Wrong'. It was always a standout performance, and I loved doing the background vocals. Like most people who know and love Sandy's songs and exceptional voice, 'Who Knows Where The Time Goes?' has a particular place in my heart.

I dared to interpret this beautiful, evocative song on a special analogue project with REGA Hi-Fi around 2004. I love singing it still.

But it was at the funeral of a well-loved public figure on the Isle of Man in 2023, where I was invited to sing one of his favourite songs at the end of the service, that I truly understood her legacy. The first song played, which set the tone for the whole service, was a live version of 'Who Knows Where The Time Goes?' from the John Peel Sessions in 1973. I know the song intimately and have heard many, many versions of it over the years, but this performance was… transcendental. It was mesmerising, a sacred, mystical experience. I was moved to tears, not only for the gathered people come to pay their respects to a decent man, but by the reverence, clarity and authenticity in Sandy's performance – in her being. That she lived, loved, laughed, wrote, and sang with such vibrancy is a gift to the world. That she left so young is a deep, abiding sorrow.

MARCUS BANKS

I turned sixteen in the summer of 1973. The world seemed young and everything was new. I began to drift away from the pop music of the era as soon as I left school in search of I knew not what. I began, with a slow-burning curiosity, to read *Sounds* magazine and the *New Musical Express* which led to a life-long love of progressive music. But despite the blaring headlines and the hype, there was a quietly persistent mention of a lady called Sandy Denny. She seemed to have a firm grip on the magazine readers' annual polls for best female singer. As I was to discover much later, there was so much more to learn!

It was several years after Sandy's death that I, fatefully, first set foot in a folk club. I immediately took to the friendly people there and the club had a lovely cosy vibe. But there was something else. 'What's the background music?' I asked and someone said, 'It's *The Best Of Fairport Convention*, mate.'

That was the first time I had ever heard Sandy Denny sing.

Sandy's voice got under my skin on that day and has always been there. Her cassettes were among the first I reached for during interminably long car journeys to work. And later, Fairport Convention's rendition of Sandy's 'Who Knows Where The Time Goes?' would bathe a precious corner of Oxfordshire at their annual festival. Sandy's voice endures and, oh, how easily it still moves me to tears.

In more recent years, it has been my pleasure to spend time lingering in the Sandy Denny Exhibition at Cropredy and my privilege to meet its curator, her daughter Georgia. It is her self-imposed mission, not only to keep Sandy's memory alive but also to provide a physical, tangible link to Sandy.

And so Sandy Denny, songwriter and singer without rival even today, remains in our collective memory. It is my firm belief that any social historian worth their salt would cement her place in our national folk memory.

For a great many of us, Sandy's music is ever present now. As for myself, there will always be a place in my heart for 'The Lady' and the unicorn she always kept.

Bless you, Sandy.

IAN BURGESS, FRIENDS OF FAIRPORT

Not listening to folk or even folk rock through the seventies, Sandy went completely under my radar. I first became aware of her when I saw in a birthday listing that we shared the same birthday. Well, day and month (I'm a few years younger). In those pre-internet days Sandy's albums were unavailable and finding them was difficult.

Rendezvous was Sandy's final album, released in 1977

In 1979, when Fairport split, Peggy joined Jethro Tull. I was a big Tull fan and decided to look out the previous history of the new boy. This led me firstly to Fairport before I started to track down the solo work of other Fairport members. At a record fair in Bristol, I found a copy of *Rendezvous*, in mint condition for £2. When I tried to put the disc back in the sleeve, something was obstructing it. I assumed it was a booklet that came with the album. Purchasing the album, I went home happy. I was even happier when I discovered that tucked away in the sleeve was a copy of the *Rendezvous* tour programme.

That was the start of some vigorous collecting, both of Sandy but recordings by all the ex-Fairporters. Gradually, and particularly with the advent of compact discs, it became easier to collect all her recordings, including the magnificent 19 disc set that included everything previously released alongside a whole lot more.

Sandy left us before I heard her sing even a note. I may have found her via another route, but I say thank you to Dave Pegg for joining Jethro Tull. I started running 'Friends Of Fairport' in 1987, and although the magazine *The Ledge* is now history, I am still promoting the Fairport family whenever I can.

MICK PETERS, FORMER FAIRPORT TOUR MANAGER

In the late sixties I had heard of Fairport Convention and was particularly impressed with Sandy's vocals. I went to a gig somewhere in the Midlands (God only knows where – it was a long time ago!) and I confess I fell madly in love with Sandy even though she was about seven years older than me.

After Sandy left Fairport, I still went to the occasional Fairport gig. In the seventies I got to know Peggy and met members of the various FC line-ups at his house in Barford. In 1976, Fairport played on the front lawn of Prescote Manor in Cropredy. Peggy asked Wayne Averill, who was an electrician and a good mate of mine, to sort out the electrics for the gig. Wayne took me along to help out.

In 1979 I was working at Freddie Bannister's Knebworth Festival. This clashed with the final Fairport gig. Wayne had asked me to help him at Cropredy, so being a mercenary youth, and having got my Knebworth t-shirt, I jumped ship and went to Peewit Farm for the 'last ever' Fairport show.

Ever since, I have worked at Cropredy, never missing a year until the

Covid layoff. I worked as a generator engineer, a rigger and a forklift driver, and then worked my way up to site manager. After the sad loss of Rob Braviner, I was asked to take over as the band's tour manager, something I really enjoyed. I held the role until 2024, when old age took over and I retired from touring.

I owe Sandy big time for introducing me to a crazy lifetime in the music and festival industries. In my humble opinion she was undoubtedly the best female vocalist ever, and always will be.

CARLA FUCHS, SINGER SONGWRITER

My exploration of Sandy Denny's lost lyrics has been one of the most exciting and profound journeys of my life. I am a musician and a Germanist. My work on Sandy Denny's unpublished lyrics followed a philological and artistic-research approach, combining close textual analysis, comparison of variants and sketches, and historically informed musical composition.

During the coronavirus pandemic, I rediscovered my deep connection to Sandy's music. It carried me through this time, and I began singing her songs, exploring them on the piano and guitar, entering her musical language more intensely than ever before. Sandy's fate, and that of her daughter Georgia, touched me deeply.

It has always been central to my work to promote the achievements of women in art and music and to contribute to their visibility within cultural history. I wrote the song 'Songbird' for Georgia and Sandy, in Sandy's spirit blended with my own songwriting – not as a copy, but as an expression of gratitude and critical reflection on the story of these two remarkable women.

Carla Fuchs worked with Georgia on an album of Sandy's unpublished lyrics

When Georgia suggested that I might create an album using unpublished lyrics by her mother, set to new music,

I did not hesitate for a moment. I had already studied Sandy's music for years: listening closely, analysing her harmonic language and phrasing, studying her lyrics, her vocal technique and her musical development.

The first step was locating the original manuscripts. When they finally arrived in Australia after their journey from the UK, we had one of our legendary day–night calls – late at night in Germany, early morning in Australia. With boundless enthusiasm, Georgia photographed everything for me while I tried to sort through the images of Sandy's diaries, until Georgia's phone overheated so badly that it had to be put into the fridge.

Then the work began: composing the music, philologically sorting and comparing versions and sketches, and developing a working process that did not follow the easiest path, but the most accurate one. This proved challenging, as some texts offered little indication of their intended final form. Passages Sandy had crossed out, I respected as an expression of authorial will, and I attempted to resolve formal problems by working with the remaining sketches rather than by adding new material.

Although I had studied Sandy's tonal language, phrasing, lyrics and musical history in great detail, I cannot fully rationalise how the songs ultimately came to me. Once the texts had been shaped into a coherent form, the music arrived with remarkable immediacy. This process corresponds to what artistic research describes as embodied or tacit knowledge: a form of understanding that emerges through long-term engagement and practice rather than through analytical reasoning alone.

I knew immediately which songs belonged to the guitar and which to the piano – which chords, which tunings my guitar required. Throughout, I aimed to remain as close as possible to Sandy's musical language without copying it.

Sharing the new songs as demos with Georgia and, together with her, bringing her mother's music into a new, living present became a journey through time – into another life that nonetheless reached deeply into our own.

One day before the anniversary of Sandy's death, my dearest person in the world passed away unexpectedly, just before the vocal recordings began. I knew I had to continue. I sang with all the strength I could summon, singing as if my heart were leaving my chest. Between hospital rooms, funeral homes, life and death, farewell and new beginnings, this album took shape as our shared connection – and as our gift to Sandy and to everyone who loves her music.

Sandy Denny's biography can be read as a woman struggling to make it in the male-dominated music industry. Many of the mechanisms that limited her recognition during her lifetime persist today, despite changed rhetoric and surface-level progress. During our work on *Songbird*, Georgia and I found ourselves confronted with the very same structures that had once contributed to Sandy's marginalisation.

These often difficult experiences ultimately brought us even closer together. We encountered them independently, and again and again we had to encourage one another not to give up – not to give in to the arrogance of those who still believe that women in the music business should not be taken seriously. Our mission to raise Sandy's visibility as a woman artist became inseparable from our own struggle for recognition within a predominantly male professional environment.

Georgia's life story is one of the most remarkable biographies I have ever encountered. Together, we have succeeded in opening a new chapter. *Songbird* is shaped by scholarly research, years of sustained engagement with Sandy's music, a deep sisterhood between Georgia and myself, and the conviction that Sandy's work must be remembered not only because she was an outstanding songwriter and singer, but because the struggle of women in the music industry remains a lived and unresolved reality.

Our *Songbird* project stands for what Sandy means to us: depth, warmth, compassion and independence – in our relationships, in our music, and in her lyrics and art.

RECORDING STUDIO
1982, SYDNEY, AUSTRALIA

MARCIA HOWARD

In 1982 we were recording our band Goanna's first album, *Spirit Of Place*, in Sydney and Melbourne, Australia. The producer of this album was Trevor Lucas from Fairport Convention. I knew of the band and I knew that Trevor had been married to the singer songwriter, Sandy Denny. I got to know Trevor and met his daughter Georgia and son Clancy and his mum, Liz. That is when I started listening to Sandy's songs. Her voice was clear and strong and tuneful and honest. The beautiful vibrato that was her vocal tone told her stories through song. Sandy was a trail blazer and a unique artist. She died sadly way too soon.

After Trevor passed away, I have always kept an eye out for Georgia. I think her mother and her father would be so very proud of the woman and mother she has become and their grandchildren who carry that talent. Clancy is there to keep an eye on his sister as well. The exhibition and book Georgia have created are a legacy for Sandy and Trevor's descendants. Well done, Georgia. You have kept your mother's musical memory alive and her songs will go on and take their place in the long history of British folk song.

My friend the brilliant Irish musician singer, Mary Black, covered Sandy's song, 'Who Knows Where The Time Goes?'. I love Mary's version and I love Sandy's song. It transports me to a place that suspends time and reminds us to savour our time here on earth. Sandy influenced my songwriting style and challenged me to be musically brave and share my vulnerabilities in my song writing on my own albums. The Denny/Lucas family hold a special place in my heart.

Marcia Howard's band's first album was produced by Trevor Lucas

THOMAS HERLING

I first heard Sandy Denny in 1983. I was working at the college radio station. The station manager had cancelled the late-night rock music show so we employees were gradually pilfering LPs from the now unused record library for the best stuff.

One of them was *The Fairport Chronicles*, a 1976 promotional double LP issued in the US by A&M Records. I'd heard *of* Fairport Convention but I don't know if I'd actually *heard* the band so the album fell into my book bag. It's a record that's pretty Sandy-heavy, since it features a number of tracks from her solo albums and The Bunch record. From there on it was a hunt for more of her records.

Back in the early eighties, finding a Sandy Denny record was a bit of a treasure hunt, especially in the US, so when I travelled, I'd be sifting through a record shop's few folk records from England. I found the *Sandy* LP while visiting London, carefully packing it in my suitcase hoping it wouldn't get damaged on the flight home. I found the *Fotheringay* record in a store in Toronto.

One song has stood out for me: 'Next Time Around'. I spent some of my childhood in Buffalo so it was interesting to hear that name sung so beautifully. It's probably the saddest song ever recorded, especially when you learn about the tragic life of the person who inspired it, her first boyfriend, Jackson C Frank, scarred by a fire at his school near Buffalo.

Then came the 1986 big box set compiled by Joe Boyd and Trevor Lucas, a four LP set only available through mail order. I can't remember how many times I played that collection when I first got it.

The mid to late eighties were difficult times. Cold, dark, and dreary days. My career as a recording engineer in New York City and then a DJ at a tiny upstate New York radio station was floundering. Money was always a real problem. I'd gotten married for a lot of wrong reasons. I had been walking around with an undiagnosed and untreated anxiety disorder, during an era when you didn't talk of such things, much less seek treatment.

'The best healers were the musicians,' The Band's Garth Hudson stated in the film *The Last Waltz*, 'they had the ability to punch through that pain.' Sandy's music could do that. Her music was a relief for my failing marriage and career, during what were some of the lowest years of my life.

Somehow, I managed to pull myself out of it, to get into graduate school, to ultimately rise above my personal demons and become a college professor, teaching filmmaking and music recording. Some of my students have gone on to work with some of Sandy's contemporaries, Richard Thompson and Linda Thompson.

Now, decades later, Sandy's records can be had by anyone with an internet connection. The giant 19 CD 'crate set' – too much to be called a mere boxed set – and re-releases of Fairport's and her solo albums, mean you can get pretty much everything she ever recorded. You can even hear her extol the virtues of butter in a radio commercial on YouTube.

I've since attended the Cropredy Festival, visited the Sandy Denny Exhibition and met Sandy's daughter, the delightful and talented Georgia Rose Lucas. Some of Georgia's art featuring her mother is on my wall. Appropriately, I think, between posters of The Beatles and Bob Dylan. I've paid my respects at Sandy's grave in Putney Vale.

I never had the chance to see Sandy in performance. I only learned about her some years after her death. I can only imagine that it was a captivating experience. The short amount of video of her singing that still exists always makes me marvel at how such a beautiful sound can come from a person.

There's so much I could say about her music. The power behind 'Nothing More'. The highwire act of 'A Sailor's Life'. The mesmerising 'Banks Of The Nile'. That her life and career were so short makes the music she left behind more valuable.

Her music still retains that power to punch through that pain. As with an old friend, there's times when you would lose contact when life got busy, but would connect again to find the voice that has always had that ability to move me. I had no idea that how finding that one album by chance way back when would make her music a part of my life all these years.

NEVILLE DALTON

I was aware of Sandy and a fraction of her work, with Fairport Convention and as a solo artist. I loved her voice but never got around to exploring further... until I became educated. A BBC work colleague, Richard Warry, was a fount of knowledge on anything music-related. He could tell you the most minute details about the most obscure artists and, as it was my pleasure to discover, was usually right.

He was an admirer of Nina Simone, but when it came to British music, he was at the front of the queue of those who held Sandy in the highest esteem.

On what would have been her 73rd birthday, he wrote in the Sandy Denny Facebook group: 'The greatest singer in British popular music.'

If Richard said it, it must be true. His enthusiasm for her work rubbed off on me and as a result, I became a little more familiar with her music, but Richard was the Denny aficionado. Unfortunately, he too died far too soon, a few years ago. He would have loved this book. And although he was never one for the limelight, he would have been thrilled to be associated with it.

JAMIE CHRISTIAN

I first heard and fell in love with Sandy's voice when I was eleven years old in 1984. My uncle put on *The History Of Fairport Convention* and the track 'Matty Groves'. I was immediately transfixed. I knew the song from an old Joan Baez album my dad owned, but here was something that sounded sexy, heavy and extremely cool. At that time, there was little still available – only the early Fairport albums and some very expensive American/Canadian imports. Thankfully, the first box set soon appeared, and now I can safely say I have everything!

LEVENT VARLIK, SANDY DENNY MAILING LIST

Istanbul is an ancient and beautiful city with a sea running through it. In April, the Judas trees on both sides of the city bloom with purple flowers, blending the purple and blue of the Bosphorus. Seagulls constantly fly over the sea, following the boatmen, their cries echoing as they join the fishermen in their catches. One day, I was going to visit a friend on the other side of the city, crossing the Bosphorus. I left the university and went to Karaköy Pier on the European side. I bought my ticket. Then I glanced at the newspapers on the pier and suddenly saw the headline in *Melody Maker* magazine: 'Sandy Denny Is Dead.' I was shocked! How could it happen…? Her melodies were in my ears for years. She was my heroine! As TS Eliot said, 'April is the cruellest month.'

I was fifteen years old in 1971 and growing up listening to musicians of that era like The Beatles, Rolling Stones, Eric Clapton, Traffic, Cream, Blind Faith, Bob Dylan, Joni Mitchell, etc. on Turkish radios. My only connection to music was radio broadcasts. There were no record stores where I lived back then. However, my brother was working in a larger city, he had bought a Garrard Turntable for me, and the seller had given him *Unhalfbricking* as a gift. It's a second-hand,

US promo copy, with elephants and a ballerina on the LP cover. It was my first-ever LP. That's how my acquaintance with Sandy's voice began fifty-five years ago, with Richard Thompson's composition, 'Genesis Hall', the first song on the record.

I listened to *Unhalfbricking* over and over again every day. The music was amazing. It had a different sound than the songs I constantly heard on the radio. Richard's guitar, Martin's drums, Swarb's violin, everything was beautiful. Above all, Sandy's voice and her songs were captivating. I was mesmerised. Now, a day hadn't passed without me listening to Sandy's voice. Then, I started looking for other Fairport Convention records. But, in Turkey, nobody knew this band. I never heard them on the radio either.

My brother and I tried to listen to BBC Radio 2, expecting to hear Sandy's singing. The technology of those days wasn't as advanced as it is now. It was hard to listen to the BBC without interference. John Peel's programmes interested me. One day, me and my brother sent a letter to John Peel requesting him to play a Fairport Convention song. We were curious whether he would play it or not. A few days later John Peel said, 'I received an interesting letter from Turkey, they want us to play Fairport Convention,' and then played 'Si Tu Dois Partir'. That was joyous!

In the early-seventies I bought Led Zeppelin's fourth album. The inside cover of the Turkish pressing had no information. I didn't know Sandy was the guest musician on it. But I was so familiar with Sandy's voice that I remember thinking, 'Hey, that's Sandy,' when I heard 'The Battle Of Evermore'" I was so happy at discovering a new song with Sandy.

Towards the mid-seventies, some radio DJs began to play Fairport Convention songs on their programmes, and the band became a bit more well-known in Turkey. So, I started buying Sandy's and Fairport's second-hand records whenever I found them. At the same time, I was gathering information about Sandy from various fanzines like *Fairport Fanatics* (later *Dirty Linen*), *The Ledge*, *Fiddlestix*, *Hokey Pokey* and *Flypaper*, collecting press cuttings, and trying to learn more about her.

However, I was hungry for more information about Sandy, her recordings, her demos, etc. Information provided by print media was limited. It was the 1990s, and the internet age had begun. I found Willem Doornkamp's website for Sandy. It was a very informative site.

Since the internet was accessible to everyone, I realised I needed to create a mailing list to reach fellow Sandy fans like myself.

I started the Sandy Denny Mailing List on 11 May 1997 with the encouragement of Willem, the original webmaster of the Sandy Denny home page, and John Penhallow. The mailing list was introduced on Willem's page. Those who wanted to join would email me, I would create the group, and I would manually forward the messages to other list members. Initially, we only had 200 people. The group shared lots of information about Sandy and her music, her lyrics, reviews, etc. Later, I transferred the mailing list to Yahoo Groups and we communicated there for ten-plus years. When Yahoo stopped their mailing list operations, I opened the list at IO Groups site. This was, and still is, a labour of love for me.

It has been a long time since we lost Sandy, but she is always in my life. Whether happy, sad or in love, I always listen to her. When I go to the seaside, the sound of the waves reminds me of her singing. When I think about the past, I remember her songs. The sound of the rain, the ticking of the clock, the sadness of November, loneliness, all remind me of her. I carry her soft, silky voice with me always.

For the last fifty-five years, a different Sandy song was my favourite every day. It's sometimes 'Who Knows Where The Time Goes?', sometimes 'Late November', sometimes 'The King And Queen Of England'. Today I don't have another fifty-five years under blue sky ahead of me, but whatever remains, I know that all my days will be filled with her songs.

BLUE 4 LP
RELEASED 1975

BUDI BUTENOP, THE TIGER LILLIES

I lived in a small town in North Germany. I loved fifties music and beat, and I played drums in a skiffle band and a blues rock band. I loathed eighties music and the dull, dated, whining lyrics of mediocre singers. There was no diversity on German radio, and the only source for creativity was nighttime AM radio.

Then Sandy Denny and Fairport came into my life. *The North Star*

Grassman and *The History Of Fairport Convention* were my first albums. I immediately started writing songs in the vein of 'Tam Lin' and 'Late November' and our blues band turned 'folkadelic'. My passion was poetry, experimenting with metaphors, settings, view point angles, words.

Sandy Denny's lyrics contained everything that I felt important. She chose the music that best transported the message, the mood, the emotion. The four-LP blue box set *Who Knows Where The Time Goes?* became the soundtrack of my nineties, and Sandy's lyrics my bible of (self) critical poetic thinking. Her lyrical perspective on life was closer to mine than many others, old and new.

My bass player and I moved to Berlin and finally life began. I studied social work, acted at a theatre and played drums in countless bands, including some Irish folk bands which brought in money and gave me a chance to exercise Dave Mattacks' routines. My bass player and I quietly wept along to 'Nothing More' and 'One More Chance'. Sandy gave us two young struggling souls comfort in the big city. We had both experienced heartbreak, losing some friends to mental hospitals, some to hard drugs. Normal life in your twenties, I guess.

In 1999 I met an inspiring young woman. While I was out working with deprived youths she listened to my records and started fiddling with my four-track tape recorder. Joni Mitchell, Bob Dylan, Janis Ian, Fiona Apple, Gillian Welch and Sandy Denny sparked her songwriting. I joined her guitar and banjo on double bass and we toured Europe for the next ten years as a folk/Americana duo.

Promoters, audiences and media called us 'niche'. Frustrating as it was, we preferred to stay true to our music rather than playing cheesy industry games. The 'John The Gun' feel and drum pattern became a fixed term in our arrangements, while 'By The Time It Gets Dark' became a lyrical and musical blueprint for folky, up tempo songs.

We had toured England and loved their enthusiasm, their open mindedness and how almost everyone knew Sandy or Fairport. We had even supported Dave Swarbrick! (To my singer's embarrassment, I brought every record of his that I owned for him to sign.) We felt so at home there that in 2015 we moved to London.

Then my singer moved to Canada and I began drumming with the Tiger Lillies, a band where music is the vehicle for the lyrics, where Sandy Denny is known and respected, where I can play what I learned from the great Dave Mattacks and Gerry Conway. Their contributions to Sandy's songs are, along with John Bonham, the main influences on my instrument.

PROMISES
RELEASED 1985

KEVIN DEMPSEY

I played in the band Whippersnapper for a number of years with Swarb. Rehearsing material for our first album, Swarb said he wanted to record 'One Way Donkey Ride', a Sandy song. He went into great detail about how Sandy came to his house and played on the piano sitting there in our rehearsal room. Apparently, it is the last song that Sandy wrote. All was well until Swarb said he wanted me to sing it! After a quick panic, I decided to have a go. Sandy never got to hear this version, but I met Trevor at Cropredy shortly after the album with our version had been released. He came up to me and said, 'Sandy would have loved it, mate.'

MARK AYNSLEY

How did I come to find Sandy? Well, it was 1984; I didn't know her voice when she was alive because I was only eleven years old when she passed. I went to see a young American band play a small gig in '85, promoting their LP. Joe Boyd had produced it and it was called *The Wishing Chair*. John Peel was playing it. That band was 10,000 Maniacs and Natalie Merchant. I chatted with Natalie afterwards and her parting shots were, 'Listen to Sandy Denny; listen to Fairport.' She was clearly healthily obsessed and I became so too.

I even called John Peel whilst he was doing his radio show and he told me just how much Sandy still meant to him, even in those post-punk years of slightly denying the past and embracing the new.

I can never focus on anything else when Sandy is singing; she's the only singer who can do that for me, without remotely sounding like she's trying to find your attention. There are so many equally great singers, and some of them, like Nina and Judy, did covers. Many voices I love were not even particularly good singers. Yet only Sandy utterly captures my attention. Right there, on the spot.

One of the things I love about her is that she isn't always trying to sound beautiful and lovely… There is a deliberate sourness and insouciance in some performances. Maybe that appeals to all of us who don't want to be categorised in any obvious way.

JOHN PENHALLOW

My first encounter with Trevor Lucas goes back to the days of 1967. I was Fairport's first manager. I was helping them transition from weekend warriors to full professional status. We were loading the band's gear into a small rehearsal room in Soho that doubled up as a storeroom for Elektra Records. Trevor was already there, rehearsing with his band Eclection. We were introduced, then Eclection left and it was Fairport's turn to rehearse.

In the seventies I saw Trevor at a couple of Fairport gigs. I can never say I had any type of friendship with Sandy. As she joined Fairport in 1968, I left, so our meetings over the following years were backstage at gigs as Simon Nicol's mate. Just 'hellos', 'enjoyed the show' and 'goodbyes'. It was kind of funny that, 30 years later, I should end up helping to look after parts of her and Trevor's musical legacy.

I moved to Sydney in 1975 and forgot all about Fairport's fortunes for a while. I even missed the Sydney Opera House gig – shame on me! My biggest regret was missing Trevor's performances at Melbourne's Troubadour Cafe. We lived in Melbourne for 15 months from 1980. Imagine my disappointment when reading the Friday night gig guide on Saturday morning, and seeing that Trevor had played there the night before!

John Penhallow (right) with Cropredy stallholder Leon (Georgia Rose Lucas)

Then in 1986, during Fairport's tour of Australia, I joined them for the Victorian and Sydney gigs. We all got invited to a barbecue at Bushwacker Dobe Newton's house in North Melbourne. Trevor's wife Elizabeth was there with Georgia and Clancy.

Trevor? Well, he was up at the Music Farm near Byron Bay, recording songs for a movie. One track from that session turned up on *The Attic Tracks Cassette Volume 4* – 'A Picture of You', so I'm grateful for that.

We finally got to see the whole Lucas family regularly when they moved to Sydney in 1987. We became good friends. It was at one of my visits that Trevor took me into his attic music room. He started saying, 'Oh, you'll love this one John!' He played me Sandy's songs: 'The King And Queen Of England', 'Easy To Slip', 'Losing Game', 'Still Waters Run Deep', 'No End' and his own wonderful version of 'Girls On The Avenue'. In an old singles box, we found 'Tears'. We copied each song onto cassette as we found them and so the first volume of the *Attic Tracks* came to be.

In 1989, after Trevor had died, Elizabeth asked me to take care of Trevor's tape and cassette collection. I assembled a tribute cassette of performances recorded by him at the Troubadour Cafe in '83 and '84 and released it in March 1989 to the readers of our Australian Friends of Fairport newsletter, *Fiddlestix* (back in the days before Facebook). Dave and Chris Pegg at Woodworm Records sold a couple of hundred copies at that year's Cropredy Festival.

More letters of encouragement from the true fans of Sandy led me to release *Attic Tracks 3* in March 1990. It catalogued 14 songs which I believe are the earliest of Sandy's recordings from 1966 and '67. I included nine tracks from the last concert performance that Sandy gave at the Royalty Theatre, London on 27 November 1977.

Finally, I compiled *Attic Tracks 4*, subtitled *Together Again*, which has 13 tracks from each of Sandy and Trevor. It took many hours of listening to songs on old reels. Some were spoilt by studio mishaps. Others had false starts, forgotten lyrics, or out-of-tune guitars. One track had the front-of-house engineer soloing the drums through the mixer in the middle of a great live version! I bounced lists back and forth with Elizabeth until we were both happy with the final selection.

I took the chosen tapes to a friend's demo studio. He equalised the levels and added a bit of tone correction to get them sounding better. Here was a bunch of songs that traced the careers of both Sandy and Trevor. Many of the songs were complete surprises to many Sandy and Fairport fans. They thought they had everything ever released.

In May 1994 I released *Attic Tracks Volume 4*. I was making copies at home on my Denon Twin Cassette Deck, as the mail orders came in from around the world.

In 1995 Raven Records in Melbourne invited me to submit a selection of songs from the four cassettes for a CD release. It would be called *Sandy Denny, Trevor Lucas and Friends: The Attic Tracks 1972–1984*.

Later on, Elizabeth and I were again in London at the same time and we met with Sue Armstrong of the Strange Fruit label. I submitted the running order to Sue and in 1997 *The BBC Sessions 1971–1973* got released. But its life was short-lived. Due to rights issues, it was withdrawn on the day of release! Around 4,000 had been shipped from the warehouse to retailers around the world. It became a highly collectible disc for a time. It's still listed on Discogs at some high prices for quality copies.

This was followed in 1998 when Denny's final performance at the Royalty Theatre, entitled *Gold Dust*, was issued by Island Records on CD. Jerry Donahue produced it. He replaced a few bum bass notes and lead lines himself. He got Simon Nicol and Chris Leslie in to add a few in-tune backing vocals where they were needed. This CD coincided with the twentieth anniversary of Sandy's passing and also brought a close to my involvement with Sandy's recordings. It's always been for the love of her and Trevor's music and for the family they left behind.

'BY THE TIME IT GETS DARK' RELEASED 1987

MARY BLACK, SINGER

As a teenager in the late sixties and early seventies I was totally obsessed with Sandy Denny and Fairport Convention. I'd spend hours listening over and over to every turn and phrase of her voice. I recorded 'Crazy Man Michael' – my party piece – back in the late seventies, very early in my career, and 'By The Time It Gets Dark' was the title track off my third album. Also on that album was 'Farewell, Farewell', a Richard Thompson song that I heard from her. The album was a turning point in my career.

Since then, I've recorded 'Moments', 'One Way Donkey Ride', 'Full

Moon' and 'Who Knows Where The Time Goes?'. Sandy's songs and voice inspired me to become a singer. I connected deeply to all of her work… I was heartbroken to hear she passed away so young... What a huge loss! I had dreamt I would at least one day get to see her live but it wasn't to be. Her spirit lives on in her music and (strange as it might sound) I sometimes have felt that spirit around me when I'm on stage!

MUSIC FARM STUDIO
1986, BYRON BAY, MULLUMBIMBY, AUSTRALIA

WAYNE GILLESPIE

Growing up in New Zealand I was massively influenced by singer songwriters of the sixties and seventies. I started writing songs in my teens and in 1979 moved to London where I saw the likes of John Martyn, Bert Jansch and Steve Ashley perform. In 1981 I returned to Auckland, New Zealand and became part of the folk/acoustic scene. I found an Island sampler album that opened with 'Late November'. It blew me away with its power, vocals and lyrics and I began immersing myself in Sandy's solo material.

My debut album made the finals of the 1984 Music Awards 'Most Promising Male Vocalist' and 'Folk Album Of The Year', leading CBS Records NZ to sign me up to make a follow up. Trevor Lucas was my first choice of producer and I sent him a demo tape. Trevor's manager, Chris Gough, called saying Trevor was interested in working with me. Trevor said, 'I had a listen to your demos and it sounded like the typical folky shite I often get sent, but there was one song that stood out that got my attention called 'Heart's For' so I'm in!'

In January 1986 I flew from Auckland to Melbourne for pre-production, staying with Trevor and his partner Liz, where I got to meet their son Clancy (then aged four) and the eight-year-old Georgia.

Trevor was super-extroverted, friendly, supportive and somewhat direct at times, possessing an almost stereotypical 'ocker' persona and with Aussie accent undiluted by his years living in the UK. (Think Paul Hogan in *Crocodile Dundee*!) He had an unbridled passion for all kinds of music and exuded an infectious confidence, which was much needed by this acoustic singer/songwriter who had never played with a drummer before. Pre-production with Trevor consisted of moments such as: 'I think this song needs a verse about the bloke drowning his sorrows at the pub. I'll just grab some lunch while you come up with the verse!'

Recording at Music Farm Studio, my lack of experience with time and click tracks showed and I was relieved of my role as rhythm guitarist. Trevor normalised my distress at not cutting it by sharing a story of his own where he was not allowed to play on his own track in his early career for the same reason.

Trevor told me that he and Joe Boyd had produced 1985's four-album box set of Sandy's music *Who Knows Where the Time Goes?* He recounted listening to the studio takes in compiling the album and answering back to Sandy's voice on the tapes: 'How was that take, Trevor?'

The experience of compiling the album seemed to have sent him right back to those times and the pain of losing her. The engineer on our project told me that late at night, when we had finished recording, he had found Trevor in the studio with tears in his eyes, playing the box set. Trevor also wrote a song which he played me (called 'Girl In The Photo' or 'Girl In The Frame'), which appeared to be about Sandy as there was a framed photo of her in the studio.

My album was released under the title *New Locations* and Trevor's favourite song from that album, 'Heart's For' made the finals of the 1988 New Zealand Music Awards under the Best Folk category.

In January 1989, Trevor came to my house in Balmain. He was very keen on the idea of producing the follow-up to *New Locations*. A week later, I got a call from his friend and ex-Fairport manager John Penhallow saying that Trevor had passed away in his sleep from a heart attack. He was 44 years old.

The funeral was a sad affair. A song we recorded, 'Old Friends Like Us Will Never Be Forgotten', was one of the songs played at his wake at his home in Epping, Sydney. Georgia and Clancy seemed to enjoy swimming in the pool that day, in that moment oblivious to the hardships and challenges that lay ahead.

I stayed in touch with Georgia and Clancy and got to visit Georgia's twin girls Jahmira and Ariel soon after they were born in 1997. Fast forward to 2025 and it was a privilege to be able to pass the baton on and produce a number of original demos for Jahmira Jade Lucas and a song of Ariel's.

Jahmira poignantly did a beautiful rendition of a favourite song of her grandmother's, Jackson C Franks' 'Blues Runs The Game'.

PETER READ

It was a 1988 BBC radio documentary to mark ten years since her death where I first heard Sandy's voice and story. I was 21. Nearly forty years later I still haven't heard another singer-songwriter that moves me more. I see Fairport, Richard Thompson and the Sandy Denny Project as much as I can, and I love it that they and others are keeping her music alive. I particularly love PP Arnold's great version of 'I'm a Dreamer' that she often includes in her setlist. If I had to choose just two favourite Sandy songs, ones in which I always hear something new in the lyrics and the music, they would be 'The Pond And The Stream' and 'Autopsy'.

GOLD DUST
RELEASED JUNE 1988

MARION FLEETWOOD

I am so fortunate to be part of The Sandy Denny Project, alongside my friends Sally, Gemma, Mat, Mark and PJ. We have all brought our favourite Sandy songs to the project and this story is about how I found mine.

Many years ago, I was given a copy of Sandy's album *Gold Dust* by a friend who wanted to share her music with me. I was singing lots of jazz

The Sandy Denny Project (PJ Wright)

and not a lot of folk music, so Sandy's music hadn't really become part of my musical library. One night / early morning in June – driving home very, very late from a gig in a far-flung corner of southern England as dawn approached – I was digging around for something to listen to on the last stretch home between Banbury and Stratford-upon-Avon. So it was that I found myself driving through the Oxfordshire countryside on a midsummer's morning at around dawn. And *Gold Dust* was unwrapped and put in the CD player.

The A422 has some beautiful spots and more than one hill, one in particular being Sun Rising Hill which, when you start your descent onto the Stratford plain, gives you a breathtaking view of the English countryside, stretching from the Malverns across to Daventry. When it is clear, even the tiniest detail of a stream or hedgerow is visible for miles. The sky as the sun rises contains every shade of blue, pink and yellow imaginable – uninterrupted by powerlines or tall buildings. Birds abound and the trees which line the road mask the glory of the countryside from time to time, meaning you catch tiny glimpses, then longer views, then glimpses again. Nature is teasing you. And then after the last bend, the view unfolds and sometimes you just have to stop in the layby there. Especially if your timing is good and, like I did that morning, you arrive there as the sun rises.

As I approached Sun Rising Hill, with great hopes for and memories of the view rising in me, track seven started. As I made my way down the hill, straining my eyes to see through the branches, and anticipating the final vista, I discovered my very favourite Sandy song. The words. The soaring melody. The simplicity. The silver tongue, the golden heart. Every word carrying meaning and resonance. I had to stop as the tears blurred my vision and I had to give all my attention to the music pouring out and filling my head and heart.

'On a beautiful morning, of silver and gold.' Life met art there as the sun rose on Sun Rising Hill and added such richness to my musical life from that moment on.

I have sung this song so many times since that day – and am honoured to sing it with The Sandy Denny Project and also on Feast of Fiddles tours. Each time I am reminded of that first hearing and the happy tears. As the last note fades, there is often a barely audible sigh from somewhere in the audience. And there is always peace and a quietness in the shared moment.

RYMAN AUDITORIUM
1988, NASHVILLE, TENNESSEE

TINA ADAIR, MUSICIAN

I became a huge fan and admirer of Sandy Denny's writing when I was introduced to her song 'By the Time It Gets Dark' in 1996 by my producer at the time, Jerry Douglas. He played me Mary Black's version from a cassette tape he had in his living room. I immediately fell in love with this song and knew I had to record it on my very first album for Sugar Hill Records. The song truly came to life in the studio with Chris Thile on mandolin, Bryan Sutton on guitar, Viktor Krauss on bass, Aubrey Haynie on fiddle, Charlie Cushman on banjo and Jerry Douglas on dobro. Alan O'Bryant and Keith Little sang the beautiful harmonies with me on it. During the session, this song was one of those magical moments in the studio that was beautifully recorded in one or two takes, played live by the band. The combination of Sandy's lyrics and melody hit me every single time I hear it. The song makes people feel good and happy when they hear it.

I was just 17 years old when I first recorded it. Fast forward to a couple of months ago and I found myself in the studio in Nashville, Tennessee, recording 'By The Time It Gets Dark' with a brand-new band that I am involved in forming. Some of these band members grew up listening to this version of the song and encouraged me to re-record it. Sandy's 'By The Time It Gets Dark' transcends time, place and genre. One of my favourite memories of playing this song live, with my family band – The Adairs – was in 1998 on the historical stage of the Ryman Auditorium, known as the Mother Church of Country Music in Nashville, Tennessee. This song will always remain as one of my favourite songs I've recorded and played live.

CROPREDY FESTIVAL
19 AUGUST 1989, CROPREDY, UK

JULIANNE REGAN, ALL ABOUT EVE

It was 1987 and I'd just played a gig at The Bull & Gate in London, when somebody stopped me and said, 'If you haven't heard of her, I think you'd love Sandy Denny.' I hadn't heard of her, or rather *thought* I hadn't, because although I'd heard 'The Battle Of Evermore', I hadn't read the sleeve notes to *Led Zep IV* so had no idea who Robert Plant's angelic counterpoint had been.

In pre-internet days, the usual way to discover music was to buy an album, and so the next day I walked out of Our Price with *The Best Of Sandy Denny* in hand. So the first time I heard Sandy sing – outside of 'The Battle Of Evermore' – was on 'Listen, Listen'. I was struck by the dynamics of her voice, how it ranged from sweet to strident, and also by that appealingly subtle huskiness, alongside her choice of vocal harmonies not always being the most obvious.

'The Lady' further cemented my appreciation. Not so much the voice, but the instrumentation put me in mind of 'The Man With The Child In His Eyes' side of Kate Bush. I then remembered I'd heard the name 'Sandy Denny' sung by Kate Bush in the song 'Blow Away'. It felt like my discovery of Sandy Denny was something of a missing piece in my musical jigsaw. Kate loved Sandy, I loved Kate, and now I loved Sandy too.

That I then went on to sing some of Sandy's songs live with Fairport Convention was incredible. Naturally, it was an honour, yet also a terrible pressure, because Sandy had become so rightfully legendary, and, as I was singing in front of a Fairport Convention audience, that audience would have known every twist and turn of every Sandy vocal. Expectations would've been sky high.

Singing 'Who Knows Where The Time Goes?', undoubtedly one of Sandy's most beloved and beautiful songs, at night time, in an enormous field, to thousands of people? Well, I'll never forget that atmosphere, nor will I forget the generosity of the reception I got. It was a genuinely very moving experience.

I remember thinking that I'd have loved to have sung 'Battle Of Evermore' with Robert Plant, who was also at Cropredy that year, but now realise that would've been exceptionally greedy. To have sung Sandy's songs, with the warm support of Fairport, both musical and emotional, was special enough, *beyond* special, and I'll never undervalue the opportunity to have done so. It was magical. Thank you chaps, and thank you Sandy.

JENNIFER CROOK, SINGER SONGWRITER

I vividly remember lying on my bed in my student accommodation in London listening to 'Who Knows Where the Time Goes?' over and over and over again. Every single ornament and vocal inflection sounded exquisite to my ears. I wanted to try and perfect every nuance for an upcoming performance – or at least try and copy it as closely as I could. It was 1990 and I wasn't keen on much of the pop music of the day. I wanted something earthy, real and beautiful. I wanted songs that could hold complex emotions. At the time I was writing a dissertation about the British Folk Revival of the 1960s – a period I felt would've suited me much better, and the doorway for my discovery of Sandy Denny as a key figure in the development of British folk rock.

I owe her a great deal. I'd been writing songs on the piano and guitar since I was a child and having been through a variety of singing teachers and styles, I'd lost my way. Hearing Sandy's voice reconnected me to a more natural form of expression. The way she sings through the consonants and makes full use of the rhythm and stress of the words, the way she allows the lyrics and phrasing to lead the musical arrangement.

She is the only singer I have ever studied in such detail (which is why I am always delighted when a reviewer says there are 'echoes of Sandy Denny' in my own work). No one compares to Sandy Denny, but she set me on my path. I gave up the singing lessons and went on to develop my own natural way of singing.

However, it is as a songwriter that her influence is most noticeable, with its narrative poetry and desire to create a sense of meaning within the melancholy and find beauty in the timeless metaphors of the sea and the changing seasons.

Fast forward 30 years and I'm once again enraptured when I discover Sandy's solo John Peel performance of 'Who Knows Where the Time Goes?' from 1973. It's 2020 and the song resonates profoundly. There is nothing in the performance or the instrumentation that places it in a particular decade, which gives it a quality that reflects the aesthetic of the song itself: timeless.

I am forever grateful to Sandy Denny for her artistry, and the legacy she left to us all.

PUTNEY VALE CEMETERY
21 APRIL 1990, WIMBLEDON, LONDON, UK

HELEN HAYS

I was a student in Dundee in 1987, when one evening, while I was working at my desk listening to *Folk On Two* through a little transistor radio, I heard the words:

They stood upon the deck, as the ship went out to sea,
The wind it took the sails, and left the land a memory

I was stunned! It was one of those unforgettable seminal moments that change everything. I immediately bought *The Best of Sandy Denny*, then the *Who Knows Where the Time Goes* box set, and anything else I could find. I was lucky enough to get in touch with Nick Pilley, who very generously helped me to find lots of live recordings.

While Sandy's songs enthralled me, nourished and supported me, knowing that I had missed my chance to see and hear her singing live was a great sadness to me. I decided I needed to do something to demonstrate my love for Sandy and my gratitude to her, and that was to place some flowers on her grave.

Helen Hays was shocked to meet Sandy's father when she visited Sandy's grave

My very understanding future husband, Mark, and I made plans to visit Sandy's grave on 21st April. I knew that Sandy was buried in Putney Vale Cemetery and that it was a huge place. I wrote to the cemetery authorities and asked if they could help me out by telling me where in the cemetery Sandy's grave was located. I paid a search fee of £4.75 to Wandsworth Borough Council. A letter came back. Sadly, they had no record of Sandy Denny being buried there, but they would keep trying.

It was a blow, but it wasn't going to stop us. In any case, we were undeterred, and I'm sure Mark realised that we would check every single gravestone in the cemetery if we had to; there was no way I wasn't going to find Sandy.

On 9 March, another letter arrived from the Principal Cemeteries Officer saying, 'We have finally traced this elusive lady's grave. As you will see her surname was not Denny but Lucas.' Of course! How could I have been so stupid? So, we knew we had to make our way to grave no 38 block V. They added some extra information: 'Our search has also revealed that her parents are buried in grave no. 299 block V.' They even sent a map with two arrows on highlighting the plots.

On 21 April 1990, we took a train from Sheffield to London, and then made our way towards Putney Vale, stopping off on the way to buy a bunch of red roses. Arriving at the cemetery, we made straight for Block V and Mark, as sensitive as ever, held back a little, knowing that this would be a hugely emotional moment for me.

My heart was beating like a drum as I walked along the path, and then I saw those words, 'The Lady'. I had found her. It was somehow overwhelming to be there, at her final resting place. I knelt to place the roses by the headstone, barely aware that a tall figure dressed in a dark coat was also standing at the graveside. Then he spoke to me, saying, 'Did you know my daughter?'

The letter from the council had said 'her parents are buried in grave no. 299' and an arrow on the map I'd been sent had labelled one of the graves as 'parents'. Still on my knees I looked up and my face must have been a picture of incredulity. For a few seconds I thought I had seen a ghost.

After the initial shock I was delighted to meet Neil, Sandy's father, and I quickly recognised him from the *Unhalfbricking* cover. He was so gracious and kind to us, thanking us for travelling so far to pay our respects to his daughter. He said he hoped that she wouldn't be forgotten, and we assured him that there was no way that would ever happen.

He said he had a tape of what was Sandy's first song, 'The Tender Years', in his car and asked us if we needed a lift anywhere. We could have gone anywhere, just to spend a little more time with Neil and to hear that recording, but I wanted to spend more time with Sandy, so we shook hands and parted. Afterwards, I regretted turning down his offer.

Meeting Neil and seeing Sandy in his eyes was more than I could have hoped for when we set out that morning. It was such a significant day that I kept a scrap book with the train tickets, the letter from the council and photos of the day. Mark and I both wrote poems about the day, mine were terrible, his less bad, but they were expressions of the deep emotions we felt on that day when we had such a close connection to Sandy.

Sandy has been the musical love of my life ever since that memorable evening in 1987. If I could thank her personally I would.

PUTNEY VALE CEMETERY
APRIL 1996, WIMBLEDON, LONDON, UK

CHRIS HOUSTON

In the late 1980s an excellent documentary entitled *It All Comes Around Again* fanned the flames of my growing interest in Fairport Convention and the band's many offshoots. One of the highlights of Paul Kovit's excellent film was grainy B&W student-shot video footage of Sandy Denny delivering an epic version of her song 'Solo', live onstage with Fairport.

Sandy's grave (Chris Houston)

My dream became to attend the Fairport Convention Cropredy Festival but a trip to the Oxfordshire countryside from my native Canada was a pricey proposition. When a dear friend landed a housesitting gig near London for a few months in the spring of 1996, I knew this was my big chance to visit the UK for the first time. My friend's housesitting gig would wrap up well before Cropredy but it was still too good an opportunity to pass up. Upon arrival, I put together a carefully curated itinerary of important Sandy and Fairport-related sites to visit.

This included Sandy's home in Wimbledon, as pictured on the cover of *Unhalfbricking*. I duly took the Tube to Wimbledon from Ealing, and in just under an hour, I was standing in the exact spot where Eric Hayes took the now iconic cover shot. Armed with my copy of the LP, it was relatively easy to sort out the location, given that St Mary's Church figures so prominently in the cover image. The brick fence was gone, replaced by a hedge – but it was great fun to be at the site where Sandy's parents had lived, and where Fairport had spent some time in the yard.

The next stop was the final resting place of Sandy herself. It was easy enough to ask for directions to the cemetery in Putney; however, I had not realised there were two different cemeteries in Putney. I found myself in the Putney Old Burial Ground first. An hour of wandering aimlessly amongst (very old) tombstones passed before I had the good sense to ask a passing worker for some assistance. Although unfamiliar with Sandy Denny, the date of her passing was enough of a clue for him to point me in the direction of Putney Vale Cemetery. However, he warned me to get moving as the gates were locked at 4pm, it was a 45-minute walk on foot – and it was now 3.10 pm!

Fortunately I was able to get into Putney Vale Cemetery before the gates were locked and, despite having no idea where to look for Sandy's grave, I found it easily. It was as if I suddenly knew where I was going. I was stunned to see 'The Lady' written on the headstone. Sandy's lovely song of the same name came to mind at once. Despite the hustle and bustle of my adventure, I had a truly tranquil moment.

Everything was suddenly very silent and peaceful; the setting was still and even the rain held off so I could enjoy a quiet communion with an artist whose work I loved and respected in equal measure. Rather than sadness (graveyards are not my thing) I felt a great relief and joy, like I had found a missing piece of a puzzle.

Since that time, my connection to the music of 'The Lady' has only deepened, and I am thankful that I was able to make this special pilgrimage to two of the places that are so much a part of Sandy's life and music.

And for anyone wondering who that young man with the backpack hopping over the fence at Putney Vale Cemetery after 4pm sometime in April 1996 was, it was me!

DARRAN MCATEER

John, Andy and I would take it in turns to play music in the office. Our music tastes differed, but occasionally they aligned, leading to the discovery of an artist or song. This happened one day when my colleagues – who both claim credit – played 'Who Knows Where The Time Goes?' by Fairport Convention for me. I was captivated instantly by the song and by Sandy's voice. I was very surprised when I found out how old the song was; it sounded so fresh! I was saddened to discover Sandy had died long ago, and before I was born which meant I'd never be able to hear that beautiful voice live.

I went away and listened to every song I could find that featured Sandy on streaming platforms. In the process, Sandy became one of my all-time favourite artists. Although I'll never get the opportunity to see her live, I have done the next best thing and been to see The Sandy Denny Project and Liege & Lief, who were both fantastic. Prior to discovering Sandy, folk music was a genre I had barely explored but she acted as a gateway and I thank her for that and for the beautiful music she has gifted to the world.

'WHO KNOWS WHERE THE TIME GOES?'

BARBARA DICKSON, SINGER

Because I lived in Scotland and didn't keep abreast of what was happening in the south, I wasn't really aware of Sandy until *Liege & Lief*. I knew she was working with Fairport Convention and was also well aware of the fact that they were the first really commercial sounding folk/rock band. She was a huge influence and inspiration to other female singers to be fronting that band at that time.

I can't remember hearing 'Who Knows Where The Time Goes?' for the first time but when Sandy died, that song took on a huge sadness and poignancy as she was no longer here and gone so young. When I recorded it in the 1990s, it had that status for me and I used the sound of a chiming clock at the outset of our arrangement on my recording. Also, Dave Mattacks played on my version. The song itself had masses of space and so there is a feeling of a person being in a remote spot and watching birds fly over, etc… it's a lovely song.

I remember vividly recording the album, *Dark End Of The Street*, as it was a seminal album for me, after all the pop music I had been associated with for almost 20 years. Danny Thompson played on 'Who Knows Where The Time Goes?' and the other musicians were just totally in the zone with the songs chosen. It's a beautiful song, well written and a great legacy for Sandy. If she'd done nothing else or written nothing else, it would be a wonderful gift to British music.

REN HARVIEU, SINGER

When I was growing up, every now and again my mum would sit on the living room floor with a glass of wine and a cigarette, listening to her favourite records. Around midnight, she would inevitably play 'Who Knows Where the Time Goes? and she used to say that she and Sandy Denny were kindred spirits and that Sandy spoke to her soul. I remember standing in the doorway in my pyjamas, listening to her sing along softly, her eyes closed.

When I was twenty, I was in a bad accident and broke my back. I remember lying on a hospital bed under stark white lights. Nurses moved around me in blurred slow motion. There were tubes and wires, and someone asking if they could cut my clothes off with scissors. Although half delirious, I knew that this was the most pivotal moment of my young life so far. My spine was split in half, and yet I felt strangely serene, as though I were floating above myself, drifting somewhere else… or perhaps returning. And then, out of nowhere, and even with a tube down my throat, I started to sing: 'Across the evening sky, all the birds are singing.'

The words slipped out like a hymn. One of the nurses looked at me and said, 'You've got a really good voice. Are you a singer?' A singer? Yes, that sounded familiar.

I remember thinking that if I kept singing, my mum would hear me. That she would appear by my bedside, take my hand, and tell me I was being very brave. That I was going to be okay. So I kept going; 'For who knows where the time goes?' I don't remember much after that.

Later, after a twenty-six-hour surgery, I thought about the words I had been singing. The birds leaving. Time slipping away. I realised then that I hadn't been calling for my mother. I had been carrying her with me all along. You might think the song would bring back painful memories. But I still listen to it regularly. It doesn't take me back to fear. It reminds me that I survived. And I think perhaps that is what Sandy gave us.

Not answers. Just the courage to keep going when time is doing what it always does. Moving on.

MARK STEVENS, THE SANDY DENNY PROJECT

It wasn't until I became a member of the Sandy Denny Project that I realised just how great a songwriter she was. Like so many people, I'd always been aware of her unique voice and her abilities as a storyteller, but the depth and intensity of her songs really came into focus for me when we started playing and recording them.

Members of the Sandy Denny Project with Georgia at the Sandy Denny Memorial Bench, Cropredy, August 2025

Our approach in the Sandy Denny Project is to interpret (not copy) Sandy's songs, sometimes changing the tempo and feel quite considerably from the original versions. As Sally Barker always tells our audience, 'We are here to keep these songs alive.' A great song is a great song no matter how it is performed and every song we have worked on has proved itself to be truly great. As Sandy's songs are broken down, they reveal moments of lyrical, melodic and harmonic brilliance and no matter how you reconstruct them, that brilliance and integrity remains, and my appreciation and love for Sandy's songs grow stronger.

CROPREDY FESTIVAL
8 & 9 AUGUST 1997, CROPREDY, UK

JULIE JULY, THE JULIE JULY BAND

Julie July's Sandy epiphany was at Cropredy

I grew up in a home filled with music: Frank Sinatra, Tony Bennett and Matt Monro spun endlessly on my dad's stereo. From them I learned phrasing, storytelling and how to fully inhabit a song, lessons that have shaped every note I've sung since. But it was the music of the sixties and seventies that first opened my heart. The harmonies of Simon & Garfunkel, the vast emotional landscapes of Joni Mitchell, the open-road poetry of Crosby, Stills & Nash; all shaped my musical instincts. I trained classically into my late teens, but something in the purity and honesty of folk rock kept calling me back.

And then, in 1997, I truly 'met' Sandy. A boyfriend took me to the Cropredy Festival, a magical year with Richard Thompson, Vikki Clayton, Ashley Hutchings, Dave Swarbrick and so many legendary players. I still remember the atmosphere: open night skies, comets, incredible musicianship, songs that seemed to shimmer in the evening air. In a stroke of surreal luck, I won the signed guitar in the raffle, a guitar I still treasure today. I took it home and started learning everything I could: 'Crazy Man Michael', 'Rising For The Moon', 'White Dress', 'Meet On The Ledge' and 'Who Knows Where the Time Goes?', a song so impossibly wise for someone of nineteen. I bought Sandy's vinyl box set shortly after and was completely smitten.

What struck me then (and still does) is the emotional truth in her voice. Sandy didn't simply sing songs; she inhabited them. She lived them. There is a warmth, a fearlessness, and honesty in her delivery that continues to guide me every time I step on stage. She could be tender, powerful, aching, or bright sometimes all in the same phrase and yet always unmistakably herself. She was, and remains, a songwriter with a rare ability to touch something universal.

When I began performing Sandy's songs over ten years ago, I couldn't have imagined the journey ahead: tours across the UK and beyond sharing these beautiful songs with audiences who hold them so dearly, witnessing the way people still lean in, still close their eyes, still feel that spark of recognition when they hear her words. I often say to the band before we perform 'Who Knows Where The Time Goes?' that we must create the space, space for people to remember, to grieve, to hope, to feel. Sandy's music asks for that respect, and we try to honour it every night.

Singing her songs for so many years has shaped not just my voice, but my writing. Her phrasing, her imagery, her quiet bravery in expressing vulnerability, all of these have influenced my own songwriting and helped me find my place as a folk artist. The new songs we write today carry threads of the emotional landscape she opened up for me. What amazes me most is how her music continues to connect with audiences of all ages. People often tell me after a show that they feel her presence in the room. Her songs still breathe. They still travel. They still speak directly to the heart.

Sandy's legacy isn't just alive; it is thriving, evolving, and inspiring new generations of musicians and listeners. I am honoured to be even a small part of the ongoing story of her music.

MAX BOLCH

Sandy Denny was my entry point into my making music. In 2013, I was 19 years old and a medical student and amateur musician in Germany, wondering which songs would be worth playing on stage. I was deeply fascinated by Sandy Denny's songwriting and, having been trained as a pianist, I was mesmerised by those spectacular chord changes she used. I acquainted a wonderful singer – Laura Dieck – who sang Sandy's songs so beautifully. Sometimes we had a drummer and a bass player too. So, the first band I was in was actually a Sandy Denny covers band. We played 'Banks Of The Nile' and 'Late November', but also rarer bits like a fairly psychedelic version of 'Setting Of The Sun'.

In the group I mostly played the guitar and we did 'Gypsy Davey' too, where I tried imitating Jerry Donahue's behind-the-nut bending on the G-string.

In her earlier songs, written between 1967-1972, Sandy wrote the tunes very freely, using modal scales and not letting the guitar or the piano disturb the tune. It feels as if the core of the songs was herself and her voice – nothing more. The result is that the chord progressions follow the tune (sometimes into very strange realms), and not the other way around. In that respect I think Sandy's songs are quite close to Lal Waterson's and Steve Ashley's. And Sandy's poems are like landscapes, very evocative, like written dreams. They blend perfectly with the sweet tunes and the ragged chords.

The great skill of Fotheringay was that they absolutely knew how to rock 'n' roll (their live versions of 'John The Gun' hit hard), but they were also masters of subtlety. When you listen to 'The Sea' or 'Two Weeks Last Summer', it is neither pop nor rock – it is very subtle. It features very delicate percussion work and there are Jerry Donahue's meandering lead guitars and Sandy's quiet, controlled voice. 'The Sea' especially touches the neo-classical realm and represents a path that the contemporary folk approach could have taken, combining Schubert, Vaughan Williams, The Beatles, medieval music and folk song into a very unusual unity which nonetheless feels natural. It feels like a new beginning, in a way. In her later works, Sandy chose a different approach and built her melodies around the piano chords – which resulted in very different songs.

ST ANN'S CHURCH
21 NOVEMBER 1998, BROOKLYN, NEW YORK

PETER HOLSAPPLE

I can pretty much pinpoint my first exposure to Sandy at age 14 and listening to a copy of *Friends*, a free A&M Records sampler LP from 1970, whose first side closed with 'Peace In The End' by Fotheringay. A great place to start! Sandy and Trevor Lucas and an interlocking choir; just heavenly. (The proximity to 'Walk Awhile' by Fairport Convention which started the same side on *Friends* certainly didn't hurt either. I bought *Full House*, then *Liege & Lief*, then *Unhalfbricking* and on backwards and forwards through their history, reintegrating Sandy into the Fairport story for me.)

Hearing her sing 'A Sailor's Life' or 'Blackwaterside' felt like being handed an admission ticket to a very different world, one based on something ancient and decidedly unfamiliar; I knew nothing of the ballads and story songs they were making contemporary with electric guitars and drums, but I made my way through the paths she and the band laid out for me, and I heard forebears, fellows and followers that have since become essential parts of my lifetime as a listener.

That voice, so rich and self-assured, and by turns gentle and tired and deeply sad, all of which can take place in one single line. One of my favourite tracks Sandy recorded was a sublime duet with Linda Thompson of the Everly Brothers' 'When Will I Be Loved' on *Rock On* by The Bunch. The tag line of each verse drops to a whisper, and you have to crane to hear Sandy and Linda as they disappear together behind acoustic guitars.

It always seemed improbable that this extraordinary voice, this passionate songwriter, should not be more widely known; Sandy's innate ability to write contemporary music which was as timeless as the folk repertoire she was steeped in was persuasive. But as time has passed, the likelihood of her comparative obscurity being rectified is growing fainter, barring some savvy music supervisor laying it over the credits of a blockbuster film. It could happen.

We of a certain time, one when Sandy was making records, may simply be the fortunate beneficiaries of that now-past world – not as far back as the ancestry of the Fairport catalogue, but historical enough in the twenty-first century. It falls upon us who know these tunes, like 'Autopsy' and 'At The End Of The Day', to make sure we've let someone else in on this unintentional secret, to keep the chain going somehow. Because, indeed, who knows where the time goes?

Twenty-eight years after I got *Friends* in the mail, I played as part of Continental Drifters at a tribute to Sandy in a dark and majestic gothic church in Brooklyn, St Ann's with my friends Don Dixon and Marti Jones, singing 'Peace In The End' near the end of the show. We filled that church with her songs, with singers like Darius Rucker, Michael Steele and Vicki Peterson from the Bangles, Robyn Hitchcock, Mike Mills and Susan Cowsill, all paying tribute to someone who did for them what she did for me. We all went down that same path, the one Sandy showed us.

28 years on from the St Ann's show, I'm still listening to and marvelling at the glory of hearing Sandy Denny sing. How she moved air; the vibrato, the volume, the bravado; like standing at the edge of a precipice. It still has me in thrall.

ANTHONY JOHN CLARKE, SINGER SONGWRITER & CROPREDY MC

The name Sandy Denny does not just rest somewhere on a long list of singer-songwriters. Her place in history was guaranteed many moons ago. I was 16 years old when I accompanied my older sister in singing a couple of Sandy's songs. It was a small village hall just outside of Belfast and an occasion I have spoken about a thousand times. Our performance was at best mediocre but the audience were silent and respectful.

I have been lucky enough to meet and chat with many of my musical heroes – my influences, my inspirations – but I never met Sandy Denny. Meeting her daughter, Georgia Rose Lucas, was such a special Cropredy moment for me. I was bold enough to proudly

Anthony John Clarke (left) with Dave Pegg, Nigel Schofield & Georgia, Cropredy 2019

introduce the lovely Georgia to many of my friends and their reactions will forever stay with me. We all realised we were tasting a beautiful history. Memories were shared, with cherished anecdotes recounted, songs and concerts remembered. Many people just politely embraced Georgia and wept. There was no reason to ask them why they wept. It was just beautiful.

When a famous songwriter pops into a conversation, the reaction is generally predictable. Memories are evoked and album tracks recalled. I think it is different when Sandy Denny's name is mentioned. It is as if she has always been there. When I listen to people who knew her well, the voices lower, there is invariably a pause; they realise that they have something very important to say and their words are chosen carefully and spoken with love and respect.

'Greatness' is a word often bandied about. Not here. Women and men who write or perform songs will always have two names in their top pocket; Sandy Denny and Bob Dylan. Writers who were born with the greatest gift of all. They wrote songs that will be respected, enjoyed and loved for generations to come.

ÁINE FUREY, SINGER

My father introduced me to the wonderful voice of Sandy Denny in the seventies, when I wasn't yet even a teenager. Dad (Finbar Furey) had met her on several occasions over the folk circuit and spoke so highly of her. I listened to the cassette recording Dad gave me of Sandy over and over and over and very much tried to sing as she did.

I recorded two tracks, 'Who Knows Where The Time Goes?' and 'Winter Winds', in the nineties on my own solo album, *Sweetest Summer Rain*, but alas I could never give the wealth of feeling and range vocalised by Sandy Denny. Having later in my teens discovered songs like 'Whispering Grass' or 'Solo', I just couldn't get enough.

What an absolute tragedy her passing was, and a huge loss to the world of music. However, her voice is timeless and shall, I am sure, inspire many generations to come.

Always the heart.

LISTEN, LISTEN: AN INTRODUCTION TO SANDY DENNY RELEASED JUNE 1999

TEL MCHARROP

I discovered Sandy on a various artists CD given away free with the music magazine *Uncut*. The track was 'Listen, Listen' and I really hadn't heard anything quite like it before. My God, what a voice. That week I went to Tower Records in Glasgow to look for a CD to introduce me to Sandy Denny and found *Listen, Listen: An Introduction To Sandy Denny*. The song 'Listen, Listen' was not a one off.

The tracks on the CD had no context. The compilation had pulled tracks from each of Sandy's four solo albums, and four of the songs – 'Solo', 'Like An Old Fashioned Waltz', 'Dark The Night' and 'No End' – all came from what would become in time my favourite Sandy album, *Like An Old Fashioned Waltz*.

In September 2020 I watched a documentary called *Sandy Denny: Folk Music's Unsung Pioneer*. This was the first time I had heard 'Who Knows Where The Time Goes?'. The very next evening, watching a TV show about the breakup of a marriage on a holiday in Europe, I heard the track again. Now knowing the name of the song, I asked Alexa to play it. This was the first Fairport song I ever played.

Five years have now passed and I have amassed a huge collection of Sandy's records, box sets and CDs, but also Fairport, Steeleye Span, Pentangle, Dave Swarbrick, The Albion Band, Martin Carthy, Richard Thompson, Feast of Fiddles, Iain Matthews, etc.

I have now heard 'Who Knows Where The Time Goes?' performed live by Fairport many times. But at Cropredy in 2022, just before the band performed it, the Cropredy crowd were treated to a video message from Sandy's daughter Georgia Rose Lucas from Australia, which made the song even more poignant.

I spoke to Dave Mattacks prior to a Feast of Fiddles gig in Kendal in April 2024. He and Richard Thompson had recently talked about how sad it was that Sandy Denny still remains unknown to most people. It is time that changed. All people have to do is 'Listen, Listen'.

NO MORE SAD REFRAINS – THE ANTHOLOGY RELEASED 2000

ROMAIN TRANCHART, PRODUCER & MUSICIAN

I remember the first time I heard Sandy Denny's voice. Just like everything that moves me, I felt I always knew her voice – and as a matter of fact I did! Being a huge Led Zeppelin fan, my heart and ears immediately recognised the town crier in 'The Battle Of Evermore'. Very quickly, the double album *No More Sad Refrains* became one of my all-time favourites. Discovering Sandy Denny's music has been a fundamental milestone, undeniably one of the strongest encounters of my life as a musician. Her work as a solo artist, as well as with Fairport Convention, Fotheringay, Srawbs, The Bunch and Led Zeppelin, is an influential goldmine. How can anyone listen to 'White Dress' (live) and not be deeply moved by it? Not a single note is off-tune, and even the notes that are ring true. Sandy, and her voice, sing directly to one's heart.

'STRANGER TO HIMSELF'

TOMMY O'SULLIVAN, MUSICIAN

I first heard the song 'Stranger To Himself' when I was around at a friend's house and they put on a Fairport record. I don't remember which album it was (*Rising For The Moon*) but 'Stranger' was on it and I'd never heard it before. It somehow grabbed me. I remember listening and thinking that the recording of the song was quite short, a little over two minutes, and there was no instrumental break either as far as I recall.

I could hear possibilities in my head and there was a bluesy undertone I thought that could be lifted to the surface so I started messing with it. It had occurred to me that if I were ever to record it, it would be a slightly less well-known Sandy Denny song too, which might be a good thing especially if I could put an original spin on it while still honouring her original version.

As it happened, shortly afterwards I was set to record an album with Paddy Keenan the great uileann piper from the Bothy Band. Paddy has a wildness to his piping and I knew he loved all things bluesy. I also knew he would add a 'cry' to it with his piping, which of course he did. We recorded it on *The Long Grazing Acre* album and have performed it live on many, many occasions.

SANDYDENNY.CO.UK
2003

STEVE LENCH

As a lad I'd always listened to all sorts of music and never really had a favourite genre – I loved it all. In the seventies I felt that Sandy was just another folk singer. But around the millennium I perked up my ears and listened more closely to Sandy's music and fell in love with her voice and her songwriting style. It was a discovery of someone who had it all – she looked great, sang and played incredibly well and had a captivating style. Her songs were emotionally charged, with subjects that I felt drew listeners toward nature and life. Folk, but not folk as I knew it.

In 2003, after I'd started my interest in the 'new' internet boom, I bought the domain sandydenny.co.uk and created a website dedicated to 'The Lady'. I felt a sense of pride, hoping to make her songs and life story reach out and appeal to wider groups of people. (I think it was successful.)

My interest allowed me to appreciate her talent more and more. In our house, Sandy's songs are what you'd mostly hear. Online I got to know some of the people she brushed shoulders or worked with, who gave me a greater insight in to how Sandy worked her magic. Songs I have written owe a lot to Sandy and her outside-the-box approach to writing a good song.

How I wish I'd met her or just heard her performing. Imagine now, had she lived longer, what gems we would be listening to. And would she still be singing along in the Fairport crew? We'll never know.

MARIA OLIVERO

I'm an Italian composer, singer-songwriter, musician and producer. I've performed in Italy and abroad, including many times in Norway and California, and twice at the Hard Rock Café in Hollywood. My music has its roots in Anglo-Saxon folk rock. I live in northern Italy, a land of noble wines. My mother is from Genoa, by the sea. Our beloved sea!

At 18, I discovered the unique and magical songs of Sandy Denny. It was one of the most important encounters of my life. I found some boxes of old LPs that belonged to my father. And I started listening... it was a revelation! The tones, the chord progressions, the atmosphere, everything, so elegant and deep... I felt so close to her, speaking directly to my heart. And she lit it, like a fire! I've performed Sandy's songs on many occasions and I think I was the first in Italy to organise a tribute to her, in 2003. I'm so happy that Fabio Rossi wrote the book, *Sandy Denny: La Regina del Folk Rock* (*The Queen of Folk Rock*). Finally, an Italian biography of one of the best singer-songwriters of all time.

Music is made of encounters, and in these 'echoes of love' I am forever grateful to have encountered Sandy Denny's music.

Maria Olivero organised Italy's first tribute concert to Sandy

'SHE'S BEEN WRITING' RELEASED 7 JULY 2003

SIMON FOWLER, OCEAN COLOUR SCENE

We used to see Ric Sanders in the Golden Lion in Solihull when we were youngsters. And Steve Cradock, guitar player in my band, would clean Ric's windows, because they lived around the corner from each other.

I was learning the guitar when I was nine and I grew up playing American folk tunes like 'Red River Valley'. I remember the very night I got into Fairport. I used to have a very lively lifestyle in Moseley. I'd come back quite late at night, and the guys I was sharing the flat with didn't want me to put on some rock and roll music, so I played this Island sampler album, *You Can All Join In*. It had people like Spooky Tooth on there (and we knew the drummer from Spooky Tooth, because he lived around the corner from us).

One of the tracks on this album was 'Meet On The Ledge'. I had imbibed several things that night, and I must have played that track twenty times that night, after which I came to the conclusion that it was the greatest song ever written. I thought it was just wonderful. I still do. We used to do it live.

I remember speaking to Dave Pegg once and I said, 'What's 'Meet On The Ledge' about? And he said, 'Well, Richard would go out and Linda was there and he'd leave the evening's meal, some meat, on a ledge just above the cooker.'

I explored Sandy's back catalogue, with Fairport, with Fotheringay and solo. 'Solo' is one of my favourite songs, as are 'Like An Old Fashioned Waltz' and 'A Sailor's Life'. She wrote some incredible songs. She originally did 'Who Knows Where The Time Goes?' with The Strawbs. I just fell in love with it and with her. I fell in love with her character as well, because I've kind of got a little bit of that within me. I actually went up to try and find the cottage that she lived in in Byfield.

We were on tour in the States. We were just going through the border to Canada. I was reading a book about Sandy and I started tearing up and I had to stop reading it. I don't think I read the last chapter with its dreadful denouement.

I wrote the song 'She's Been Writing' (on the Ocean Colour Scene album *North Atlantic Drift*). It's one of my favourite songs I've ever written because I think the lyrics work really, really nicely. I found it a fascinating story and I just wanted to pay a tribute to her.

THE SANDY DENNY SONGBOOK JANUARY 2005

KARENT.CO.UK

I was a young child when Sandy died. I discovered her music 34 years ago when I was 19. I remember as if it were yesterday my ex-boyfriend Tiny, the lead singer with Ultrasound, putting on the Sandy Denny box set. It starts with a live version of 'The Lady' and I lay on the floor in student digs watching the most amazing spectacle of cloud activity outside the window, whilst this dreamy piano playing and voice teleported me to an alternative dimension.

Over the years Sandy's music has saved me, inspired me and intrigued me. With every listen I've felt a closer appreciation of understanding this giant of a soul – the healer. Sandy's sadder and more reflective songs capture me the most. Her acoustic versions, when she's pared down and at her most vulnerable, is where I find the true magic. Like Billie Holiday, that haunting beauty can capture and hold you in a delicate cocoon of fragility.

Sandy's songs have become a soundtrack intertwined with my life. Those songs have seen me through so much, like a security blanket I can pull over and lose myself in.

Karen discovered the Sandy Denny songbook, compiled by Maartin Allcock

I have made some unexpected friendships with some of Sandy's closest friends. In the late 1990s I met Miranda Ward and we went on to forge a strong friendship which lasted many years. Through Miranda, I also became friends with Bambi Ballard and David Sanderson. I recall one year we were all invited to Miranda's house in Stroud for a few days. They all reminisced about Sandy and it was one of many beautiful times I had with this group appreciating Sandy. Miranda and I had endless chats, down to random things like Sandy's favourite perfume being Mitsouko and the last record she had listened to being Andy Fairweather Low's 'Wide-Eyed And Legless'.

We spoke of Sandy often and it frequently felt like she was in the room with us. Miranda often said that Sandy and I would have got on like a house on fire. It inspired Miranda to tell me how well Sandy had got on with Mama Cass when Miranda had introduced them.

I also find it very healing and inspiring to sing Sandy's songs. I've spent endless hours singing along with her as her music plays. I've also learned to play some of her songs on the guitar. I bought *The Sandy Denny Songbook*, put together by Maartin Allcock, in 2005. My now tattered and torn copy has been through a life journey. I occasionally sang a Sandy cover to Miranda or another of Sandy's friends, Philippa Clare. It's surreal singing Sandy's songs to her friends.

Now I sing publicly, I often include a cover version of at least one of Sandy's songs. It's a real insight as to just how much people love her songs. 'Who Knows Where The Time Goes?' has become somewhat an anthem for a lot of people. They tell me what the song means to them, how it's become entwined in their life story, or how they could listen to it every single day.

My life experience has been enriched by this beautiful lady's output. I find great teachings in her music, her lyrics, her being. There's a spiritual saying that when the student's ready, the teacher arrives. I often wonder if Sandy was brought to me as a teacher. I can't envisage how my life would have been without her presence.

SANDY DENNY ANNIVERSARY TRIBUTE THE TROUBADOUR
20 APRIL 2008, LONDON, UK

PHILIP WARD

To my infinite regret, I never actually saw Sandy live, much less begged for an autograph or shook her hand after a concert to thank her for a job well done. Though I owned a couple of her records as a schoolboy in the 1970s, I was more into classical music in those days (it was that sort of school) and failed to separate her out from the other girl singers with long blonde hair and folky voices. In the years since, she became a siren voice in my head; often I would hear another voice and think that it reminded me of something very precious from the past. Eventually I yielded to that siren voice, immersed myself in her entire recorded output and realised what the schoolboy should have known: that she was one of the greatest British singers of her generation. But she never realised it herself, so perhaps my oversight was excusable.

Philip Ward's book about Sandy

Keen to make up for lost time – and who knows where *that* goes? – in 2008 I co-organised an anniversary tribute to Sandy at the Troubadour Club, London. It had to be the Troubadour – she'd played there often enough in the sixties. Through that and later events, I've made so many new friends: interesting, creative people she introduced me to from beyond the grave. And, as the subject of my earliest writings on popular music, she also kickstarted a sideline for me in music journalism. In 2011

I put all this together to publish a book about Sandy's music, *Sandy Denny: Reflections On Her Music* (Matador).

FOTHERINGAY 2
RELEASED 30 SEPTEMBER 2008

COLIN RANDALL, JOURNALIST

Just when it seemed there could surely be nothing more to say or hear, that every radio and television library, record label archive and attic had been combed for material to satisfy the fascination with her life and work, another Sandy Denny album has surfaced. The story of Fotheringay's *2*, the follow-up record that took 38 years to complete and release, is an extraordinary one. Who, indeed, knows where the time went?

In 1970, having left Fairport Convention, the pioneers of British folk-rock, after the first of her two stints with the band, Denny created Fotheringay. She was the undoubted star, and eyes focused naturally on her. But she saw it in more democratic terms, considering her colleagues – two former members of Eclection, Trevor Lucas and Gerry Conway, and two former members of Poet and the One Man Band, Jerry Donahue and Pat Donaldson – as equal components of the band.

There were similarities between the group Denny formed and the one she had left: traditional songs and wistful country ballads meeting rock and finding glorious expression in superior musicianship and breathtaking vocals.

Fotheringay 2 was released in September 2008

Even the name of the band was resonant of Denny's recent past. 'Fotheringay', her song about Mary, Queen of Scots, had been a treasured part of Fairport's repertoire.

Fotheringay's eponymous debut album is regarded by folk-rock connoisseurs today as a masterpiece. Even in 1970, when the weight of expectation led to cooler appraisal, the hope was that Fotheringay would take the genre to new heights of subtlety and substance. Work soon began on a follow-up.

Despite the bouts of self-doubt that dogged her career, the young Denny, far from being confined to the tight ghetto of folk, was viewed within the pop music industry as highly marketable. There was pressure to embark on a solo career and, during a break for Christmas from recording the new album, it became irresistible.

When the band returned to the studios in Chelsea, west London, early in January 1971, she was in tears as she announced her decision to leave. The album was abandoned, and the tapes of what had already been recorded disappeared into record company archives.

And there they would have stayed but for the stubborn resolve of one of Denny's Fotheringay colleagues, American guitarist Jerry Donahue. It was not quite a case of a dog refusing to let go of a bone, since the bone was buried; Donahue nevertheless kept on digging until, five years ago, he unearthed it. Eventually, in exchanges with Joe Black, an executive from Universal, which long ago absorbed Fotheringay's label, Island, it became clear that the work in progress was likely to have survived. And so it turned out to be; even though the tapes had been shunted around on to different reels, Black was able to assemble all the material.

'I was so happy,' says Donahue, whose own career path had led him, post-Fotheringay, into production. 'It was just so great not only to hear these long-lost recordings, but to find them in such good condition.'

The remaining snag was that the timing of the break-up of the band meant nothing was a finished product. Donahue set about piecing together the jigsaw using the best elements of each track Black had located. Denny's most appealing version of a song might be on one tape, the strongest guitar solo or bass line on another. 'I wanted everything to be the absolute best,' he says.

It was quickly evident that some additional work would be needed. Denny was long dead, of course, as was Trevor Lucas, her estranged husband at the time of her passing in April 1978 and the father of their daughter, Georgia.

Donahue, who divides his time between California and the northern England town of Clitheroe, quickly recruited the others. Gerry Conway was living near London, and working regularly with Fairport, and also his wife Jacqui McShee's band Pentangle. Pat Donaldson was lured from his retreat in the south of France.

Both travelled to Donahue's studio in Clitheroe to add the sequences needed to complete the album. 'Wild Mountain Thyme', a traditional ballad widely acclaimed as one of the most gripping tracks of the newly released album, was a good example; Denny had recorded it as a guide for the others, with just voice and guitar. On the version buyers of the new album hear, all three of Fotheringay's surviving musicians are featured.

The result of the extra recording, and the process of mixing and matching the best segments of each track from a variety of contemporary sources, is a set with key differences from what Denny and Fotheringay's fans have previously encountered, even though other versions of the same material have appeared since her death.

'These are not only among the very first versions of those songs,' says Donahue. 'They are totally different takes, different performances from those that made their way to vinyl and/or CD in the years that followed the 1970 sessions. Once the doors were finally opened to us, it was like pursuing a known treasure with limited expectations – and, upon finding it, uncovering totally unexpected gems that were either forgotten or presumed lost forever.'

So how good is it? Few would claim that sounds essentially recorded nearly 40 years ago could be seen as the cutting edge of modern music. 'Listening to my own performances from all that time ago, I can hear the enthusiasm,' says Conway, Fotheringay's drummer. 'And I can also hear where it was flawed. Generally speaking, though, it is a great thing of its time. We had all given up hope of seeing it happen and to our amazement it has come out, warts and all.'

What the passage of time has not removed, as Conway's comments imply, is the passion with which Fotheringay approached their music. Beyond that, the individual performances are compelling. Lucas's tones, which dominate several tracks, are lugubrious, but seem utterly right for the context; if the classic male folk-rock voice of the era existed, he had it. From Denny, there is yet another melancholy reminder of that magical combination of emotion, purity and vulnerability.

Despite two awards as female singer of the year, as voted by readers of a respected pop music weekly, *Melody Maker*, the solo career was not a resounding success. Denny was to descend into the rock pitfalls of drink and, reportedly, drugs, weaknesses that introduced a self-destructive aspect into her final years. But those who knew or admired her prefer to remember the exceptional vocal gifts, which make '*Wild Mountain Thyme*' and '*Silver Threads And Golden Needles*' not only the outstanding tracks of *2*, but as fresh as if recorded last week.

'I have such fond memories of that time,' says Donaldson from his French home. 'It was a wonderful band, extraordinarily together. For Sandy to leave was a huge dilemma for her, and I think it stayed one in the back of her mind for the rest of her life. She never seemed settled in any way, as a solo artist or on a personal level. But it was an absolute privilege to work with her. She is way up there on the top rung of the ladder of people I've played with.'

'Sandy is still probably the most special singer I have known,' says Donahue. 'I have heard technically better, but when she was into a song, especially when recording a guide track without interference from nerves, or from people telling her how it should be sung, it was the most beautiful thing I have heard.'

IAN WALTON

Sandy has been part of my musical life since 1970. I still remember the after-dinner coffee conversation in St Salvator's Hall at the University of St Andrews where we were introduced to the newly-released *Fotheringay* album. Since dinners were formal affairs in those days, we were probably all wearing the red undergraduate gowns that featured on the album gatefold. Sadly, I missed the Fotheringay show at the Younger Hall in St Andrews – except for walking past and hearing the last few minutes on my way back from a climbing weekend in the Highlands. At that point, I somehow managed to be completely unaware of Fairport Convention.

Several years later, when I was located in Santa Cruz, California with its wonderful Logos book and record store, it was Sandy's voice on the *Rising For The Moon* album that instantly turned me into a life-long Fairport fan and Cropredy attendee. I set about buying every recording I could find. I also managed to miss her Fairport show in the nearby San

Lorenzo Valley by not finding out about it until the week after the show.

But despite never hearing or seeing 'The Lady' in live performance, her songs have been a big part of my life – playing the records and then playing my own version of them at assorted open mics over the years. I often introduce myself as playing 'depressing Celtic ballads from around the world', but Sandy's songs include many of my and my audience's favourites. They're depressing, yes, but also beautiful and haunting and enigmatic and uplifting all at the same time. And I love all the later renditions by her fellow musicians at Cropredy and on the technically astonishing *Fotheringay 2*. I've introduced a lot of my friends to her brilliance and I still have a few of her songs to learn how to play.

ROMEO NATHAN BUMANN

I first heard Sandy's voice on an LP sampler issued by Island Records in Germany in 1969 called *London Pop News*. It had tracks from various bands, including Fairport Convention's 'Mr Lacey' which was sung by Sandy. Her impressive singing stayed in my ear for longer than the song lasted.

During the 1990s, I discovered new Sandy Denny songs, which became constant companions when I divorced the mother of my two daughters at the turn of the millenium. 'Ecoute, Ecoute' reminds me of staying on the flank of the volcano on the island of Stromboli with my two daughters, watching the beautiful eruptions.

Songs like 'Listen Listen' and 'Solo' have stood the test of time. Sandy's music was not mainstream. It was often very personal, almost intimate, but always direct. Even when she sang other people's compositions, it came from deep within her. Many songs still move me today, so much so that I would like to give Sandy a big hug from the bottom of my heart.

In fall 2008 I spent a month at Sands school in Ashburton, Devon doing a teaching internship in order to prove my proficiency as an English teacher in Switzerland. In my spare time, I visited record shops to discover new releases or find bootlegs. That's where I came across the newly-released *Fotheringay 2* CD. It was so fitting that I discovered this CD in England, in magical Devon and right after its release.

QUEEN ELIZABETH HALL
1 DECEMBER 2008, SOUTH BANK, LONDON, UK

LISA KNAPP, SINGER SONGWRITER

I first heard Sandy Denny's soaring vocal on 'The Battle Of Evermore', a duet with Robert Plant on Led Zep *IV*, sometime in my late teens and was struck by the powerful, intriguing female vocal delivery. Fast forward a year to sitting in the bedroom of my friend, singer Naomi Bedford, in her mansion flat in Putney. She had a vast and immensely varied record collection that featured folk records inherited from her parents. *Liege & Lief* by Fairport Convention hit the deck: 'Come all ye rolling minstrels, and together we will try…' and out poured Sandy Denny.

An extraordinary voice, a strong voice, soulful, spirited and a bit wild yet skilful, beautiful. 'A holiday, a holiday and the first one of the year…'. A voice that could hold you, suspended, through an entire story, through all the joy, grief, character and action, with style, vitality and also tenderness. 'Tam Lin', 'Reynardine', 'Matty Groves'. What stories!

The first thing I did was get hold of a CD copy of *Liege & Lief* and learn Sandy Denny's version of 'Reynardine' word for word, note for note, ornament for ornament. She had a wonderful way with ornamentation, a slight Celtic influence and sort of local, honest pronunciation. I was delighted when I read she'd spent her childhood not too many miles from my neck of the woods in south London and even more delighted that she sounded like it, sort of grounded.

Fast forward again to 2007. I had just released my own first album of mostly folk songs, *Wild & Undaunted*. A year later I was asked if I would join a cosmic cast of singers and musicians to celebrate the music of Sandy Denny in a tribute concert at the Queen Elizabeth Hall.

I'm not sure if I can quite explain the mix of emotion, from some sort of surreal wonder to abject glee, of going from singing at local sessions to being asked to sing the songs of one's musical hero on the stage of one of the biggest concert halls in the country. It is my lasting pleasure and a career highlight to have got to sing her version of 'Quiet Joys Of Brotherhood' alongside the legendary Dave Swarbrick and then join the rest of the evening's stellar company of musicians and singers which featured Mark Almond, PP Arnold, Jerry Donahue, most of Bellowhead, Jim Moray and Mary Epworth among many others for the finale. Together we sang the seminal 'Who Knows Where The Time Goes?', a song and a half to have written, pure pleasure to sing.

'IT'LL TAKE A LONG TIME' RELEASED 30 APRIL 2009

STEPHEN MILLER, MUSICIAN

It was 1974. I was 15. I lived in a country town called Goulburn, New South Wales. The local newsagent sold budget LPs. The Australian label that produced these records was called Summit. Amongst the usual commercial recorded fare was a curious album with a garish fluorescent pink and red cover credited to Sandy Denny and The Strawbs called *All Our Own Work*. It jumped out at me. I was already enamoured with music and songwriting so took a chance.

I took it home and played it loud on the family Pye three-in-one. The sound jumped out of the speakers, crystal clear and powerful. The songs were fabulous, in particular 'Who Knows Where The Time Goes?'. This was the most beautiful, heartfelt yet very sad voice I had ever heard. It has moved me to tears many times. A simple, plaintive guitar, a voice and a spectacular song. I was hooked.

I went searching for this wonderful woman and found a record called *Sandy*. This album saved me from mundanity and pushed aside an ever-growing depression that has haunted me all my life: 'And the music he weaves is so gentle and sad but freedom he has anyway.' It captured my heart.

Stephen Miller's home made badge

I found all of Sandy's records and love every single one of them. I also became a huge Strawbs fan and bought all their albums as well. My band The Winter Station recorded 'It'll Take A Long Time' on an album called *Brickwork* in 2009. I have played Sandy's songs live over all these years.

Back then I'd tape those records

and sit in fields on cold, foggy nights outside Goulburn, playing them on a battery-driven cassette player and immersing myself in the wonder.

How slowly the colours change
We feel the drops of rain
Mists of evening rise again
We rarely stroll the shadowed lanes
As autumn night draws in

Sandy and her songs have shaped who I am.

AN ALL-STAR FAIRPORT CONVENTION CONCERT, BARBICAN
18 JULY 2009, LONDON, UK

LINDE NIJLAND, SINGER SONGWRITER

As a child growing up in the north of The Netherlands in the late seventies and early eighties, I first heard Sandy Denny's breathtaking music as part of my parents' record collection. I guess her voice and songs were part of my musical DNA.

When I was about 16, taking up singing and guitar playing myself, I searched the flea markets for more of her albums to complete the collection. Sandy became my favourite singer (beloved songs included 'The North Star Grassman And The Ravens' and 'Nothing More') and she remains so up to this day. It's because of the loving melancholy of her lyrics, which seem to tremble on a very familiar frequency and because of her voice, vulnerable and strong at the same time.

Linde Nijland recorded a solo tribute album to Sandy (Alıreza Sakaki)

I started recording and performing with my own harmony singing duo, Ygdrassil, at the age of 18 and we became successful in The Netherlands. My musical career got more directly inspired by Sandy when I recorded a solo tribute album to her, which also made me dive deeper into folk music in general. It felt best not to try to copy her but to respect and love the essence of the originals (both her own wonderful songs, as well as the traditionals and covers recorded by her).

When recording *Linde Nijland Sings Sandy Denny*, I met my current partner, multi-instrumentalist Bert Ridderbos. I got invited to sing at a book launch by Joe Boyd (producer of four of Sandy's albums) and you can imagine how happy I felt when he 'approved'. Eventually this led to guest lead vocals on 'Fotheringay' and 'Si Tu Dois Partir' at Fairport's all-star reunion concert in 2009. And I was interviewed by Bob Harris for the BBC2 radio documentary about Sandy.

On UK tours, it always struck me how many people still love her sincere music, all these years after her sad passing. Sandy's songs are still part of my repertoire, even though I'm more focused on my own songwriting. 'No End' and 'Who Knows…' are always in the set and it feels like a privilege to play them. They seem fresh and never old. The atmosphere becomes slow and silent... people have a moment of reflection and the themes of time and timelessness seems to particularly touch the audience, even the ones who have not heard of Sandy before.

But many of her other songs are equally a joy to sing, feeling almost as familiar to me as my own. And who knows? Perhaps I'll record a second tribute album one day. 'For who knows how my love grows…'.

Thank you, Sandy.

'WHO KNOWS WHERE THE TIME GOES?'

ANDREW FLOWER

I hit university at the end of September 1969. It was there that fellow student Keith pulled out his copy of *Unhalfbricking*, which has become my all-time favourite album. If I ever was on BBC's Desert Island Discs, the version of 'Who Knows Where The Time Goes?' from this album would top my list. But is it because of the soft ripple of Sandy's voice as she tells her tale? The sudden power bursting forth that speaks of the depth of emotion beneath still waters? Or the quiet melancholy of love that echoes in your head even when the song has come to an end?

What strikes one is the sheer authenticity of her singing. She never holds back or flinches from exposing her own heart. And in doing so, it is as if she is holding a mirror up to one's own frailty and sensitivity. You are there with her. The tugs on your own heart are real.

When a band gels, they feed off each other's intuitive feel. This is the magical connection you can hear so solid and clear from the very first notes of *Unhalfbricking*.

My Stones albums went to the boot fair 20 years ago and my original Beatles LPs were passed on to our son-in-law a while ago. But Sandy has outlasted six changes of stereo and the birth of three totally captivating daughters. They have got to know Sandy. She was with us shortly after the birth of my first daughter, Eleanor, in 1980, when I fired up a pair of newly-built transmission-line speakers.

When my third daughter, Georgina, arrived on the scene, in 1993, Sandy was a leading contributor to my new CD collection. And Sandy was there in 2000, when I went on an extended business trip. Georgina and my middle daughter, Aimée, produced a drawing of the lyrics for my favourite song to take with me.

So, Sandy's message has universal appeal, and my daughters see the truth of this song: it speaks of love that is not possessive or demanding, but a thing of shared growth and development along life's path.

In 2010, Sandy made it into the few boxes of personal possessions I took with me when I moved to Austria. She was one of the first artists to be digitised for my PC and mobile phone and listened to in my home office or driving my car. But there is nothing I like more than turning up the volume in the living room, as Sandy sings out through those transmission-line speakers I built 45 years ago. She is like a welcome old friend I can share a happy moment with, or talk through my deeper thoughts.

For my seventieth birthday, Aimée produced a recording of herself playing guitar and singing my favourite all time song, 'Who Knows Where The Time Goes?'. What a wonderful sentiment – echoing the timelessness of Sandy's eternal words.

FAIRPORT'S CROPREDY CONVENTION
13 AUGUST 2010

BUDDY WOODWARD, THE DIXIE BEE-LINERS

Some of my earliest memories of being especially moved by singers are of hearing Appalachian Gospel, with its mysterious-sounding modal cadences that echo their Scots-Irish forbears and their stone, high-ceilinged churches. Any time I hear reflections of those 'ancient tones' (as Bill Monroe called them), I sit up and take notice.

It was in 1987, at a party in San Francisco, that I first encountered the phenomenon that was Fairport Convention via the newly released video cassette, *It All Comes 'Round Again*. And that's where I first heard it. That Voice. Sandy.

I immediately recognised her as the female singer that I'd heard years ago on Led Zeppelin's 'The Battle Of Evermore'. She was someone who could have really done justice to 'Precious Mem'ries', 'Jacob's Ladder' or 'Gloryland', with an intonation as keen as iron, yet immersive as water. A voice like quicksilver: shimmering, fluid… and ultimately corrosive to the artist who possesses it. A voice with the stark quality of someone who has gazed into the depth and darkness of the old stone well at the back of the garden and knows never to venture there again.

I sought out her albums through catalogues, libraries and indie record stores: all of her work in and out of Fairport, obscure Strawbs' wax, reissues and BBC live sessions, solo albums and the all-too-brief association with Fotheringay.

I devoured it all, obsessively. And then I put it all away for several years, while I pursued my own musical journey. It was on this journey, with my bluegrass band The Dixie Bee-Liners, that I was able to revisit my love for the mixolydian modulations of Appalachian Gospel and work them into our own sound. Our liberal use of DADGAD and drop-D tunings and Celtic fiddle were largely inspired by my favourite British folk performers, who themselves found some measure of inspiration from our American string band performers. So, a nice little mutual admiration society/circular firing squad was formed… a 'clusterfolk' continuum.

When The Dixie Bee-Liners received an invitation to play Fairport's Cropredy Festival in 2010, I was stunned. It was a surreal moment, and yet it seemed like a very real continuation of something – what our musical elders sometimes pithily referred to as 'the folk process'.

There I was, in Oxfordshire, hearing those 'ancient tones' pouring from the Cropredy stage and echoing around the glen, desperately wishing I could sing 'Drifting Too Far From The Shore' with Sandy.

So, after our set, I snuck off by myself with my mandolin and sang it to her.

SANDY DENNY BOX SET RELEASED 22 NOVEMBER 2010

DENNIS LEE CLEVEN

I live in Madison, Wisconsin. I recall seeing Sandy's solo albums in the cut-out bins in the record shops around 1975-77 when I was in my late teens but I had no idea who she was. It was Judy Collins who had a big hit with 'Who Knows Where the Time Goes?'. While I got into doing research for fun on the sixties and seventies Brit Girls, it was focused on pop beat acts like Dusty, Sandie Shaw, Lulu and Cilla and others like Twinkle, Marianne Faithfull, Kiki Dee and Elkie Brooks.

I was working in a bookstore in the eighties, playing music I liked, when a customer asked if I knew of Sandy Denny. (He bought music newspapers like *Melody Maker*.) He gave me a tape of Sandy Denny, but the sound quality was not that great. I was a fan of Melanie and others, so I became intrigued by Steeleye Span and Pentangle and that led me to Fairport Convention. The best Fairport Convention albums are those with Sandy Denny without a doubt and the sets released posthumously have superior sound quality. I found myself transfixed by her voice and the demos are so pure and gorgeous. The big, boxed set was announced and it was very limited in

Judy Collins covered 'Who Knows Where The Time Goes?' in 1968

its release, so it was a command to splurge and get it before it became unavailable. I had become an addict and I did not want a twelve-step programme. I got the huge boxed set. I love her singing enormously.

'WHO KNOWS WHERE THE TIME GOES?'

RONDI CHARLESTON, SINGER SONGWRITER

I can remember the moment I first heard the Judy Collins' recording of this powerful and haunting song by the brilliant Sandy Denny. It was the 1970s and I was a teenager playing guitar, singing and dreaming big dreams in our Chicago South Side apartment.

I can see my young self, sitting in my bedroom, figuring out the chord changes on my guitar as I listened to Judy's album, staring at the ethereal photo of her on the cover, and being absolutely mesmerised by this one particular song. What was it that compelled me to listen to it over and over? Was it because it made me feel something extraordinary as it transformed my little sphere of space and sound into a vast wide world full of possibility and hope? I felt fully embraced by peace, acceptance, forgiveness, and love. Pretty powerful stuff delivered in a mere four minutes and twenty seconds.

That's great songwriting right there. No two ways about it. Judy sang it beautifully but Sandy created it – from scratch – from her own vivid imagination. She painted that opening imagery of restless birds, winter fire and lovers dreaming – images that linger in our minds long after the song is over, and live somewhere between hope and melancholy, in an almost liminal space that manages to be both healing and therapeutic, as well as thought-provoking. There's a certain genius to that. It doesn't come around very often, but when it does, you know.

Fast forward forty years to 2011, and I'm recording my fourth solo jazz album for Motema Music in New York. It became clear to me almost in a dream state that I needed to explore the ephemeral passage of time, as it pertained to my own life. I was no longer young. I had experienced life's ups and downs, and I knew love and loss. It was time to revisit and reinvent 'Who Knows Where The Time Goes?' as a mature artist, and to discover where it would lead me.

And it led me to the river of creativity. The songs I chose for the album were knit together through the lens of the passage of time, and made a powerful statement about the movement of time as a whole, spearheaded by Sandy's masterpiece, which, like any great song, lends itself to endless layers of interpretation. Fleshing out the new arrangement, I felt a deep gravitational pull, which led me and my brilliant collaborator, Dave Stryker, to the grounding, expansive bass line that anchors our version. It was as if the circle of time had come to embrace me – uniting my young and innocent self with my mature and knowing self, and still having the same mysterious power over me.

'Who Knows Where the Time Goes?' is a prayer, a meditation, and a kind of healing balm that you can return to again and again. It somehow manages to fill your particular emotional needs, whether it's comfort and solace after a setback or loss, or hope and promise at a new stage of life. Sandy, if you're up there listening, eternal thanks to you for this beautiful gift.

DON'T STOP SINGING
RELEASED 7 NOVEMBER 2011

THEA GILMORE

I grew up in the shadow of folk rock. Not academically, no liner notes or timelines. I've never been that kind of music fan. But geographically. Living in Oxfordshire, Cropredy Festival was close enough to feel like part of the annual weather system. Fairport Convention, Sandy Denny, that whole constellation of sound lived somewhere between hedgerows and car radios, in my dad's record collection, in the air of the place. Sandy's voice in particular didn't feel like an artist you discovered, more a river or a range of hills. Something already there when you arrived.

I was born in late '79, the year after Sandy died. By the time I hit my teens in the mid-nineties, my listening habits were promiscuous, the way teenagers' ears always are. *The North Star Grassman And The Ravens* sat happily next to Tori Amos, Oasis, Leonard Cohen, Blur, Elastica. Bob Dylan shared shelf space with Bros. I didn't see any contradiction in that. I still don't. It all just went into the same bloodstream.

So when I was approached about working on what became *Don't Stop Singing*, my first instinct wasn't excitement, it was terror. It felt like the job should belong to someone else. Someone with footnotes. Someone who could quote session musicians, studio locations, catalogue numbers, release dates. Someone who might have been able to look Sandy Denny in the eye and say with authority, 'This is what you meant here'. I had none of that. What I had was reverence and instinct and those can be unreliable companions when you're standing near something sacred.

There was another fear too, less noble of course but very real. Her fans. People who loved her fiercely, knowledgeably. People who'd built lives around that voice. I assumed that many would ask, quite reasonably, why I had been chosen at all. I asked it myself. More than once. I said no to the project repeatedly.

Don't Stop Singing was Thea's tribute to Sandy

Then the booklet arrived. Bound photocopies of handwritten lyric sheets. I opened it, because anyone would. It fell open at 'Song No. 4' and within five minutes, the melody had written itself. And I knew I was lost.

There's no mystical explanation for that and I'm suspicious of them anyway. It wasn't channelling or communion. Just the way certain words lean towards music if you let them breathe. I didn't feel particularly clever, more… conscripted!

I carried the work with enormous caution. I was conscious the whole time that Sandy wasn't here to argue with me. That she couldn't tell me she hated a chorus or that a bridge was indulgent or I'd misunderstood the weather inside a line. Her absence hung over everything. You can't collaborate with the dead. You can only approach with your hat in your hand and hope that your footsteps are light.

Of course I brought myself to it anyway. There's no such thing as a pure artist. We drag our own ghosts into every room we enter. My history, my damage, my preferences, my voice. I'm sure now that my fingerprints and the fingerprints of others are all over that record in ways I didn't consciously intend or particularly like.

Are there things I would change? Of course. Like every artist I know, I'm in constant dialogue with my past selves.

Do I feel like I did Sandy justice? Honestly, no. Not in the grand, impossible sense of the word.

What it felt like was trying to ballet dance through beautiful, broken glass. Maybe that's what respect feels like. Tentative movement through something fragile and luminous and dangerous. I've never thought that you finish songs like that, you just hold them for a while. These were no exception.

When I'm asked about my relationship to Sandy's work now, I still don't reach for analysis, I reach for geography. Her voice was my musical mountains and sea. Something vast and familiar that framed my childhood. You don't ever stand back from landscapes when you're young. You just live inside them and only later realise how extraordinary the backdrop was.

When I was asked if I might contribute to this book, I felt the same mix of gratitude and hesitation. I can't offer a scholar's take. But I can offer the testimony of someone who grew up with Sandy's voice woven into the ordinary fabric of life. Someone who approached her words with fear, awe, reluctance and instinct in equal measure. Someone who definitely didn't feel entitled to stand alongside them but was changed by touching them anyway.

SANDY DENNY TRIBUTE ROYAL CONCERT HALL
20 MAY 2012, NOTTINGHAM, UK

DAVID BELBIN

The show started so promptly (7.30pm) that we missed the opening remarks. Each of the acts was introduced by Andrew Batt who put the tour together and also worked on all the recent Sandy re-issues including compiling and mixing the 19 CD boxset. All credit to him, but I'm not sure this was a good idea. At one point my companion said that it reminded him of a sixth form concert. Certainly, there was plenty of awkwardness which could have been dispelled had one of the musicians acted as compere. But presumably Jerry Donahue was only prepared to take the Richard Thompson role on guitar. And while it was great to see Swarb again, he isn't comfortable with being a frontman. Indeed, he ambled off stage long before everybody took their final bow.

I wanted to see this show partly because I never got to see Sandy sing. Her last Nottingham gig was in 1975, the year before I came here. I vividly remember the night in Easter 1978 when a friend had come round and was about to go when I put on the John Peel show. Instead of the usual introduction, John played three Sandy songs back-to-back, concluding with 'Who Knows Where The Time Goes?'. The pair of us sat and listened, then heard that Sandy had just died, after a fall down the stairs. There's more on her life and death here.

The tribute show, even one with an august a line-up as this, is a peculiar, fragile beast. Too much reverence, it's like being in church. Too little, and the acts can blow the mood even worse. Opening with 'A Sailor's Life', Sandy's old band-mate Dave Swarbrick playing violin, Trembling Bells' Lavinia Blackwall could hardly go wrong, and one of my favourites, the lovely 'Late November', suited her Denny-esque voice too.

But nobody can capture the sad, timeless vulnerability that made Sandy's voice unique and it was often the people who sounded least like her who came off best. Scritti Politti's Green Gartside gave us a choice three songs, 'Like An Old Fashioned Waltz', 'Run For Cover' and a great 'The North Star Grassman'.

The best solo number of the show, though, was Joan As Policewoman's unique take on 'No More Sad Refrains'. Alone at the piano, in a dress rather than her trademark leathers, she gave a mesmerising, transformative performance. In the first half, she gave strong performances of 'By The Time It Gets Dark' and 'The Lady'.

Maddy Prior sang a strong 'Fotheringay', the song which gave the name to Sandy's short-lived band, although her trademark dancing in the middle spoiled the mood of the song somewhat (and what was the point of introducing it afterwards? More amateurishness.) Guitarist Jerry Donahue played lovely lead Thompson-esque throughout, apart from one moment during PP Arnold, when he went a bit Eric Clapton. Thea Gilmore was lively and likeable. She has the right, rich voice to give Sandy songs a contemporary twist. She did two of the songs she's written with her music to Sandy's lyrics. They were a bit different, but in a good way. By contrast, while soul singer PP Arnold is still great; here, she felt out of place. To justify her presence, it was pointed out to us that she had sung with Nick Drake. Well, sort of, but Nick hated those backing vocals on 'Poor Boy' – with good reason, some would say.

Other members of the band got a song each, all enjoyable, including a fun 'Matty Groves' (not a Denny song, but never mind) and Blair Dunlop's 'The Sea' and 'It'll Take A Long, Long Time'. The other most memorable moment came with a traditional song, when the voices of Thea, Maddy and Lavinia were joined just by Swarb on violin for a beautiful 'The Quiet Joys Of Brotherhood'. Magic.

The ending, of course, was what the vicar described as 'the inevitable', an effective 'Who Knows Where The Time Goes?'. It was more than OK, with good moments, but not quite great, which probably sums up the evening. For those of us who are too young to have seen Sandy Denny, though, it was great to be able to hear many of these songs live. It's a legacy well worth celebrating.

THE LADY: A HOMAGE TO SANDY DENNY BARBICAN THEATRE 23 MAY 2012, LONDON, UK

JOAN WASSER (AKA JOAN AS POLICEWOMAN)

Sandy Denny has that 'thing' I love in a songwriter who sings her own songs. She sings to soothe her own sorrow, that blank space inside her, and in doing so, brings the listener great comfort. Our spaces may vary slightly or greatly, but we've all got them; that place where things get lost, where life doesn't and won't make sense, where loneliness exists and feels as if it will never retreat.

Because we all know that Denny ultimately died from the complications from a fall, while inebriated. We know that she had her share of this kind of pain, as well. Is this why she didn't become a bigger star at the time? I don't know. No one can know this. Certainly, if she had lived longer, she'd have had more time to show the world how stunningly talented she was.

I do feel that the cream always rises to the top, no matter how isolated or adverse to success or appreciation one might be. In this case, a songwriter and singer of her calibre seemed surely ready to experience renewed interest, especially because her songs are classics. They are timeless and enduring; simple enough to be sung and interpreted by others, distinct enough to be undoubtedly hers.

I was interested in this project because what Denny created is what I am interested in doing in my own life as a songwriter and singer. I want to sing from that place we all share; from the space that can feel indescribably painful and confusing but also unites us all. Learning through living in another's songs makes me a protégé and a believer of her truth.

And I do believe in Sandy Denny.

The Lady - A Homage to Sandy Denny

OLYMPIC STADIUM
12 AUGUST 2012, STRATFORD, LONDON

TIM EDMONDS

I was aware that Sandy had left a considerable number of unfinished songs – in many cases just lyrics on scraps of paper. In 2011, I read that Thea Gilmore had composed tunes to a selection of these songs and recorded them with some excellent musicians, including John Kirkpatrick and Nigel Stonier. These were released on her album *Don't Stop Singing*, which I bought immediately. The following year, the Olympic Games came to London and my wife and I managed to get tickets for several events. We watched much more on TV, and were watching TV when Gary Lineker ended the coverage with a short montage of highlights. This had a musical accompaniment and, as soon as the intro began, I recognised it as 'London' from the Thea Gilmore album. The song made a superb soundscape for the montage. Sandy had become a London 2012 Olympic star!

ACROSS THE PURPLE SKY
RELEASED 2013

BRYONY HOLDEN, TINKERSCUSS

In 2005 we played a Gloucestershire gig where we met festival organiser Bob Porter. After our set, he remarked on similarities between mine and Sandy's voices, adding that 'Who Knows Where The Time Goes?' was his and his wife Carol's 'song' throughout their courtship and still pivotal to them. We agreed to do the song for him at some point, little knowing how busy we were going to be kept for the next few years, touring and recording.

We'd been joined temporarily by a third member and, after she moved on, we found ourselves thinking about the next project. In the intervening years many a comment or song suggestion had been made and, remembering our promise, we began with a list. Not wishing to just replicate, we approached most of the songs as if they were being done for the present.

My sister Erin wanted 'Two Weeks Last Summer' for its lazy summer feel. I'd been performing 'Reynardine' a cappella. We wanted to give it something futuristic whilst keeping the ethereal dark theme. Most instruments were played by Erin with harp, piano and all vocals from me. As a harmony fiend, 'Quiet Joys' was a must. I enjoyed unravelling the vocal lines, then reassembling. All it needed was a string outro; and a spellbinding effort from Aly Rainey (Dryadic) was the finishing touch. For the opening track, we went for a straight take of 'Banks Of The Nile', with Vincent Salzfaas (ex Gigspanner) adding noteworthy percussion.

The gaps closed rapidly once 'Who Knows…' and a favourite, 'The Sea', were done. Erin and I had first encountered Sandy duetting with Robert Plant on Zeppelin *IV*'s epic 'The Battle Of Evermore'. Could we find our own Robert? Several tribute band 'Plants' around the country auditioned and we chose Whole Lotta Led's Lee Pryor for his fluidity. So successful was the pairing, we also recorded 'Going To California' and went on to open for the band on several occasions with our take on Zeppelin classics from the source. Of course, that included Jimmy Page's 'Black Mountainside' and so 'Black Waterside' was added to the album. 'Gypsy Davey' got the slide guitar treatment, and 'John The Gun' showed Erin's rock guitar roots: we were almost done.

Across The Purple Sky was released digitally in 2013 on the 35th anniversary of Sandy's death. A mutual friend of Elizabeth Hurtt (Trevor Lucas's third wife) passed the album to her and we had a letter back saying she was 'blown away' and that Georgia had flown home with it on her iPod. It was a wonderful acknowledgement of the work we'd put in. And the album was later pared down and re-released as *Who Knows Where The Time Goes?*

INTERVIEW
2013

DAVE SWARBRICK, FIDDLE PLAYER, FAIRPORT CONVENTION

You've got to understand, I have never got over her dying. It's very hard to listen to her stuff. I did these two Sandy tours and I found it very hard. You know, it occurred to me the other day that if she was alive now, she would have grandchildren, possibly she'd be a great grandmother... and it was very weird. It seems weird because Sandy was one of those who fell in the war. 'Age shall not weary them as we that are left grow old' and all that. She'll never be any older than she was.'

Were you close?

Very close.

Were you her boyfriend?

Yes, I was her boyfriend... Well, I wouldn't call myself a boyfriend. It was more casual than that. She had a fierce upbringing, you know. Her mother was a fierce woman and Sandy herself was very unsure of what she was doing. She didn't have a lot of confidence. She was the kind of person who if you said, 'I really liked that, Sandy,' she would say, 'Why, didn't you like the other?' She was very loving and super smart, she saw through people very quickly: she was a real character.

A lot of her lyrics are about loneliness.

Well yes. But to an extent most touring musicians are lonely and if you are a woman, it's worse because probably you're torn between being at home and being on the road. Admittedly Sandy often toured with her husband... but that brought its own difficulties. I've been in bands with other women and it's always been difficult for them. I mean, what do they do? Do they become one of the boys?

UNDER THE BRIDGE
19 JUNE 2015, CHELSEA, LONDON, UK

JOHN DEOL

In the late nineties I moved to Fulham. Somebody mentioned to me that a folk singer had lived just around the corner, in Parsons Green. I knew nothing of Sandy Denny and I didn't really know Fairport either. Before streaming sites, you had to buy the records if you wanted to hear the music, so I went and ordered a new Sandy compilation that had just come out. It was around the same time as Clinton Heylin's biography of her was published. The compilation starts with tracks from *The North Star Raven And The Grassmen* and I just loved it from the beginning.

There's just so much melancholy in her music. It's quite a dark record, and the songs just resonated with me. And it was through listening to Sandy Denny and then buying the solo albums and then getting to know Fairport that I got into folk music. I was years too late to see her live, but

Dave Swarbrick, Richard Thompson & Sandy working on *Liege & Lief,* 1969 (Eric Hayes)

in 2003 I saw Simon Nicol and Dave Swarbrick play a gig at the Putney Half Moon, and I saw Richard Thompson not long after.

But the gig for me was in 2015 when Fotheringay reformed, obviously without Trevor and Sandy, but with three out of the five original members. I believe Jerry Donahue put the band together with Gerry Conway and Pat Donaldson. They played at Under The Bridge in Chelsea. It was really poignant, right next to Fulham, not far from where Sandy and Trevor used to live in Parsons Green, but, even more poignant, it was pretty much across the road from where they got married. Those photos of them outside the Fulham Registry Office in 1973 were kind of in my mind as well.

It was really poignant to hear those songs again with three out of the five original Fotheringay members but also sad that Sandy and Trevor weren't there. The *Fotheringay* album is probably one of my favourites that Sandy's been involved in. It's got some of her strongest songs: 'The Sea', 'Nothing More', 'The Pond And Stream'.

What is it about Sandy? As for a lot of people, once you hear her music, you can't quite believe she wasn't huge and isn't huge. It's not just the songwriting, it's the voice and the universal themes of longing and pathos and melancholy and sadness in her songs that are all so relatable even today. I can't quite believe she never made it big.

Also, I now live in Wimbledon, so I'm literally around the corner from two of her childhood homes. I've been up to the grave up at Putney Vale a fair few times, I go past the hospital where she was born and past what was then the hospital where she passed away as well. There's lots of reminders of her around Wimbledon when I'm there.

I encourage anyone I know to get into her music. I've bought lots of her CDs and given them out as presents to people who, like me, feel the same thing when they hear her music. They can't quite believe she wasn't huge and isn't a household name. And maybe that makes it more special for those of us who are into her. The music isn't spoiled by being overplayed, and that's okay.

NIGEL SCHOFIELD

In 2008, Jerry Donahue completed work on a true labour of love, the abandoned *Fotheringay 2* album. It was extremely well received, not least because it finally placed several refugee songs that had been released in later contexts back in their rightful place. The interest generated in long-gone, short-lived band led, on 30 March 2015, to the release of *Nothing More*, yet another four disc booklet-box featuring Sandy. It included the two Fotheringay albums, plus demos and out-takes, all the band's BBC recordings, a complete concert in Rotterdam, and four songs from a German TV broadcast.

To tie in with the release, the band's three surviving members – Jerry Donahue, Pat Donaldson and Gerry Conway – recruited Sally Barker, Kathryn Roberts and PJ Wright to tour once more as Fotheringay. The line-up lasted 18 months off and on and evolved into The Sandy Denny Project which plays a wider selection of Sandy's material and still draws packed houses whenever its many members can get together.

SALLY BARKER, SINGER SONGWRITER, THE SANDY DENNY PROJECT

I never knew Sandy. I sang 'Who Knows Where the Time Goes?' in folk clubs around the Midlands in the seventies but only started listening to her albums after she passed. When I left school at the age of 18 in 1978, I briefly attended university at Worcester and it was there I met fellow student Robin Shepherd (now known as actor Robin Kingsland). He asked me if I had heard Sandy's music and proceeded to play me *The North Star Grassman And The Ravens*, Sandy's first album from 1971. He then told me that she had left this world too soon but had left an intriguing body of work.

My favourite song of hers is 'No End', her song about two friends meeting up in winter after a long hiatus. I find it quite beautifully English in character with its talk of snow on the motorway, and the song ends in positive mood. After talking through the night, the visitor (presumably Sandy?) has inspired the painter to resume his art.

I was honoured to be asked to sing Sandy's songs when Jerry Donahue reformed Fotheringay in 2015 with the other surviving members. I knew the guys in Fairport Convention, having played Cropredy quite a few times in the nineties and again after I had been on *The Voice UK* in 2014, so was familiar with Sandy's body of work and her story. And I sang again when a blue plaque was unveiled at Byfield Village Hall to commemorate the last concert Sandy played, in the village where she had lived with Trevor and baby Georgia.

With Georgia's blessing, my friends and I now perform as The Sandy Denny Project in Byfield every April at what we call *SandyFest*. I also sing Sandy's songs alongside those of Joni Mitchell in my solo show, 'Joni, Sandy & Me', where I talk of both Sandy and Joni, their song writing styles and their influence on my own songs.

I come to Sandy's songs from a recognisable place; I am lost in the gracious wonder and glory of her individual artistic expression and I daydream and contemplate her inspirations, frustrations and musical changes, that sometimes follow a different path than the expected.

BBC RADIO 2 FOLK AWARDS ROYAL ALBERT HALL

27 APRIL 2016, KENSINGTON, LONDON, UK

RUFUS WAINWIGHT

I never met her, sadly, but Sandy loomed large in my household. My mother, the late great Kate McGarrigle, knew her. And, of course, my dear friend Linda Thompson knew her very, very well.

I chose to sing 'Who Knows Where The Time Goes?' at the awards ceremony because that song was so poignant for me. On one hand, my mother understood and appreciated Fairport Convention and got it in a lot of ways. But there was always a little bit of rivalry between the different folk factions, you know – Canadian folk, British folk, and so forth.

My mother could be quite on and off about a lot of artists. She was a very competitive woman. But that song always touched her deeply and was kind of her emblem for why Sandy was so great. My mother would sing it. I think what my mother loved about Sandy with that whole Fairport thing was that it was very kind of masculine – 'who was the best guitar player?' – and there was a really tough sound to it, and a sexiness to it which was very male. But Sandy really gave it this female touch, a vulnerability and a more mystical tone. And my mother very much gravitated towards that and appreciated it on a deep level.

'Who Knows Where The Time Goes' was one of the very first songs Sandy wrote. My aunt Anna (McGarrigle) has the same blessing or curse, because one of her first songs was 'Heart Like A Wheel'. It's the same for Edith Piaf and 'La Vie En Rose'. 'Who Knows Where The Time Goes?' is so iconic and came so early and really set the stage.

FAIRPORT'S CROPREDY CONVENTION
9-11 AUGUST 2018, CROPREDY, UK

MICK MONK

I will never forget the moment Cropredy remembered the fortieth year of Sandy's passing. Fairport stopped playing mid-set and the sound of Sandy singing 'Quiet Joys Of Brotherhood' rose in volume and filled the night sky. Heaven was sending the best it could send.

I have attended almost every SandyFest, staged by the superb Sandy Denny Project, at the Byfield Village Hall where Sandy made her last performance.

I am humbly grateful to Georgia Rose, especially, for maintaining and heightening the legacy of Alexandra Elene McLean Denny through the exhibitions of her mum's personal effects, the Carla Fuchs album *Songbird* based on unused Sandy lyrics and other promotions.

And if I had to pick a memory that stands out since Sandy left us, it would be meeting Georgia Rose face-to-face for the first time after getting to know and, in my own small way, work with her remotely.

I will always view Thursday 10 August 2023 as my 'Georgia Rose Lucas Day'. She was running her first Sandy Denny Exhibition at the Brasenose Arms in Cropredy whilst nursing a damaged ankle. She struck me as a humble, kind, friendly superwoman, a survivor. Balancing family with enhancing her mum's legacy and running charity fund-raisers, while being so thoughtful to all. I know first-hand how thoughtful she is when she, as a creative talent, voluntarily created an artwork of my mum when my family's maternal head passed.

Her own mum deserves legendary status as a singer/songwriter/performer. She stands comparison to any vocalist to draw breath. And always will.

KIP WINTER, WINTER WILSON

We sing songs. It's what we do. Mainly songs we've written ourselves (mostly Dave Wilson), but just a few covers now and then. As a result, we both think we know a good song when we hear one. We had of course both been aware of Sandy's music and the tremendous role she played in the UK folk revival since we were young, but it was when we were invited to tour with Fairport Convention in early 2018 that we really began to realise the impact her songs had on audiences. Every evening, Simon Nicol would sing 'Who Knows Where the Time Goes?' and packed houses would melt. It was hard to fathom that Sandy had written such a deep and powerful song aged just 19.

For Cropredy in August that year, the guys planned a special tribute concert, celebrating Sandy's life and work 40 years after her untimely death, and we were invited to contribute. We chose to perform 'It'll Take A Long, Long Time' and walked out on stage in front of who knows how many thousands of people to play and sing, backed by Fairport. Once

Kip Winter & Dave Wilson with Georgia, Cropredy 2019

again, the reaction was palpable. The crowd sang along beautifully and we had so many amazing comments afterwards.

Subsequently, a chain of weird coincidences led to Sandy's daughter Georgia turning up at a gig we played in Sydney, New South Wales, and we sang for her. We have since become good friends but equally we have become more and more aware of Sandy's impact on not only the British, but the world's folk scene.

NICKY MANSFIELD

My brother Michael bought *The History Of Fairport Convention* in 1976 and we loved it. I was 13. He then got *What We Did On Our Holidays*, *Unhalfbricking*, *Liege & Lief* and the *Sandy* album. I was very taken with Sandy's songs and her voice, and spent many hours working out the chords to her songs on my guitar. They were often tricky as many of the melodies have beautiful, unusual chord patterns.

When I heard Sandy had died, I was shocked. I remember thinking how I would never see her play live and there would be no more songs. The obituary I read in the music press was spot on.

I bought the *Fotheringay* album, *Rising For The Moon* and all but one of the solo albums. When I wrote to Island Records to ask about *Like An Old Fashioned Waltz,* I got a very snotty reply. The solo work is a mixed bag but the best songs are gems.

The 40-year anniversary tribute at Cropredy was wonderful and it was worth getting utterly soaked to hear it, and to share the moment with fellow fans. Great songs live eternally and Sandy's legacy is assured.

'LIKE AN OLD FASHIONED WALTZ'

JUDITH ANTONIDES

My father introduced me to Sandy Denny's music, and it has held a special place in our hearts ever since, especially her song 'Like An Old Fashioned Waltz'. Her song helped us through difficult times when my father was ill in 2018. It gave us comfort and strength when we needed it most. Even now, it still gives me strength and brings back precious memories of my childhood.

SEAFORD THEATRE
24 NOVEMBER 2018, EASTBOURNE, UK

PHIL JONES, HATFUL OF RAIN

I never met Sandy – Lord, I wish I had – but she was in my life since the age of 14. I was music mad. I hung on every word of the older boys in school, who were a couple of years ahead of my excitement. I had gone to see Steeleye Span and was talking about how much I liked Maddy's voice. One of the assembled company literally grabbed me by the collar and said, 'You need to hear Sandy Denny!'

A few weeks later, I was in Woolworths in the small South Wales valley town where I lived and saw *All Our Own Work* by Sandy and the Strawbs which I snapped up. I loved it but – wow! – 'Who Knows'! I thought I'd discovered the source of the Nile! To me that's always been my favourite version by some distance – I just loved Sandy's guitar accompaniment.

Roll forward 45 years or more. My band were opening for the Acoustic Strawbs in Eastbourne. Backstage was the great man himself, Dave Cousins, looking tired and careworn to be honest. He clearly wanted to be left alone and of course I obliged. After our soundcheck he approached me to say how much he liked our singer Chloe Overton's voice. I thanked him and, as we chatted about female singers for a little while, I saw my chance. I told him how I would repeatedly reread the story of the Denmark trip which led to *All Our Own Work*. He smiled softly and a look of reverie came over his face. 'What a wonderful time,' he said. 'Sandy was wonderful, and great company.'

It wasn't much, but it was all I needed.

WOODWORM STUDIOS
BARFORD ST MICHAEL, UK

CHARLES WARNER

Fairly early on in his association with Fairport, my brother Clive invited me to the Barford pub and then down to Woodworm's Hilton. Now I was a very shy teenager. I had been to the Cropredy Festival a couple of times but I had also seen Tull. It was quite a big deal to be in Peggy's house. I had just started to learn to play guitar and I had a little pamphlet called the 'Three Chord Trick', but I couldn't really play. Mat Davies invited us into the studio. Clive could play drums a bit and Mat just said to take a guitar off the wall and come and join them for a jam.

In my shyness, and coupled with the fact that I couldn't really play, I chose a battered acoustic and plinked away for a bit before giving up as Mat did all that thunderous slap bass and Clive bashed out a rhythm on the drums. While this was happening Peggy entered, plugged in a gleaming white Stratocaster and smashed out an amazing blues solo. I had no idea he even played lead. He then unplugged the Strat and walked past me. He looked me up and down, looked at the guitar I was cradling and said, 'That was Sandy's guitar.'

I just wanted to melt into the floor.

'WHO KNOWS WHERE THE TIME GOES ?'

JON AND LUCY, HONEY & THE BEAR

Sandy's incredible legacy came in to sharp focus for us in lockdown. Her name and music had been present in both our lives from as far back as we can remember. It's strange to reflect on those years of the Covid pandemic now that life has fully reverted to the way it was before everything came to an abrupt stand still in March 2020. Live music was stopped in its tracks in the UK so, instead, we took to people's screens for a weekly livestream performance each and every Sunday night.

Jon and Lucy (Honey & the Bear) with Georgia, Les Cousins 60th Anniversary, FolkEast, August 2025 (Dawn Kemp)

We would perform an hour or more of our own material, as well as a selection of traditional songs or covers suggested by our faithful audience. It's important to say that the community that formed around our online events got us through lockdown as much as our performances were, hopefully, a reliable beacon for the listeners in a troubled and turbulent time. We kept the livestream going for over 51 weeks in all. During that time, we could give our full attention to the songs that people suggested we research and learn.

One of the early suggestions was 'Who Knows Where The Time Goes?'. The lyrics resonated with us both straight away, as they did with our online audience. It was clear that this was a song that was a lifelong favourite for many of our viewers. How do you tackle a cover that has held such a treasured place in people's hearts with Sandy's incredible voice defining it? Well, luckily for us, the realisation of its profound imprint on the world of folk didn't dawn on us until we had interpreted it for the following Sunday's livestream.

We had under a week to have it rehearsed and ready, so in reality our cover is a musical photograph of that day in 2020, a snapshot in time. If we knew then what we know now about the revered status of Sandy's recording, we might never have dared to venture near it, but we are very grateful that it has been received so well. Mark Radcliffe's introduction on the BBC Radio 2 Folk Show was generous, and so too have our audience reactions been to our countless live performances since. In fact, it often gets requested. Says Jon, 'It remains a treasured moment in our live set, as Lucy's soaring vocal invokes so many emotions and memories, it always casts a spell over me. But then, that just goes to show how well it was written. It can be as evocative and relevant today as the day Sandy put pen to paper.'

Lucy adds, 'I always find singing 'Who Knows Where the Time Goes?' incredibly grounding. There is a quiet beauty and poignance to the lyrics that fills me with peace. Having said that, I always say a silent prayer before I begin that my voice manages to do the song justice.'

CLAY WORLEY

Amongst my parents' records, one album stood out even to me as a toddler. Its title felt like both a riddle and a lullaby: *Who Knows Where The Time Goes?* I remember tugging at my mother's sleeve, asking her to play the title track again (the Judy Collins version). As she smiled and exhaled, Pall Mall smoke drifted through the morning light in our living room, and my mom quietly went along.

I plunged headlong into the thunder and mystique of Led Zeppelin. 'The Battle Of Evermore' flooded my imagination with visions of ancient landscapes, forgotten kingdoms and adventures that felt both impossibly distant and strangely familiar.

Woven through Robert Plant's vocals was another voice — one that didn't simply harmonise, but seemed to rise from some older, deeper place. It rang through the song like a medieval bell echoing from the stone walls of a cathedral. Her voice carried a kind of ancestral summons – a folksy call to arms that made you want to fasten your armour, tighten your scabbard and saddle your warhorse, beckoning me toward battles fought in an ancient past.

Sandy's voice remained ever present in the winds that carried me toward adulthood and, eventually, into military service. Whether I was peacekeeping in Bosnia or fighting in Iraq, I often remembered something my mother once told me, that I was 'the sum of all my pluses and minuses'. It was her way of reminding me that strength and vulnerability coexist, and that both would shape the man I was becoming.

Back home, my parents were still fighting their own battles. My mother was diagnosed with clinical depression, a ghastly beast that clawed at her spirit and frayed the seams of the life my parents had built together. Its torment was relentless, and it cast a long shadow over our family.

Ten years after my return from Iraq – after sheathing my sabre for the last time, tying it off with a yellow ribbon and promising my family I would never again take up arms – my own demons rose up like spectres from the darkest cave walls of a child's nightmare. PTSD had been gathering quietly across multiple tours, and now it stepped fully into the light. In its wake lay two broken marriages and an unrelenting inner claxon calling for the higher purpose I had once known in uniform… a seemingly useless figure: the warrior without a war.

I refused to cave into the call, the harkening of phantasms in distorted glory. I threw myself into a new career instead, determined to build something meaningful out of the pieces I still carried, looking for a new way to serve. It took years before I could finally see that I had ended up exactly where I needed to be – not by accident, but by endurance.

And then came the warm rains of final discovery: learning, at last, about the genius of Sandy Denny. The magnificence of music that had soothed me in childhood, stirred my imagination in adolescence and accompanied me through war and its aftermath suddenly had a name, a history and a life of its own. It felt as though a longlost thread had been placed back into my hands, completing a circle I hadn't even known I was tracing.

Through Pandora, Sandy finally pulled back the curtains and revealed herself. Her strength, her originality and the sheer range of her voice entranced and pitched me through a portal in time. I began researching everything I could find – who she was, how she lived, what shaped her. I ordered every CD I could get my hands on and filled the compartments of my car with her music. Her voice lived through the emotions that washed over me like warm summer tides, steadying me in ways I hadn't known I still needed.

I was driving north one afternoon, after one of the worst arguments I'd ever had with my closest friend. My heart was drenched and stained with tears, the painful echo of harsh words burning like the unforgiving Texas heat. I needed someone or something to listen to my desolation. And Sandy did. I played the same song from my earliest childhood repeatedly, but this time it was Sandy, not Judy. Her voice kissed my tears away.

When I returned home after that long drive to Temple, I felt calm for the first time in so very many days. Something inside me had settled. I felt equipped with the unassailable resolve of someone who finally understood he wasn't all that bad at his core. It felt like a spiritual rebirth.

I think of Sandy Denny in the way of stars of morning skies – how their light and their galactic ballads travel the universe for eons after they go dark. Yet, you see what look like frozen fires, suspended in their stellar silence from distances that will surely outlive us all. That is the perpetual cascade of Sandy's brilliant benevolence, immortal like the stars themselves. Her voice, her art, her spirit — all of it still soaring, landing, and illuminating lives long after her earthly flame began to fade. And truly… who knows where the time goes?

PASQUALE DI RESTA, MUSICIAN

A song whispered to the heart, a flute-like melody in the moor, a light rain in spring, a gust of wind, the sound of the sea waves, the sun piercing the soul... This is what I felt the first time I heard her singing, and the sensations I experience listening to Sandy's voice remain unchanged, my great inspiration and teacher, on how to let heart and soul flow in song, a river that expands from its source into the sea. I love her compositions and the way she interpreted them is just wonderful.

Pasquale Di Resta collaborated with Carla Fuchs on *The North Star Grassman And The Ravens*

I met Georgia through Carla Fuchs, with whom I collaborated in early 2022 on her version of Sandy Denny's 'The North Star Grassman And The Ravens', and I had the opportunity to appreciate her talent as an artist and her touching love for her mother. I am united with Georgia in memory and in the feeling for the many emotions conveyed by Sandy's music, and so it will always be.

LIEGE & LIEF TURNS 50 DECEMBER 2019

TONY HARDY

It's hard to believe but this album, often lauded as the greatest folk-rock record of them all, is 50 years old this month. It is up there, too, in my all-time greats list, so it was a pleasure to blow the cobwebs off this particular masterpiece and remind myself just how good it really was, and indeed still is.

Liege & Lief was the band's fourth album and their third with the never surpassed Sandy Denny as lead singer. The album came to define the movement known as folk-rock and while three of the eight songs were actually contemporary, the composite effort sounds pretty much traditional, yet with the benefit of a radical makeover.

Like the prog-rockers of their day, Fairport were not averse to extended pieces of music, and two songs here get the full treatment: 'Tam Lin' and 'Matty Groves' clock in at seven and eight minutes respectively. Of course, being folk ballads, there are lots of verses to fit in, but both songs feature storming instrumental sections, with the denouement to 'Matty Groves' being the absolute highlight. The musicianship is rock solid and at times brims with true virtuosity. The second half of 'Matty Groves' is a sheer delight with Richard Thompson interweaving guitar licks with Dave Swarbrick's soaring violin, while the rhythm guitar of Simon Nicol, bass of Ashley Hutchings and Dave Mattacks' immaculate drumming hold the whole thing together expertly.

Much of the recording has a live feel, and Sandy Denny's singing is, as always, top notch. Her premature death in 1978, after an accident at home, was a tragic loss to her family, friends and the whole music world. What made Denny such a great singer can be heard in abundance on this album. Her vocals can be clean and pure, soft or strong, and imbued with a rustic timbre all their own. The legendary Island production and engineering team of Joe Boyd and John Wood were also absolutely key to how good *Liege & Lief* still sounds today. The beauty and richness of analogue recording shines through in these days of digital compression.

Opening with the infectious 'Come All Ye', written by Denny and Hutchings, you could be listening to a trad song given a fresh reworking until Thompson's angular electric lead kicks in and the song builds by introducing the band in a folk equivalent of 'Sgt. Pepper'! The album includes quiet moments, like the mournful 'Reynardine' and contemplative 'Farewell, Farewell', plus a joyfully slick medley of jigs and reels. There's the simple beauty of 'The Deserter' and the landmark folk-rock anthems of 'Matty Groves' and 'Tam Lin', before closing with an original Thompson-Swarbrick composition, 'Crazy Man Michael', on which Sandy Denny once again shines with rare delicacy.

As a complete package that broke new ground in the UK and stills provides inspiration for new generations of folk musicians, *Liege & Lief* remains unsurpassed. Listen to it on some decent equipment and see if you agree.

FAIRPORT'S CROPREDY CONVENTION
11-13 AUGUST 2022, CROPREDY, UK

SORREL NATION, SINGER SONGWRITER

I was first asked to sing 'Who Knows Where The Time Goes' back in 2022 whilst performing in The Magic Teapot venue at Fairport's Cropredy Convention. You could hear a pin drop as I sung what I believe to be a truly timeless and perfect piece of music, completely acoustically, next to the fire. This was a truly wonderful moment for me as a grassroots artist trying to make her way, for the room was filled with so many lifelong Sandy Denny fans and seeing the smiles on their faces is something I will never forget.

Sorrel Nation has grown to truly love 'Who Knows Where The Time Goes?'

My love for this song has continued over the past few years as my career has progressed and this song has been on tour with me and is sung at every single show. I get shivers every time I sing it and it brings on new meanings to myself and others as time passes, as loved ones are lost and memories are shared. I released a live solo version on my EP, *Thirty Summers*, in memory of my beloved rescue dog Gracie and have performed the song in various formats over the years including the addition of cello and violin. I plan to record and release a studio version of this song to include on my second studio album and wish to keep the beauty of this emotional, important and classic song alive and bring it to new generations as long as my career allows.

HIGH SCHOOL
SEPTEMBER 2022, POLAND

NATALIA KUPIS

In September 2022 I began the final year of my high school. I felt lonely, sad, and helpless. I struggled to find my voice, or rather – to deliver my voice to others. To make them listen to me. What really was making me upset was that strong conviction that no one cared about my music. I went to the school rock band audition – I sang a beautiful rock ballad and got accepted. All would have been perfect, but the teacher asked me to prepare an AC/DC song for the following week. I felt defeated. No one cared about the gentle beauty of ballads. For me singing folk-rock songs and traditional music was the core of my existence, the sense of my teenage life. For a year and a half, I had been in love with Fairport Convention and the voice of Sandy Denny. In harsh moments it was soothing.

My ambition was to sound like my role model – Sandy. I wanted the whole world to hear her songs and maybe become a bit more tender. One Saturday, after a few hours of listening to 'Who Knows Where The Time Goes?', and after having considered it a perfect ballad, with such a deep and moving meaning, I went for a walk. Strolling through the streets of my neighbourhood is quite boring, so I turned my thoughts towards the lyrics of Sandy's masterpiece and thought how it would sound like in Polish.

That day, I began my fascinating adventure of translating songs. It did not matter that on Monday I had a maths test planned. The only thing that interested me was bringing the spirit of the song 'Who Knows…' into my first language. I really, really wanted to present it to my parents who did not understand English easily. I wanted them to experience the song, its beauty, its strength, just as I did. By evening the draft was ready. The next day was the great day of the first performance. Both Mum and Dad loved it. I was so proud of myself. I brought the melancholy and the quiet hope of this song to life in my native language.

Sandy's work could be now admired by people who don't know English. Two months later I had an amazing opportunity to perform my translation of the song in front of a bigger audience. I participated in the Youth Song Festival in one of the high schools in my city; I presented Sandy's 'Who

Knows Where the Time Goes?' and 'Crazy Man Michael'. I remember people waving their phones with lights turned on. It was… magical.

As a short introduction to the songs I was going to sing, I said that my hope was to deliver the beauty hidden in these ballads to the Polish audience. That evening I felt… complete. People were listening.

That night I also met the boy who changed my life, but that's another story. Or, maybe not so much, because if it hadn't been for Sandy's song, I wouldn't have gone to the festival and wouldn't have met him.

Sandy Denny's music was with me when I was at my worst. It helped me to believe in myself. It gave me the sense of purpose. Although I never had the opportunity to see her live, I am grateful for her work, for all the beauty she left. Her music is for me like a warm hearth, giving me a sense of safety. Listening to her songs I feel understood. And I think that's the power of her music.

Thank you, Sandy.

BRASENOSE ARMS
10-12 AUGUST 2023, CROPREDY, UK

ESTELLE JACKSON

Trying to summarise Sandy's importance in my life is like trying to explain the importance of air; of matter; of a heartbeat. Her words and music are part of me now.

I first heard about Fairport Convention in 1992. My school GCSE music class put together an eclectic concert, comprising instrumental solos, duets and group items, solo singers, rock and blues songs, improvisation, and all of us singing some of the hits from *Grease*. We toured local care homes and primary schools, performing our concert eight times in a week. I had recently acquired a collection of tin whistles, and had been learning to play all kinds of folk tunes on them, and writing music for them too. My class teacher wrote an arrangement of 'The Wraggle Taggle Gypsies' for me to play with my violinist friend. We absolutely loved performing it, and it proved to be an extremely popular item.

At the end of the week, my teacher lent me his copy of *Full House*, which he thought I 'might enjoy'. Enjoy was an understatement – I was transfixed. Unfortunately, back in the early 1990s, we didn't have Internet, and the only information I could find about Fairport was in reference books in the library. Nevertheless, my enthusiasm was undimmed, and I hoped to be able to see them one day.

In November 1994 when I was 17, *Folk on Two* (a British radio show) broadcast a weekly programme for four weeks, about the history of English folk rock. It was here that I first heard about Sandy, and heard that magical voice. The very same day, I found out that she had sadly passed away many years before. I recorded the shows onto cassette and played them obsessively. I began to visit the library more frequently and managed to listen to records by Fairport, Sandy, Fotheringay, the Strawbs and so on.

The following year, I began a relationship with the man who would eventually become my husband. A big early factor uniting us was our love of folk rock and 1970s music. We swapped records all the time. I saved up for all the Fairport and Sandy CDs, and as much vinyl as I could lay my hands on. Wanting to listen to everything of Sandy's was probably one of the reasons for my first big purchase as a young adult – a hi-fi system including a turntable, CD player, radio and two cassette decks.

While still 18, I went off to university to study music and psychology. Being shy and in a long-distance relationship, I struggled at times, particularly with loneliness. Sandy and the Fairports felt like friends I had never met. They became the soundtrack to my life.

My passion for anything folk rock or Celtic expanded to encapsulate Runrig, The Levellers, Bellowhead, Dylan, Richard Thompson, Jackson C Frank, Perkelt, Seth Lakeman and more – many of whom I have been fortunate enough to see live. While I was studying at the University of London, my mum took me to visit Sandy's grave, and it was there that I was finally able to thank her for all the music.

I attended my first Cropredy in 2012. It's where I feel closest to Sandy (and Trevor), and it's also where I have met the Fairports many times. There is always an amazing atmosphere – it's just the best festival, and the music is fantastic. We saved up and took the kids in 2017 – Fairport's fiftieth birthday party.

My husband and I were having a wander around the village and followed our noses into the Brasenose Arms. I got the shock of my life when I discovered we had wandered straight into a Sandy Denny exhibition. It was like all my birthdays and Christmases had come at once! Seeing so much of her memorabilia – including notebooks, childhood toys, press releases and clothing – blew my mind. I tried to drink it all in, while taking as many photos as I could, to cherish later. (I was especially pleased to see on her passport, her height listed as five foot two – the same as me. I've always thought it would be useful to be a little bit taller, but now I embrace it completely! Something small but significant that we have in common.)

While we were looking around, my husband said, 'Is that her daughter?' I heard the Australian accent before I was able to peep through the throng and see Georgia. 'Yes!' I exclaimed, and my shyness went into overdrive. I was too overwhelmed to go over and speak, but knew that if I didn't, I would regret it for the rest of my life.

I slowly edged towards the table, perusing items for sale and trying to pluck up the courage to speak. Other people were asking Georgia to sign their purchases, so I did the same. She was friendly and kind, and took the time to chat to me.

I am so grateful for her friendship, which came about because of the mother neither of us remembers, but who has given the world so much.

GEMMA SHIRLEY, THE SANDY DENNY PROJECT

When I was first asked to join The Sandy Denny Project, I have to confess that I didn't know much about Sandy or her songs, just the few I had seen Fairport perform at Cropredy over the last 20 years or so. I had roughly three months to learn around 30 songs and spent each weekend rehearsing with a different band member, which became affectionately known as Sandy Bootcamp. It was a challenge and a hard, fast learn for me as keys aren't my natural habitat but I was determined to get there. I watched many hours of footage to help me get a flavour of Sandy's songwriting and, of course, that voice.

As I immersed myself in the songs it became clear that I was playing some really interesting stuff, some unusual chord progressions and lyrical themes that were particular to Sandy's music, and inevitably it struck me then how few female artists of that time have such a remarkable and consistent body of work.

So after a 2023 spring tour and a few months of gigs, we played at the Brasenose Arms in Cropredy as part of the fringe festival. It happened to be the first year that Georgia had curated the Sandy Denny exhibition there in tandem with the album launch for *Songbird* by Carla Fuchs which set Sandy's lyrics to new music. As part of my research, I had been particularly taken by one of Sandy's performances from a show called *One In Ten*, just her at the piano singing 'Late November' and 'The North Star Grassman And The Ravens'. The clothes she was wearing stuck in my mind too, the fabric being a black and white background with a print of red flowers. At the exhibition there were all kinds of artefacts, notebooks, photos, lyrics, jewelry, her guitar and, most poignantly of all, her daughter Georgia.

But it was the black, white and red outfit hanging in the corner that suddenly brought it all overwhelmingly in to focus for me. Here was a real person, a real woman, a real artist and not just a list of songs I had to learn.

KEVIN SMITH

I wasn't really familiar with Sandy during her lifetime. I was more interested in Hawkwind, ELP, Pink Floyd and Led Zeppelin. It wasn't until later years that I became familiar with Fairport Convention, a band I have now enjoyed and followed for many years. This also exposed me to a lot more of Sandy's work including with The Strawbs and Fotheringay for example.

With the formation of the band Listen Listen, later to become The Sandy Denny Project, I again became further aware of her material and started to listen to a lot more of her music. What an incredible talent and remarkable voice. Her lyrics, her playing were like no other. A wonderful musical discovery.

In 2019 I bumped into Sandy's daughter Georgia at a Fairport soundcheck and we popped over to Pizza Calzoni in Banbury for a bite to eat. We talked a lot about Fairport, her mother and life. I mentioned to Georgia that I never knew her mother and her reply was, 'Neither did I.' I felt awful as it had never crossed my mind. I realised we were both discovering Sandy, but in different ways. Needless to say, we spoke a lot as we both learned things over time.

It was shortly after this that I was working in Kingston-upon-Thames. Realising that Sandy was buried just around the corner from my customers, I popped into the local ASDA, grabbed some flowers and made my way to the cemetery. Having located the grave, it was nice to see it was obviously still being cared for. A few dead flowers and a couple of cuddly toys showed how much she was still loved. I tidied up the leaves and other wind-blown debris, then swapped over the flowers for the fresh ones. I also did likewise to the other family plot behind. It was quite a strange experience, as I had never done this for a person I'd never known in life. It was however nice to pay my respects and say thank you for the music I had begun to really enjoy.

Later, in 2023, Georgia organised the first Sandy Denny Exhibition at the Brasenose pub in Cropredy to link in with the Cropredy Festival. I popped along to lend a hand in setting things up. To see and handle Sandy's most special treasures was incredibly emotional and something I wasn't expecting. Over the years of discovering Sandy, I had become more attached to her than I had realised. To hold her toys, her handwritten lyrics, her awards, even her passport was quite a surreal experience. Seeing her dresses was also strange as I didn't realise how small she was. It was something I had never really thought about. The exhibition was a huge success with people visiting from all over the world. Many seemed equally touched by it all.

Sandy at home, Twistle, Byfield, 1975 (Sandy Denny Archive) (Brian Cooke)

Sandy played what was to be her final gig at Byfield Village Hall in April 1978. There is now a blue plaque placed there commemorating her life. She had a house there too. As I only live two miles from Byfield, I offered to take Georgia to visit both. Firstly, we visited the plaque and it was lovely to see Georgia's smile at seeing it.

Kevin, Georgia & Lisa at The Twistle, Byfield

The next stop was her house. I had been to the house before, but only to see the outside. This was Georgia's first time. We parked opposite and started taking some snaps. It was then that a lady inside started to wave to us through the window, beckoning us to come over. We walked over to the side door to be greeted by a lovely kind lady who asked if we were Sandy Denny fans. When Georgia mentioned she was Sandy's daughter, the woman just gasped. Having recovered from the obvious shock, we were invited in. She rushed to find her daughter, who in turn rushed to call her husband. They couldn't believe who was visiting.

What followed was an hour of lovely conversation, a tour of the property and garden and a look at some interesting memorabilia. It was both lovely and quite moving seeing Georgia trying to take everything in. When she sat by the window where Sandy was once photographed with her piano, it was a bit of a moment. I immediately grabbed a snap. Later we did some general snaps for Georgia to remember the visit by.

Many years ago, when I started my journey discovering Sandy Denny, I had no idea it would take me to her house, with her daughter, holding her possessions and taking in so many things that made Sandy Denny 'The Lady'. It's been a wonderful journey and her music lives on.

FAIRPORT'S CROPREDY CONVENTION
8-10 AUGUST 2024, CROPREDY, UK

PAULA ANN SAVAGE

I only discovered Sandy Denny in 2024, God knows how. I thought I'd heard all the greats by now, but it opened up another world and level of music for me. Her pure talent of raw vocals, simple but genius songwriting, with lyrics that take you to an unforgettable time and place. I can play her songs like 'Fotheringay' and 'The Sea' over and over again and never tire of them. I feel as if I know her, like there is a connection between us, that's how her songs leave me feeling.

For Paula Ann Savage, Sandy's writing is up there with that of Nick Drake

I was lucky enough to meet her daughter Georgia that summer, during a Sandy Denny exhibition, where I saw her handwritten lyrics, guitars she composed on and clothing she wore on and off stage. It was one of the most enchanting days of my life. Sandy Denny is up there with Nick Drake for me. Their song writing is from the core of their souls, laid bare for us all to escape into, stirring those beautiful emotions in a way that only certain musicians can.

MARC BUCKLEY

Every August for as long as I can remember, my family and I have attended the Fairport Convention festival in Cropredy. After my mother's passing in 2016 we had a plaque put on Jonah's Oak by the festival field. In 2024 I went to the oak to say a few words and remember my mum and I met a lady who said she was remembering her

Marc Buckley met Georgia at Jonah's Oak at Cropredy

mum as well. We talked for a while and she asked which plaque was my mother's so I pointed it out. When she pointed to her mum's plaque, it was to none other than Sandy Denny. I had by sheer luck met and been chatting with Georgia Rose Lucas. Having been brought up on Sandy's music with Fairport, Fotheringay and solo, I was completely overwhelmed to meet this lovely lady. We spent some time together talking and agreed to meet the following day on the festival field where she gave me one of her Jonah's Oak artworks and signed it for me. I will remember it forever.

PETER BUCKLEY

Chatting with Georgia Rose Lucas in 2024 at the Cropredy Festival, I mentioned that my late wife Geraldine's favourite song was 'Who Knows Where The Time Goes?' and how it brought tears to her eyes every time she heard it. I explained the reason for this and how she had requested that we played it at her funeral which, of course, we did. Georgia put her arms around me and we had a few sad words about losing loved ones. She then gave me a copy of the lyrics in her mother's handwriting and signed it for me. This now has pride of place in my music room.

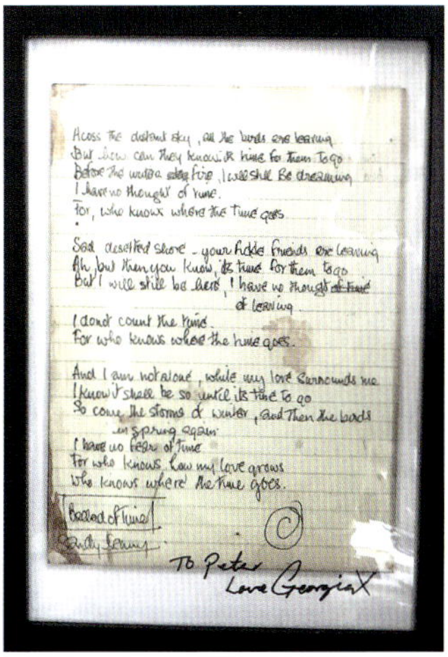

Across the distant sky, all the birds are leaving
But how can they know it's time for them to go
Before the winter fire, I will still be dreaming
I have no thought of time.
For, who knows where the time goes

Sad deserted shore - your fickle friends are leaving
Ah, but then you know, its time for them to go
But I will still be here, I have no thought of leaving
I don't count the time.
For who knows where the time goes.

And I am not alone, while my love surrounds me
I know it shall be so until its time to go
So come the storms of winter, and then the birds in spring again
I have no fear of time
For who knows how my love grows
Who knows where the time goes.

Ballad of Time
Sandy Denny
©
To Peter
Love Georgia X

Peter Buckley got Georgia to sign a copy of the lyrics to his late wife's favourite song

GABRIEL LUIZ

I am 21 years old and I am from Brazil. Who would have thought that someone so young and far from the United Kingdom could be a fan? But I have a great love for old British music and I found Sandy's music at the beginning of 2024 through the internet and I ended up falling in love with her music. She quickly became one of my favourite artists. Her gentle voice makes life so much lighter. There are still so many of her songs that I want to explore and imprint on my mind. My favourites are 'Nothing More', 'Late November', 'It Suits Me Well', 'Fotheringay' and especially her cover of 'Knockin' On Heaven's Door'. One of my dreams is to be able to visit her in Putney Vale, and leave a flower as beautiful as she is at her resting place.

PAUL SMITH, RECORDING ENGINEER

Sadly, I never met Sandy in person. When she passed in 1978, I was 19 years old and a student at North Staffordshire Polytechnic (now Staffordshire University). I was already a huge fan of Fairport Convention, Steeleye Span, Lindisfarne, Led Zeppelin, etc. and I got involved with the student union events. Most of the big shows were hosted at Keele University in the big hall there. We booked Fairport many times but back then they were in a bit of turmoil and had almost called it a day, especially after Sandy's earlier passing.

I already knew Dave Pegg as he lived only seven miles away from me in Sutton Coldfield. I also knew Ric Sanders from back then too. He didn't join Fairport until 1986 but was playing a lot around the folk scene and jazz scene in this area.

Fairport called their shows the *Farewell* tour but then decided to do a reunion. 1979 was the first big Cropredy reunion weekend and it all went on from there. Peggy was already in Jethro Tull which gave Fairport a huge leap back onto the touring scene. Around that time, I'd already cut my teeth in live audio engineering and I met Dave Cousins and The Strawbs. We did quite a few tours together, including a few in the USA, and Dave became one of my best friends ever. We toured the world until Dave became too ill to perform and then sadly passed. I really do miss him. I was pretty cut up when I got the sad news. Although I knew he hadn't got long left it still hurts.

Dave knew Sandy well before she got involved with Fairport. He really opened the door for her. Fairport escalated her career, and then she and Trevor built the great band Fotheringay. I had the great pleasure of meeting Trevor a lot of times.

Fairport is more than just a band. It's a beautiful family and they have an amazing bond with loyal fans the world over who are all part of that family. I don't want to wish myself older but there are times I wish I had been around a little earlier and had got to know Sandy. I do feel I know her through her music, through Fairport, via Dave Cousins and through Georgia, who is keeping a beautiful legacy alive.

WHAT WE DID IN OUR SCHOOL HOLIDAYS

KEVIN ROGERS

She sang Suzanne I remember,
At the Country Club; Belsize Park.
North star, singing of Eastern Rain.
Down from some barricade or other,
Your voice telling me; catch a breath.

Dread Queens, in harsh stone-grey castles,
Enamelled birds in gossamer cage.
Nurture these untutored errant ears
Narrate this too-fast fleeting youth.
Yonder, into your soft Highland eyes.

Kevin Rogers wrote a poem

IAN DE SILVA, LA NOUVELLE MUSIQUE

I first heard Sandy Denny's music on an Island Records compilation about ten years ago. I was instantly captivated by her voice. It just has such a compelling depth and seems effortlessly able to channel the emotion of generations of past folk singers, while at the same time being unique and personal to her. I was so struck by her voice and songs that I remember making a pilgrimage to Putney Vale cemetery to pay my respects.

THE TWISTLE
2025, BYFIELD, UK

LISA & KEVIN

We love knowing that we live in Sandy's beautiful house. We've heard so many stories about Sandy. We go to Cropredy. When Sandy and Fairport were rehearsing in the barn, Sandy was getting a bit chilly and a local gentleman called Maurice had his old station coat and he loaned it to Sandy and he never got it back. To this day he still goes on about it. We've lived in this house 27 years and we understand why she and Trevor moved here. And to make music in that barn and in this, our front room, must have been magical.

ENZO BOERI

I remember reading the sad news of Sandy's passing in an Italian music magazine. Over time, I appreciated her greatness as a songwriter and wanted to translate her lyrics into Italian. The cost of obtaining authorisation to translate the lyrics for commercial purposes forced me to publish the book with the phrase 'free copy, not for sale'. I titled it *The Rich Tapestry Of Life*, using an expression of Sandy's. I gave away the few copies I had published to fans.

JIM FOGARTY, NO GREY FAITH

In the early eighties, long before I'd as much as thought of picking up an instrument, much less becoming a professional musician, I was a total music geek. Every spare dime went to the Record Cellar, a used shop inhabited by fellow geeks and wise, older vinyl pushers who seemed to know everything about every band in the history of everything. There, and in the music mags I devoured, the names Richard and Linda Thompson were starting to be mentioned often, and in hushed tones. I took a chance and bought *Pour Down Like Silver*, despite the daunting quasi-religious cover, and had no idea what to make of it. But there was enough mystery, sublime female vocals, crystalline guitar fragments and dark, alluring, dangerous lyrics to keep me on the hook. Within weeks, the Thompsons were all I consumed.

Needing more, more, more, I found Fairport Convention, then Fotheringay, the Strawbs, Albion Band, etc. Some I liked, some I loved… and then there was Sandy.

Liege & Lief is one of the few perfect albums. Not a note misplaced, no excess, but still wide open, unrushed and majestic. Most importantly, at the centre was Sandy Denny, not just an amazing voice, but a presence drifting over, through and inside the tales of murder, illicit sex, wolves and faeries. While clear as a bell, Sandy also had the vocal depth and gravitas to mesh it all together, and hold her own amongst the swirling fiddle, keening electric guitars and just-shy-of-heavy rock rhythm section. She lived and breathed those stories and held them out for the rest to observe.

I was hooked and went on to find everything she did. Sometimes it was used albums, sometimes cassettes advertised in the back of fanzines and sent away for. I marinated in it all and was changed for the better by doing so. I think it was the mystery of it all that kept me searching for more. Sandy wasn't just a pretty voice. She was both mystery and light personified.

In that time (my teens), my mother died way too young, and I found something in both the sadness and fragility, but also the strength and occasional joy, in Sandy's music that kept me going through that hellish time. I also found the guitar.

Forward a few years, and I've begun playing in a cool, eclectic rock band, living in a hovel and going wherever music took me. But, in the back of my mind, I wanted to also be doing something more acoustic, more folk-rock and more organic. Lo and behold, in the wanted section of a local trade rag, an ad popped up: 'Female vocals looking for guitar/ mandolin for acoustic project. Folk, pop, Fairport, Sandy Denny, etc.' Through that, I met Lindsay Gilmour, a stunning New Zealand vocalist and writer, fellow Sandy devotee, and for 35-plus years, my wife and musical partner. We bonded playing and singing 'Who Knows Where the Times Goes?'. Karma.

Over our career, Lindsay and I have been lucky enough to share stages with so many legends and outstanding artists. Along the way, via festivals and house concerts, Iain (nee Ian) Matthews became a friend and occasional musical co-conspirator (after I stopped picking his brain for FC, RT and Sandy stories!). We spoke at length about doing some kind of album together, and with Lindsay and Iain's haunting voices, a tribute to Sandy was the obvious choice. It's coming out later this year via Pat Thomas' Heyday Again record company in America under Iain's name and the title *No Grey Faith*. (Hmm… what's that an anagram for?)

So, for me, while I've got tons of more music in me, it feels like a full circle moment. I couldn't be prouder and more excited for people to hear our take on Sandy's inspired songs. I hope the love comes through.

Thank you, Music Weaver.

MARTIN SIMPSON, MUSICIAN

It is rare and wonderful when one person's voice becomes the very essence of a time, the signifier of a style of music and the vehicle for delivering that music's greatest performances. Sandy's voice and indeed her compositions represent the best of folk rock's blooming years.

Martin Simpson, Ric Sanders, Graham (Sharpy) Sharpe, Richard Digance & Chris, Cropredy 2019

EDWIN TOMEI

If only I had the opportunity of seeing Sandy in concert. Unfortunately, I came to her music later in life as I was too young at the time to fully appreciate her music. I have however tried to make up for lost time and am collecting as many vinyls of hers as possible, whether with Fairport, Fotheringay or solo. When my son and I were in Glasgow in December 2025, I did pick up an original pressing of her collaboration with The Strawbs, which is a great album. My favourite song of hers is 'Banks Of The Nile' with Fotheringay, which chokes me up with every listen.

VLAD POPOV

Unlike my fellow Bulgarians, I didn't come to the UK with ambition to make a career or to chase a better life. It was music that led me here. I believe in a humble life, knowing that no matter what I achieve or whatever I earn, buy or find as a physical or material thing, I will not be able to take it with me when my days on earth end. The purpose of life is to focus on precious moments and to cherish the love, the true friendship, the real joy of making someone, somewhere happy – but without proclaiming it loud, without expecting something in return, and quietly enjoying those moments.

One morning in London, I was reviewing my music library and really felt the need to hear Sandy's voice. The voice that had already captured me, the voice that was so strongly anchored in my heart. 'Who knows where the time goes?' or 'who knows how long our days will last?' I heard the song that became the reason for so many things to follow, a song possibly triggered lyrically by pain. It was 'I'm A Dreamer'. I had never thought so much before on the impact that someone could have, transcended through notes guided by such beautiful harmony.

When I get into something I can become so emotionally tied to it that I might not let go. This all made sense when I was diagnosed last year with autism and attention deficit hyperactivity disorder. I'm exploring what it is and possibly the reason causing it, but one thing I always get high on dopamine from is Sandy's voice. It's healing, it's refreshing, it's happy and sad. It's a well of wisdom, it's a lesson, an example, a guide, a reason to open the heart. It is provoking to think about the important things in life – those that money cannot buy.

That star that shines on me through supernatural, divine presence might not be the biggest or the brightest of them all, but it shone on me and changed my life. We don't choose what music to like – it either resonates with us or not.

'And the truth is I don't think I'll ever go!'

ALAN BETHELL

I have a unique experience of enjoying Sandy's work. I underwent a hernia operation under local anaesthetic eighteen months ago. To palliate the pain under the knife (I could feel the instrument inside my innards at times) a nurse asked me what I would like to hear. The answer was Sandy's voice, of course. He played (via Spotify, I assume) 'The Sea', 'The Ballad Of Easy Rider', 'Percy's Song', 'I'll Keep With Mine', 'Like An Old Fashioned Waltz and 'It'll Take A Long Time'. Only one member of the operating team had heard any of her work, but they were beguiled by it. I gave them a potted history of her life story and stated, not entirely untruthfully, that I enjoyed the experience so much that I wouldn't mind coming back every week!

BRUCE ROWLAND, FAIRPORT CONVENTION

Sandy was mesmerising. Pete Townshend put his finger on it: no vibrato at all. The expressiveness of her voice, the wonderful songs, and the problem for all of us that she was endlessly forgivable. She only had to open her mouth and sing and the synchronised weeping would start. Her tragedy was that she never really understood how well loved she was both by the punters and the band and other musicians.

COLIN RANDALL, JOURNALIST

Sandy Denny was one of the artists most responsible for changing forever my outlook on music. From the gloriously enhanced traditional ballads and spellbinding self-compositions to the forays into French ('Si Tu Dois Partir' of course, but also 'Écoute, Écoute'), she simply stole my heart.

MADDY PRIOR, STEELEYE SPAN

My thoughts on Sandy are largely snapshots. It's a very long time ago and draped in a mist of alcohol! When Rick Kemp and I lived in Muswell Hill, she rang and asked us to go to Banbury (or somewhere out that way) to help Peggy (Dave Pegg) out on a gig he'd organised, but with seemingly no performers turning up. The urgency is all that stays with me now.

There was a sunny afternoon out in the Folk Rock Belt (Northampton to Oxfordshire) and I remember singing on a flatbed truck, terrified, but feeling reassured by the trees wafting gently, and knowing they didn't care and would be there long after I had gone. I see in my mind's eye Dave Swarbrick and Sandy.

Rick has reminded me that Sandy had tickets to see the Eagles but couldn't go, and offered the tickets to us. How kind.

In Essex we saw Sandy perform a solo gig at a small sunny open-air festival. It was a lovely day.

Rick and I sat with Ralph McTell at another solo gig in an old theatre in London.

The first solo tour that I did, Trevor and Sandy came to a gig in Wembley. I was so chuffed that they came, but also a bit embarrassed because it was not well attended. The whole tour was a disaster. But they were both generous and Trevor gave me the advice to stay in charge, which, although I didn't necessarily follow it, I remembered ever after.

Sandy was always an impressive singer. Always a little reticent, but so unique. Her voice had a quality I've never heard from anyone else. When she sang high, instead of softening, she brought in an edge that was really distinctive, and her ornamentation was also unlike anyone else.

She was a vibrant personality in the room. She was witty and urbane. Matched with Linda Thompson, they were like two castles lined up in a chess game. Formidable.

In an interview once I was asked if Sandy was a friend of mine. I replied that I knew her, but wasn't presumptuous enough to call her a friend. In those days there was very little coverage of music, so everyone saw everything that was printed in the music press. Sandy startled me by ringing me the next day to say what did I mean 'not her friend?'

'WHO KNOWS WHERE THE TIME GOES?'

MARY GILES

When my husband Alan died we played Sandy's 'Who Knows Where the Time Goes?' at his funeral. It's just a beautiful and moving song, and she had a pure and amazing voice. I've got goosebumps just thinking about it.

MAT DAVIES, BASS PLAYER, SANDY DENNY PROJECT

I grew up in Barford St Michael, which will be familiar to many as for many years it was the home of Woodworm Records and the engine room of the Cropredy Festival. As a teenager, I used to help out at Woodworm with odd jobs, which included regular envelope-stuffing for festival mailshots and putting together the mix tapes to play between bands at Cropredy.

Sandy has been part of the soundtrack of Mat's life

At that stage, I had only known Fairport with the *Gladys' Leap* line-up, featuring Simon's vocal, and wasn't aware of the rich history of the many and varied line-ups. When I dropped the needle on the vinyl, pressed play/record on the tape deck and heard 'Come All Ye' for the very first time, I was blown away. It stopped me in my tracks. I had never heard anything like it; the purity, the soul.

While I never met Sandy personally, she has been with me ever since – whether watching the moon come up to the soundtrack of 'Rising', or raging to 'John The Gun' played at neighbour-bothering volume! I grew my collection, and Sandy has genuinely been part of my life's soundtrack.

Spool forward almost 40 years from the 'Come All Ye' moment, and I find myself in the job of my dreams. Standing alongside my dear chums Mark Stevens and PJ Wright, from my Little Johnny England days, with the awesome vocals of Sally Barker, Marion Fleetwood and Gemma Shirley collectively working as The Sandy Denny Project.

Each of us is a Sandy super-fan. You won't hear slavish facsimiles of the originals, but more our personal interpretations of Sandy's amazing songs, reflecting what the songs mean to us, and our love for them. Each gig I get shivers down my spine as we celebrate 'The Lady' and her incredible legacy. My favourite track changes from time to time, but currently is 'The Sea'.

If Sandy is watching over us now, I truly hope that she feels the love that we feel for her work, each and every show.

JOHN GRIMLEY

My story is simple and short. It's been almost 60 years since 'Who Knows Where the Time Goes?' was released on record. I was 19 then. I'm 77 now. And still, every time I hear it, I weep. I'm a little teary now just thinking of it. RIP Sandy. We so miss you still.

MILICA THEESSINK, PROMOTER

As a teenager, I loved The Beatles and was totally crazy about Donovan! But the greatest influence on my life, and thus on my path in life, was the voice and music of Sandy Denny. She had such a transcendent voice. I loved listening to her, and through her, I was hooked on folk music.

I was so enthusiastic about the music that it inspired me to start my folk music agency, Open Road Management, in Vienna in 1974. I started with Andy Irvine and Dougie McLean and organized the Vienna Celtic Festival in 1980, followed by the Vienna Folk Festival in 1981. I booked Fairport Convention, Richard & Linda Thompson, Donovan, Melanie, Arlo Guthrie, The Dubliners, and my now husband Hans Theessink.

After all these years, I am still active in organising concerts and booking artists. Thank you so much, Sandy Denny. You infected me with the music that has enriched my life so much.

RICHARD WILLIAMS, JOURNALIST

There are plenty of fine singers, but Sandy Denny was a great one. Not only were her tone and phrasing lovely and distinctive, but she sang from the inside of a song and she had the gift of slowing your heartbeat to match the pulse of her music. What she didn't possess were the attributes that often propel lesser artists to a higher plane: a powerful sense of focus, a rock-solid self-confidence, and the right team around her at the right time.

I knew her a little, and even four decades after her death I find it hard to accept that, although she achieved recognition in some respects, somehow she didn't manage to build the sort of career that everyone expected her to have, and then fell so fast and so conclusively that she was dead at 31.

Two linked episodes – the aftermath of Fairport Convention's motorway tragedy and the saga of Fotheringay – stand out as pivotal. One night in May 1969 the van carrying members of Fairport Convention back to London from a gig in Birmingham crashed down an embankment on the M1, killing Martin Lamble, their drummer, and Jeannie Franklyn, the girlfriend of Richard Thompson, their lead guitarist.

The traumatised band recruited a new drummer, Dave Mattacks, and a fiddler, Dave Swarbrick, and threw themselves into a different kind of project: the album *Liege & Lief*, in which they applied advanced rock band techniques to traditional material. It was released in December of that year, and its instant critical acceptance as a benchmark in the evolution of folk rock diverted them from the musical path they would surely have followed had the accident never happened and the fast-evolving songwriting of Sandy and Richard remained the core of their activity.

Eventually the pair left in frustration, both keen to stretch their wings. Sandy put together the five-piece Fotheringay in 1970 with her new boyfriend, the Australian singer/guitarist Trevor Lucas. Joe Boyd, who had mentored and produced the Fairports, firmly believed that Sandy's future was as a solo artist, not as a member of another group – particularly not one organised, as she insisted, along strictly democratic and non-hierarchical lines. He distrusted the charismatic but headstrong

Lucas, and he was appalled by the way the record company's large advance - originally predicated on a solo album – was being blown on such things as an oversized PA system and a Bentley in which they made their way to gigs.

But although Fotheringay's first album, and their uncompleted second effort, may have been recorded under Boyd's disapproving gaze, out of those sessions came the finest moment of Sandy's career. Within the highly original and starkly dramatic arrangement of 'Banks Of The Nile', a traditional ballad telling the story of the reaction of a young girl to the imminent departure of her soldier lover, Sandy seems to summon centuries of English history.

As the singer Dick Gaughan said on the subject, in an eloquent note in the booklet accompanying *A Boxful Of Treasures*, the five-CD anthology released by Fledg'ling Records in 2004: 'The raw, aching agony which she brings to her reading of it makes it impossible not to feel the fear and grief of the young woman at the separation from her loved one and the uncertainty of his return from the horrors of war… It is the supreme example of the craft of interpreting traditional song and is the standard every singer should be aiming for.'

Sandy didn't write 'Banks Of The Nile' but she did write 'Who Knows Where The Time Goes?', 'Late November', 'John The Gun', 'It'll Take A Long Time' and other songs that showed her gift for taking a sudden but invariably graceful left turn with a melody or finessing an unexpected chord change with perfect logic, and for lyrics that often contained affectionate but clear-eyed portraits of friends and fellow musicians (Anne Briggs in 'The Pond And The Stream', for example, or Richard Thompson in 'Nothing More'). But to me 'Banks Of The Nile' indicates most clearly what might have been, had a combination of internal and external pressures not provoked the disintegration of Fotheringay after less than a year.

Chronic insecurities were beginning to hinder her career, particularly after the rupture with Boyd, who had provided support and decisiveness. The biggest blow to Fotheringay was dealt by the Royal Albert Hall concert of October 1970.

Disastrously, they invited Elton John to open the show, at the very moment when his career was taking off. He hadn't yet grown into his full on-stage flamboyance, but his performance was powerful enough to put his hosts in the shade. When they came out after the intermission, it was somehow like the colour on a TV set had been suddenly turned off – and the audience, which had come to acclaim Sandy and her band, found themselves present at an epic anti-climax. Three months later, demoralised by that event and by the unsatisfactory sessions for their projected second album, the band broke up – thanks largely to a simple misunderstanding between Sandy and Joe Boyd over the terms on which he would produce her first solo effort.

In fact Boyd never produced her in the studio again, and the four solo albums released between 1971 and 1977 chronicle a diminishing ability to identify and present the essence of who she really was. The overproduced (by Lucas) cover version of Elton John's 'Candle In The Wind' on the final album, *Rendezvous*, represented some sort of nadir. The record company – Island – did its best, which in this case too often turned out to be not so good. She found herself agreeing to be photographed by David Bailey, to be dressed up in a 1930s costume, and to be airbrushed and wind-machined in an effort to create an image more superficially glamorous than that represented by her own true self. As Island grew too quickly and had its head turned by success, her career became, to some extent, collateral damage.

When she was voted Britain's top female singer by the readers of the *Melody Maker* not once but twice, in 1970 and 1971, it was assumed that commercial success would take care of itself. But after Boyd, she didn't get much constructive help – for which, now, I must partially blame myself, since I was running Island's A&R department between 1973 and 1976. But the artists inherited from Boyd's Witchseason stable were somehow thought to be a law unto themselves in terms of musical direction, and although Sandy was loved within the company for her warmth of her personality as well as for her artistry, she was not biddable. Nor, in those days, were real artists supposed to be.

I like the remark by Mick Houghton, her biographer, that her first solo release, *The North Star Grassman And The Ravens*, is 'the only album on which Sandy steadfastly stands her ground – usually by the seashore or the riverbank – and invites her audience to come to her.' And he writes of Trevor Lucas, five years later, working on the production of the ill-starred *Rendezvous*, 'doing such protracted overdubs that it was almost as if he was subconsciously trying to bury the sentiments of the songs.'

Had she lived, perhaps she'd have encountered another manager, producer or A&R person capable of earning her trust, focusing her talent, calming her self-doubt, curbing her destructive tendencies, nurturing the elements that made her unique and presenting them to the world in the right package. Who knows how much great music was left in her? I like to think of Sandy coaxing Anne Briggs out of seclusion and inviting Kate Rusby to join them both on stage.

Her old folk-club mate Ralph McTell told Houghton that, as difficult as she could be, he didn't know anyone who didn't love her. And you didn't have to know her to love her. You only have to listen to any of her sisters – Judy Collins, Nina Simone, Eva Cassidy, Nanci Griffiths, Kate Rusby, Susanna Hoffs – unpeeling the emotional layers of 'Who Knows Where The Time Goes?', a song she wrote when she was 18. Or, in my case, to listen to 'Banks Of The Nile', over and over and over again.

ROSIE JONES, SINGER SONGWRITER

'Who Knows Where The Time Goes?' came into my orbit a few years ago, and I listened to it often, soothed by the sunny, mellow instrumentation and wistfulness in Sandy's vocals. The chorus is perfection – the first time she asks the question it's arresting, a high melody arc and a long-held plea, but the second is smaller, lower and neatly finished, accepting the sweet ache of nostalgia.

I began to work on a cover, preparing for a gig, but truly found my version deep in production mode in my bedroom studio. A happy accident – pitching my mandolin down an octave and washing it out with a pedal gave me the watery, oceanic version I needed to make. From there, the found sounds and bird-like synths built the world out for me.

Sandy manages to say just enough in the lyrics (harder than it looks), which I think gives it its place amongst the classic songs of our time. I fell in love over the course of working on this song – and James had a large hand in it, mixing the track in our little home studio. Sitting there with our cat on my lap, watching him tweak and polish and massage the sounds into something better, I kept smiling at Sandy's line: 'And I am not alone, while my love is near me.'

TREVOR TALL

I wish I had a story of seeing Sandy do a gig or of how I had met her. I was nine when she died and when I was older, I had a few Fairport albums that I didn't listen to closely enough to appreciate. All this changed thanks to Richard Thompson's *Beeswing* memoir. He talked so glowingly of her that I had to explore further. And I did, deeply.

I was 52 when the Denny penny dropped, and by the time I was 53 I had everything that was ever officially released. I also bought numerous bootlegs, read every book about her, had seen three bands that play her music, been on pilgrimages (to Wimbledon, Byfield and elsewhere) and made sure I met Georgia (at Cropredy) when she visited the UK.

I'd imagine anyone reading this knows how beautiful Sandy's voice is. She moves me in a way no other singer has. I can't listen to her version of 'Tomorrow Is A Long Time' without tearing up. I love her songwriting too. She managed to write deeply moving music with words that added even more depth, whilst carrying an earthy humour. Not many songwriters can balance the amusing with the sad.

In psychotherapy, there's a term known as 'rippling' which is used to help people with death anxiety. The concept is that we live on after we die in countless ways. These can include the memories and reminiscences of those that live, who then pass them on to others. Will my kids tell theirs about Sandy? I hope so. What a gift she is to this world.

Richard Thompson has said words to the effect of, 'If I can turn even one person on to the magnificence of Sandy Denny, I will have done my job.' Job done, Richard. Thank you.

ZÖE WREN, SINGER SONGWRITER

One day, in my mid-teens, I heard 'Who Knows Where The Time Goes?' for the first time, performed live by Josienne Clarke and Ben Walker in a pub basement somewhere in Cambridgeshire. At that time, I had no idea that this was one of the most iconic songs of its era, or that it had been voted 'Favourite Folk Track Of All Time' by BBC Radio 2 listeners. All I knew was that at the first notes a hush came over the room, and I was immediately transfixed. And I knew that I needed to learn the song. So, I rushed to find the original version (and along the way became familiar with Judy Collins, Eva Cassidy and Nina Simone's renditions). Fifteen years later, it is still one of my most frequently performed and requested covers, and its magic is that I never ever tire of singing or hearing it.

There is something about the way it's written that seems to bring out the best in whatever voice sings it, and I felt like I was somehow becoming a better writer just by getting to inhabit this particular song. There is so much to learn from Sandy about where to leave space in a song, how to gently unfold a melody, how to say so much with fewer words. I have come to know and love a lot of other Sandy Denny tracks, both from her solo albums and with Fairport Convention, but I will never forget that first experience of hearing 'Who Knows Where The Time Goes?'. Many great songs have become victims of their own popularity on the live folk circuit, but it is safe to say that audiences cannot hear this one, or indeed any Sandy Denny cover, too many times. Sandy's songs have been with me right at the start of my journey as a songwriter and I have no doubt I'll be listening to them until the end.

WILLIAM HIGGINS

She was a singer and composer with great emotional range and phrasing. She also understood the atmospheric silence between the notes. Couple that with her timeless lyrics and arrangements and you have a voice for the ages. She left us early, but left us a legacy that will always be forever…

JAMES DENNY

Our times on the planet may not have been destined to collide, yet the legacy of Sandy – and by extension that of her dad, Neil, who I was fortunate to know – has had a broad and wonderful impact on me.

I had known about Sandy's music and influences from a young age, but it was during the early 2000s that I started to follow the 'Fairport family tree and associated shrubbery'.

The specific moment where something snapped was watching Simon Care dance and play the 'Bacca Pipes Jig' as part of the Cecil Sharp Centenary Collective, an Ashley Hutchings production, in 2003. I was spellbound.

I was attending Crawley College and found that Hobgoblin had a musical instrument shop nearby. I promptly marched down there on a lunch break, stated that, 'I know nothing about melodeons but I really want to buy one,' waited for Neil the manager to stop laughing, handed over a large bundle of my hard-earned, and walked away with a shiny new melodeon of my own.

The universe seems to have a habit of throwing areas of my life together and, in this case, one of my tutors at the college was Jim Barclay. When he saw my new purchase, Jim said he had danced the Morris for the late, great William Kimber. Since the best way to learn to play a melodeon was to play it for Morris dancers, why didn't I come and join Thames Valley Morris Men?

Twenty-three years later, I'm still a Morris musician and sometime dancer for Thames Valley, with happy memories of playing for a variety of other sides over the years. I also founded the Croydon Night Of Dance (CNOD), an annual festival of Morris dance with up to 16 sides attending in any given year. And I was privileged beyond words to join Fairport, contributing melodeon to 'Genesis Hall' at a couple of their stops on one of their winter tours.

None of this would have happened without Sandy. When she joined Fairport Convention and took part in the invention of the genre of folk rock, Sandy was an instrumental part of a worldwide shift in how folk music was played. It may well be that a parallel universe exists where Fairport didn't take this course, perhaps with similar results for music, perhaps not… But in *our* variant, Sandy was hugely influential – globally, and personally. For that, and for the music, I am forever grateful.

At the time of writing, I'm 40 and my daughter Emily is nearly the age I was when I started fully enjoying Sandy's legacy. Her music has now become something that not only Emily and I, but also her partner Annie, can bond over, and we're looking forward to a Fairport Convention concert in March. Again, none of this would have been without Sandy.

Spending half of my working days in theatre and live arts (shared with a career on the railway), I have found multiple ways in which Sandy's music was just right. One of my first plays (set in the thirties) included Sandy's hauntingly beautiful cover of 'Whispering Grass' as the audience entry music. My (occasional) band is appropriately-to-us named 'The Optimist'. And my recent production of the Charles Dickens story *The*

Signalman concluded with the demise of The Visitor being underscored to suitably aching effect by 'Nothing More'.

My friend I know you've suffered,
Although you are still young.
Why was it you who'd not take help
From anyone?

Without Sandy's influences, my life would have been immeasurably different.

DONNA HINGSTON

Sandy's music has soothed me, thrilled me, echoed my thoughts and feelings, touched me deeply, made me smile, and brought me to tears. I identified with her lyrics, admiring her honesty, her language, and her dignity and grace. When I felt despondent and alone or wanted to ache over an old boyfriend or simply see and hear my own reflection in her songs (in any of her career's incarnations), I knew I could turn to Sandy's exceptional voice, arrangements, interpretations, and depth of consciousness and emotion for satisfaction.

I hope that's what a performer, an artist, a poet, a musician hopes to achieve; a lasting, indelible place in the hearts of their audience, a respect for their talent, an appreciation of their being and the baring of their soul, a connection to like-minded people, and to the stars.

In my heart and in my mind, I believe Sandy has exceeded those hopes. Her work has certainly captivated me and supported me in my personal journey through life, love and healing and I am eternally grateful for the gifts she brought to the quality of my life.

JOSIENNE CLARKE, SINGER SONGWRITER

I was about 18 when I first heard her name – I was at a folk sing-around, doing a version of 'Lily Of West' I'd learnt from a Joan Baez CD. An older lady remarked that I sounded like Sandy Denny. I didn't know who that was but I could tell by how she'd said it that she had just bestowed a great compliment upon me. Very intrigued, I went home to look it up and what I found was my favourite music, such beautiful singing and among the best songwriting I've ever heard. Her deep sense of melancholy resonated with me to such a degree I have been a devoted follower ever since and no other artist has had as profound an effect on my own artistic output.

So few artists can balance light and shade that perfectly or be both so nostalgically old-fashioned and utterly modern. Singing her songs is a thrilling challenge vocally and a huge honour. It also feels like a great responsibility, for these are songs that mean so much to people. They are the soundtrack to big life events, they underscore important emotional moments and thus must be treated carefully. These songs feel personal and they are personal to each of us. For me, singing her songs is like finding a gorgeous vintage coat that fits so perfectly you just want to wear it all the time.

ANDREW BATT, PRODUCER

I can't even remember the very first time I hard Sandy: somehow it feels like she has always been with me, but the earliest moment I can remember is playing her recordings with my close friend Rupert when we were at university. He and I spent hours listening to all sorts of music and we would become obsessed with particular musical artists and embarked on deep dives into their catalogue. With Sandy it was love at first listen and we quickly realised we would have to collect it all.

I remember the thrill we had in finding releases in second hand record stores and sharing rare Sandy recordings with each other when we got them. I particularly recall listening to the *Attic Tracks* cassette and that incredible demo version of 'One More Chance' which blew us away. Little did I realise that, just a few years later, I would be working on Sandy's catalogue and helping to bring her music back to public attention.

Being involved in the re-issue of Sandy's work would become one of the most fulfilling projects of my life and undoubtedly established my career in music. I had started work in music doing PR and websites which led to my working with Marianne Faithfull in the early 2000s. I remember listening to the Nick Drake re-issues with her and we both thought, 'What about Sandy?' She introduced me to Island's PR Rob Partridge who continued to represent Marianne after she left Island.

After that it all moved very quickly.

I was put in touch with Mick Houghton, one of the leading PRs at the time, who had worked with Richard Thompson since the seventies, and Sue Armstrong at Universal Catalogue. As it turned out the department had vague plans to do something with Sandy's music, pockets of which were long out of print.

Our first project was *Live At The BBC*. What had started out as basically a one-disc collection mirroring Sue's withdrawn BBC release for the Strange Fruit label, I was able to expand into a four-disc boxset. This was principally due to acetates, cassettes and reels including World Service transcripts and off-air recordings in my collection and from other collectors I was in touch with. These additional recordings allowed me to compile a much broader representation of her solo work, and at that time, it represented pretty much Sandy's entire surviving solo sessions for the broadcaster.

The cherry on top was the inclusion of the *One In Ten* TV broadcast – an incredible archive find that we thought lost. I'll never forget the day we found that and watching the playback for the first time. To see Sandy on screen as an almost living breathing personality in the throes of her muse was a deeply moving experience. The artwork was designed by Phil Smee who created a beautiful collage of sketches and lyrics from Sandy's notebooks that boldly did not have her face on the cover. The Sandy renaissance was underway.

The *Live At The BBC* boxset was such a great critical and commercial success that it basically green lit my entire re-issue programme. Joining Phil, Mick and myself was product manager Joe Black, and the writers Patrick Humphries and Philip Ward, who all made significant contributions to Sandy's legacy. So it was that 'Team Sandy' was born. We were a passionate group of committed individuals that all had our own field of expertise and most importantly we all cared deeply about the music.

I had a clear vision of what the reissues should be and what they should communicate. When you work on reissue projects you always need to think of the broader remit. What's the story? How can the material connect with the buyer, satisfy the existing fan base and expand out into new listeners?

With Sandy the story was obvious to me; her talent as one of Britain's leading songwriters was still not widely known, and her instrumental role in the emergence of the folk-rock sound was still underestimated. I remember being furious at a CD reissue of *Liege & Lief* in *Q* magazine that didn't even mention Sandy by name, despite namechecks to other members. Her talent as a solo artist and gifts as a songwriter therefore became the leading message of Mick Houghton's PR campaign.

When I started work on Sandy's music, interest in her catalogue had started to rekindle, so the opportunity was there to capitalise on the work that had been done and consolidate her position as Britain's foremost female singer songwriter. David Suff had done *Boxful Of Treasures*, a five-disc set on his Fledgling label which was the first indication to many, myself included, that a cache of unreleased material was out there, but it was clear that it would take a major label to turn the tide and bring her to a wider audience.

Following the massive success of the *Live At The BBC* boxset, we jumped straight in to one of the most ambitious projects the Universal catalogue team had ever produced. The 19 CD boxset was the brainchild of Sue Armstrong, and aimed to represent Sandy's complete recorded work. The project was a massive undertaking and I spent many months going through every single reel in the Island archive.

In those days there was a studio on Belsize Park Road where I could have the reels delivered and then go and listen to them before deciding which to transfer. The tape report was at that time not particularly detailed as the box covers housing the tapes did not necessarily specify the full content of the reel or what versions of the songs were contained within. I quickly understood that the only way I was going to find the kind of rare and unreleased material I was looking for was to listen to everything, from beginning to end.

Studio engineer Jared Hawkes and I spent many hours going through all the tapes and it paid dividends. One particular track that Sandy had been known to attempt in the studio was the traditional 'Lord Bateman', and although it was listed on some of the tape boxes, the track had either been cut out or was only an instrumental.

Finally, one day, we were listening to a reel and after a couple of tracks at the front of the tape there was ten minutes of silence before unexpectedly Sandy's voice rang out - backwards! We quickly flipped the tape and there was 'Lord Bateman'. As an archivist and researcher, these are the sorts of moments you live for! And it was a salutary lesson to listen to reels from beginning to end.

Another key ambition for the 19 CD boxset was that I wanted it to be as much a visual record of Sandy's career as a musical one. I well remember being told at Island that this would be an uphill battle as 'Sandy wasn't photographed much' but given her copious coverage in the pages of the *NME* and *Melody Maker* I knew this not to be the case. But did those images survive?

So began my second archival journey, where I contacted every photographer or representative that I knew to have shot her and any other photographers active in that period. A pattern swiftly emerged. Sandy had actually been photographed a lot and most of the photographers still had their negatives or vintage prints. In this way, I was able to use literally hundreds of previously unseen photos of Sandy, or better-quality versions of those images already familiar to us.

Sandy's estate also had an archive of both professional and personal images, many of which had never been reproduced. They had a duplicate print of Bailey's famous black and white portrait of Sandy. It was a long-cherished dream of mine to get Sandy into the National Portrait Gallery.

I already knew Terence Pepper, who was then curator of photography at the NPG, and I had successfully got a photograph of Kate Bush added to the collection the previous year. They were keen to include more female artists, so I knew my pitch as to why Sandy should take her rightful place alongside all those public figures who had excelled in their respective fields would fall on receptive ears. The gallery accepted the donation that Sandy's estate agreed to make, and I'm still so proud that fans can now see Sandy's photo on public display.

Following the 19 CD boxset, I conceived and worked on a whole range of Sandy and Sandy-related reissues, all of which included unreleased gems and new photos, etc. These included *Nothing More – The Collected Fotheringay* boxset, which also contained the full video tape of the band's performance on the German TV show *Beat Club* (although the programme only broadcast 'Too Much Of Nothing' the tape also included 'Nothing More' and two further songs earmarked for *Fotheringay 2*; 'John The Gun' and 'Gypsy Davey'), some Fairport Convention releases including the *Rising For The Moon* deluxe edition, which included the LA Troubadour show, and the boxset *Come All Ye: The First Ten Years*.

Further Sandy releases included the acoustic compilation *I've Always Kept A Unicorn,* which coincided with Mick Houghton's definitive biography on Sandy of the same name, and a vinyl edition of Sandy's final concert *Gold Dust – Live At The Royalty*, which restored Sandy's between song chat and the original applause and also utilised only those songs Sandy and Trevor had indicated on the reel boxes as the best performances. This allowed me to get as close as possible to what would have been released at the time.

In 2012 I worked on deluxe editions of all four of Sandy's solo albums on Island, which coincided with a tribute tour I produced with Music Beyond Mainstream and the Sage Gateshead called *The Lady: An Homage To Sandy Denny*. Back in 2008 I had produced a show commemorating the thirtieth anniversary of Sandy's death at the Queen Elizabeth Hall on the South Bank. My focus then was to tie in to the message of the wider reissue programme and highlight Sandy's own compositions, demonstrating their timeless beauty, and how effectively they could be interpreted by artists beyond the world of folk.

The show sold out and I planned to take it on the road, but getting the financial backing took time; in the interim years, a plan was hatched to set Sandy's many unused lyrics to music. I had noted several when I was researching the 19 CD boxset and in 2010 I collated all the unrecorded lyrics and these were offered to Thea Gilmore who released a highly successful album of a selection of them called *Don't Stop Singing*. Due to the cost of replicating the songs live, Thea decided not to take the album on the road, and I saw the opportunity to bring her into my plans for the tour. With Thea on board, financial backing was secured, and I put together a show of a diverse group of artists from different genres, generations and backgrounds to recreate Sandy's music in a live setting. With Bellowhead as the house band and artists like Maddy Prior, Sam Carter, Joan As Policewoman and PP Arnold, we played eight joyful sold-out shows, and the London date at the Barbican was televised on BBC4.

Being involved in re-issuing Sandy's work was a very meaningful and rewarding experience for me; it's not often you get the opportunity to work on something that means so much to you and which made a tangible difference to that person's legacy. It fills me with such pride that Sandy is now part of the culture, namechecked in the music press on a regular basis as a reference point, a style, or someone to aspire to.

I made so many new friends on these projects whom I've continued to work with and it also brought me together with many that had known and worked with Sandy, who became my friends too. Although I am too young to have ever met her, Sandy will always be one of the most important people in my life.

PAT THOMAS

I first heard Sandy Denny from a friend who handed me a cassette of her first two Fairport Convention albums. The year was 1982 and I was immediately entranced. Back then, most of her albums (with or without Fairport) weren't easy to find in America – they were mostly out of print. However, A&M Records (Fairport and Sandy's American label) had assembled an expansive double LP compilation titled *Fairport Chronicles* complete with detailed liner notes, some non-Fairport Sandy material and a cover image of Stonehenge – just to give it an old-world English feel. Despite being superseded a dozen times over by other compilations in the CD age, it remains one of my favourite overviews of that clan and ideally would still be in print.

Just a few years after my personal discovery, Joe Boyd via his Carthage Records reissue label (part of his Hannibal empire) began reissuing vintage Fairport and Sandy solo albums in America in the mid-1980s. I was able easily to fill in some major gaps in my collection.

In '85 Boyd and company also unleashed a Sandy Denny 4-LP box set *Who Knows Where The Time Goes?* with many rarities. I, for one, was in heaven. The Nick Drake *Fruit Tree* 4-LP collection followed a year later. That kick-started Nick's posthumous career (a worldwide fanboy obsession) that continues to this day. While I love both Sandy and Nick, I've remained batshit puzzled why Sandy has never gotten the due that Nick has in recent decades. The Freak Folk youngsters never name drop her in interviews. *Mojo* and *Uncut* have occasionally done a detailed Sandy article or two, but not with the regularity Nick's legacy enjoys.

I'm still waiting for some young aspiring singer/songwriter to say, 'Sandy Denny is my Beatles!'

Anyone else remember a cassette series known as *The Attic Tracks* (available only via mail order from Australia) in 1988-89? Keep in mind, that was well before the internet, email or Paypal. The nerd in me had to track those folks down (it was an official release by her estate – not a bootleg) and figure out a way to send them the money through the post. You really had to want this stuff!

Other gems cropped up along the way, such as the five-CD *A Boxful of Treasures* compiled by David Suff in 2004. Disc five of that collection containing previously unreleased Sandy home demos from the mid-1970s remains for me the single greatest collection of Sandy solo material ever. Do whatever it takes to acquire it.

Interesting to note, it was Sandy who first brought traditional folk songs to the attention of her fellow Fairport Convention band members – which they devoured via the eleven-minute 'A Sailor's Life' on *Unhalfbricking*. Fairport's definitive concept album of trad material, *Liege & Lief*, set bandmate Ashley Hutchings on a lifetime of exploration after that, including forming Steeleye Span and The Albion Band to focus specifically on that goal. Sandy never fully turned her back on folk songs, but her own songwriting became so strong she neither needed, nor wanted, to rely on that – hence she exited Fairport right after *Liege & Lief*.

For years, I assumed that Sandy's recording of 'Who Knows Where the Time Goes?' with The Strawbs was the first recorded version of her best-known composition. It was a revelation to hear not one, but two versions – a '67 tape that pre-dates the Strawbs recording by a few months while a '68 version would be recorded after The Strawbs' 1967 sessions that resulted in the 1973 album *All Our Own Work* – which has been reissued a few times since then.

Fellow Fairporter Richard Thompson – needless to say, a well-established songwriter in his own right (understatement) – has long proclaimed Sandy as an unsung songwriter who deserves more due, and he calls her the best female singer England ever produced. Thompson, not known for covering other people's material, still plays 'Who Knows Where the Time Goes?' in his own sets – and during his years with his sublime vocalist wife Linda Thompson they performed Sandy's 'I'm A

Dreamer'. This is the ultimate testament to Denny's greatness.

As dark and intense as Sandy's music could be, it's important to remember as Steeleye Span's extraordinary frontwoman Maddy Prior points out, Denny could be quite entertaining:

Sandy Denny and Linda Thompson were a fearsome couple. You wanted to keep your head down if those two were about, especially if drink had been taken. Very witty at anybody's expense. Great fun!

I'm honoured to be the bridge between the Sandy Denny estate and Earth Recordings in London – we've already released Sandy's early home demos on vinyl and CD. And we have some 1970s era solo live treats coming.

LAZY THINKING
14 FEBRUARY 2026, SYDNEY, AUSTRALIA

SACHIKO KANENOBU

The music of Sandy Denny touches my heart very deeply. What a beautiful song is 'Who Knows Where The Time Goes?'. It has a special feeling I know very well. When I met Sandy's daughter, the lovely Georgia Rose, on my 2026 Australian tour we had such a lovely talk. Over dinner she pointed out that the lyrics share some imagery with my own song 'Misora'. I had never thought about it before. That night, at the beginning of my show in Sydney, I dedicated my song 'Misora' to Georgia Rose and her brilliant mother.

A dog runs through a flock of doves taking flight
The sky is an endless, beautiful blue
Suddenly my hands reach infinity
I am embraced by a moving cloud
Flying over a magical sea
The sun sits on soft silk
Watching fairies dance and play
The sky is an endless blue
A dove lands on my shoulder

Leaving his footprints as he flies away
Green gods put up sails, getting ready to
Sail away to a paradise of green
'Please take me with you...
To that green paradise'
Look up, the sky is beautiful
The sky is beautiful

Thank you, Sandy, for your beautiful songs. You will be near us always, your songs will stay in our hearts forever.

Big Sky Love to you and dear Georgia Rose.

RIC SANDERS, FAIRPORT CONVENTION

I think I may be the only long-time member of Fairport who never met Sandy, or Trevor. I so wish I had. I do remember the first time I ever heard Sandy's magical voice, and in fact the first time I ever heard Fairport. When we were still at school I was at the house in Birmingham of my dear pal (to this day), the legendary Chris 'Myring Wiring', techno wizz and pedalboard maker to the stars, who would years later tour with the *Rising For The Moon* line-up. He played me not a Fairport album but an Island Records sampler album called *Nice Enough To Eat*. The first track, on side one, was 'Cajun Woman' and I was hooked. The year was 1969.

Ric Sanders with Georgia

In the mid-nineties, Fairport made the album *Who Knows Where The Time Goes?*. Chris Leslie had just joined us and so we could play live with two violins – brilliant! I think my first string arrangement for us was 'Who

Knows…' and it's stayed in the repertoire ever since, which makes me very happy. Playing with Chris was and is an absolute delight, and at the end of the song we go free and improvise, so it's never exactly the same!

Over the forty or so years I've been in Fairport I've played lots of Sandy's beautiful songs, and so although I never met her, I feel in a pretty damn cosmic way that I do in fact know her, and count her as a friend.

GEORGIA ROSE LUCAS

Living in Australia while so many of my mum's friends were in the UK has meant real relationships have been hard to build, but whenever I saw Danny, I always felt his love and a fatherly presence that stayed with me long after I'd gone home. I wanted him to be included in these memories of my mum.

Sandy & Trevor's wedding, September 1973, with Danny Thompson pictured right

Georgia and Danny, Cropredy, 2019

Danny Thompson, Birmingham Town Hall Sandy's last tour, 16 November 1977 (Birmingham Music Archive/Robin Jones)

Danny Thompson (Georgia Rose Lucas)

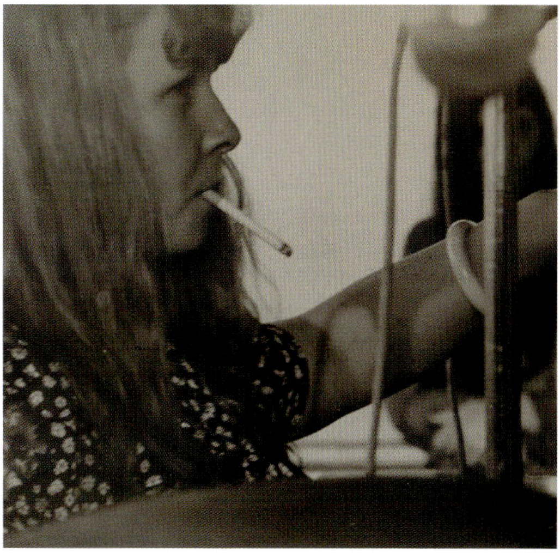

Sandy (Esther)

Danny was best man at my mum and dad's wedding. He was a big part of their everyday life, often visiting their home at Chipstead Street, even helping to tidy and clean the flat. I smile at Danny recalling, 'Sandy was notorious for lighting 200 fags at once and leaving them burning standing up like candles. There were all these cork tips on the mantelpiece. The fact that Trevor never sorted that out really got to me… but nobody was going to be any good for her in my eyes… I was a bit like her dad, I suppose.' He once said Sandy was 'hypersensitive and lived more vividly than the rest of us' which feels to me like one of the truest descriptions of her.

In one of his emails to me about the *Songbird* album I brought out with Carla Fuchs, he said it was 'a wonderful achievement… releasing the warmth and beauty of Sandy, it gives me a great feeling of joy to see her words brought to life again.' In a message he sent me a few weeks before he died in September 2025, he said how happy he was to see 'all my work being rewarded' and how glad he felt that 'my mum was still surrounded by love and support'. He signed off with, 'May her resting place be forever perfumed with love, light, music and laughter.'

And yours Danny – I will treasure your love and kindness always. x

CHRIS MYRING

If you asked me to say in a couple of sentences what I remember about Sandy, I would say, 'Firstly, when Sandy gave me her copy of Bob Dylan's *Blood On The Tracks*, and when she played Steely Dan's *Pretzel Logic* for me at The Twistle in Byfield. Secondly, in April 1978, I was on tour in Germany with Joan Armatrading. One day, I dropped my old wristwatch on a tiled floor, and it stopped working. That was the day we heard that Sandy had died.'

But to begin at the beginning…

At the end of junior school, and moving on to high school, Ric (Sanders) arrived at the same time from his junior school, so we have known each other since then. In sixth form, I was listening to music mostly from the USA, some 'folky' such as Tom Paxton and Leonard Cohen (Joni came later!), some from bands like Velvet Underground and Jefferson Airplane: 'It's A Beautiful Day'. (You get the picture.) A school friend had a copy of *Unhalfbricking* and when I heard it, I was captivated by the singer's voice, although not on the obvious song; it was 'Percy's Song'. I bought my own copy and pre-ordered *Liege & Lief* for the day of release, the only time I have done that for an album. What would happen a few years later was not even imagined.

Spooling forward through school and college, Ric was working at a violin shop in Birmingham (Swarb would drop by sometimes), and I set up my own business providing technical support for the creative arts. Through those connections, we met Steve Cross who played in the Brierley Cross duo with Marc Brierley. I was retained by Marc to build a PA system they could use for their gigs, with the primary criterion that it would fit in the back of their Morris Minor van and leave space for some guitar cases. Somehow, Marc persuaded Jeff Byers of a fledgling company to build him a small mixer in a black metal box. That company (whatever happened to them?) was called Midas.

In the Birmingham music scene, everyone knew everyone, so Marc Brierley knew Dave Pegg. Fairport had recently, in 1973, been on tour in Australia, using the Jands sound system. High import duties at the time had the effect (no doubt intended by the authorities) of encouraging local manufacturing and Jands made their own stage monitor speakers, which Dave was hoping to duplicate. I got the job and the connection was established. Joining the Fairport family is either a life membership or a life sentence. Possibly both.

Sandy was back in the fold for 1974 and Fairport toured extensively. I worked with the Fairport crew – Phil, Roger and Big George – and they brought various tasks to be completed in between my touring with Wizzard, Black Sabbath and The Sweet. Roger asked me to join the touring crew for 1975, which made sense because I had by then built half of the equipment!

Rehearsals began in January 1975 at Island Records in British Grove, although the first day was Sandy's birthday and I have a note that we went to the Speakeasy Club to celebrate. It was the *Rising For The Moon* lineup with Bruce Rowland. Sandy was playing piano, if not out front, and we had a Helpinstill pickup which we fitted each night to the house or hired-in piano, instead of using microphones. Roger ran FOH and I ran the monitor desk. Normal for bands at the time, Fairport owned their own complete PA system, which we drove round the UK and Europe and set up every night. Local sound companies, of varying quality, were used in the USA and Australia.

1975 was a whirlwind year. Fairport toured Europe, the UK, Australia and New Zealand, the USA and performed at festivals and TV shows. Jo Lustig (and not forgetting Dee) took over the management. The title track from *Rising For The Moon* and others on the album tell the tale of life on the road and the tensions that develop when living close, travelling and performing for months on end. That was our fortune, but it didn't make a fortune. At the end of the year, we went our separate ways.

Brought together by Glyn Johns, who was working at Olympic Studios on her album as well as Fairport's, Jerry Donahue, Dave Mattacks and Pat Donaldson became Joan Armatrading's backing band. Jerry called me and 1976 turned into another whirlwind year.

I was on tour with Joan in April 1978 when we heard that Sandy had died. Roger was with me on that tour and he had phoned home.

Rising for the moon,
the sun has set and it is dark,
But the star of the enchanted tune,
is bright as any spark.
The chorus of the dusk,
regale the evening lark,
Whose every day does start,
rising for the moon. S.D.

In 2019, Georgia came to Cropredy. It was the first time we met, but it seemed to me that we had met before...

RALPH MCTELL

I knew of Sandy before I met her. She had carved out a reputation as an extraordinary singer and writer on our scene, and her first tenure with Fairport had already ended when I got to know the band.

We were at the same parties and events, and our orbits crossed a few times before we properly met. We of course had a lot of friends in common; she had a riotous friendship with the late, great double bass player Danny Thompson, and her driver and 'bodyguard', Gordon 'Doon' Graham, recalled his stints as an ad hoc hairdresser, straightening her wild curls with an iron before driving her to shows in Trevor Lucas's beast of a Daimler.

Ralph McTell in 1964 (Brian Shuel)

She was a ball of energy; a little clumsy, loud, sexy, insecure, chaotic, funny and quite witty.

Sandy was, on stage, very much one of the lads. She had to be. Endless tours, freezing vans, primitive sound equipment and inevitable battles with promoters and agents to get paid were extremely common pitfalls for all musicians. With many years perspective, I don't doubt harassment would have impacted a youthful Sandy (and other young women in music).

Ralph McTell with Georgia, 2023

I got to know Sandy much better when I became friends with her husband Trevor Lucas. Trevor was truly devoted to Sandy and had utmost faith in her work and potential. His efforts to showcase Sandy's range and skill in the albums he produced proved Trevor was correct in his belief that she could have broken into the mainstream.

Others will have anecdotes of nights of drinking and mayhem, but I treasure the memories of her songs. I still find her performance of 'White Dress' incredibly tough to listen to, as beautiful as it is – a song of reconciliation? Resignation? A modern-day ghost song, made more poignant with Sandy's untimely passing? It breaks my heart to this day.

Sometimes it's hard not to feel angry at the wicked waste of talent, the mundanity of the accident that took her life, all the music that was yet to come. And especially the loss that denied a baby her mother.

Looking back over 50 years, it's inevitable and easy to romanticise some of those that left us so early and so young. But Sandy's talent and potential deserves every single posthumous plaudit given.

FAIRPORT'S CROPREDY CONVENTION
1993-2025, CROPREDY, UK

GEORGIA ROSE LUCAS

I first went to Cropredy in 1993, when I was sixteen. My mum's friend Miranda Ward took me and she suggested I probably shouldn't tell anyone who I was. The atmosphere on The Field was brilliant, everyone was so happy and lively. When Fairport came on stage (Fairport, my mum and dad's band!) and the first song was 'Come All Ye', one of my mum's, I couldn't take it all in. At the end, I found myself up on stage singing 'Meet On The Ledge' for the very first time. I didn't know all the words, but I was there – part of it all. Afterwards I got to spend time with Dave Swarbrick at the annual cricket game. He was like a crazy uncle – very funny and full of stories about my mum.

It was to be twenty-six years before I returned. In 2019, I became a director of my mum's estate and that year my friend Tracey persuaded me Cropredy was 'the' place to be to feel the power of my mum's songs and to be with people who love her.

After the last night of the warm-up gigs I was in my hotel room and I wrote a poem for my mum. The next morning Peggy and AJ (Anthony John Clarke) asked if it could be read on stage on the first day of the Festival. I knew I wouldn't be able to read it myself so AJ read it for me.

I stood behind him, hugging Peggy, just watching The Field as my words were spoken. The tears rolled down my face.

There was lots of joy and fun too. Ric Saunders and I even managed a dancing in the rain routine down at the Brasenose – it was hilarious, we laughed so much!

On the last night, the band dedicated their entire set to my mum and dad. At the end, the lights came up, and the stage came down faster than I expected. One moment I was enjoying the most incredible weekend of my life, and the next I was sobbing in Ellen (Mamma Bear) Pegg's arms, watching it all disappear. Bittersweet doesn't cover it.

In 2023 I had the chance to make my own contribution to Cropredy. The weekend didn't get off to the best start: on the first day I fractured my ankle when my foot got caught in a rabbit hole. Resting up wasn't an option; there was too much to do and see. I hobbled through the festival.

I had brought some of my mum's collection of writings, photos, costumes and instruments and put on the first ever Sandy Denny Exhibition. It was at The Brasenose Arms in Cropredy village. I met lots of my mum's fans and we were all very emotional – we certainly went through an awful lot of tissues together! Ralph McTell, Simon and Debs, Ric and Chris, Richard Digance and AJ all visited – I was overwhelmed by the response.

That year my friend, the musician Carla Fuchs, and I also launched the CD *Songbird* at the Cropredy Fringe with Malcolm from Talking Elephant Records. It was a collaboration we had worked on over Covid, with Carla setting to music some of my mum's unpublished writings and me creating the CD cover design, using my mum's sketches and drawings. Carla sang some tracks from the album playing my mum's Gibson – it was spine-tingling.

In 2024 I was properly on The Field. We ran a raffle in Gerry Conway's name for MND, I sold my artworks of my mum and dad and their musical buddies and I camped on Field 6A with Tracey and the Croppers family. I felt truly part of Cropredy – no longer an 'outsider'.

In 2025 I put on the second Sandy exhibition at The Brasenose, helped by a close group of my closest friends – Sian, Cathy, Karen, Vlad and Dawn. The exhibition included more about my mum's music and the amazing musicians who inspired her and who she played with.

We unveiled a memorial bench for my mum, put together by Chris and Cathy, with the Sandy Denny Project playing Swarb's 'White Dress' to 'christen' it – a beautiful moment. We stayed at Cathy's thatched roofed cottage in Byfield, a stone's throw from the village hall where my mum performed her last concert. It was such a special connection. We all felt Sandy's spirit cheering us on.

The MND raffle for Gerry on The Field raised over a thousand pounds. My mum's songs rang out: 'Come All Ye', 'Fotheringay', 'Rising For The Moon' and other classics from her Fairport years. Simon dedicated 'Who Knows Where The Time Goes' to me. Singing along to 'Meet On The Ledge' at the end, arms linked with my Cropredy team, was one of the most emotional moments I have ever experienced on The Field.

Thank you: Simon, Peggy, Ric, Chris, DM, AJ, Debs, Ellen, Angie, Linda, Julia, Chris, Gareth and Milly. Thank you for all your support and kindness to me over the years, and for making a place for me in the Fairport family. Thank you for Cropredy – one of the best music festivals in the world. It is the place on earth I feel closest to my mum and dad. I love you all.

'Uncle Kev' Smith & Georgia

John O'Regan & Georgia

Mick Monk & Georgia

Rupert Kirque (Sandy's godson), Chris & Linda Leslie with Georgia, Cropredy 2024

Vlad, Dawn, Georgia, Cathy & Sian, Cropredy 2025

ACKNOWLEDGEMENTS

The publisher would like to thank: Pamela Murray Winter for the Hilary English (née Jones) anecdote (page 21); Dawn Kemp for the Stephen Stathers anecdote (page 79); Colin Davies, for the Jerry Donahue quote (page 92); John Tobler for the Elton John interview extract (page 177); Jerry Gilbert for the Gerry Conway *Sounds* 10 October 1970 interview extract (page 100), and for the Paul Simon *Sounds* 9 May 1973 interview extract (page 180); Joan As Policewoman, whose views on Sandy originally appeared in drownedinsound.com (page 333); Neil Atherton for the extract from his blog at nealatherton.com (page 160); Emma Hartley for the Dave Swarbrick interview from her blog at theglamourcave.blogspot.com; Neil Storey for the John Wood and Chris Blackwell stories; Stephen J Birkill for permission to reproduce Clive James' article, 'In A Lonely Moment', originally published in *Let It Rock* in March 1974 and reprinted in *Fiddlestix*, the Australian Fairport Convention fanzine, Issue 38, Spring 1995.

Thanks go to the authors of the following for permission to reproduce extracts from their books: Dave Cousins, *Exorcising Ghosts: Strawbs And Other Lives* (Witchwood Media Limited, 2014); Oliver Gray, *Volume: A Cautionary Tale Of Rock and Roll Obsession* (Sarsen Press, 2006); Chris Groom, *Rockin' And Around Croydon,* (Unknown, 1998); Ray Stevenson, Not Just Punk (Cadiz Music, 2025).

The publisher would also like to thank the following for their help: Andrew Batt, Elspeth Cowie, Robin Denselow, Jerry Gilbert, Annie Haslam, Mick Houghton, Patrick Humphries (patrickhumphries.co.uk); Steve Lench, Iain Matthews, Alan McGee, Simon Nicol, Colin Randall (former *Daily Telegraph* folk writer, now editor of Salutfolk.com); Levent Varlik, Barrie Wentzell, Richard Williams, Dawn Kemp and Kate Sullivan.

SPECIAL THANKS

Øivind Berne, Adam Blake, Adam Denning, Adrian Chant, Adrian Sales, Adrian Wright, Alan Burant, Alan Davidson, Alan Giles, Alan James, Alan Marsh, Alan Pearson, Alan Smith, Alasdair Wylie, Alison Brown, Alison Wagstaff-Dorrian, Allan Frewin, Allen John Herbert, Allen Walker, Andreas Steurer, Andrew Leonard, Andrew Adams, Andrew Bracey, Andrew Collingwood, Andrew Dyer, Andrew Flower, Andrew Hull, Andrew Kirk, Andrew Mellor, Andrew Turner, Andy Green (The Saloon/Radio Warrington), Andy Morton, Andy Nagy, Anthony Walker, April Phillips, Arie Euwijk, Arthur Crispo, Arthur Hardigg, Þórdís Bjarney Hauksdóttir, Bart van Poppel, Bartleby from the Isle of Man, Bastiaan van der Plas, Bernie Baldwin, Bill, Bill Sandalls, Bob Bettendorf, Bob Mackintosh, Bob Young, Brian Cranston, Brian Lowe, Brian McKibbin, Carroll Hillhouse, Celia Hall, Charlotte Le Blond, Chris, Chris Bates, Chris Harding, Chris Inkpen, Chris Saunders, Christian Globisch, Christopher Ellis, Christopher Shutty, Christopher Taberham, Ciaran Mallon, Claire Louise Seeds, Claudie Layden, Clay Worley, Colin George, Colin Norton, Colm McKenna, Darran McAteer, Dave Kenyon, Dave Allaway, David Pollard, David Blake, David Brooke, David Chick, David Crozier, David Farrar, David Francis, David Jacks, David James, David Magnuson, David Monk, David Schwartz, David Spittle, David Tester, David Todd, David Woolven, Dawn Broadhead, Dawn Kemp, Denyse Anger, Derek BS McAllister, Dermot Ferguson, Dick Greener, Donald McCombie, Edwin Tomei, Edwin Wallage, Elise Bettendorf, Elsie Macrae, Elspeth Cowie, Enzo Boeri, Eric Huet, Estelle Jackson, Eugene Czauderna, Eugene McGarrigle, Frank Vlaskamp, Gary Smith, Gordon Palmer, Graeme Carney, Graham Dumble, Graham Hawkins, Graham Warren, Graham Weston, Greg Borgartz, Greg Sinclair, Harald Tomren, Heather Roberts, Helen Hays, Herman Gilligan, Howard Brindle, Howard Earl, Iain Race, Ian Dearden, Ian Johnson, Ian Jones, Ian Lawrence, Ian McLean, Ian Nilo-Walton, Ian Oxley, Ian Walton, Ian Waters, Ioan James, J R Bickhart Jr, Jack H Hirschorn, James Franey, James McCrimmon, James Noury, Jamie Pipe, Jamie Taylor, Jason Denny, Jeff Gigon, Jeffrey Cooper, Jem Laugharne, Jen & Simon Banks, Jennifer Wilson, Jeremy Rutter, Jerry Pryke, Jim

Hockenhull, Jim Marlow, John Clare, John Deol, John Ellison, John Farrar, John H Perry, John Harris, John Leversuch, John Penhallow, John Smallshaw, John Whiting, Jon Callas, Jonas Söderström, Jonny Wah Wah, Joseph McLaughlin, Juan Manuel Escrihuela Ruíz, Wild Bill, Katrina Swift, Katy Skinner, Keith Chick, Keith J McCarthy, Kevan Taplin, Kevin O'Donnell, Kim McBride, Lee Sargent, Leslie Smith, Linda & Ian Albert, Lindsey M Lindley, Llyr Otto, Lucy Sheldrake, Lynne Winter, Malcolm Goode, Malcolm Howes, Marc Reynolds, Marcus Banks, Margo Rye, Mark Aynsley, Mark Kuykendall, Mark Moerman, Martin Abernethy, Martin Ashe, Martin Vincent, Martyn Bone, Mary Veazey, Matt Deighton, Mauro Regis, Melody Joanna Hatch, Michael Frankel, Michael Harrison, Michael Howlett, Michael Jackson, Michael James Murphy, Michael John Thompson, Michael Monk, Michael Phillips, Michael Rogers, Michael Slagter, Michael Steptoe, Michael Walsh, Michael Watts, Michael Webb, Mike Andrews, Mike Donovan, Neil Parison, Neville Dalton, Nic Potts, Nicholas Turner, Nicholas Dowding, Nick Clancy, Nick Pilley, Nick Weinreb, Nicky Mansfield, Nicole Ebers, Nigel Banks, Nigel Chitty, Nigel Trotman, Nik Williams, No'am Newman, Noreen Romano, Oddbjorn Wessel, Pat Swayne, Paul Bacon, Paul Brownbill, Paul Burgess, Paul Chesterman, Paul Gaudynski, Paul Hillock, Paul Sampson, Paul Sandy, Paul Walsh, Paula Savage, Penny Davies, Pete Somers, Peter & Chris Branson, Peter Brennand, Peter Cowley, Peter Hall, Peter Harrar, Peter Roe, Peter Stansfield, Peter Turner, Peter Wilson, Phil Coldham, Phil Gallo, Phil McMullen, Phil Parker, Philip Bagge, Philip Bentley, Philip French, Philip Parry, Philip Ward, Pim van der Kleij, Ren Hudspith, Richard Parry, Richard Singleton, Richard Gleave, Richard Gould, Richard Hall, Richard Lewis, Richard Pearl, Richard Scott, Richard Smith, Rick Jones, Rob Bodger, Rob Bostock, Rob McGrath, Rob Whitmarsh, Robert Mackreth, Robert Mazur, Robert Osman, Robin Whittaker, Roger Baxter, Roger Haydock, Roger Machin, Romain Tranchart, Romeo Nathan Bumann, Ronald Pease, Ronald Shepcar, Ross Cowie, Roy Omond, Roy Sysum, Russell Allan, Sally Maybury, Sam Garrett-Jones, Sarah Webb, Siebolt Visser, Simon Armstrong, Simon Chislett, Simon Sharrock, Simon Vernon, Skey Skey, Slava Nekrasov, Steen Jørgensen, Stephen Pepperall, Stephen Royston, Stephen Clark, Stephen

Mummery, Stephen Stathers, Stephen Taylor, Steve Baxter, Steve Clarke, Steve Hamilton, Steve Harvey, Steve Higgins, Steve Sheldon, Steve Warrillow, Steve West, Steven Southgate, Stuart Kesting, Suki Swindale, Susan Tobias, Suzanne DeCory, Sverre Knustad, Ted Harris, Terry Bidle, Terry Harrop, Terry Potter, Thomas Byrne, Thomas Herling, Thomas Huth, Thomas Lotti, Thomas Plath, Tim Edmonds, Tim Halliday, Tim Whitmarsh, to the memory of Geraldine Buckley, Tom Casey, Ton Schuringa, Tony Neel, Tor-Erik Nord, Trevor Guppy, Trevor Tall, Twinkle Newton, Ulli vom Scheidt, Ulrich Henrichs, Vincent Carolan, Wayne Gillespie, Wayne & Jane Smith, William (Bill) Windsor, William Messing

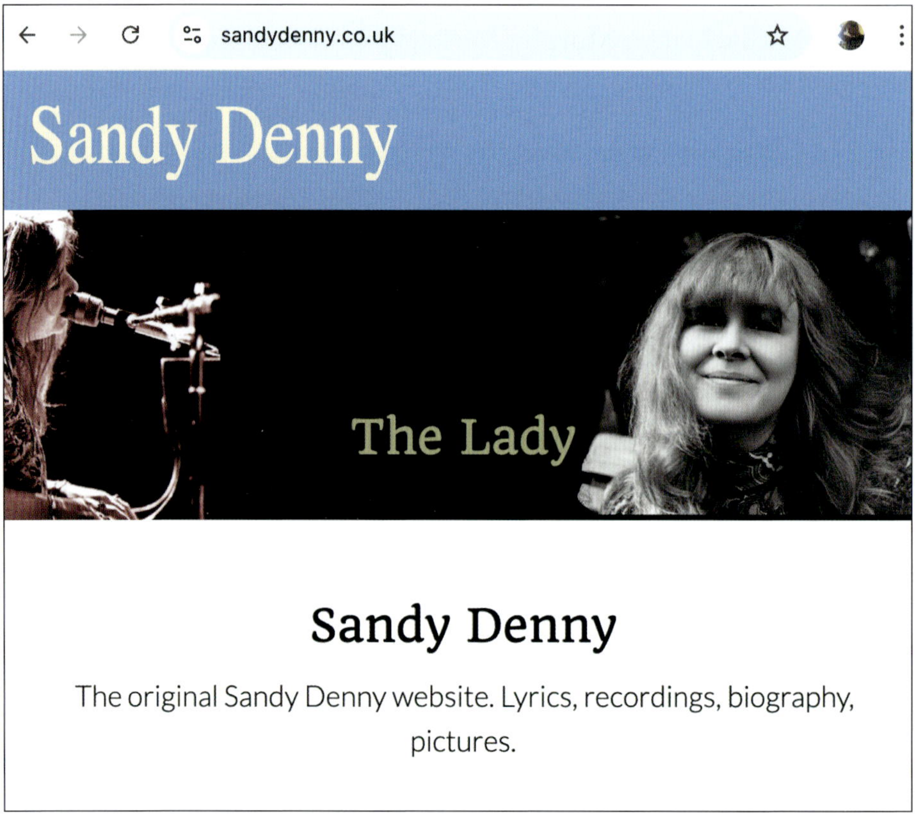

№ 9347
6pm to 10am Saturday August 31st
25/-
THE GREAT SOUTH COAST BANKHOLIDAY POP FESTIVITY
designed by dave roe solent-G
IWISPA
SATURDAY
ANGLERS, TEDDINGTON. Blues
Mafioso (retired).
IAN ANDERSON
AT COUSINS, 49 Greek Street.
.30-11. Two Lovely Ladies.
SANDY DENNY
ANN BRIGGS
Next week Dave Van Ronk. All
night sessions.
DAVY GRAHAM
AL JONES
yorkshire folk, blues & jazz festival
KRUMLIN, BARKISLAND
Nr. HALIFAX, Yorkshire
57262
14th, 15th and 16th August 1970
E DOME, BRIGHTON
AT., 5 DECEMBER, 1970
at 8 p.m.
(Doors open 7.30 p.m.)
FOTHERINGAY
and
THE COLOSSEUM
NOW THROUGH FEB. 7th
Friday, February 5 1972, 8:30 P.M.
SANDY DENNY
A&M Recording Artist
And ★ JACKSON BROWNE
Asylum Recording Artist
ALSO: SAGEWORTH
Coming: Feb. 9 to 14 - Merry Clayton & Bobby Gosh
TALENT SHOWCASE EVERY TUESDAY NIGHT
THE BITTER END
147 BLEECKER STREET
GREENWICH VILLAGE, N.Y.
RES. GR 5-7804
017614
THE BITTER
147 Bleecker
ADMIT
$4.0
$4.00 + 1 DRINK
SANDY DENNY with FAIRPORT CONVENTION & BROCK WALSH
SANDERS THEATRE
MAIN FLOOR
Friday Eve. 8:30 P.M.
MAY 10 1974
FRIDAY, MAY 10, 1974
Australian Festival of The Performing Arts presents
FAIRPORT CONVENTION
Melbourne Festival Hall
25 January '74
Sydney Opera House
CONCERT ARTS presents
THE FAIRPORT CONVENTION WI
SANDY DENNY & GUEST
CRIS WILLIAMSON
N 124
ORCHESTRA
MAY
18
Saturday Eve., at 8:0
Admission $5.5
LISNER AUDITORIU
Fairpo
Convent
WITH
SANDY DENN
PERTH CONCERT HALL WED.
APOLLO STADIUM FRI.
DALLAS BROOKS HALL SAT.
STATE THEATRE SUN.